Contents

Introduction

Introduction	v
Studying A2 physics	vii
How science works	viii

Unit 4
Fields and further mechanics 2

1 Force and momentum

1.1	Momentum and impulse	4
1.2	Impact forces	8
1.3	Conservation of momentum	11
1.4	Elastic and inelastic collisions	14
1.5	Explosions	16
	Examination-style questions	18

2 Motion in a circle

2.1	Uniform circular motion	22
2.2	Centripetal acceleration	24
2.3	On the road	26
2.4	At the fairground	28
	Examination-style questions	30

3 Simple harmonic motion

3.1	Oscillations	34
3.2	The principles of simple harmonic motion	36
3.3	More about sine waves	38
3.4	Applications of simple harmonic motion	40
3.5	Energy and simple harmonic motion	44
3.6	Forced oscillations and resonance	47
	Examination-style questions	50

4 Gravitational fields

4.1	Gravitational field strength	54
4.2	Gravitational potential	56
4.3	Newton's law of gravitation	59
4.4	Planetary fields	62
4.5	Satellite motion	66
	Examination-style questions	68

5 Electric fields

5.1	Field patterns	72
5.2	Electric field strength	76
5.3	Electric potential	80
5.4	Coulomb's law	83
5.5	Point charges	86
5.6	Comparison between electric and gravitational fields	89
	Examination-style questions	90

6 Capacitors

6.1	Capacitance	94
6.2	Energy stored in a charged capacitor	96
6.3	Charging and discharging a capacitor through a fixed resistor	98
	Examination-style questions	102

7 Magnetic fields

7.1	Current-carrying conductors in a magnetic field	106
7.2	Moving charges in a magnetic field	110
7.3	Charged particles in circular orbits	113
	Examination-style questions	116

8 Electromagnetic induction

8.1	Generating electricity	120
8.2	The laws of electromagnetic induction	123
8.3	The alternating current generator	127
8.4	Transformers	130
	Examination-style questions	133

Unit 4 examination-style questions 137

Unit 5
Nuclear physics, thermal physics plus an optional topic   146

Section A Nuclear and thermal physics

9   Radioactivity

9.1	The discovery of the nucleus	148
9.2	The properties of α, β and γ radiation	151
9.3	More about α, β and γ radiation	156
9.4	The dangers of radioactivity	159
9.5	Radioactive decay	162
9.6	The theory of radioactive decay	165
9.7	Radioactive isotopes in use	168
9.8	More about decay modes	172
9.9	Nuclear radius	176
	Examination-style questions	178

10   Nuclear energy

10.1	Energy and mass	182
10.2	Binding energy	185
10.3	Fission and fusion	188
10.4	The thermal nuclear reactor	191
	Examination-style questions	195

11   Thermal physics

11.1	Internal energy and temperature	198
11.2	Specific heat capacity	202
11.3	Change of state	205
	Examination-style questions	208

12   Gases

12.1	The experimental gas laws	210
12.2	The ideal gas law	212
12.3	The kinetic theory of gases	215
	Examination-style questions	219

Unit 5 examination-style questions   222

Section B Optional topics, student course notes and support materials are available on kerboodle!

Unit 6
Investigative and practical skills   228

13   Practical work in A2 physics

| 13.1 | Comparison of physics practical work at A2 and AS level | 230 |
| 13.2 | More about measurements | 233 |

14   Internal assessment in A2 physics

| 14.1 | The ISA/PSA scheme at A2 (scheme T) | 236 |
| 14.2 | The AQA-marked scheme at A2 (scheme X) | 239 |

15   Mathematical skills for A2 physics

15.1	Trigonometry	242
15.2	Algebra	245
15.3	Logarithms	247
15.4	Exponential decrease	250
15.5	Areas and integration	253

For reference

1.	Useful data for A2 physics	256
2.	Glossary	260
3.	Answers to summary questions	267
4.	Index	271

Introduction

Nelson Thornes has worked in partnership with AQA to ensure this book and the accompanying online resources offer you the best support for your A Level course.

All resources have been approved by senior AQA examiners so you can feel assured that they closely match the specification for this subject and provide you with everything you need to prepare successfully for your exams.

These print and online resources together **unlock blended learning**; this means that the links between the activities in the book and the activities online blend together to maximise your understanding of a topic and help you achieve your potential.

These online resources are available on **kerboodle!** which can be accessed via the internet at www.kerboodle.com/live, anytime, anywhere. If your school or college subscribes to this service you will be provided with your own personal login details. Once logged in, access your course and locate the required activity.

For more information and help visit **www.kerboodle.com**

Icons in this book indicate where there is material online related to that topic. The following icons are used:

💡 Learning activity

These resources include a variety of interactive and non-interactive activities to support your learning.

✅ Progress tracking

These resources include a variety of tests that you can use to check your knowledge on particular topics (Test yourself) and a range of resources that enable you to analyse and understand examination questions (On your marks…).

🔎 Research support

These resources include WebQuests, in which you are assigned a task and provided with a range of web links to use as source material for research.

🔖 Study skills

These resources support you develop a skill that is key for your course, for example planning essays.

Weblinks

Our online resources feature a list of recommended weblinks, split by chapter. This will give you a head start, helping you to navigate to the best websites that will aid your learning and understanding of the topics in your course.

🔬 How science works

These resources are a mixture of interactive and non-interactive activities to help you learn the skills required for success in this new area of the specification.

⚠ Practical

This icon signals where there is a relevant practical activity to be undertaken, and support is provided online.

■ How to use this book

This book supports the specification for your course and is arranged in a sequence approved by AQA. The course consists of two theory units (4 and 5) and a practical skills unit (6).

The book content is divided to match the compulsory content of the specification: Unit 4 (Fields and further mechanics), Unit 5 Section A (Nuclear and thermal physics) and Unit 6 (Investigative and practical skills). Note that Unit 5 Section B (An optional topic) is provided as on-line support material. Each of the units in the book is divided into chapters and then topics, making the content clear and easy to use.

Unit openers for the theory units give you a summary of the content you will be covering and a recap of ideas from AS level that you will need.

The features in this book include:

Learning objectives

At the beginning of each section you will find a list of learning objectives that contain targets linked to the requirements of the specification. The relevant specification reference is also provided.

Key terms

Terms that you will need to be able to define and understand are highlighted in bold blue type within the text, e.g. **binding energy**. You can look up these terms in the Glossary (page 260).

Hint

Hints to aid your understanding of the content.

How science works

'How science works' is a key part of the new A Level physics specifications. As with the specification, 'How science works' is integrated throughout the content of the book. This feature highlights 'How science works' as it occurs within topics, so that it is always relevant to what you are studying. You will not be examined on the exact information provided in this book with relation to 'How science works'. The ideas provided in these features are intended to teach you the skills you will need to tackle this part of the course, and give you experience when dealing with applying your knowledge to different contexts. See the 'How science works' spread on page viii for more detail.

Summary questions

Short questions that test your understanding of the subject and allow you to apply the knowledge and skills you have acquired to different scenarios. Answers are supplied at the back of the book (page 267).

AQA Examiner's tip

Hints from AQA examiners to help you with your studies and to prepare you for your exam.

AQA Examination-style questions

Questions in the style that you can expect in your exam, including the new 'How science works' strand. These occur at the end of each chapter to give practice in examination-style questions for a particular topic. They also occur at the end of each unit; the questions here may cover any of the content of the unit.

When you answer the examination-style questions in this book, remember that quality of written communication (QWC) will be assessed in any question or part-question in the Unit 4 and 5 papers where extended descriptive answers are required. So make sure your answers to such questions are of good quality in terms of QWC as well as in terms of physics.

AQA examination questions are reproduced by permission of the Assessment and Qualifications Alliance.

Nelson Thornes is responsible for the solution(s) given and they may not constitute the only possible solution(s).

Link

Synoptic questions or part-questions are a key feature of your A2 examination papers. Such a question may require you to:

- draw on knowledge, understanding and skills from AS level that underpin the A2 topic which the question is about,
- to link knowledge, understanding and skills from topics in the A2 theory unit on which the question is set, perhaps in a new context which is described in the question.

Synoptic links are highlighted in the margin near the relevant text using the links icon accompanied by brief notes which include page references to where the linked topics are to be found in this book or the AS book.

Stretch and challenge

Some of the questions in the papers for Units 4 and 5 are designed to test the depth of your knowledge and understanding of the subject. Such questions may require you to:

- solve a problem where you have to decide on a suitable strategy and appropriate methods, possibly linking different ideas from within the Unit,
- discuss in an extended written answer a controversial issue involving physics, perhaps in terms of advantages and disadvantages, that affects people or society at large.

The questions test your ability to think deeply and clearly about physics and to provide solutions and answers that are coherent and clear.

Web links in the book

As Nelson Thornes is not responsible for third party content online, there may be some changes to this material that are beyond our control. In order for us to ensure that the links referred to in the book are as up-to-date and stable as possible, the websites are usually homepages with supporting instructions on how to reach the relevant pages if necessary.

Please let us know at **kerboodle@nelsonthornes.com** if you find a link that doesn't work and we will do our best to redirect the link, or to find an alternative site.

Studying A2 Physics

This book is written for students who are following or about to follow the AQA A2 Physics (Specification A) course. It provides the main content of the A2 course including information and advice about practical assessment. In addition, essential maths skills for A2 Physics are provided. Support for the optional topics is available online.

In studying the main content of the specification, you will:

- learn more about force and energy in the contexts of collisions and explosions, circular motion and oscillations, electric, gravitational and magnetic fields, thermal physics and nuclear energy,

- revisit important ideas such as electric potential and meet new ideas and theories such as binding energy in nuclear physics and the kinetic theory of gases,

- study important applications and devices including capacitors, electric generators and transformers, and nuclear reactors,

- gain further practical skills and greater expertise in analysing measurements and evaluating results.

In studying an optional topic, you will build on relevant topics in the main content of the A2 specification to gain a deeper insight into physics:

Option A Astrophysics shows how fundamental principles of physics and key devices such as charged coupled devices (CCDs) and instruments such as telescopes are used to gain knowledge and understanding of the Universe, including objects such as quasars and black holes and concepts such as dark energy.

Option B Medical physics shows how the application of physics principles and techniques underpins a broad range of techniques used for diagnosis of sight defects and hearing problems, for cardiac monitoring and endoscopy and for ultrasonic and X-ray imaging.

Option C Applied physics develops knowledge of mechanics and thermal physics by studying, respectively, the dynamics of rotating objects including moments of inertia, and the principles of heat engines and heat pumps in the context of applications such as the four-stroke petrol engine, the Diesel engine and the refrigerator.

Option D Turning points in physics involves the study of key experiments, discoveries and conceptual shifts in the subject, including the discovery of the electron and the measurement of its charge/mass ratio and its charge, the principles and consequences of special relativity including time dilation and wave particle duality including quantum tunnelling.

This book covers all the main topics in the A2 specification.

A2 Course Structure (A2 % weighting of each unit shown in brackets)

Unit 4 Fields and further mechanics (40%)
　　Chapters 1–8

Unit 5 Nuclear physics, thermal physics plus an optional topic (40%)

　　Section A Nuclear and thermal physics
　　Chapters 9–12

　　Section B An optional topic
　　AQA A2 Physics A on *Kerboodle!*

Unit 6 Investigative and practical skills (20%)
　　Chapters 13–14

Each of the units starts with two opening pages that outline the key topics in each unit and the links between topics in each Unit. In addition, a useful list of key elements from the AS course that underpin the Unit are provided. Notes on the optional topics which comprise Unit 5 section B are provided on Kerboodle. Unit 4 is examined through a written examination offered in January or June. Unit 5 is examined through a written examination offered in June only.

Practical skills for A2, assessed internally in Unit 6, are described in Chapters 13–14 and plenty of opportunities are provided to develop these skills as you progress through the topics in Units 4 and 5A. Chapter 15 Mathematical skills for A2 Physics provides valuable mathematical support for the topics in the A2 Physics course.

The reference section provides useful data, a glossary, answers to numerical questions, and a comprehensive index. In addition, a full list of the formulae you will be provided with in your A2 examination papers is provided at the end of the book.

This book is written to help you pass the A level examination and then move on successfully to the next stage of your career, especially if you intend to pursue a career in science or engineering. More importantly, I hope it will give you a lasting interest in physics and on-going enthusiasm for this exciting and vital subject!

How science works

As you progress through your A2 Physics course, you will develop your scientific skills further and learn more about important new ideas and applications through the 'How science works' component of your A level course. These skills are a key part of how every scientist works. Now you will develop them further and gain new skills as you progress through the course. The following notes are intended as a reminder.

'How science works' at A level has several different strands (summarised in Table 1) and these are brought out in your course as appropriate in different topics. These strands include practical and investigative skills in science. They also consider the implications of scientific work in terms of how science is used not just by scientists and engineers but also by society at large.

Most of the strands, such as those relating to practical work and the ability to communicate scientific ideas have always been part of science courses and contributed to the total course mark. Science courses have always included the aspects of 'How science works' that deal with major scientific discoveries too, for example the discovery of the atomic nucleus by Ernest Rutherford.

The strands relating to the implications of science are new at A level. They are important because what scientists do affects us all, and ethical issues are often associated with their work. For example:

- Should children be banned from using mobile phones because of concerns about the effects of mobile phone radiation?
- Should scientists working on the use of radiation to treat cancer use patients to test the effectiveness of new treatments?

These strands are in all A level science courses and can be examined. So you need to be able to discuss in depth a scientific issue by considering the benefits and the risks or the advantages and disadvantages. You will develop the necessary skills for these strands as you progress through your course and meet topics that touch on issues that show how and why science affects us all.

'How science works' is developed in this book through relevant features in the main content of the book and are highlighted accordingly. All the 'How science works' strands of AQA's A level science specifications are the same. The 'How science works' features in this book will help you to develop the relevant 'How science works' skills necessary for examination purposes but more importantly these features should give you a thorough grasp of how scientists work and what they do, as well as a deeper awareness of how science is used to improve the quality life for everyone.

Table 1 *How science works specification summary*

Strands	Skills
A **Theories, models and ideas** are used to develop and modify scientific explanations.	Scientists make progress when validated evidence is found that supports a new theory or model.
B **Predictions from a hypothesis** (i.e. untested idea) or a theory need to be tested by experiment. If a reliable experiment does not support a hypothesis or theory, the hypothesis or theory must be changed.	Scientists use their knowledge and understanding in forming a hypothesis and when questioning the explanations of themselves or of other scientists.
C **Appropriate methodology**, including ICT, is used to make observations and measurements. Experiments are the key links between the 'real world' and the abstract ideas of science.	When scientists plan and carry out investigations, they need to: • identify the dependent and independent variables in the investigation and the control variables, • select appropriate apparatus and methods, including ICT, • choose measuring instruments according to their sensitivity and precision and carry out reliable measurements.

continued

Table 1 *(continued)*

Strands	Skills
D The range of experimental skills needed to carry out scientific investigations include manual and data skills (tabulation, graphical skills, etc.).	Scientists have to follow appropriate experimental procedures in a sensible order, use appropriate apparatus and methods to make accurate and reliable measurements, identify and minimise significant sources of experimental error and identify and take account of risks in carrying out practical work.
E Data must be analysed and interpreted to provide evidence, recognising correlations and causal relationships. When experimental data confirm predictions from a theoretical model, scientists become more confident in the theory.	Scientists look for patterns and trends in data as a first step in providing explanations of phenomena. They need to know how to: • process measurement data, • use equations and carry out appropriate calculations, • plot and use appropriate graphs to establish or verify relationships between variables, • relate the gradient and the intercepts of straight line graphs to appropriate linear equations.
F The methodology used, evidence and data must be evaluated and conflicting evidence resolved. The validity of new evidence is a stimulus for further scientific investigation, which involves refinements of experimental technique or development of new hypotheses.	Scientists need to be able to distinguish between systematic and random errors, make reasonable estimates of the errors in all measurements, use data, graphs and other evidence from experiments to draw conclusions and to use the most significant error estimates to assess the reliability of conclusions drawn.
G The tentative nature of scientific knowledge needs to be considered. Scientific knowledge changes when new experimental evidence provides a better explanation of scientific observations.	Scientists need to know that if evidence that is reliable and reproducible does not support a theory, the theory must be modified or replaced with a different theory.
H Research findings need to be communicated to the scientific community to see if they can be replicated, thus either confirming new explanations or refuting them.	Scientists need to provide explanations using correct scientific terms, and support arguments with equations, diagrams and clear sketch graphs when appropriate.
I The applications and implications of science and their associated benefits and risks need to be considered.	Scientists apply their scientific knowledge to develop technologies that improve our lives. We all need to appreciate that the technologies themselves may pose significant risks that have to be balanced against the benefits.
J The ethical issues associated with scientific developments need to be considered.	Scientists have a duty to consider ethical issues associated with their findings. Scientists provide solutions to problems but the solutions often require society to form judgements as to whether the solution is acceptable in view of moral issues that result. Issues such as the effects on the planet, and the economic and physical well being of the living things on it should be considered.
K The scientific community itself validates new knowledge and ensures integrity.	Scientists need a common set of values and responsibilities. They should know that scientists undertake a peer-review of the work of others. They should know that scientists work with a common aim to progress scientific knowledge and understanding in a valid way and that accurate reporting of findings takes precedence over recognition of success of an individual.
L Decision makers are influenced in many ways, including their prior beliefs, their vested interests, special interest groups, public opinion and the media, as well as by expert scientific evidence.	Scientific evidence should be considered as a whole. Media and pressure groups often select parts of scientific evidence that supports a particular viewpoint and that this can influence public opinion which in turn may influences decision makers. Consequently, decision makers may make socially and politically acceptable decisions based on incomplete evidence.

Fields and further mechanics

Chapters in this unit

1 Force and momentum

2 Motion in a circle

3 Simple harmonic motion

4 Gravitational fields

5 Electric fields

6 Capacitors

7 Magnetic fields

8 Electromagnetic induction

Introduction

This unit consists of two main areas: further mechanics and fields. Both areas depend on a good understanding of AS studies on force and energy.

Further mechanics

Further mechanics develops the AS link between force and acceleration to establish force as rate of change of momentum before moving on to the important principle of conservation of momentum and its application to explosions and collisions. Force is also considered in the context of the motion of objects moving in circular motion at constant speed and those oscillating in simple harmonic motion. All these topics develop an awareness of the wide application of Newton's laws of motion and the conservation of energy. The first three chapters explore all the above topics in a range of contexts including vehicle impacts, fairground rides and bridge stability. In addition, the study of mechanics in this unit covers effects such as damping and resonance which are found not just in mechanical systems but also in acoustic, atomic and electrical systems. By studying the further mechanics topics in this unit, you should establish a solid basis for further studies in physics and engineering and hopefully gain an appreciation of the historical importance of Newton's laws in providing the key principles behind the design, construction and use of the machines and engines that powered the industrial revolution and of the machines we rely on in our own scientific age.

Fields

Fields also extends AS studies on force and energy through in-depth studies of the force of gravity, the electrostatic force between charged objects and the forces that magnetic fields exert on current-carrying conductors. In all these situations, objects exert forces on one another without being in direct contact so we say these forces 'act at a distance'. We describe action at a distance in terms of a 'field' surrounding an object due to its mass or charge or due to an electric current passing through it and exerting a force on any similar object in the field. You will have gained some appreciation of how such forces act in your studies of exchange particles in Unit 1 of the AS course. In Unit 4, the properties of gravitational, electric and magnetic fields in terms of force and energy are studied in depth. The strength of each type of field is defined and measured and the potential of gravitational and electric fields to do work is considered in detail. In addition, Newton's law of gravitation and its application to satellite motion is considered in depth as is Coulomb's law of force between charged objects. The study of electric and magnetic fields applies knowledge and understanding of a range of applications and devices including the capacitor, a device that stores charge and is used in radio circuits and timing circuits, and alternating current generators and transformers which are used, respectively, to generate and supply the electricity we use at home.

What you already know:

From your AS studies on mechanics, you should know that:

- A vector quantity has magnitude and direction and a scalar quantity has magnitude only.
- Displacement, velocity, acceleration and force are vector quantities.
- A force F can be resolved parallel and perpendicular to a line at angle θ to the direction of the force into a parallel component $F\cos\theta$ and a perpendicular component $F\sin\theta$.
- Velocity = rate of change of displacement = the gradient of a displacement–time graph.
- Acceleration = rate of change of velocity = the gradient of a velocity–time graph.
- An object continues at rest or at constant velocity unless acted on by a resultant force.
- The resultant force on an object = its mass × its acceleration and its weight = its mass × g.
- The symbols s, u, v, a, t and F represent displacement, initial velocity, velocity at time t, acceleration and force.
- The equations for uniform acceleration $v = u + at$, $s = \frac{1}{2}(u + v)t$, $s = ut + \frac{1}{2}at^2$ and $v^2 = u^2 + 2as$ and $F = ma$ can be applied to predict the motion of an object moving along a straight line.
- The work done W on an object is given by $W = Fs\cos\theta$, where θ is the angle between the direction of the force and the displacement of the object.
- For an object of mass m, its kinetic energy at speed $v = \frac{1}{2}mv^2$ and its change of gravitational potential energy = $mg\Delta h$ when moved up or down through a vertical distance Δh.
- Power = rate of transfer of energy.

From your AS studies on electricity, you should know that:

- Charge = current × time.
- An electric current in a metallic conductor is a flow of 'free' electrons due to a pd across the ends of the conductor.
- The potential difference (pd) between two points = work done per unit charge to move a charged object from one point to the other.
- Electrical power = current × pd.
- Resistance = pd/current.
- The symbols Q, I, t, V, P and R respectively represent charge, current, time, pd, power and resistance.
- For components in series, the current is the same in each component and the sum of the pds across the components is equal to the total pd.
- For components in parallel, the pd is the same across each component and the sum of the currents through the components is equal to the total current.
- The emf of a source of pd is the electrical energy per unit charge produced by the source.

1.1 Momentum and impulse

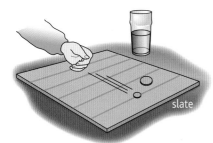

Figure 1 *Momentum games*

Momentum

If you have ever run into someone on the sports field, you will know something about momentum. If the person you ran into was more massive than you, then you probably came off worse than the other person. When two bodies collide, the effect they have on each other depends not only on their initial velocities but also on the mass of each object. You can easily test the idea using coins, as shown in Figure 1. You might already have developed your skill in this area! It is not too difficult to show that when a large coin and a small coin collide, the motion of the small coin is affected more.

Sir Isaac Newton was the first person to realise that a **force** was needed to change the velocity of an object. He realised that the effect of a force on an object depended on its mass as well as on the amount of force. He defined the **momentum** of a moving object as its mass × its velocity and showed how the momentum of an object changes when a force acts on it. In the AS course, you learned that the force needed to give an object a certain acceleration can be calculated from the equation 'force = mass × acceleration'. In the A2 course, we consider the ideas that Newton established in full.

How science works

Universal laws

Although Newton put forward his ideas over 300 years ago, his laws continue to provide the essential mathematical rules for predicting the motion of objects in any situation except inside the atom (where the rules of quantum physics apply) and at speeds approaching the speed of light or in very strong gravitational fields (where Einstein's theories of relativity apply). For example, the launch of a rocket is carefully planned using **Newton's laws of motion** and his **law of gravitation** which we will study in Chapter 4. However, the laws do not for example predict the existence of black holes, a confirmed prediction of Einstein's theory of general relativity. In fact, Einstein showed that his theories of relativity simplify into Newton's laws, where gravity is weak and the speed of objects is much less than the speed of light.

The momentum of an object is defined as its mass × its velocity.

■ The unit of momentum is $\mathrm{kg\,m\,s^{-1}}$. The symbol for momentum is p.

■ Momentum is a vector quantity. Its direction is the same as the direction of the object's velocity.

■ For an object of mass m moving at velocity v, its momentum $p = mv$.

For example, a ball of mass 2.0 kg moving at a velocity of $10\,\mathrm{m\,s^{-1}}$ has the same amount of momentum as a person of mass 50 kg moving at a velocity of $0.4\,\mathrm{m\,s^{-1}}$.

▦ Momentum and Newton's laws of motion

Newton's first law of motion: An object remains at rest or in uniform motion unless acted on by a force.

In effect, Newton's first law tells us that a force is needed to change the momentum of an object. If the momentum of an object is constant, there is no resultant force acting on it. Clearly, if the mass of an object is constant and the object has constant momentum, it follows that the velocity of the object is also constant. If a moving object with constant momentum gains or loses mass, however, its velocity would change to keep its momentum constant. For example, a cyclist in a race who collects a water bottle as he or she speeds past a 'service' point gains mass (i.e. the water bottle) and therefore loses velocity.

Newton's second law of motion: The rate of change of momentum of an object is proportional to the resultant force on it. In other words, the resultant force is proportional to the change of momentum per second.

At AS level, Newton's second law was presented in the form 'force = mass × acceleration'. At A2, we look at how this equation is derived from Newton's second law in its general form as stated above.

Consider an object of constant mass m acted on by a constant force F. Its acceleration causes a change of its speed from initial speed u to speed v in time t without change of direction:

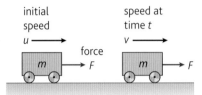

Figure 2 *Force and momentum*

▦ its initial momentum = mu, and its final momentum = mv

▦ its change of momentum = its final momentum (mv) – its initial momentum (mu).

According to Newton's second Law, the force is proportional to the change of momentum per second.

Therefore, force $F \propto \dfrac{\text{change of momentum}}{\text{time taken}} = \dfrac{mv - mu}{t}$

$$= \dfrac{m(v - u)}{t} = ma$$

where $a = \dfrac{v - u}{t}$ = the acceleration of the object.

This proportionality relationship (i.e. $F \propto ma$) can be written as $F = kma$, where k is a constant of proportionality.

The value of k is made equal to 1 by defining the unit of force, **the newton**, as the amount of force that gives an object of mass 1 kg an acceleration of $1\,\mathrm{m\,s^{-2}}$ (i.e. force $F = 1\,\mathrm{N}$, mass $m = 1\,\mathrm{kg}$, acceleration, $a = 1\,\mathrm{m\,s^{-2}}$ so $k = 1$).

Therefore, with $k = 1$, the equation $\boldsymbol{F = ma}$ follows from Newton's 2nd law provided the mass of the object is constant.

In general, the change of momentum of an object may be written as $\Delta(mv)$, where the symbol Δ means 'change of'. Therefore, if the momentum of an object changes by $\Delta(mv)$ in time Δt, the force F on the object is given by the equation

$$F = \dfrac{\Delta(mv)}{\Delta t}$$

1   If m is constant, then $\Delta(mv) = m\Delta v$, where Δv is the change of velocity of the object.

$$\therefore F = \dfrac{m\Delta v}{\Delta t} = ma \text{ where acceleration } a = \dfrac{\Delta v}{\Delta t}$$

AQA⁄ Examiner's tip

The unit of momentum may be either $\mathrm{kg\,m\,s^{-1}}$ or (more neatly) N s.

The equation $F = \dfrac{\Delta(mv)}{\Delta t}$ always applies but $F = ma$ applies only to objects of constant mass.

2 **If *m* changes at a constant rate** as a result of mass being transferred at constant velocity, then $\Delta(mv) = v\Delta m$, where Δm is the change of mass of the object.

$$\therefore F = \frac{v\Delta m}{\Delta t} \text{ where } \frac{\Delta m}{\Delta t} = \text{change of mass per second.}$$

This form of Newton's second law is used in any situation where an object gains or loses mass continuously.

For example, if a rocket ejects burnt fuel as hot gas from its engine at speed *v*, the force *F* exerted by the engine to eject the hot gas is given by

$$F = \frac{v\Delta m}{\Delta t} \text{ where } \frac{\Delta m}{\Delta t} = \text{mass of hot gas lost per second.}$$

An equal and opposite reaction force acts on the jet engine due to the hot gas, propelling the rocket forwards.

The **impulse** of a force is defined as the force × the time for which the force acts. Therefore, for a force *F* which acts for time Δt,

$$\text{the impulse} = F\Delta t = \Delta(mv)$$

Hence the impulse of a force acting on an object is equal to the change of momentum of the object.

Force–time graphs

Suppose an object of constant mass *m* is acted on by a constant force *F* which changes its velocity from initial velocity *u* to velocity *v* in time *t*. As explained earlier in this topic, Newton's second law gives

$$F = \frac{mv - mu}{t}$$

Rearranging this equation gives $Ft = mv - mu$

Figure 3 is a graph of force v. time for this situation. Because force *F* is constant for time *t*, the area under the line represents the impulse of the force *Ft* which is equal to $mv - mu$. In other words,

the area under the line of a force–time graph represents the change of momentum or the impulse of the force.

Link

Use of $F = \dfrac{mv - mu}{t}$ is another way to calculate an impact force.

See *AS Physics* Topic 9.5.

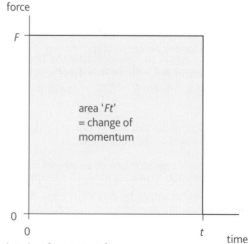

Figure 3 *Force against time for constant force*

Note: The unit of momentum can be given as the newton second (N s) or the kilogram metre per second (kg m s^{-1}). The unit of impulse is usually given as the newton second.

*Worked example:*_____

A force of 10 N acts for 20 s on an object of mass 50 kg which is initially at rest.

Calculate:

a the change of momentum of the object,

b the velocity of the object at 20 s.

Solution

a Change of momentum = impulse of the force = Ft = 10 × 20 = 200 N s

b Momentum at 20 s = 200 N s as the object was initially at rest.

$$\therefore \text{Velocity} = \frac{\text{momentum}}{\text{mass}} = \frac{200}{50} = 4.0\,\text{m s}^{-1}$$

Summary questions

1 a Calculate the momentum of:

   i   an atom of mass 4.0×10^{-25} kg moving at a velocity of $3.0 \times 10^{6}\,\text{m s}^{-1}$,

   ii a pellet of mass 4.2×10^{-4} kg moving at a velocity of $120\,\text{m s}^{-1}$,

   iii a bird of mass 0.56 kg moving at a velocity of $25\,\text{m s}^{-1}$.

  b Calculate:

   i   the mass of an object moving at a velocity of $16\,\text{m s}^{-1}$ with momentum of $96\,\text{kg m s}^{-1}$,

   ii the velocity of an object of mass 6.4 kg that has momentum of $128\,\text{kg m s}^{-1}$.

2 A train of mass 24 000 kg moving at a velocity of $15.0\,\text{m s}^{-1}$ is brought to rest by a braking force of 6000 N. Calculate

  a the initial momentum of the train,

  b the time taken for the brakes to stop the train.

3 An aircraft of total mass 45 000 kg accelerates on a runway from rest to a velocity of $120\,\text{m s}^{-1}$ when it takes off. During this time, its engines provide a constant driving force of 120 kN. Calculate:

  a the gain of momentum of the aircraft,

  b the 'take off' time.

4 The velocity of a vehicle of mass 600 kg was reduced from $15\,\text{m s}^{-1}$ by a constant force of 400 N which acted for 20 s then by a constant force of 20 N for a further 20 s.

  a Sketch the force v. time graph for this situation.

  b i   Calculate the initial momentum of the vehicle.

   ii Use the force v. time graph to determine the total change of momentum.

   iii Hence show that the final velocity of the vehicle is $1\,\text{m s}^{-1}$.

1.2 Impact forces

- What happens to the impact force (and why?) if the duration of impact is reduced?

- How do we calculate $\Delta(mv)$ for a moving object which stops or reverses?

- What happens to the momentum of a ball when it bounces off a wall?

Specification reference: 3.4.1

Figure 1 *A golf ball impact*

A sports person knows that the harder a ball is hit, the further it travels. The impact changes the momentum of the ball in a very short time when the object exerting the impact force is in contact with the ball.

- If the ball is initially stationary and the impact causes it to accelerate to speed v in time t, the gain of momentum of the ball due to the impact $= mv$, where m is the mass of the ball.

  Therefore, the force of the impact $F = \dfrac{\text{change of momentum}}{\text{contact time}} = \dfrac{mv}{t}$

- If the ball is moving with an initial velocity, u, and the impact changes its velocity to v in time t, the change of momentum of the ball $= mv - mu$.

  Therefore, the force of impact $F = \dfrac{\text{change of momentum}}{\text{contact time}}$,

  $$F = \frac{mv - mu}{t}$$

Link

Use of $F = ma$ and $a = \dfrac{v-u}{t}$ is another way to calculate an impact force.

See *AS Physics*, Topic 9.5.

Worked example:

A ball of mass 0.63 kg initially at rest was struck by a bat which gave it a velocity of 35 m s⁻¹. The contact time between the bat and ball was 25 ms. Calculate:

a the momentum gained by the ball,

b the average force of impact on the ball.

(**Note** The 'm' in ms stands for milli.)

Solution

a Momentum gained $= 0.63 \times 35 = 22 \text{ kg m s}^{-1}$

b Impact force $= \dfrac{\text{gain of momentum}}{\text{contact time}} = \dfrac{22}{0.025} = 880 \text{ N}$

Application and How science works

Vehicle safety reminders

The AS specification looks at the physics of vehicle safety features such as crumple zones, seatbelts, collapsible steering wheels, and airbags. These and other features such as side-impact bars are all designed to lessen the effect of an impact on people in the vehicle. As explained at AS level, the essential idea is to increase the time taken by an impact so the acceleration or deceleration is less and therefore the impact force is less. The result is the same using the idea of momentum; for a given change of momentum, the force is reduced if the impact time is increased. However, as explained in Topic 1.3, the ideas can be developed much further by using the concept of momentum.

Force–time graphs for impacts

The variation of an impact force with time on a ball can be recorded using a force sensor connected using suitably long wires or a radio link to a computer. The force sensor is attached to the object (e.g. a bat) that causes the impact. Because equal and opposite forces act on the ball, the force on the ball due to the bat varies in exactly the same way as the force on the bat due to the ball. The variation of force with time is displayed on the computer screen.

Figure 3 shows a typical force–time graph for an impact. The graph shows that the impact force increases then decreases during the impact. As explained in Topic 1.2, the area under the graph is equal to the change of momentum. The average force of impact can be worked out from the change of momentum divided by the contact time.

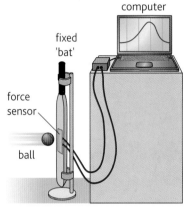

Figure 2 *Investigating an impact force on a ball*

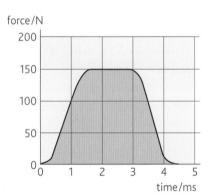

area under curve = 9 blocks
Ft for 1 block = $50\,N \times 1\,ms$
$= 5.0 \times 10^{-2}\,N\,s$

change of momentum
$= 9 \times 5.0 \times 10^{-2}$
$= 0.45\,N\,s$

Figure 3 *Force against time for an impact*

Rebound impacts

When a ball hits a wall and rebounds, its momentum changes direction due to the impact. If the ball hits the wall normally, it rebounds normally so the direction of its momentum is reversed. The velocity and therefore the momentum after the impact is in the opposite direction to the velocity before the impact and therefore has the opposite sign. Figure 4 shows the idea.

Suppose the ball hits the wall normally with an initial speed u and it rebounds at speed v in the opposite direction. Since its direction of motion reverses on impact, a sign convention is necessary to represent the two directions. Using + for 'towards the wall' and – for 'away from the wall', its initial momentum = $+mu$, and its final momentum = $-mv$.

Therefore,

its change of momentum = final momentum – initial momentum

$$= (-mv) - (mu)$$

The impact force $F = \dfrac{\text{change of momentum}}{\text{contact time}} = \dfrac{(-mv) - (mu)}{t}$

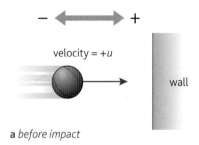

a *before impact*

velocity = $+u$

wall

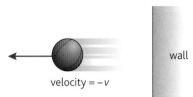

wall

velocity = $-v$

b *after impact*

Figure 4 *A rebound*

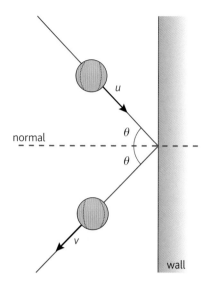

Figure 5 *An oblique impact*

Notes:

1 If there is no loss of speed on impact, then $v = u$ so the impact force

$$F = \frac{(-mu) - (mu)}{t} = \frac{-2mu}{t}$$

2 If the impact is oblique (i.e. the initial direction of the ball is not perpendicular to the wall), the normal components of the velocity must be used. For an impact in which the initial and final direction of the ball are at the same angle θ to the normal and there is no loss of speed (i.e. $u = v$), the normal component of the initial velocity is $+u\cos\theta$ and the normal component of the final velocity is $-u\cos\theta$. The change of momentum of the ball is therefore $-2\,mu\cos\theta$.

Worked example:

A tennis ball of mass 0.20 kg moving at a speed of 18 m s⁻¹ was hit by a bat, causing the ball to go back in the direction it came from at a speed of 15 m s⁻¹. The contact time was 0.12 s. Calculate:

a the change of momentum of the ball,

b the impact force on the ball.

Solution

a Mass of ball $m = 0.20$ kg, initial velocity $u = +18$ m s⁻¹, final velocity $= -15$ m s⁻¹.
   Change of momentum $= mv - mu = (0.20 \times -15) - (0.20 \times 18)$
   $= -3.0 - 3.6 = -6.6$ kg m s⁻¹

b Impact force $= \dfrac{\text{change of momentum}}{\text{time taken}} = \dfrac{-6.6}{0.12} = -55$ N

Note: The minus sign indicates the force on the ball is in the same direction as velocity after the impact.

Summary questions

1 A 2000 kg lorry reversing at a speed of 0.80 m s⁻¹ backs accidentally into a steel fence. The fence stops the lorry 0.5 s after the lorry first makes contact with the fence. Calculate:

a the initial momentum of the lorry,

b the force of the impact.

2 A car of mass 600 kg travelling at a speed of 3.0 m s⁻¹ is struck from behind by another vehicle. The impact lasts for 0.40 s and causes the speed of the car to increase to 8.0 m s⁻¹. Calculate:

a the change of momentum of the car due to the impact,

b the impact force.

3 A molecule of mass 5.0×10^{-26} kg moving at a speed of 420 m s⁻¹ hits a surface at right angles to the surface and rebounds at the same speed in the opposite direction in an impact lasting 0.22 ns. Calculate:

a the change of momentum,

b the force on the molecule.

4 Repeat the calculation in Q3 for a molecule of the same mass at the same speed which hits the surface at 60° to the normal and rebounds without loss of speed at 60° to the normal as shown in Figure 6. You will need to work out the component of the molecule's velocity parallel to the normal before and after the impact. Assume the contact time is the same.

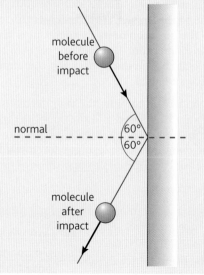

Figure 6

1.3 Conservation of momentum

Learning objectives:

- Is momentum ever lost in a collision?

- What do we mean by *conservation of momentum*?

- What condition must be satisfied if the momentum of a system is conserved?

Specification reference: 3.4.1

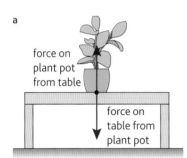

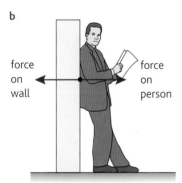

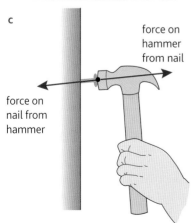

Figure 1 *Examples of Newton's third law*

Newton's third law of motion

When two objects interact, they exert equal and opposite forces on each other.

In other words, if object A exerts a force on object B, there must be an equal and opposite force acting on object A due to object B.

For example,

- an object resting on a table exerts a force on the table which exerts an equal and opposite force on the object;

- a person leaning against a wall exerts a force on the wall which exerts an equal and opposite force on the person;

- a hammer hitting a nail exerts a force on the nail which exerts an equal and opposite force on the hammer;

- the Earth exerts a force due to gravity on an object which exerts an equal and opposite force on the Earth;

- a jet engine exerts a force on hot gas in the engine to expel the gas; the gas being expelled exerts an equal and opposite force on the engine.

The Principle of Conservation of Momentum

When an object is acted on by a resultant force, its momentum changes. If there is no change of its momentum, there can be no resultant force on the object. Now consider several objects which interact with each other. If no external resultant force acts on the objects, the total momentum does not change. However, interactions between the objects can transfer momentum between them. But the total momentum does not change.

The Principle of Conservation of Momentum states that for a system of interacting objects, the total momentum remains constant, provided no external resultant force acts on the system.

Consider two objects that collide with each other then separate. As a result, the momentum of each object changes. They exert equal and opposite forces on each other when they are in contact. So the change of momentum of one object is equal and opposite to the change of momentum of the other object. In other words, if one object gains momentum, the other object loses an equal amount of momentum. So the total amount of momentum is unchanged.

Let's look in detail at the example of two snooker balls A and B in collision, as shown in Figure 2 overleaf.

The impact force F_1 on ball A due to ball B changes the velocity of A from u_A to v_A in time t

Therefore, $F_1 = \dfrac{m_A v_A - m_A u_A}{t}$, where t = the time of contact between A and B, and m_A = the mass of ball A.

11

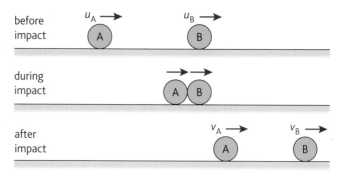

Figure 2 *Conservation of momentum*

The impact force F_2 on ball B due to ball A changes the velocity of B from u_B to v_B in time t.

Therefore, $F_2 = \dfrac{m_B v_B - m_B u_B}{t}$, where t = the time of contact between A and B, and m_B = the mass of ball B.

Because the two forces are equal and opposite to each other, $F_2 = -F_1$

Therefore, $\dfrac{m_B v_B - m_B u_B}{t} = -\dfrac{(m_A v_A - m_A u_A)}{t}$

Cancelling t on both sides gives

$$m_B v_B - m_B u_B = -(m_A v_A - m_A u_A)$$

Rearranging this equation gives

$$m_B v_B + m_A v_A = m_A u_A + m_B u_B$$

Therefore,

the total final momentum = the total initial momentum

Hence the total momentum is unchanged by this collision, i.e. it is conserved.

Note:

If the colliding objects stick together as a result of the collision, they have the same final velocity. The above equation with V as the final velocity may therefore be written

$$(m_B + m_A)V = m_A u_A + m_B u_B$$

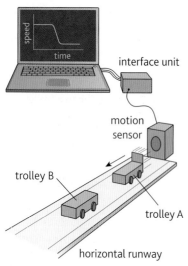

Figure 3 *Testing conservation of momentum*

Testing conservation of momentum

Figure 3 shows an arrangement that can be used to test **conservation of momentum** using a motion sensor linked to a computer. The mass of each trolley is measured before the test. With trolley B at rest, trolley A is given a push so it moves towards trolley B at constant velocity. The two trolleys stick together on impact. The computer records and displays the velocity of trolley A throughout this time.

The computer display shows that the velocity of trolley A dropped suddenly when the impact took place. The velocity of trolley A immediately before the collision, u_A, and after the collision, V, can be measured. The measurements should show that the total momentum of both trolleys after the collision is equal to the momentum of trolley A before the collision. In other words,

$$(m_B + m_A)V = m_A u_A$$

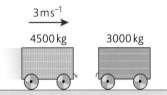

Figure 4

Worked example:

A rail wagon of mass 4500 kg moving along a level track at a speed of 3.0 m s⁻¹ collides with and couples to a second rail wagon of mass 3000 kg which is initially stationary. Calculate the speed of the two wagons immediately after the collision.

Solution

Total initial momentum = initial momentum of A + initial momentum of B

$$= (4500 \times 3.0) + (3000 \times 0) = 13\,500 \text{ kg m s}^{-1}$$

Total final momentum = total mass of A and B × velocity V after the collision

$$= (4500 + 3000)V = 7500V$$

Using the Principle of Conservation of Momentum,

$$7500V = 13\,500$$
$$V = \frac{13\,500}{7500} = 1.8 \text{ m s}^{-1}$$

Head-on collisions

Consider two objects moving in opposite directions that collide with each other. Depending on the masses and initial velocities of the two objects, the collision could cause them both to stop. The momentum of the two objects after the collision would then be zero. This could only happen if the initial momentum of one object was exactly equal and opposite to that of the other object. In general, if two objects move in opposite directions before a collision, then the vector nature of momentum needs to be taken into account by assigning numerical values of velocity + or − according to the direction.

For example, if a car of mass 600 kg travelling at a velocity of 25 m s⁻¹ collides head-on with a lorry of mass 2400 kg travelling at a velocity of 10 m s⁻¹ in the opposite direction, the total momentum before the collision is 9000 kg m s⁻¹ in the direction the lorry was moving. As momentum is conserved in a collision, the total momentum after the collision is the same as the total momentum before the collision. Prove for yourself that if the two vehicles were to stick together after the collision, they must have had a velocity of 3.0 m s⁻¹ in the direction the lorry was moving immediately after the impact.

Application and How science works

Crash barriers

Crash barriers on motorways are designed to stop out-of-control vehicles from entering the opposite carriageway. There were no crash barriers on the first major UK motorway, the M1, when it was opened in 1959. There was no speed limit either. EC regulations require that the strongest barriers are designed to withstand the impact of a 38 tonne heavy goods vehicle hitting the barrier at an angle of 20° at a speed of 18 m s⁻¹ (40 mph). Motorcycles are very vulnerable to crash barriers, particularly wire rope barriers. In 2007, the UK government rejected an e-petition sent by thousands of people to replace these barriers with stronger conventional barriers.

Summary questions

1 A rail wagon of mass 3000 kg moving at a velocity of 1.2 m s⁻¹ collides with a stationary wagon of mass 2000 kg. After the collision, the two wagons couple together. Calculate their speed immediately after the collision.

2 A rail wagon of mass 5000 kg moving at a velocity of 1.6 m s⁻¹ collides with a stationary wagon of mass 3000 kg. After the collision, the 3000 kg wagon moves away at a velocity of 1.5 m s⁻¹. Calculate the speed and direction of the 5000 kg wagon after the collision.

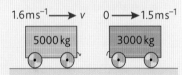

Figure 5

3 In a laboratory experiment, a trolley of mass 0.50 kg moving at a speed of 0.25 m s⁻¹ collided with a trolley of mass 1.0 kg moving in the opposite direction at a speed of 0.20 m s⁻¹. The two trolleys couple together on collision. Calculate their speed and direction immediately after the collision.

4 A ball of mass 0.80 kg moving at a speed of 2.5 m s⁻¹ along a straight line collided with a ball of mass 2.5 kg which was initially stationary. As a result of the collision, the 2.5 kg ball was given a velocity of 1.0 m s⁻¹ along the same line. Calculate the speed and direction of the 0.80 kg ball immediately after the collision.

1.4 Elastic and inelastic collisions

- What is the difference between an elastic collision and an inelastic collision?

- What is conserved in a perfectly elastic collision?

- Are any real collisions ever perfectly elastic?

Specification reference: 3.4.1

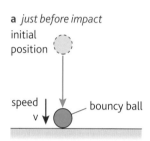

a *just before impact*

initial position

speed v

bouncy ball

b *just after impact*

ball returns to initial height

speed v

bouncy ball

Figure 1 *An elastic impact*

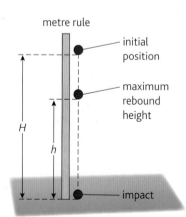

metre rule

initial position

maximum rebound height

H

h

impact

Figure 2 *Testing an impact*

Drop a bouncy rubber ball from a measured height onto a hard floor. The ball should bounce back almost to the same height. Try the same with a cricket ball and there will be very little bounce! An **elastic** ball would be one that bounces back to exactly the same height. Its **kinetic energy** just after impact must equal its kinetic energy just before impact. Otherwise, it cannot regain its initial height. There is no loss of kinetic energy in an **elastic collision**.

An elastic collision is one where there is no loss of kinetic energy.

- A squash ball hitting a hard surface bounces off the surface with little or no loss of speed. If the ball is perfectly elastic, there is no loss of speed on impact and no loss of kinetic energy.

- A very low speed impact between two cars is almost perfectly elastic, provided no damage is done. Some of the initial kinetic energy of the two vehicles may be converted to sound. If the collision causes damage to the vehicles, however, the kinetic energy after the collision is less than before the collision, so the collision is not elastic and may be described as **inelastic**.

A totally inelastic collision is one where the colliding objects stick together.

- A railway wagon that collides with and couples to another wagon is an example of a totally inelastic collision. Some of the initial kinetic energy is converted to other forms of energy.

- A vehicle crash in which the colliding vehicles lock together is another example of a totally inelastic collision. The total kinetic energy after the collision is less than the total kinetic energy before the collision.

A partially inelastic collision is where the colliding objects move apart, and have less kinetic energy after the collision than before.

To work out if a collision is elastic or inelastic, the kinetic energy of each object before and after the collision must be worked out.

Examples

1 For a ball of mass m falling in air from a measured height H above the floor and rebounding to a height h,

   i the kinetic energy immediately before impact = loss of potential energy through height $H = mgH$,

   ii the kinetic energy immediately after impact = gain of potential energy through height $h = mgh$.

So the height ratio h/H gives the fraction of the initial kinetic energy that is recovered as kinetic energy after the collision.

2 For a collision between two objects, the kinetic energy of each object can be worked out using the kinetic energy formula $E_K = \frac{1}{2}mv^2$, where m is the mass of the object and v is its speed. Using this formula, the total initial kinetic energy and the total final kinetic energy can be worked out if the mass, initial speed and speed after collision of each object is known.

Worked example:

A railway wagon of mass 8000 kg moving at 3.0 m s⁻¹ collides with an initially stationary wagon of mass 5000 kg. The two wagons separate after the collision. The 8000 kg wagon moves at a speed of 1.0 m s⁻¹ without change of direction after the collision. Calculate:

a the speed and direction of the 5000 kg wagon after the collision,

b the loss of kinetic energy due to the collision.

Solution

a The total initial momentum = 8000 × 3 = 24 000 kg m s⁻¹

The total final momentum = (8000 × 1.0) + 5000V, where V is the speed of the 5000 kg wagon after the collision.

Using the Principle of Conservation of Momentum

$$8000 + 5000V = 24\,000$$

$$5000V = 24\,000 - 8000 = 16\,000$$

$$V = \frac{16\,000}{5000} = 3.2\,\text{m s}^{-1}$$

b Kinetic energy of the 8000 kg wagon before the collision

$$= \tfrac{1}{2} \times 8000 \times 3.0^2 = 36\,000\,\text{J}$$

Kinetic energy of the 8000 kg wagon after the collision

$$= \tfrac{1}{2} \times 8000 \times 1.0^2 = 4000\,\text{J}$$

Kinetic energy of the 5000 kg wagon after the collision

$$= \tfrac{1}{2} \times 5000 \times 3.2^2 = 25\,600\,\text{J}$$

∴ loss of kinetic energy due to the collision = 36 000 − (4000 + 25 600)

$$= 6400\,\text{J}$$

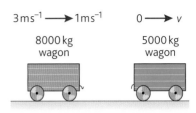

Figure 3

AQA Examiner's tip

Momentum is always conserved in collisions. Total energy is always conserved, but kinetic energy may be converted to other forms.

Link

Excitation by collision in a gas occurs when the gas molecules undergo collisions and are excited to higher energy states. Such a collision is inelastic because the kinetic energy of the colliding particles is less after the collision than before. See AS Physics Topic 3.3, page 35.

Summary questions

1 a A squash ball is released from rest above a flat surface. Describe how its energy changes if:

i it rebounds to the same height,

ii it rebounds to a lesser height.

b In (a) (ii), the ball is released from a height of 1.20 m above the surface and it rebounds to a height of 0.90 m above the surface. Show that 25% of its kinetic energy is lost in the impact.

2 A vehicle of mass 800 kg moving at a speed of 15.0 m s⁻¹ collided with a vehicle of mass 1200 kg moving in the same direction at a speed of 5.0 m s⁻¹. The two vehicles locked together on impact. Calculate:

a the velocity of the two vehicles immediately after impact,

b the loss of kinetic energy due to the impact.

3 An ice puck of mass 1.5 kg moving at a speed of 4.2 m s⁻¹ collides head on with a second ice puck of mass 1.0 kg moving in the opposite direction at a speed of 4.0 m s⁻¹. After the impact, the 1.5 kg ice puck continues in the same direction at a speed of 0.80 m s⁻¹. Calculate:

a the speed and direction of the 1.0 kg ice puck after the collision,

b the loss of kinetic energy due to the collision.

4 The bumper cars at a fairground are designed to withstand low-speed impacts without damage. A bumper car of mass 250 kg moving at a velocity of 0.90 m s⁻¹ collides elastically with a stationary car of mass 200 kg. Immediately after the impact, the 250 kg car has a velocity of 0.10 m s⁻¹ in the same direction as it was initially moving in.

a i Calculate the velocity of the 200 kg car immediately after the impact.

ii Show that collision was an elastic collision.

b Without further calculations, discuss the effect of the impact on the driver of each car.

1.5 Explosions

Learning objectives:

- What energy changes take place in an explosion?

- What can we always say about the total momentum of a system that has exploded?

- What are the consequences when, after the explosion, only two bodies move apart?

Specification reference: 3.4.1

Figure 1 *The gun barrel recoils when the shell is fired. Large springs fitted to the barrel take away and store the kinetic energy of the barrel as it recoils*

When two objects fly apart after being initially at rest, they recoil from each other with equal and opposite amounts of momentum. So they move away from each other in opposite directions. Consider Figure 2 where a trolley of mass m_A and a trolley of mass m_B, initially at rest and in contact, move apart at speeds v_A and v_B respectively when the rod is tapped to release the spring-loaded bolt in trolley A.

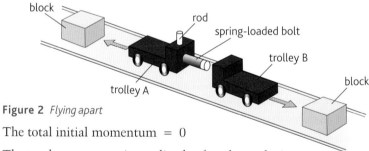

Figure 2 *Flying apart*

The total initial momentum $= 0$

The total momentum immediately after the explosion

$$= \text{momentum of A} + \text{momentum of B}$$

$$= m_A v_A + m_B v_B$$

Using the Principle of Conservation of Momentum, $m_A v_A + m_B v_B = 0$

$$\therefore \qquad m_B v_B = -m_A v_A$$

The minus sign means that the two masses move apart from each other in opposite directions.

For example, if $m_A = 1.0\,\text{kg}$, $v_A = 2.0\,\text{m s}^{-1}$ and $m_B = 0.5\,\text{kg}$,

$$\text{then } v_B = -\frac{m_A v_A}{m_B} = -4.0\,\text{m s}^{-1}$$

So A and B move apart at speeds of $2.0\,\text{m s}^{-1}$ and $4.0\,\text{m s}^{-1}$ in opposite directions.

Link

The α particles from a given isotope are always emitted with the same kinetic energy because they are emitted with the same speed. This is because each α particle and the nucleus that emits it move apart with equal and opposite amounts of momentum. This isn't the case with β particles because a neutrino or antineutrino is emitted as well. See *AS Physics* Topic 1.2.

Testing a model explosion

In Figure 2, when the spring is released from one of the trolleys, the two trolleys, A and B, push each other apart. The blocks are positioned so that the trolleys hit the blocks at the same moment. The distance travelled by each trolley to the point of impact with the block is equal to its speed × the time taken to travel that distance. As the time taken is the same for the two trolleys, the distance ratio is the same as the speed ratio. Because the trolleys have equal (and opposite) amounts of momentum, the ratio of their speeds is the inverse of the mass ratio. The distance ratio should therefore be equal to the inverse of the mass ratio. In other words, if trolley A travels twice as far as trolley B, then the mass of A must be half the mass of B (so they carry away equal amounts of momentum).

Note: In this experiment, the kinetic energy of the two trolleys immediately after they separate from each other is equal to the energy stored in the spring when it was originally compressed. For two or more objects that fly apart due to an explosion, their total kinetic energy immediately after the explosion is less than the total chemical energy released in the explosion because heat, light and sound all carry away energy.

Summary questions

1 A shell of mass 2.0 kg is fired at a speed of 140 m s⁻¹ from an artillery gun of mass 800 kg. Calculate the recoil velocity of the gun.

2 In a laboratory experiment to measure the mass of an object X, two identical trolleys A and B, each of mass 0.50 kg, were initially stationary on a track. Object X was fixed to trolley A. When a trigger was pressed, the two trolleys moved apart in opposite directions at speeds of 0.30 m s⁻¹ and 0.25 m s⁻¹.

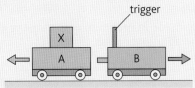

Figure 3

   a Which of the two speeds given above was the speed of trolley A? Give a reason for your answer.

   b Show that the mass of X must have been 0.10 kg.

3 Two trolleys, X of mass 1.20 kg and Y of mass 0.80 kg, are initially stationary on a level track.

   a When a trigger is pressed on one of the trolleys, a spring pushes the two trolleys apart. Trolley Y moves away at a velocity of 0.15 m s⁻¹.

      i Calculate the velocity of X.

      ii Calculate the total kinetic energy of the two trolleys immediately after the explosion.

   b In part **a**, if the test had been carried out with trolley X held firmly, calculate the speed at which Y would have recoiled, assuming the energy stored in the spring before release is equal to the total kinetic energy calculated in **a ii**.

4 A person in a stationary boat of total mass 150 kg throws a rock of mass 2.0 kg out of the boat. As a result, the boat recoils at a speed of 0.12 m s⁻¹. Calculate **a** the speed at which the rock was thrown from the boat, **b** the kinetic energy gained by **i** the boat, **ii** the rock.

1   ISA

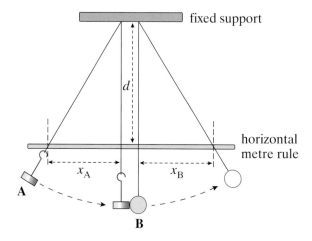

Figure 1
In an impact investigation by two students, a mass hanger **A** suspended on a thread
was displaced from its equilibrium position by a certain distance and released so it
collided with a ball **B** suspended on a thread. A horizontal metre ruler fixed in a clamp
(not shown) was used to measure the horizontal displacements x_A and x_B of each
thread from its equilibrium position at the level of the metre ruler, as shown in the
diagram. The vertical distance, d, of the ruler below the upper end of the threads was measured.

The measurement of x_B was repeated without changing x_A and d for different
additional masses added to the mass hanger.

(a) The measurements shown in Table 1 were made in preliminary tests using a total
     mass m for the mass of the hanger and the additional mass.

Table 1

m/kg	x_B/mm	
0.100	60	62
0.200	77	75
0.300	80	78

The students decided to make further measurements between 0.100 and 0.200 kg
and above 0.300 kg. Why do you think they made this decision?   *(4 marks)*

(b) Table 2 shows all their measurements.

Table 2

m/kg	x_B/mm	x_B/mm				$<x_B>$/mm	$\theta/°$
0.100	60	62	58	58	60	59.6	8.47
0.120	67	68	68	65	62	66.0	9.37
0.150	68	73	70	68	70	69.8	9.90
0.200	77	75	78	71	76	75.4	10.67
0.300	80	78	79	80	80	79.4	11.22
0.600	86	85	88	85	88		

$d = 400$ mm, $x_A = 60$ mm

The maximum angular displacement θ of the thread from equilibrium can be calculated using the equation $\tan\theta = \langle x_B\rangle/d$, where $\langle x_B\rangle$ is the mean value of x_B. This has been done in Table 2 for all the rows except the last one.

Copy and complete Table 2 by calculating $\langle x_B\rangle$ and θ for $m = 0.600$ kg.

(2 marks)

(c) (i) By considering the energy changes of B after the impact, show its velocity V immediately after the impact is given by $V = \surd(2gh)$ where h is B's maximum height gain from its equilibrium position. *(2 marks)*

(ii) The height gain h can be calculated using the trigonometry formula $h = l(1 - \cos\theta)$ where l is the distance along the thread from the point of suspension of the ball to its centre. This distance was measured to be 575 mm. For each mass m, Table 3 shows the results of these calculations except for the last row. Copy the table and complete this last row. The last 2 columns are for the next question.

Table 3

m/kg	$\theta/^\circ$	h/mm	V/m s^{-1}		
0.100	8.47	6.27	0.351		
0.120	9.37	7.67	0.388		
0.150	9.90	8.56	0.410		
0.200	10.67	9.95	0.442		
0.300	11.22	11.00	0.465		
0.600					

(2 marks)

(d) The students found a theoretical analysis of the impact which gave the following equation relating V and m:

$$\frac{1}{V} = \frac{kM}{m} + k$$

where M is the mass of the ball and k is a constant.

(i) Plot a suitable graph to see if this relationship is correct. Show the results of any further calculations you carry out in the last two columns of your own Table 3.

(ii) Using your graph or otherwise, determine values for k and M. *(9 marks)*

(e) (i) What conclusions do you draw from the graph?

(ii) Use your results to evaluate your conclusions.

(3 marks)

Extension question

The theoretical analysis is based on the diagram below in which an object (**A**) of mass m moving at velocity v collides with a stationary object (**B**) of mass M. After the impact, the two objects move apart at velocities v and V in the same direction as A's initial direction.

i) before

ii) after

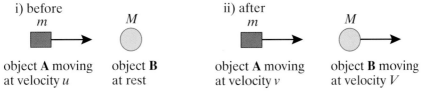

object **A** moving   object **B**   object **A** moving   object **B** moving
at velocity u at rest   at velocity v at velocity V

Figure 2

The theoretical analysis assumed that the velocity of **B** relative to **A** after the collision $(V - v) = eu$, where e is a constant that depends on the two objects.

(f) Combine the equation above with the equation representing conservation of momentum to derive the theoretical equation given in question 3

where $k = \dfrac{1}{(1 + e)u}$ *(5 marks)*

2 (a) Collisions can be described as *elastic* or *inelastic*.
State what is meant by an inelastic collision. *(1 mark)*

(b) A ball of mass 0.12 kg strikes a stationary cricket bat with a speed of 18 m s⁻¹. The ball is in contact with the bat for 0.14 s and returns along its original path with a speed of 15 m s⁻¹. Calculate:

(i) the momentum of the ball before the collision,

(ii) the momentum of the ball after the collision,

(iii) the total change of momentum of the ball,

(iv) the average force acting on the ball during contact with the bat,

(v) the kinetic energy lost by the ball as a result of the collision. *(6 marks)*

AQA, 2001

3 Two carts **A** and **B**, with a compressed spring between them, are pushed together and held at rest, as shown in **Figure 3**. The spring is not attached to either cart. The carts are then released.

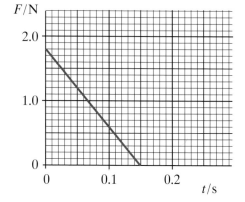

Figure 3   **Figure 4**

Figure 4 shows how the force, F, exerted by the spring on the carts varies with time, t, after release.

When the spring returns to its unstretched length and drops away, cart **A** is moving at 0.60 m s⁻¹.

(a) Calculate the impulse given to each cart by the spring as it expands.

(b) Calculate the mass of cart **A**.

(c) State the final total momentum of the system at the instant the spring drops away. *(5 marks)*

AQA, 2004

4 A railway engine is about to couple with a stationary carriage of mass 4.0×10^4 kg. When they have joined up, the engine and the carriage move at a constant speed. The engine has a mass of 6.2×10^4 kg and is moving at 0.35 m s⁻¹ just before coupling.

(a) (i) Calculate the momentum of the engine.

(ii) Calculate the speed of the engine and carriage after coupling. *(5 marks)*

(b) **Figure 5** shows the engine and carriage as they strike a buffer with an initial speed of 0.15 m s⁻¹. Assuming that the buffer behaves like a spring of stiffness 320 kN m⁻¹, calculate the maximum compression of the 'spring'. *(4 marks)*

engine   carriage   buffer spring

Figure 5

AQA, 2007

5 (a) State two quantities that are conserved in an elastic collision. *(2 marks)*

   (b) A gas molecule makes an elastic collision with the walls of a gas cylinder. The molecule is travelling at $450\,\mathrm{m\,s^{-1}}$ at right angles towards the wall before the collision.

      (i) What is the magnitude and direction of its velocity after the collision?

      (ii) Calculate the change in momentum of the molecule during the collision if it has a mass of $8.0 \times 10^{-26}\,\mathrm{kg}$. *(4 marks)*

   (c) Use Newton's laws of motion to explain how the molecules of a gas exert a force on the wall of a container. *(4 marks)*

   AQA, 2006

6 (a) When an α particle is emitted from a nucleus of the polonium isotope $^{210}_{84}\mathrm{Po}$, a nucleus of lead (Pb) is formed. Complete the equation below.

$$^{210}_{84}\mathrm{Po} \longrightarrow \alpha + \mathrm{Pb}$$ *(2 marks)*

   (b) The α particle in part (a) is emitted at a speed of $1.6 \times 10^7\,\mathrm{m\,s^{-1}}$.

      (i) The mass of the α particle is $4.0\,\mathrm{u}$. Calculate the kinetic energy, in MeV, of the α particle immediately after it has been emitted. Ignore relativistic effects.

      (ii) Calculate the speed of recoil of the daughter nucleus immediately after the α particle has been emitted. Assume the parent nucleus is initially at rest. *(6 marks)*

   AQA, 2006

7 **Figure 6** shows how the force, F, on a steel ball varies with time, t, when the ball is dropped onto a thick steel plate and rebounds. The kinetic energy of the ball after the collision is the same as it was before the collision.

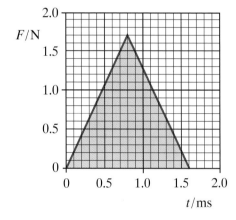

   Figure 6

   (a) State the name of the quantity that is obtained by determining the shaded area.

   (b) Use the graph **Figure 6** to determine the initial momentum of the ball.

   (c) Sketch a graph to show how the momentum of the ball varies between times $t = 0$ and $t = 2.0\,\mathrm{ms}$. *(6 marks)*

   AQA, 2006

8 (a) Explain what is meant by the principle of conservation of momentum. *(2 marks)*

   (b) A hose pipe is used to water a garden. The supply delivers water at a rate of $0.31\,\mathrm{kg\,s^{-1}}$ to the nozzle which has a cross-sectional area of $7.3 \times 10^{-5}\,\mathrm{m^2}$.

      (i) Show that water leaves the nozzle at a speed of about $4\ \mathrm{m\,s^{-1}}$.

      density of water $= 1000\,\mathrm{kg\,m^{-3}}$

      (ii) Before it leaves the hose, the water has a speed of $0.68\ \mathrm{m\,s^{-1}}$. Calculate the force on the hose.

      (iii) The water from the hose is sprayed onto a brick wall the base of which is firmly embedded in the ground. Explain why there is no overall effect on the rotation of the Earth. *(7 marks)*

   AQA, 2005

2.1 Uniform circular motion

Learning objectives:

▨ How can we recognise uniform motion in a circle?

▨ What do we need to measure to find the speed of an object moving in uniform circular motion?

▨ What is meant by angular displacement and angular speed?

Specification reference: 3.4.1

Figure 1 *In uniform circular motion*

Figure 2 *The London Eye*

In a cycle race, the cyclists pedal furiously at top speed. The speed of the perimeter of each wheel is the same as the cyclist's speed, provided the wheels do not slip on the ground. If the cyclist's speed is constant, the wheels must turn at a steady rate. An object rotating at a steady rate is said to be in **uniform circular motion**.

Consider a point on the perimeter of a wheel of radius r rotating at a steady speed.

▨ The circumference of the wheel $= 2\pi r$

▨ The frequency of rotation $f = \dfrac{1}{T}$, where T is the time for one rotation.

The speed v of a point on the perimeter = circumference/time for 1 rotation $= \dfrac{2\pi r}{T} = 2\pi r f$

$$v = \frac{2\pi r}{T}$$

Worked example:

A cyclist is travelling at a speed of 25 m s⁻¹ on a bicycle which has wheels of radius 750 mm. Calculate:

a the time for one rotation of the wheel,

b i the frequency of rotation of the wheel,

  ii the number of rotations of the wheel in 1 minute.

Solution

a Rearranging speed $v = \dfrac{2\pi r}{T}$ gives the time for 1 rotation, $T = \dfrac{2\pi r}{v}$

  Therefore, $T = \dfrac{2\pi \times 0.75}{25} = 0.19\,\text{s}$

b i Frequency $f = \dfrac{1}{T} = \dfrac{1}{0.19} = 5.3\,\text{Hz}$

  ii Number of rotations in 1 min $= 60 \times 5.3 = 318$

▨ Angular displacement and angular speed

The London Eye is a very popular tourist attraction. The wheel has a diameter of 130 m and takes passengers high above the surrounding buildings, giving a glorious view on a clear day. Each full rotation of the wheel takes 30 min. Each capsule therefore takes its passengers through an angle of 0.2° each second ($= \pi /900$ radians each second). Therefore, each capsule turns through an angle of

▨ 2° in 10 s,

▨ 20° ($= \dfrac{2\pi}{18}$ radians) in 100 s,

▨ 90° ($= \dfrac{\pi}{2}$ radians) in 450 s.

For any object in uniform circular motion, the object turns through an angle of $\frac{2\pi}{T}$ radians each second where T is the time taken for 1 complete rotation. In other words, the angular displacement of the object each second is $\frac{2\pi}{T}$.

The **angular displacement** of the object in time t is therefore given by

θ (in radians) $= \frac{2\pi t}{T} = 2\pi f t$ where T is the time for one rotation and $f\left(= \frac{1}{T}\right)$ is the frequency of rotation.

The **angular speed, ω,** is defined as the angular displacement per second.

Hence, ω = angular displacement, θ /time taken, $t = \frac{2\pi}{T} = 2\pi f$

The unit of ω is the radian per second (rad s^{-1})

Worked example:

A cyclist travels at a speed of 12 m s^{-1} on a bicycle which has wheels of radius 0.40 m. Calculate:

a the frequency of rotation of each wheel,

b the angular speed of each wheel,

c the angle the wheel turns through in 0.10 s in

    i radians,   ii degrees.

Solution

a Circumference of wheel $= 2\pi r = 2\pi \times 0.4 = 2.5$ m

    Time for 1 wheel rotation, $T = \dfrac{\text{circumference}}{\text{speed}} = \dfrac{2.5}{12} = 0.21$ s

    Frequency $f = \dfrac{1}{T} = \dfrac{1}{0.21} = 4.8$ Hz

b Angular speed $\omega = \dfrac{2\pi}{T} = 30$ rad s^{-1}

c i Angle the wheel turns through in 0.10 s, $\theta = \dfrac{2\pi t}{T} = \dfrac{2\pi \times 0.10}{0.21} = 3.0$ rad

    ii $\theta = 3.0 \times \dfrac{360}{2\pi} = 172°$

Summary questions

1 Calculate the angular displacement in radians of the tip of the minute hand of a clock in:

    a 1 second,   b 1 minute,   c 1 hour.

2 An electric motor turns at a frequency of 50 Hz. Calculate:

    a its time period,

    b the angle it turns through in radians in

      i 1 ms,   ii 1 s.

3 The Earth takes exactly 24 h for 1 full rotation. Calculate:

    a the speed of rotation of a point on the equator,

    b the angle the Earth turns through in 1 s in

      i degrees,   ii radians.

    The radius of the Earth = 6400 km.

4 A satellite in a circular orbit of radius 8000 km takes 120 minutes per orbit. Calculate:

    a its speed,   b its angular displacement in 1.0 s in

      i degrees,   ii radians.

Note

1 In time t, an object in uniform circular motion at speed v moves along the arc of the circle through a distance

$$s = vt = \frac{2\pi r t}{T} = \theta r$$

2 Speed $v = \dfrac{2\pi r}{T} = \omega r$ (as $\omega = \dfrac{2\pi}{T}$)

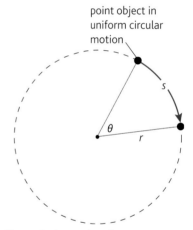

Figure 3 *Arcs and angles*

2.2 Centripetal acceleration

Learning objectives:

▨ Why is the velocity not constant when a body is travelling uniformly in a circle?

▨ In which direction does the acceleration take place?

▨ How can we calculate the centripetal force?

Specification reference: 3.4.1

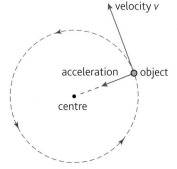

Figure 1 *Centripetal acceleration*

Note

▨ Proof of this equation is not required for the A2 specification. However, a proof is given here to provide a better understanding of the idea of centripetal acceleration.

▨ As the speed $v = \omega r$, then

$$a = \frac{v^2}{r} = \frac{(\omega r)^2}{r} = \omega^2 r$$

The equation for centripetal acceleration can then be written in terms of ω and r as $a = \omega^2 r$

Link

Remember that acceleration and velocity are vectors and that the direction of acceleration of an object is always the same as the direction of the resultant force on the object. See *AS Physics* Topic 9.1.

The **velocity** of an object moving round a circle at constant speed continually changes direction. Because its velocity changes, the object therefore accelerates. If this seems odd because the speed is constant, remember that acceleration is change of velocity per second. Passengers on the London Eye might not notice they are being accelerated but if the wheel rotated much faster, they undoubtedly would.

The velocity of an object in uniform circular motion at any point is along the tangent to the circle at that point. The direction of the velocity changes continuously as the object moves round on its circular path. The change in the direction of the velocity is towards the centre of the circle. So its acceleration is towards the centre of the circle and is referred to as **centripetal acceleration**. Centripetal means 'towards the centre of the circle'.

For an object moving at constant speed v in a circle of radius r, it can be shown that

$$\text{its centripetal acceleration, } a = \frac{v^2}{r}$$

Proof of $a = \frac{v^2}{r}$

▨ Consider an object in uniform circular motion at speed v moving in a short time interval δt from position A to position B along the perimeter of a circle of radius r. Therefore the distance AB along the circle, $\delta s = v\delta t$. Figure 2 shows the idea.

▨ The line from the object to the centre of the circle at C turns through angle $\delta\theta$ when the object moves from A to B. The velocity direction of the object turns through the same angle $\delta\theta$, as shown in Figure 2.

▨ The change of velocity, δv = velocity at B – velocity at A, is shown in the velocity vector triangle in Figure 2.

▨ The triangles ABC and the velocity vector triangle have the same shape because they both have two sides of equal length with the same angle $\delta\theta$ between the two sides.

Provided $\delta\theta$ is small, then $\qquad \dfrac{\delta v}{v} = \dfrac{\delta s}{r}$

Because $\delta s = v\delta t$, then $\qquad \dfrac{\delta v}{v} = v\dfrac{\delta t}{r}$

Therefore, acceleration, $a = \dfrac{\text{change of velocity}}{\text{time taken}} = \dfrac{\delta v}{\delta t}$

$$= \frac{v^2}{r} \text{ towards the centre}$$

▨ Centripetal force

To make an object move round on a circular path, it must be acted on by a resultant force which changes its direction of motion.

The resultant force on an object moving round a circle at constant speed is referred to as the **centripetal force** because it acts in the same direction as the centripetal acceleration, which is towards the centre of the circle.

▨ For an object whirling round on the end of a string, the tension in the string is the centripetal force,

■ For a satellite moving round the Earth, the force of gravity between the satellite and the Earth is the centripetal force,

■ For a planet moving round the Sun, the force of gravity between the planet and the Sun is the centripetal force,

■ For a capsule on the London Eye, the centripetal force is the resultant of the support force on the capsule and the force of gravity on it.

■ In Chapter 7, you will meet the use of a magnetic field to bend a beam of charged particles (e.g. electrons) in a circular path. The magnetic force on the moving charged particles is the centripetal force.

Any object that moves in circular motion is acted on by a resultant force which always acts towards the centre of the circle. The resultant force is the centripetal force and therefore causes a centripetal acceleration.

Equation for centripetal force

For an object moving at constant speed v along a circular path of radius r,

its centripetal acceleration $a = \dfrac{v^2}{r} = \omega^2 r \left(\text{where } \omega = \dfrac{v}{r} \right)$

Therefore, applying Newton's second law for constant mass in the form '$F = ma$' gives

$$\text{centripetal force } F = \frac{mv^2}{r} = m\omega^2 r$$

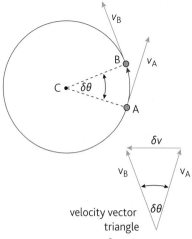

Figure 2 Proving $a = \dfrac{v^2}{r}$

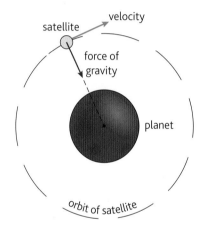

Figure 3 A satellite in uniform circular motion

Summary questions

1 The wheel of the London Eye has a diameter of 130 m and takes 30 minutes for a full rotation. Calculate:

a the speed of a capsule,

b i the centripetal acceleration of a capsule,

ii the centripetal force on a person of mass 65 kg in a capsule.

2 An object of mass 0.15 kg moves round a circular path of radius 0.42 m at a steady rate once every 5.0 s. Calculate:

a the speed and acceleration of the object,

b the centripetal force on the object.

3 a The Earth moves round the Sun on a circular orbit of radius 1.5 × 10^{11} m, taking 365¼ days for each complete orbit. Calculate:

i the speed,

ii the centripetal acceleration of the Earth on its orbit round the Sun.

b A satellite is in orbit just above the surface of a spherical planet which has the same radius as the Earth and the same acceleration of free fall at its surface. Calculate:

i the speed,

ii the time for 1 complete orbit of this satellite.

Radius of the Earth = 6400 km   Acceleration of free fall = 9.8 m s^{-2}

4 A hammer thrower whirls a 2.0 kg hammer on the end of a rope in a circle of radius 0.80 m. The hammer took 0.60 s to make one full rotation just before it was released. Calculate:

a the speed of the hammer just before it was released,

b its centripetal acceleration,

c the centripetal force on the hammer just before it was released.

Note

1 If the object is acted on by a single force only (e.g. a satellite in orbit round the Earth), that force is the centripetal force and causes the centripetal acceleration.

2 The centripetal force is at right angles to the direction of the object's velocity. Therefore, no work is done by the centripetal force on the object because there is no displacement in the direction of the force. The kinetic energy of the object is therefore constant, so its speed is unchanged.

2.3 On the road

Learning objectives:

- Why do we seem to be thrown outwards if a car rounds a bend too quickly?

- What happens to the force between a passenger and his seat on a curved bridge?

- What forces provide the centripetal force on a banked track?

Specification reference: 3.4.1

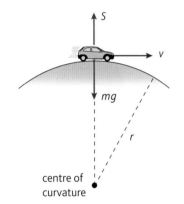

Figure 1 *Over the top*

Even on a very short journey, the effects of circular motion can be important. For example, a vehicle that turns a corner too fast could skid or topple over. A vehicle that goes over a curved bridge too fast might even lose contact briefly with the road surface. To make any object move on a circular path, the object must be acted on by a resultant force which is always towards the centre of curvature of its path.

Over the top of a hill

Consider a vehicle of mass m moving at speed v along a road that passes over the top of a hill or over the top of a curved bridge.

At the top of the hill, the support force S from the road on the vehicle is directly upwards in the opposite direction to its weight, mg. The resultant force on the vehicle is the difference between the weight and the support force. This difference acts towards the centre of curvature of the hill as the centripetal force. In other words,

$$mg - S = \frac{mv^2}{r},$$

where r is the radius of curvature of the hill

The vehicle would lose contact with the road if its speed is equal to or greater than a certain speed, v_0. If this happens, then the support force is zero (i.e. $S = 0$) so $mg = \frac{mv_0^2}{r}$.

Therefore, the vehicle speed should not exceed v_0, where $v_0^2 = gr$, otherwise the vehicle will lose contact with the road surface at the top of the hill. Prove for yourself that a vehicle that travels over a curved bridge of radius of curvature 5 m would lose contact with the road surface if its speed exceeded 7 m s^{-1}.

On a roundabout

Consider a vehicle of mass m moving at speed v in a circle of radius r as it moves round a roundabout on a level road. The centripetal force is provided by the force of friction between the vehicle's tyres and the road surface. In other words,

$$\text{force of friction } F = \frac{mv^2}{r}$$

For no skidding or slipping, the force of friction between the tyres and the road surface must be less than a limiting value F_0 which is proportional to the vehicle's weight.

Therefore, for no slipping, the speed of the vehicle must be less than a certain value v_0 which is given by the equation,

$$\text{limiting force of friction } F_0 = \frac{mv_0^2}{r}$$

Note: As F_0 is proportional to the vehicle's weight, then $F_0 = \mu mg$, where μ is the coefficient of friction.

Therefore $\mu mg = \frac{mv_0^2}{r}$.

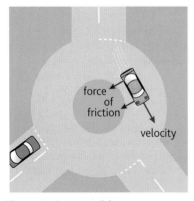

Figure 2 *On a roundabout*

The maximum speed for no slipping, $v_0 = (\mu g r)^{1/2}$

(μ is not on this A2 specification, but you might meet it if you are studying A level maths.)

On a banked track

A race track is often banked where it curves. Motorway slip roads often bend in a tight curve. Such a road is usually banked to enable vehicles to drive round without any sideways friction on the tyres. Rail tracks on curves are usually banked to enable trains to move round the curve without slowing down too much. Imagine you are an engineer and you have to design a banked track for a horizontal motorway curve.

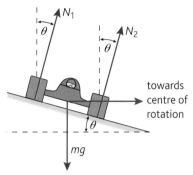

■ Without any banking, the centripetal force on a road vehicle is provided only by sideways friction between the vehicle wheels and the road surface. As explained in the previous example, the vehicle on a bend slips outwards if its speed is too high.

towards centre of rotation

Figure 3 *A racing car taking a bend*

■ On a banked track, the speed can be higher. To understand why, consider Figure 3 which represents the front-view of a racing car of mass m on a banked track, where θ = the angle of the track to the horizontal. For there to be no sideways friction on the tyres due to the road, the horizontal component of the support forces N_1 and N_2 must act as the centripetal force.

Resolving these forces into horizontal components $(= (N_1 + N_2) \sin\theta)$ and a vertical component $(= (N_1 + N_2) \cos\theta)$, then

- because $(N_1 + N_2) \sin\theta$ acts as the centripetal force,

  then $(N_1 + N_2) \sin\theta = \dfrac{mv^2}{r}$,

- because $(N_1 + N_2) \cos\theta$ balances the weight (mg), then

$(N_1 + N_2) \cos\theta = mg$

Therefore $\tan\theta = \dfrac{(N_1 + N_2) \sin\theta}{(N_1 + N_2) \cos\theta} = \dfrac{mv^2}{mgr}$

Simplifying this equation gives the condition for no sideways friction:

$\tan\theta = \dfrac{v^2}{gr}$

In other words, there is no sideways friction if the speed v is such that
$$v^2 = gr\tan\theta$$

Prove for yourself that if the banking angle θ is not to exceed 5° and the radius of curvature is 360 m, the speed for zero sideways friction is 18 m s⁻¹.

> **Link**
>
> The horizontal and vertical components of a force F which is at angle θ to the vertical must be F sin θ and F cos θ respectively. See *AS Physics* Topic 7.1.

Summary questions

$g = 9.8\,\text{m s}^{-2}$.

1 A vehicle of mass 1200 kg passes over a bridge of radius of curvature 15 m at a speed of 10 m s⁻¹. Calculate:

a the centripetal acceleration of the vehicle on the bridge,

b the support force on the vehicle when it was at the top.

2 The maximum speed for no skidding of a vehicle of mass 750 kg on a roundabout of radius 20 m is 9.0 m s⁻¹. Calculate:

a the centripetal acceleration,

b the centripetal force on the vehicle when moving at this speed.

3 Explain why a circular athletics track is banked for sprinters but not for marathon runners.

4 At a racing car circuit, the track is banked at an angle of 25° to the horizontal on a bend which has a radius of curvature of 350 m.

a Use the formula $v^2 = gr \tan\theta$ to calculate the speed of a vehicle on the bend if there is to be no sideways friction on its tyres.

b Discuss and explain what could happen to a vehicle that took the bend too fast.

2.4 At the fairground

Learning objectives:

■ When is the contact force on a passenger greatest on a 'big dipper'?

■ What condition applies when a passenger just fails to keep in contact with his seat?

Specification reference: 3.4.1

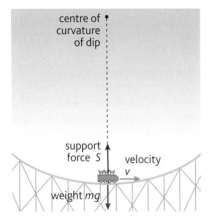

Figure 1 In a dip

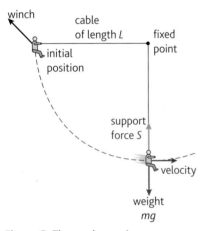

Figure 2 The very long swing

Many of the rides at a fairground or amusement park take people round in circles. Some examples are analysed below. It is worth remembering that centripetal acceleration values of more than 2–3 g can be dangerous to the average person.

The Big Dipper

A ride that takes you at high speed through a big dip pushes you into your seat as you pass through the dip. The difference between the support force on you (acting upwards) and your weight acts as the centripetal force.

At the bottom of the dip, the support force S on you is vertically upwards, as shown in Figure 1.

Therefore, for a speed v at the bottom of a dip of radius of curvature r,

$$S - mg = \frac{mv^2}{r}$$

So the support force $S = mg + \dfrac{mv^2}{r}$

The extra force you experience due to circular motion is therefore mv^2/r.

The very long swing

In this 'ride', a person of mass m on a very long swing of length L is released from height h above the equilibrium position. The maximum speed is when the swing passes through the lowest point. This can be worked out by equating the gain of kinetic energy to the loss of potential energy.

$$\tfrac{1}{2}mv^2 = mgh$$

where v is its speed as it passes through the lowest point.

Therefore $v^2 = 2gh$

The person on the swing is on a circular path of radius L. At the lowest point, the support force S on the person due to the rope is in the opposite direction to the person's weight, mg. The difference, $S - mg$, acts towards the centre of the circular path and provides the centripetal force. Therefore

$$S - mg = \frac{mv^2}{L}$$

Because $v^2 = 2gh$, then $S - mg = \dfrac{2mgh}{L}$

In other words, $\dfrac{2mgh}{L}$ represents the extra support force the person experiences due to circular motion. Prove for yourself that for $h = L$ (i.e. a 90° swing), the extra support force is equal to twice the person's weight.

The Big Wheel

This ride takes its passengers round in a vertical circle on the inside of the circumference of a very large wheel. The wheel turns fast enough to stop the passengers falling out as they pass through the highest position.

At maximum height, the reaction R from the wheel on each person acts downwards. So, the resultant force at this position $= mg + R$. This reaction force and the weight provide the centripetal force. Therefore, at the highest position when the wheel speed is v,

$mg + R = \dfrac{mv^2}{r}$ where r is the radius of the wheel

$\therefore R = \dfrac{mv^2}{r} - mg$

At a certain speed v_0 such that $v_0^2 = gr$, then $R = 0$ so there would be no force on the person due to the wall.

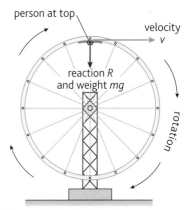

Figure 3 *The Big Wheel*

Application and How science works

Safe rides

Amusement rides are checked regularly to ensure they are safe. Accidents on such rides in the United Kingdom have to be investigated by the Health and Safety Executive (HSE). A passenger on a ride may experience 'g-forces' in different directions that may be back and forth, side to side or normal to the track. HSE have found that the g-forces in accidents were found to be within acceptable limits for amusement rides and other factors such as passenger behaviour and passenger height in relation to compartment design were more significant. In particular, a passenger should be able to sit back in their seat with their feet on the foot rests or floor and be able to comfortably reach the hand holds.

Figure 4 *g-forces at work*

Summary questions

$g = 9.8\,\mathrm{m\,s^{-2}}$.

1 A train on a fairground ride is initially stationary before it descends through a height of 45 m into a dip which has a radius of curvature of 78 m, as shown in Figure 5.

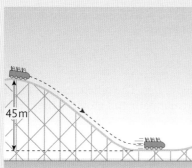

Figure 5

a Calculate the speed of the train at the bottom of the dip, assuming air resistance and friction are negligible.

b Calculate

  i   the centripetal acceleration of the train at the bottom of the dip,

  ii   the extra support force on a person of weight 600 N in the train.

2 A very long swing at a fairground is 32 m in length. A person of mass 69 kg on the swing descends from a position when the swing is horizontal. Calculate:

a the speed of the person at the lowest point,

b the centripetal acceleration at the lowest point,

c the support force on the person at the lowest point.

3 The Big Wheel at a fairground has a radius of 12.0 m and rotates once every 6.0 s. Calculate:

a the speed of rotation of the perimeter of the wheel,

b the centripetal acceleration of a person on the perimeter,

c the support force on a person of mass 72 kg at the highest point.

4 The wheel of the London Eye has a diameter of 130 m and takes 30 minutes to complete 1 revolution. Calculate the change due to rotation of the wheel of the support force on a person of weight 500 N in a capsule at the top of the wheel.

1   **Figure 1** shows a cross-section of an automatic brake fitted to a rotating shaft. The brake pads are held on the shaft by springs.

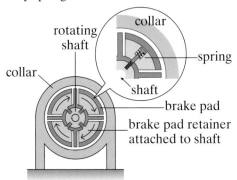

Figure 1

(a) Explain why the brake pads press against the inner surface of the stationary collar if the shaft rotates too fast. *(3 marks)*

(b) Each brake pad and its retainer has a mass of 0.30 kg and its centre of mass is 60 mm from the centre of the shaft. The tension in the spring attached to each pad is 250 N. Calculate the maximum frequency of rotation of the shaft for no braking. *(4 marks)*

(c) Automatic brakes of the type described above are used on ships to prevent lifeboats falling freely when they are lowered on cables onto the water. Discuss how the performance of the brake would be affected if the springs gradually became weaker. *(2 marks)*

2   (a) A particle that moves uniformly in a circular path is accelerating yet moving at a constant speed.

   Explain this statement by reference to the physical principles involved. *(3 marks)*

(b) A 0.10 kg mass is to be placed on a horizontal turntable that is then rotated at a fixed rate of 78 revolutions per minute. The mass may be placed on the table at any distance, r, from the axis of rotation, as shown in **Figure 2**.

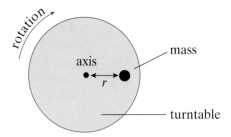

Figure 2

If the maximum frictional force between the mass and the turntable is 0.50 N, calculate the maximum value of the distance r at which the mass would stay on the turntable at this rate of rotation. *(4 marks)*

AQA, 2007

3   **Figure 3** shows a dust particle at position **D** on a rotating vinyl disc. A combination of electrostatic and frictional forces act on the dust particle to keep it in the same position.

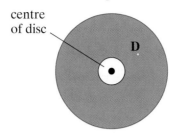

Figure 3

The dust particle is at a distance of 0.125 m from the centre of the disc. The disc rotates at 45 revolutions per minute.

(a) Calculate the linear speed of the dust particle at D.   *(3 marks)*

(b) (i)   Copy the diagram and mark an arrow to show the direction of the resultant horizontal force on the dust particle.

     (ii) Calculate the centripetal acceleration at position D.   *(3 marks)*

(c) On looking closely at the rotating disc it can be seen that there is more dust concentrated on the inner part of the disc than the outer part. Suggest why this should be so.   *(3 marks)*

AQA, 2002

4   A strimmer is a tool for cutting long grass. A strimmer head such as that shown in **Figure 4a** is driven by a motor. This makes the plastic line rotate causing it to cut the grass. To simplify analysis, the strimmer line is modelled as the arrangement shown in **Figure 4b**. In this model the effective mass of the line is considered to rotate at the end of the line.

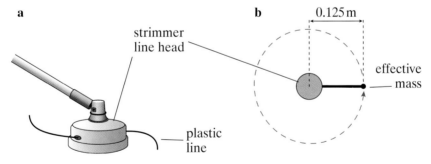

Figure 4

In one strimmer the effective mass of 0.80 g rotates in a circle of radius 0.125 m at 9000 revolutions per minute.

(a) Show that the angular speed of the line is approximately 9.4×10^2 rad s^{-1}.   *(2 marks)*

(b) (i)   Explain how the centripetal force is applied to the effective mass.

     (ii) Calculate the centripetal force acting on the effective mass.   *(4 marks)*

(c) The line strikes a pebble of mass 1.2 g, making contact for a time of 0.68 ms. This causes the pebble to fly off at a speed of 15 m s^{-1}.

Calculate the average force applied to the pebble.   *(3 marks)*

AQA, 2007

5   **Figure 5** shows a toy engine moving with a constant speed on a circular track of constant radius.

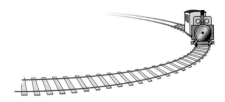

Figure 5

(a) (i) Explain why the engine is accelerating even though its speed remains constant.

    (ii) Mark on a copy of **Figure 5** the direction of the centripetal force acting on the engine. *(3 marks)*

(b) The total mass of the toy engine is 0.14 kg and it travels with a speed of $0.17 \, \text{m s}^{-1}$. The radius of the track is 0.80 m. Calculate the centripetal force acting on the engine. *(2 marks)*

Figure 6 shows a close up of a pair of wheels as the engine moves towards you in the forward direction shown in **Figure 5**.

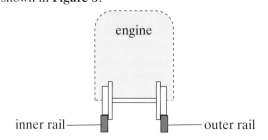

Figure 6

(c) (i) State and explain on which wheel the centripetal force acts at the instant shown. You may use **Figure 6** to help your explanation.

    (ii) For the toy engine going round a curved track, state and explain the two factors which determine the stress on each wheel. *(5 marks)*

AQA, 2004

6   A mass of 30 g is attached to a thread and whirled in a circle of radius 45 cm. The circle is in a horizontal plane. The tension in the thread is 0.35 N.

(a) Calculate:

    (i) the speed of the mass,

    (ii) the period of rotation of the mass. *(4 marks)*

(b) The mass M is now whirled in a circle in a vertical plane as shown in **Figure 7**.

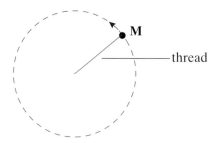

Figure 7

    (i) On a copy of **Figure 7**, label the forces acting on the mass, and use arrows to show their direction.

    (ii) Without performing calculations, state and explain the difference between the tension in the thread when M is at the top of the circle and when it is at the bottom. *(6 marks)*

AQA, 2007

7   **Figure 8** shows the initial path taken by an electron when it is produced as a result of a collision in a cloud chamber.

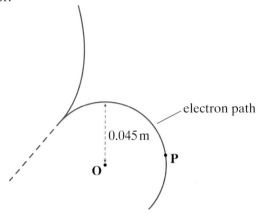

Figure 8

The path is the arc of a circle of radius 0.045 m with centre O.

The speed of the electron is 4.2×10^7 m s^{-1}. The mass of an electron is 9.1×10^{-31} kg.

(a) Calculate the momentum of the electron.   *(2 marks)*

(b) Calculate the magnitude of the force acting on the electron that makes it follow the curved path.   *(2 marks)*

(c) Show on a copy of **Figure 8** the direction of this force when an electron is at point P.   *(1 mark)*

AQA, 2002

8   **Figure 9** shows a simple accelerometer designed to measure the centripetal acceleration of a car going round a bend following a circular path.

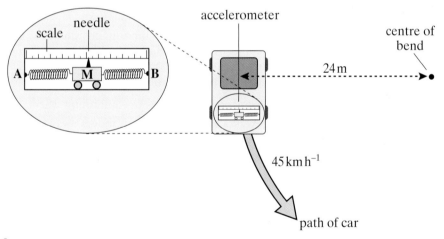

Figure 9

The two ends A and B are fixed to the car. The mass M is free to move between the two springs.

The needle attached to the mass moves along a scale to indicate the acceleration.

In one instant a car travels round a bend of radius 24 m in the direction shown in **Figure 9**. The speed of the car is 45 km h^{-1}.

(a) State and explain the direction in which the pointer moves from its equilibrium position.   *(3 marks)*

(b) (i)   Calculate the acceleration that would be recorded by the accelerometer.

(ii) The mass M between the springs in the accelerometer is 0.35 kg. A test shows that a force of 0.75 N moves the pointer 27 mm.

Calculate the displacement of the needle from the equilibrium position when the car is travelling with the acceleration in part (i).   *(4 marks)*

AQA, 2003

3 Simple harmonic motion

3.1 Oscillations

Learning objectives:

▨ What is meant by one complete oscillation?

▨ How are amplitude, frequency and period defined?

▨ What is the phase difference between two oscillators that are out of step?

Specification reference: 3.4.1

▨ Link

The displacement of an object from a fixed point is its distance from that point in a certain direction. See *AS Physics* Topic 8.1.

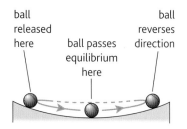

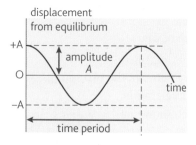

Figure 1 *Oscillating motion*

AQA Examiner's tip

Make sure you know how to apply these definitions.

▨ Measuring oscillations

There are many examples of oscillations in everyday life. A car that travels over a bump bounces up and down for a short time afterwards. Every microcomputer has an electronic oscillator to drive its internal clock. A child on a swing moves forwards then backwards repeatedly. In this simple example, one full cycle of motion is from maximum height at one side to maximum height on the other side and then back again. The lowest point is referred to as the **equilibrium** position, as it is where the child eventually comes to a standstill. The child in motion is said to **oscillate** about equilibrium.

Further examples of oscillating motion include:

▨ an object on a spring moving up and down repeatedly,

▨ a pendulum moving to and fro repeatedly,

▨ a ball bearing rolling from side to side,

▨ a small boat rocking from side to side.

An oscillating object moves repeatedly one way then in the opposite direction through its equilibrium position. The **displacement** of the object (i.e. distance and direction) from equilibrium continually changes during the motion. In one full cycle after being released from a non-equilibrium position, the displacement of the object:

▨ decreases as it returns to equilibrium, then

▨ reverses and increases as it moves away from equilibrium in the opposite direction, then

▨ decreases as it returns to equilibrium

▨ increases as it moves away from equilibrium towards its starting position.

The **amplitude** of the oscillations is the maximum displacement of the oscillating object from equilibrium. If the amplitude is constant and no frictional forces are present, the oscillations are described as **free oscillations**. See Topic 3.5.

The **time period**, T, of the oscillating motion is the time for one complete cycle of oscillations. One full cycle after passing through any position, the object passes through that same position in the same direction.

The **frequency** of oscillations is the number of cycles per second made by an oscillating object.

The unit of frequency is the hertz (Hz), which is 1 cycle per second.

For oscillations of frequency f, the time period $T = \dfrac{1}{f}$

Note: The **angular frequency** ω of the oscillating motion is defined as $\dfrac{2\pi}{T}$ ($= 2\pi f$). The unit of ω is the radian per second (rad s^{-1}). Although angular frequency is not part of the A2 physics specification, you may meet it if you are studying A level mathematics.

Phase difference

Imagine two children on adjacent identical swings. The time period, T, of the oscillating motion is the same for both, as the swings are identical. If one child reaches maximum displacement on one side a certain time, Δt, later than the other child, they oscillate out of phase. Their **phase difference** stays the same as they oscillate, always corresponding to a fraction of a cycle equal to $\Delta t/T$. For example, if the time period is 2.4 s and one child reaches maximum displacement on one side 0.6 s later than the other child, the later child will always be a quarter of a cycle (= 0.6 s/2.4 s) behind the other child. Their phase difference, in radians, is therefore 0.5π (= $2\pi\Delta t/T$).

In general, for two objects oscillating at the same frequency,

$$\text{their phase difference, in radians } = \frac{2\pi\Delta t}{T}$$

where Δt is the time between successive instants when the two objects are at maximum displacement in the same direction.

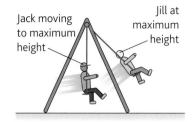

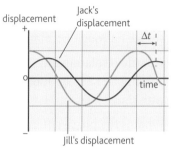

Figure 2 *Phase difference*

Notes

1 2π radians = 360° so the phase difference in degrees is $360 \times \dfrac{\Delta t}{T}$

2 The two objects oscillate in phase if $\Delta t = T$. The phase difference of 2π is therefore equivalent to zero.

3 Table of phase differences

Δt	0	0.25T	0.50T	0.75T	T
phase difference in radians	0	$\dfrac{\pi}{2}$	π	$\dfrac{3\pi}{2}$	2π
phase difference in degrees	0	90	180	270	360

Summary questions

1 Describe how the velocity of a bungee jumper changes from the moment he jumps off the starting platform to the moment he next returns to the platform.

2 a What is meant by free oscillations?

   b A metre rule is clamped to a table so that part of its length projects at right angles from the edge of the table, as shown in Figure 3. A 100 g mass is attached to the free end of the rule. When the free end of the rule is depressed downwards then released, the mass oscillates. Describe how you would find out if the oscillations of the mass are free oscillations.

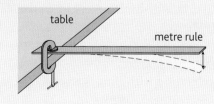

Figure 3

3 An object suspended from the lower end of a vertical spring is displaced downwards from equilibrium. It takes 9.6 s to undergo 20 complete cycles of oscillation. Calculate:

   a its time period,

   b its frequency of oscillation.

4 Two identical pendulums X and Y each consist of a small metal sphere attached to a thread of a certain length. Each pendulum makes 20 complete cycles of oscillation in 16 s. State the phase difference, in radians, between the motion of X and that of Y if

   a X passes through equilibrium 0.2 s after Y passes through equilibrium in the same direction,

   b X reaches maximum displacement at the same time as Y reaches maximum displacement in the opposite direction.

3.2 The principles of simple harmonic motion

Learning objectives:

■ What are the two fundamental conditions about acceleration that apply to simple harmonic oscillations?

■ How do displacement, velocity and acceleration vary with time?

■ What is the phase difference between displacement and (i) velocity (ii) acceleration?

Specification reference: 3.4.1

An oscillating object speeds up as it returns to equilibrium and it slows down as it moves away from equilibrium. Figure 1 shows one way to record the displacement of an oscillating pendulum.

The variation of displacement with time is shown in Figure 2(i). Provided friction is negligible, the amplitude of the oscillations is constant.

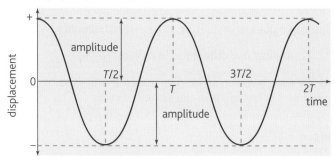

Figure 2(i) *Displacement against time*

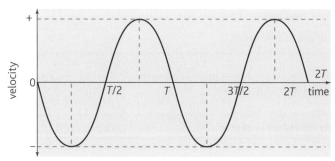

Figure 2(ii) *Velocity against time*

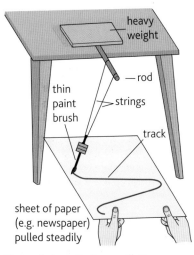

Figure 1 *Investigating oscillations*

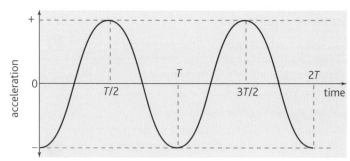

Figure 2(iii) *Acceleration against time*

The variation of velocity with time is given by the gradient of the displacement v. time graph, as shown by Figure 2(ii).

■ The velocity is greatest when the gradient of the displacement–time graph is greatest (i.e. at zero displacement when the object passes through equilibrium).

■ The velocity is zero when the gradient of the displacement–time graph is zero (i.e. at maximum displacement).

The variation of acceleration with time is given by the gradient of the velocity–time graph, as shown by Figure 2(iii).

Link

The gradient of a displacement v. time graph gives velocity. The gradient of a velocity v. time graph gives acceleration. See *AS Physics* Topic 8.5.

- The acceleration is greatest when the gradient of the velocity–time graph is greatest. This is when the velocity is zero and occurs at maximum displacement in the opposite direction.
- The acceleration is zero when the gradient of the velocity–time graph is zero. This is when the displacement is zero.

By comparing Figures 2(i) and 2(iii) directly, it can be seen that

the acceleration is always in the opposite direction to the displacement.

In other words, if one direction is referred to as the positive direction and the other as the negative direction, the acceleration direction is always the opposite sign to the displacement direction.

Simple harmonic motion is defined as oscillating motion in which the acceleration is

1 proportional to the displacement,

2 always in the opposite direction to the displacement

$$\text{acceleration, } a = -\text{ constant} \times \text{displacement, } x$$

The minus sign tells us the acceleration is in the opposite direction to the displacement. The constant of proportionality depends on the time period T of the oscillations. The shorter the time period, the faster the oscillations, which means the larger the acceleration at any given displacement. So the constant is greater the shorter the time period. As shown in Topic 3.3, the constant in this equation is $(2\pi f)^2$, where f, the frequency, $= 1/T$

Therefore the defining equation for simple harmonic motion is

$$\text{acceleration, } a = -(2\pi f)^2 x,$$

where x = displacement
and f = frequency.

AQA Examiner's tip

Acceleration is zero when speed is a maximum, and vice versa.

Hint

1 The time period is independent of the amplitude of the oscillations.

2 Maximum displacement $x_{max} = \pm A$, where A is the amplitude of the oscillations. Therefore,

- when $x_{max} = +A$, the acceleration $a = -(2\pi f)^2 A$, and
- when $x_{max} = -A$, the acceleration $a = +(2\pi f)^2 A$

3 The acceleration equation may also be written as $a = -\omega^2 x$, where angular frequency $\omega = \dfrac{2\pi}{T}$.

Summary questions

1 A small object attached to the end of a vertical spring oscillates with an amplitude of 25 mm and a time period of 2.0 s. The object passes through equilibrium moving upwards at time $t = 0$. What is the displacement and direction of motion of the object:

a ¼ cycle later,

b ½ cycle later,

c ¾ cycle later,

d 1 cycle later?

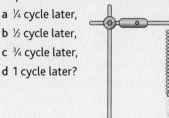

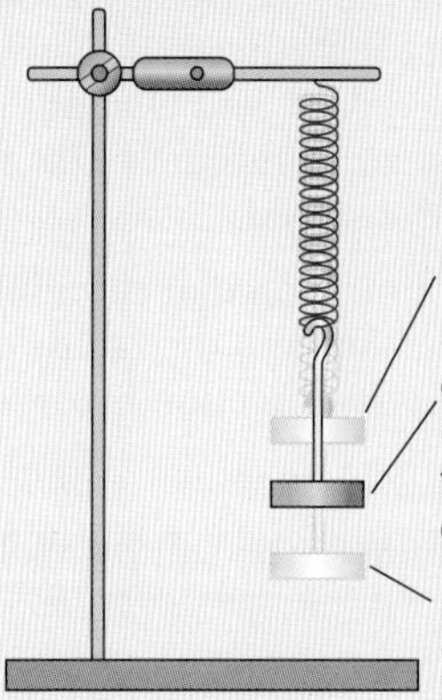

maximum upward displacement

object passing upwards through equilibrium

maximum downward displacement

Figure 3

2 For the oscillations in Q1, calculate:

a the frequency,

b the acceleration of the object when its displacement is

   i +25 mm,   **ii** 0,   **iii** −25 mm.

3 A simple pendulum consists of a small weight on the end of a thread. The weight is displaced from equilibrium and released. It oscillates with an amplitude of 32 mm, taking 20 s to execute 10 oscillations. Calculate:

a its frequency,

b its initial acceleration.

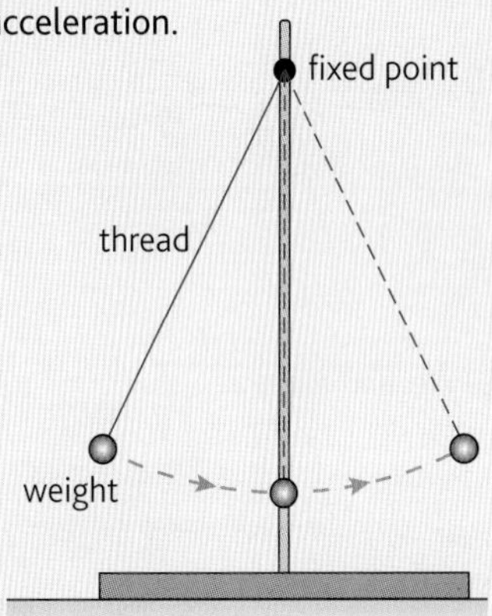

fixed point

thread

weight

Figure 4

4 For the oscillations in Q3, the object is released at time $t = 0$. State the displacement and calculate the acceleration when

a $t = 1.0$ s,

b $t = 1.5$ s.

3.3 More about sine waves

- What equation relates displacement to time for a body moving with simple harmonic motion?

- At what point must the oscillations start for this equation to apply?

- How can we calculate the velocity for a given displacement?

Specification reference: 3.4.1

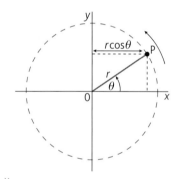

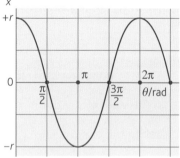

Figure 1 *Circles and waves*

Circles and waves

Consider a small object P in uniform circular motion, as shown in Figure 1. Measured from the centre of the circle at O, the coordinates of P are therefore $x = r \cos\theta$ and $y = r \sin\theta$, where θ is the angle between the x-axis and the radial line OP. The graph shows how the x-coordinate changes as angle θ changes. The curve is a cosine wave. It has the same shape as the simple harmonic motion curves in Figure 2 in Topic 3.2.

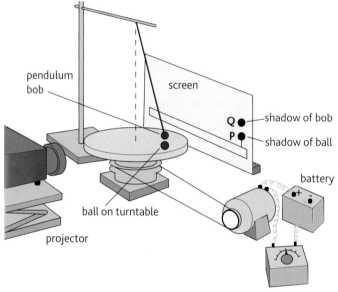

Figure 2 *Comparing simple harmonic motion with circular motion*

To see directly the link between simple harmonic motion and sine curves, consider the motion of the ball and the pendulum bob in Figure 2. A projector is used to cast a shadow of the ball (P) in uniform circular motion on to a screen alongside the shadow of the oscillating bob (Q). The two shadows keep up with each other exactly when their time periods are matched. In other words, P and Q at any instant have the same horizontal motion. So the acceleration of Q is the same as the acceleration of P's shadow on the screen.

- Because the ball (P) is in uniform circular motion, its acceleration $a = -v^2/r$ where v is its speed and r is the radius of the circle. Note that the minus sign indicates its direction is towards the centre.

Since speed $v = 2\pi rf$ (see Topic 2.1), then $a = -(2\pi f)^2 r$

- The component of acceleration of the ball parallel to the screen, $a_x = a \cos\theta$,

  ∴ the acceleration of the ball's shadow, $a_x = -(2\pi f)^2 r \cos\theta = -(2\pi f)^2 x$, where $x = r\cos\theta$ is the displacement of the shadow from the midpoint of the oscillations.

- Because the bob's motion is the same as the motion of the ball's shadow,

the acceleration of the bob (Q), $a_x = -(2\pi f)^2 x$

This is the defining equation for simple harmonic motion and it shows why the constant of proportionality is $(2\pi f)^2$.

Sine wave solutions

For any object oscillating at frequency f in simple harmonic motion, its acceleration a at displacement x is given by

$$a = -(2\pi f)^2 x$$

The variation of displacement with time depends on the initial displacement and the initial velocity (i.e. the displacement and velocity at time $t = 0$).

As explained under Figure 3, if $x = +A$ when $t = 0$ and the object has zero velocity at that instant, then its displacement at time t later is given by

$$x = A\cos(2\pi ft)$$

Notes:

1   In the above equation, x is the displacement of the bob from its equilibrium position. Its value changes from $-r$ to $+r$ and back again as the bob oscillates. Therefore the amplitude of oscillation of the bob, $A = r$.

2   The displacement of the bob from equilibrium is given by $x = A\cos\theta$, where θ is the angle the ball moves through from its position when $x = A$.

At time t after the ball passes through this position,

$$\theta \text{ (in radians)} = \frac{2\pi t}{T} = 2\pi ft.$$

Therefore, the displacement of the bob at time t is given by

$$x = A\cos(2\pi ft)$$

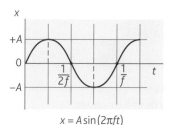

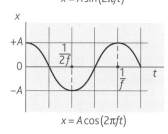

$x = A\sin(2\pi ft)$

$x = A\cos(2\pi ft)$

Figure 3 *Graphical solutions*

Summary questions

1   An object oscillates in simple harmonic motion with a time period of 3.0 s and an amplitude of 58 mm. Calculate:

a its frequency,

b its maximum acceleration.

2   The displacement of an object oscillating in simple harmonic motion varies with time in accordance with the equation $x/\text{mm} = 12\cos 10t$, where t is the time in seconds after the object's displacement was at its maximum positive value.

a Determine:

i   the amplitude,   ii the time period.

b Calculate the displacement of the object at $t = 0.1$ s.

3   An object on a spring oscillates with a time period of 0.48 s and a maximum acceleration of 9.8 m s^{-2}. Calculate:

a its frequency,

b its amplitude.

4   An object oscillates in simple harmonic motion with an amplitude of 12 mm and a time period of 0.27 s. Calculate:

a its frequency,

b its displacement and its direction of motion

i   0.10 s,

ii   0.20 s after its displacement was +12 mm.

More on sine waves

1   The shape of the curves in Figure 3, described as **sinusoidal curves**, is the same as the shape of the simple harmonic motion curves in Figure 2 in Topic 3.2.

2   The general solution of $a = -(2\pi f)^2 x$ is $x = A\sin((2\pi ft) + \phi)$, where ϕ is the phase difference between the instants when $t = 0$ and when $x = 0$. If timing were to start at the centre with oscillations going +ve, the x–t equation would become $x = A\sin 2\pi ft$ as $\phi = 0$. The general solution is not required in the A2 physics specification.

3   The time period T does *not* depend on the amplitude of the oscillating motion. For example, the time period of an object oscillating on a spring is the same, regardless of whether the amplitude is large or small.

AQA Examiner's tip

Remember that $2\pi ft$ has to be in radians. So check your calculator is in radian mode when you use the equation $x = A\cos(2\pi ft)$.

3.4 Applications of simple harmonic motion

Learning objectives:

- What conditions must be satisfied for a mass–spring system or simple pendulum to oscillate with simple harmonic motion?

- How does the period of a mass–spring system depend on the mass?

- How does the period of a simple pendulum depend on its length?

Specification reference: 3.4.1

For any oscillating object, the resultant force acting on the object acts towards the equilibrium position. The resultant force is described as a **restoring force** as it always acts towards equilibrium. Provided the restoring force is proportional to the displacement from equilibrium, the acceleration is proportional to the displacement and always acts towards equilibrium. Therefore the object oscillates with simple harmonic motion.

The oscillations of a mass–spring system

Use two stretched springs and a trolley, as shown in Figure 1. When the trolley is displaced then released, it oscillates backwards and forwards.

- The first half-cycle of the trolley's motion can be recorded using a length of ticker tape attached at one end to the trolley. When the trolley is released, the tape is pulled through a ticker timer that prints dots on the tape at a rate of 50 dots per second.

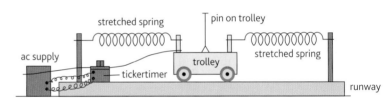

Figure 1 *Investigating oscillations*

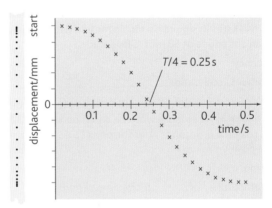

tape with dots at 50 Hz

Figure 2 *Displacement–time curve from a tickertape*

- A graph of displacement against time for the first half-cycle can be drawn using the tape, as shown in Figure 2. The graph can be used to measure the time period which can be checked (see Notes opposite) if the trolley mass m and the combined spring constant k are known.

- A motion sensor linked to a computer can be used to record the oscillating motion of the trolley. See Topic 1.3.

■ What determines the frequency of oscillation of a loaded spring?

In the above investigation, the frequency of oscillation of the trolley can be changed by loading the trolley with extra mass or by replacing the springs with springs of different stiffness. The frequency is reduced by:

1   **Adding extra mass.** This is because the extra mass increases the inertia of the system. At a given displacement, the trolley would therefore be slower than if the extra mass had not been added. Each cycle of oscillation would therefore take longer.

2   **Using weaker springs.** The restoring force on the trolley at any given displacement would be less so the trolley's acceleration and speed at any given displacement would be less. Each cycle of oscillation would therefore take longer.

To see exactly how the mass and the spring constant affect the frequency, consider a small object of mass m attached to a spring.

■ Assuming the spring obeys Hooke's law, the tension T_s in the spring is in proportion to its extension ΔL from its unstretched length. This relationship can be expressed by means of the equation $T_s = k\Delta L$, where k is the spring constant.

■ When the object is oscillating and is at displacement x from its equilibrium position, the change of tension in the spring provides the restoring force on the object. Using the equation $T_s = k\Delta L$, the change of tension ΔT_s from equilibrium is therefore given by $\Delta T_s = -kx$, where the minus sign represents the fact that the change of tension always tries to restore the object to its equilibrium position.

■ Hence the restoring force on the object $= -kx$

■ Therefore the acceleration, $a = \dfrac{\text{restoring force}}{\text{mass}} = \dfrac{-kx}{m}$

This equation may be written in the form $a = -(2\pi f)^2 x$, where $(2\pi f)^2 = \dfrac{k}{m}$

The object therefore oscillates in simple harmonic motion because its acceleration $a = -(2\pi f)^2 x$.

Notes:

1   Rearranging the equation

$(2\pi f)^2 = \dfrac{k}{m}$ gives $f = \dfrac{1}{2\pi}\sqrt{\dfrac{k}{m}}$.

This equation may used to calculate f if k and m are known. The equation also shows that the frequency is increased if k *is* increased or if m is reduced.

2   The time period of the oscillations $T = \dfrac{1}{f} = 2\pi\sqrt{\dfrac{m}{k}}$.

The time period does not depend on g. A mass–spring system on the Moon would have the same time period as it would on Earth.

3   The tension in the spring varies from $mg + kA$ to $mg - kA$, where A = amplitude.

■ Maximum tension is when the spring is stretched as much as possible (i.e. $x = -A$)

■ Minimum tension is when the spring is stretched as little as possible (i.e. $x = +A$)

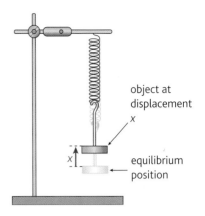

object at displacement
x

equilibrium position

Figure 3 *The oscillations of a loaded spring*

■ **How science works**

Investigating the oscillations of a loaded spring

Measure the oscillations of a loaded spring for different masses and verify the formula

$$T = 2\pi\left(\dfrac{m}{k}\right)^{\frac{1}{2}}$$

■ **Link**

Since $T^2 = 4\pi^2 m/k$, plotting a graph of T^2 on the y-axis against m on the x-axis should give a straight line through the origin with a gradient of $4\pi^2/k$ in accordance with the general equation for a straight line graph $y = mx + c$.

See *AS Physics* Topic 16.4.

*Worked example:*_____

$g = 9.8\,\text{m}\,\text{s}^{-2}$

A spring of natural length 300 mm hangs vertically with its upper end attached to a fixed point. When a small object of mass 0.20 kg is suspended from the lower end of the spring in equilibrium, the spring is stretched to a length of 379 mm. Calculate:

a (i) the extension of the spring at equilibrium,

(ii) the spring constant,

b the time period of oscillations that the mass on the spring would have if the mass was to be displaced downwards slightly then released.

Solution

a (i) Extension of spring at equilibrium, $\Delta L_0 = 79\,\text{mm} = 0.0790\,\text{m}$

(Ii) Spring constant $k = \dfrac{mg}{\Delta L_0} = \dfrac{0.20 \times 9.8}{0.079} = 25\,\text{N}\,\text{m}^{-1}$

b $T = 2\pi\left(\dfrac{0.20}{25}\right)^{\frac{1}{2}} = 0.56\,\text{s}$

■ The theory of the simple pendulum

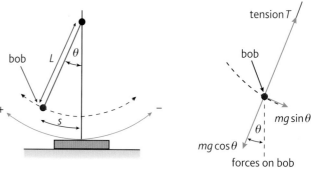

Figure 4 *The simple pendulum*

Consider a simple pendulum that consists of a bob of mass m attached to a thread of length L, as shown in Figure 4. If the bob is displaced from equilibrium then released, it oscillates about the lowest point. At displacement s, from the lowest point, when the thread is at angle θ to the vertical, the weight, mg, has components

■ $mg\cos\theta$ perpendicular to the path of the bob, and

■ $mg\sin\theta$ along the path towards the equilibrium position.

The restoring force $F = -mg\sin\theta$, so the acceleration,

$$a = \frac{F}{m} = \frac{-mg\sin\theta}{m} = -g\sin\theta$$

Provided θ does not exceed about 10°, then $\sin\theta = \dfrac{s}{L}$,

therefore the acceleration $a = -\dfrac{g}{L}s = -(2\pi f)^2 s$, where $(2\pi f)^2 = \dfrac{g}{L}$

So the object oscillates with simple harmonic motion because its acceleration is proportional to the displacement from equilibrium and always acts towards equilibrium.

AQA Examiner's tip

When timing oscillations, use a fiducial mark at the centre of oscillations and start counting with 0 as the oscillating object passes the mark.

How science works

Investigating the simple pendulum

Measure the oscillations of a simple pendulum for different lengths and verify the formula $T = 2\pi\left(\dfrac{L}{g}\right)^{\frac{1}{2}}$

Link

Plotting a graph of T^2 on the y-axis against L on the x-axis should give a straight line through the origin with a gradient of $\dfrac{4\pi^2}{g}$.

See the earlier link in this topic.

Notes

1 The time period $T = \dfrac{1}{f} = 2\pi\sqrt{\dfrac{L}{g}}$

   provided the angle of the thread to the vertical does not exceed about 10°.

2 The time period, T, can be increased by increasing the length L of the pendulum. The length of the pendulum is the distance from the point of support to the centre of the bob.

3 As the bob passes through equilibrium, the tension T_s acts directly upwards. Therefore the resultant force on the bob at this instant

$$T_s - mg = \frac{mv^2}{L},$$

   where v is the speed as it passes through equilibrium.

Summary questions

$g = 9.8\,\mathrm{m\,s^{-2}}$.

1 An object was suspended from the end of a vertical spring and set into oscillating motion along a vertical line. The amplitude of its oscillations was 20 mm and it took 6.5 s to perform 20 oscillations. Calculate

   a i   its time period,

      ii its frequency

   b its acceleration when its displacement was

      i   0 mm,

      ii   10 mm,

      iii 20 mm.

2 In the arrangement described in Q1, the object was replaced by an object of different mass. When the second object was oscillating vertically, its acceleration a at displacement x was given by $a = -360x$.

   a Calculate:

      i   the frequency,

      ii the time period of the oscillations.

   b By comparing the frequency of the oscillations of the second object with that of the first, discuss whether or not the mass of the second object is greater than or less than the mass of the first object.

3 The upper end of a vertical spring of natural length 250 mm is attached to a fixed point. When a small object of mass 0.15 kg is attached to the lower end of the spring, the spring stretches to an equilibrium length of 320 mm.

   a Calculate:

      i   the extension of the spring at equilibrium,

      ii the spring constant.

   b The object is displaced vertically from its equilibrium position and released. Show that it oscillates at a frequency of 1.9 Hz and calculate its period of oscillation.

4 A mass of 0.50 kg is attached to the lower end of a vertical spring which has a spring constant of 25 N m^{-1}. The mass is displaced downwards by a distance of 50 mm then released.

   a Calculate:

      i   the force on the object at a displacement of 50 mm,

      ii the acceleration of the object at the instant it was released.

   b i   Show that the acceleration a at displacement x is given by $a = -50x$

      ii Calculate the frequency of the oscillations and the displacement of the mass 0.050 s after it was released.

5 Calculate the time period of a simple pendulum

   a of length

      i   1.0 m,

      ii 0.25 m,

   b of length 1.0 m on the surface of the Moon where $g = 1.6\,\mathrm{m\,s^{-2}}$.

6 A simple pendulum and a mass suspended on a vertical spring have equal time periods on the Earth. Discuss whether or not they would have the same time periods on the surface of the Moon where $g = 1.6\,\mathrm{m\,s^{-2}}$.

3.5 Energy and simple harmonic motion

Learning objectives:

- In simple harmonic motion, how do kinetic energy and potential energy vary with displacement?

- How do these energies vary with time, if damping is negligible?

- What is the effect of damping on the characteristics of the oscillations?

Specification reference: 3.4.1

Free oscillations

A freely oscillating object oscillates with a constant amplitude because there is no friction acting on it. The only forces acting on it combine to provide the restoring force. If friction was present, the amplitude of oscillations would gradually decrease and the oscillations would eventually cease.

Observe the oscillations of a simple pendulum over many cycles and you should find that the decrease of amplitude from one cycle to the next is scarcely measurable. Nevertheless, over many cycles the amplitude does decrease noticeably. So friction is present, even if its effect is insignificant over a single cycle.

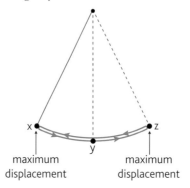

position	E_p	E_k
x	E_{TOTAL}	0
y	0	E_{TOTAL}
z	E_{TOTAL}	0

Figure 1 *The energy changes of a simple pendulum*

Consider the example of a small object of mass m oscillating on a spring. The energy of the system changes from kinetic energy to potential energy and back again every half cycle after passing though equilibrium. Provided friction is absent, the total energy of the system is constant and is equal to its maximum potential energy.

- The potential energy E_p changes with displacement x from equilibrium, in accordance with the equation $E_p = \frac{1}{2}kx^2$, where k is the spring constant of the spring.
- The total energy, E_T, of the system is therefore $\frac{1}{2}kA^2$, where A is the amplitude of the oscillations.
- Because the total energy, $E_T = E_K + E_p$, where E_K is the kinetic energy of the oscillating mass, then $E_K = E_T - E_p = \frac{1}{2}k(A^2 - x^2)$

Note:

The simple harmonic motion speed equation

Using $E_K = \frac{1}{2}mv^2$ gives $\frac{1}{2}mv^2 = \frac{1}{2}k(A^2 - x^2)$ where v is the speed of the object at displacement x.

As $(2\pi f)^2 = k/m$, the above equation can be written as $v^2 = (2\pi f)^2(A^2 - x^2)$

Hence $v = \pm(2\pi f)\sqrt{(A^2 - x^2)}$

Note that making $x = 0$ in this equation gives the maximum speed $= 2\pi fA$.

Link

The energy stored in a spring stretched by extension x from its equilibrium length is $\frac{1}{2}kx^2$ where k is the spring constant. See *AS Physics* Topic 11.2.

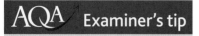

Examiner's tip

Take the total energy to be equal to E_K at $x = 0$ (i.e. $E_p = 0$ when $x = 0$).

Energy–displacement graphs

1 The potential energy curve is parabolic in shape, given by $E_p = \frac{1}{2}kx^2$

2 The kinetic energy curve is an inverted parabola, given by
$E_K = E_T - E_p = \frac{1}{2}k(A^2 - x^2)$

The sum of the kinetic energy and the potential energy is always equal to $\frac{1}{2}kA^2$ which is the potential energy at maximum displacement. This is the same as the kinetic energy at zero displacement. So the two curves add together to give a flat line for the total energy.

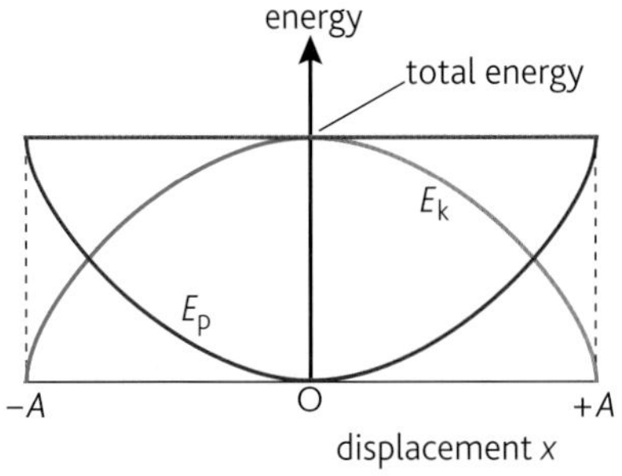

Figure 2 *Energy curves*

Damped oscillations

The oscillations of a simple pendulum gradually die away because air resistance gradually reduces the total energy of the system. In any oscillating system where friction or air resistance is present, the amplitude decreases. The forces causing the amplitude to decrease are described as **dissipative forces** because they dissipate the energy of the system to the surroundings as thermal energy. The motion is said to be **damped** if dissipative forces are present.

▦ **Light damping** The time period is independent of the amplitude so each cycle takes the same length of time as the oscillations die away. Figure 3 shows how the displacement of a lightly damped oscillating system decreases with time. The amplitude gradually decreases, reducing by the same fraction each cycle.

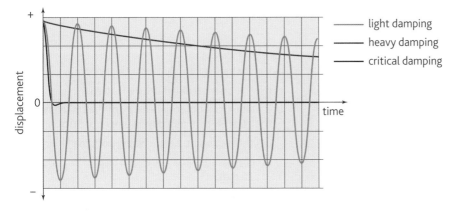

light damping
heavy damping
critical damping

Figure 3 *Damping*

▦ **Critical damping** is just enough to stop the system oscillating after it has been displaced and released from equilibrium. The oscillating object returns to equilibrium in the shortest possible time without overshooting if the damping is critical. Such damping is important in mass–spring systems such as a vehicle suspension system where an uncomfortable ride would be experienced if the damping was too light or too heavy. Figure 3 also shows how the displacement changes with time when the damping is critical.

▦ **Heavy damping** is where the damping is so strong that the displaced object returns to equilibrium much more slowly than if the system is critically damped. No oscillating motion occurs. For example, a mass on a spring in thick oil would return to equilibrium very slowly after being displaced and released.

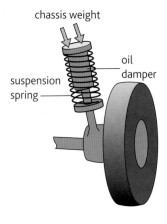

chassis weight

oil damper

suspension spring

cross-section of oil damper

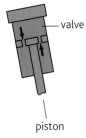

valve

piston

Figure 4 *Car suspension*

Application

A car suspension system

The suspension system of a car includes a coiled spring near each wheel between the wheel axle and the car chassis. When the wheel is jolted, for example on a bumpy road, the spring smoothes out the force of the jolts. An oil damper fitted with each spring prevents the chassis from bouncing up and down too much.

Without oil dampers, the occupants of the car would continue to be thrown up and down until the oscillations died away. The flow of oil through valves in the piston of each damper provides a frictional force which damps the oscillating motion of the chassis. The dampers are designed to ensure the chassis returns to its 'equilibrium' position in the shortest possible time after each jolt with little or no oscillations. The suspension system is therefore at or close to critical damping.

Summary questions

$g = 9.81\,\mathrm{m\,s^{-2}}$

1 A simple pendulum consists of a small metal sphere of mass 0.30 kg attached to a thread. The sphere is displaced through a height of 10 mm with the thread taut then released. It takes 15.0 s to make 10 complete cycles of oscillation.

  a Calculate:

  i the time period of the pendulum,

  ii the length of the pendulum,

  iii the initial potential energy of the pendulum relative to its equilibrium position.

  b Sketch graphs on the same axes to show how the potential energy and the kinetic energy of the pendulum varies with its displacement from equilibrium.

2 A glider of mass 0.45 kg on a frictionless air track is attached to two stretched springs at either end, as shown in Figure 5. A force of 3.0 N is needed to displace the glider from equilibrium and hold it at a displacement of 50 mm. The glider is then released and it oscillates freely on the air track.

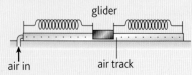

glider

air in   air track

Figure 5

Calculate:

  a i the spring constant k for the system,

  ii the time period of the oscillations,

  b i the initial potential energy of the system when the glider is held at a displacement of 50 mm,

  ii the maximum kinetic energy of the glider,

  iii the speed of the glider at a displacement of 25 mm.

3 a State if the damping in each of the following examples is light, critical or heavy:

  i a child on a swing displaced from equilibrium then released,

  ii oil in a U-shaped tube displaced from equilibrium then released,

  b Discuss how effective a car suspension damper would be, if the oil in the damper was replaced by oil that was much more viscous.

4 The amplitude of an oscillating mass on a spring decreases by 4% each cycle from an initial amplitude of 100 mm. Calculate the amplitude after:

  a 5 cycles of oscillation,

  b 20 cycles of oscillation.

3.6 Forced oscillations and resonance

Learning objectives:

■ Under what circumstances does resonance occur?

■ What is the difference between free vibrations and forced vibrations?

■ Why does a resonant system reach a maximum amplitude of vibration?

Specification reference: 3.4.1

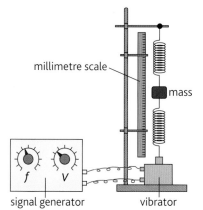

millimetre scale

mass

signal generator

vibrator

f   V

Figure 1 *Forced oscillations*

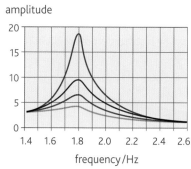

amplitude

20

15

10

5

0

1.4 1.6 1.8 2.0 2.2 2.4 2.6

frequency / Hz

Figure 2 *Resonance curves*

Forced oscillations

Imagine pushing someone on a swing at regular intervals. If each push is timed suitably, the swing goes higher and higher. The pushes are a simple example of a **periodic force** which is a force applied at regular intervals.

■ When the system oscillates without a periodic force being applied to it, its frequency is referred to as its **natural frequency**.

■ When a periodic force is applied to an oscillating system, the response depends on the frequency of the periodic force. The system undergoes **forced oscillations** when a periodic force is applied to it.

Figure 1 shows how a periodic force can be applied to an oscillating system consisting of a small object of fixed mass attached to two stretched springs.

The bottom end of the lower spring is attached to a mechanical oscillator which is connected to a signal generator. The top end of the upper spring is fixed. The mechanical oscillator pulls repeatedly on the lower spring at a frequency that can be adjusted by adjusting the signal generator. The frequency of the oscillator is the **applied frequency.** The response of the system is measured from the amplitude of oscillations of the object. The variation of the response with the applied frequency is shown in Figure 2.

Consider the effect of increasing the applied frequency from zero:

As the applied frequency approaches the natural frequency of the mass–spring system,

■ the amplitude of oscillations of the object increases more and more,

■ the phase difference between the displacement and the periodic force increases from zero to $\frac{1}{2}\pi$ at the natural frequency.

Resonance

When the applied frequency is equal to the natural frequency of the mass–spring system,

■ the amplitude of oscillations becomes very large. The lighter the damping in the system, the larger the amplitude becomes. The system is in **resonance** when the applied frequency equals the natural frequency,

■ the phase difference between the displacement and the periodic force is $\frac{1}{2}\pi$ at resonance. The periodic force is then exactly in phase with the velocity of the oscillating object.

As the applied frequency becomes increasingly larger than the natural frequency of the mass–spring system,

■ the amplitude of oscillations decreases more and more,

■ the phase difference between the displacement and the periodic force increases from $\frac{1}{2}\pi$ until the displacement is π radians out of phase with the periodic force.

The amplitude of oscillations is greatest when the applied frequency is equal to the natural frequency, provided the damping is light.

For an oscillating system with little or no damping, at resonance,

applied frequency of periodic force = natural frequency of system

More examples of resonance

Barton's pendulums

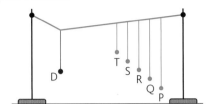

Figure 3 *Barton's pendulums*

Figure 3 shows five simple pendulums, P, Q, R, S and T, of different lengths hanging from a supporting thread which is stretched between two fixed points. A single 'driver' pendulum D of the same length as one of the other pendulums is also tied to the thread.

The driver pendulum D is displaced and released so it oscillates in a plane perpendicular to the plane of the pendulums at rest. The effect of the oscillating motion of D is transmitted along the support thread, subjecting each of the other pendulums to forced oscillations. Pendulum R responds much more than any other pendulum. This is because it has the same length and therefore the same time period as D. So its natural frequency is the same as the natural frequency of D. Therefore, R oscillates in resonance with D because it is subjected to forced oscillations of the same frequency as its own natural frequency of oscillations. The response of each of the other pendulums depends on how close its length is to the length of D.

Bridge oscillations

A bridge span can oscillate due to its 'springiness' and its mass. If a bridge span is not fitted with 'dampers', it can be made to oscillate at resonance if subjected to a suitable periodic force.

1 A crosswind can cause a periodic force on a bridge span because of eddy currents created by the wind along the bridge span. If the wind speed is such that the periodic force is equal to the natural frequency of the bridge span, resonance can occur in the absence of damping. The dramatic collapse of the Tacoma Narrows Bridge in the United States in 1940 was due to such resonance.

Figure 4 *The collapse of the Tacoma Narrows Bridge*

2 A steady trail of people in step with each other walking across a footbridge can cause resonant oscillations of the bridge span if there is insufficient damping. Soldiers marching in columns are taught to break step when crossing a footbridge to avoid causing resonance. Shortly after it was opened, the Millennium Bridge in London had to be closed and fitted with a suitable damping system because it swayed in resonance when people first walked across it.

Figure 5 *The Millennium Bridge, London*

Summary questions

1 a A mass suspended on a vertical spring is made to oscillate by applying a periodic force of natural frequency f_0.

   i   What is meant by resonance?

   ii Explain why the frequency of the periodic force needs to be f_0 to cause resonance.

   b With reference to the mass–spring system shown in Figure 1, state and explain what the effect would be on the resonant frequency of

   i   increasing the mass,

   ii replacing the springs with stiffer springs.

2 A 0.12 kg mass suspended on a vertical spring is made to resonate by applying a periodic force of frequency 2.4 Hz to it. Calculate:

   a the spring constant of the system,

   b the frequency at which the system would resonate if the mass were doubled.

3 The panel of a certain washing machine vibrates loudly when the drum rotates at a certain frequency. Explain why this happens only when the drum rotates at this frequency.

4 A vehicle of mass 850 kg has a suspension system that is lightly damped. When it is driven without extra load by a driver of mass 50 kg over speed bumps spaced 15 m apart at a speed of 3.0 m s^{-1}, the vehicle resonates.

   a Explain why this effect happens.

   b At what speed would resonance take place over the same speed bumps if the vehicle had also been carrying an extra load of 130 kg?

1 In an investigation, a small object was suspended from the lower end of a vertical steel spring which was fixed at its upper end, as shown in **Figure 1**.

A horizontal marker pin P was attached to the lower end of the spring. The vertical position, x, of the pin was measured against the millimetre scale of a metre rule clamped vertically in a fixed position. The measurement was made three times without, then with, the small object suspended from the spring.

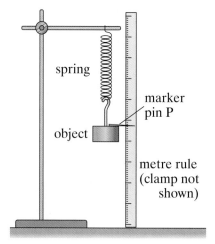

Figure 1

(a) The readings obtained are shown in Table 1.

Table 1

	x/mm			mean x/mm	extension e/mm
without the object on the spring	2	2	2	2.0	0
with the object on the spring	71	72	73		

    (ii) Copy and complete Table 1 by calculating the mean vertical position of P and the extension of the spring when the object was placed on it.

    (iii) The readings were taken to a precision of 0.5 mm using a millimetre ruler. Estimate the percentage 'uncertainty' in the extension. *(2 marks)*

(b) The time period, T, of small vertical oscillations of the object on the spring was also measured by timing 20 oscillations three times.

    The timing readings for 20 oscillations were 10.98 s, 11.11 s and 10.97 s.

    (i) Calculate the time period T.

    (ii) Use the readings to estimate the percentage 'uncertainty' in T. *(2 marks)*

(c) (i) Give an expression for the extension e of the spring in terms of the mass m of the object and the spring constant k of the spring.

    (ii) Hence show that $T = 2\pi\sqrt{\dfrac{e}{g}}$ *(3 marks)*

(d) The experiment was repeated with objects of different mass suspended from the spring. The measurements obtained are given in Table 2.

Plot a suitable graph using the above measurements to confirm the equation and to determine g.

Table 2

object	e/mm	T/s
1	70	0.551
2	139	0.761
3	205	0.923
4	271	1.062
5	341	1.187
6	409	1.291

(9 marks)

(e) Discuss the accuracy of your determination of g. *(4 marks)*

2   The tuning fork shown in **Figure 2** is labelled 512 Hz and has the tip of each of its two prongs vibrating with simple harmonic motion of amplitude 0.85 mm.

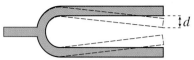

Figure 2

(a) (i) **Figure 2** shows the extreme positions of the prongs. How is the distance marked d related to the amplitude of the prongs?

   (ii) Sketch a graph to show how the displacement of one tip of the tuning fork changes with time. Mark each axis with an appropriate scale. *(4 marks)*

(b) (i) Calculate the maximum speed of the tip of a prong.

   (ii) Calculate the maximum acceleration of the tip of a prong. *(4 marks)*

AQA, 2007

3   A simple pendulum consists of a 25 g mass tied to the end of a light string 800 mm long. The mass is drawn to one side until it is 20 mm above its rest position, as shown in **Figure 3**. When released it swings with simple harmonic motion.

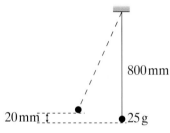

Figure 3

(a) Calculate the period of the pendulum. *(2 marks)*

(b) Show that the initial amplitude of the oscillations is approximately 0.18 m, and that the maximum speed of the mass during the first oscillation is about 0.63 m s^{-1}. *(4 marks)*

(c) Calculate the magnitude of the tension in the string when the mass passes through the lowest point of the first swing. *(2 marks)*

AQA, 2003

4   (a) **Figure 4a** shows a demonstration used in teaching simple harmonic motion. A sphere rotates in a horizontal plane on a turntable. A lamp produces a shadow of the sphere. This shadow moves with approximate simple harmonic motion on the vertical screen.

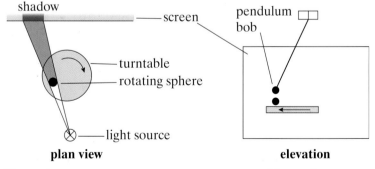

Figure 4a   **Figure 4b**

   (i) The turntable has a radius of 0.13 m and the teacher wishes the time taken for one cycle of the motion to be 2.2 s. The mass of the sphere is 0.050 kg.

   Calculate the magnitude of the horizontal force acting on the sphere.

   (ii) State the direction in which the force acts. *(3 marks)*

(b) **Figure 4b** shows how the demonstration might be extended. A simple pendulum is mounted above the turntable so that the shadows of the sphere and the pendulum bob can be seen to move in a similar way and with the same period.

(i) Calculate the required length of the pendulum.

(ii) Calculate the maximum acceleration of the pendulum bob when its motion has an amplitude of 0.13 m. *(3 marks)*

(c) **Figure 5** is a graph of displacement against time for the pendulum.

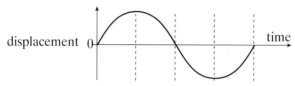

Figure 5

Sketch, for the same interval, graphs of:

(i) acceleration against time for the bob, and

(ii) kinetic energy against time for the bob. *(4 marks)*

AQA, 2005

5   (a) Simple harmonic motion may be represented by the equation

$$a = -(2\pi f)^2 x$$

(i) Explain the significance of the minus sign in this equation.

(ii) Copy **Figure 6** and sketch the corresponding v–t graph to show how the phase of velocity v relates to that of the acceleration a. *(2 marks)*

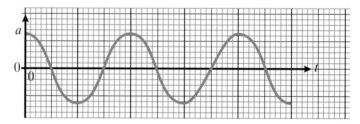

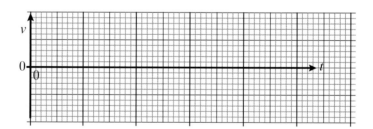

Figure 6

(b) (i) A mass of 24 kg is attached to the end of a spring of spring constant 60 N m^{-1}. The mass is displaced 0.035 m vertically from its equilibrium position and released. Show that the maximum kinetic energy of the mass is about 40 mJ.

(ii) When the mass on the spring is quite heavily damped its amplitude halves by the end of each complete cycle. Sketch a graph to show how the kinetic energy, E_k, /mJ, of the mass on the spring varies with time, t/s, over a single period.

Start at time, $t = 0$, with your maximum kinetic energy.

You should include suitable values on each of your scales. *(8 marks)*

AQA, 2004

6   To celebrate the Millennium in the year 2000, a footbridge was constructed across the River Thames in London. After the bridge was opened to the public it was discovered that the structure could easily be set into oscillation when large numbers of people were walking across it.

(a) What name is given to this kind of physical phenomenon, when caused by a periodic driving force?   *(1 mark)*

(b) Under what condition would this phenomenon become particularly hazardous? Explain your answer.   *(4 marks)*

(c) Suggest **two** measures which engineers might adopt in order to reduce the size of the oscillations of a bridge.   *(2 marks)*

AQA 2002

7   **Figure 7** shows how the displacement of the bob of a simple pendulum varies with time.

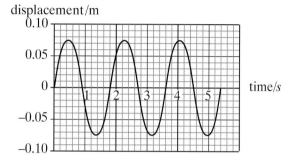

Figure 7

(a) (i) Calculate the frequency of the oscillation.

   (ii) State the magnitude of the amplitude of the oscillation.

   (iii) State how the frequency and amplitude of a simple pendulum are affected by increased damping.   *(5 marks)*

(b) Draw on a copy of **Figure 7** the displacement–time graph for a pendulum that has the same period and amplitude but oscillates 90° ($\pi/2$ radian) out of phase with the one shown.   *(2 marks)*

(c) The pendulum bob has a mass of 8.0×10^{-3} kg. Calculate:

   (i) the maximum acceleration of the bob during the oscillation,

   (ii) the total energy of the oscillations.   *(5 marks)*

AQA, 2006

8   (a) A spring, which hangs from a fixed support, extends by 40 mm when a mass of 0.25 kg is suspended from it.

   (i) Calculate the spring constant of the spring.

   (ii) An additional mass of 0.44 kg is then placed on the spring and the system is set into vertical oscillation. Show that the oscillation frequency is 1.5 Hz.   *(4 marks)*

(b) With both masses still in place, the spring is now suspended from a horizontal support rod that can be made to oscillate vertically, as shown in **Figure 8**, with amplitude 30 mm at several different frequencies.

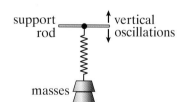

Figure 8

Describe fully, with reference to amplitude, frequency and phase, the motion of the masses suspended from the spring in each of the following cases.

   (i)   The support rod oscillates at a frequency of 0.2 Hz.

   (ii) The support rod oscillates at a frequency of 1.5 Hz.

   (iii) The support rod oscillates at a frequency of 10 Hz.   *(6 marks)*

AQA, 2006

4 Gravitational fields

4.1 Gravitational field strength

Learning objectives:

- How can we represent a gravitational field?

- What do we mean by the strength of a gravitational field?

- What is a radial field and what is a uniform field?

Specification reference: 3.4.2

Figure 1 *Earth in space*

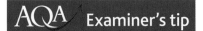
Examiner's tip

Remember that g is a vector, even though it is called 'strength'.

Link

See *AS Physics* Topic 8.4 for more about the measurement of g.

'What goes up must come down' or must it? Throw a ball into the air and it returns to you because of the Earth's gravity. The force of gravity on the ball pulls it back to Earth. The force of attraction between the ball and the Earth is an example of gravitational attraction, which exists between any two masses. It isn't obvious that there is a force of attraction between you and any object near you, but it is true. Any two masses exert a gravitational pull on one another. But the force is usually too weak to be noticed unless at least one of the masses is very large.

The mass of an object creates a force field around itself. Any other mass placed in the field is attracted towards the object. The second mass also has a force field around itself and this pulls on the first object with an equal force in the opposite direction. The force field round a mass is called a **gravitational field.**

If a small 'test' mass is placed close to a massive body, the small mass and the body attract each other with equal and opposite forces. However, this force is too small to move the massive body noticeably. The small mass, assuming it is free to move, is pulled by the force towards the massive body. The path which the smaller mass would follow is called a **field line** or sometimes a **line of force**. Figure 2 shows the field lines near a planet. The lines are directed to the centre of the planet as a small object released near the planet would fall towards its centre.

The strength of a gravitational field, g, is the force per unit mass on a small test mass placed in the field.

The test mass needs to be small, otherwise it might pull so much on the other object that it changes its position and alters the field. In general, the force on a small mass in a gravitational field varies from one position to another. If a small test mass, m, is at a certain position in a gravitational field where it is acted on by a gravitational force F, the gravitational field strength at that position is given by

$$g = \frac{F}{m}$$

The unit of gravitational field strength is the newton per kilogram ($N\,kg^{-1}$). For example, the gravitational field strength of the Earth at the surface of the Earth is $9.8\,N\,kg^{-1}$.

Free fall in a gravitational field

The weight of an object is the force of gravity on it. If an object of mass m is in a gravitational field, the gravitational force on the object $F = mg$, where g is the gravitational field strength at the object's position. If the object is not acted on by any other force, it accelerates with an

$$\text{acceleration } a = \frac{\text{force}}{\text{mass}} = \frac{mg}{m} = g$$

The object therefore falls freely with acceleration, g. Thus g may also be described as the acceleration of a freely falling object.

An object that falls freely is unsupported. Although the object in this situation is commonly described as being weightless, it is better to describe it as 'unsupported' as it is acted on by the force of gravity alone.

The unit of gravitational field strength is $N\,kg^{-1}$ and the unit of the acceleration of free-fall is $m\,s^{-2}$.

■ Field patterns

1 A **radial field** is where the field lines are like the spokes of a wheel, always directed to the centre. Figure 2 shows an example of a radial field. The force of gravity on a small mass near a much larger spherical mass is always directed to the centre of the larger mass. For example, the force on a small object near a spherical planet always acts towards the centre of the planet, regardless of the position of the object. The magnitude of g in a radial field decreases with increased distance from the massive body.

2 A **uniform field** is where the gravitational field strength is the same in magnitude and direction throughout the field. The field lines are therefore parallel to one another and equally spaced.

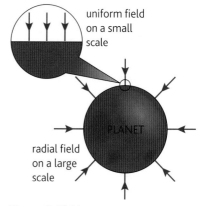

Figure 2 *Field patterns*

Is the Earth's gravitational field uniform or radial?

The force of gravity due to the Earth on a small mass decreases with distance from the Earth so the gravitational field strength of the Earth falls with increasing distance from the Earth. The field is therefore radial. However, over small distances which are much less than the Earth's radius, the change of gravitational field strength is insignificant. For example, the measured value of g has the same magnitude $(= 9.8\,N\,kg^{-1})$ and direction (downwards) 100 m above the Earth as it is on the surface. In theory, g is smaller higher up, but the difference is too small to be noticeable – provided we don't go too high! Only over distances which are small compared with the Earth's radius can the Earth's field be considered uniform.

■ Summary questions

1 a What is meant by a field line or a line of force of a gravitational field?

  b With the aid of a diagram in each case, explain what is meant by

   i   a radial field,

   ii a uniform field.

2 a Calculate the gravitational force on:

   i   an object of mass 3.5 kg in a gravitational field at a position where $g = 9.5\,N\,kg^{-1}$,

   ii an object of mass 100 kg in a gravitational field at a position where $g = 1.6\,N\,kg^{-1}$.

  b Calculate the gravitational field strength at a position in a gravitational field where

   i   an object of mass 2.5 kg experiences a force of 40 N,

   ii an object of mass 18 kg experiences a force of 72 N.

3 Show that the acceleration of an object falling freely in a gravitational field is equal to g, where g is the gravitational field strength at that position.

4 Figure 3 represents a small part of the Earth's surface. Sketch the lines of force near this part of the Earth's surface

  a if the density of the Earth in this part is uniform,

  b if there is a large mass of dense matter under this part of the surface.

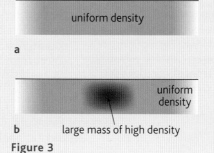

Figure 3

4.2 Gravitational potential

Learning objectives:

- What do we mean by gravitational potential?

- How do we calculate the gravitational potential difference between two points?

- Where would an object have to be placed for its gravitational potential energy to be zero?

Specification reference: 3.4.2

Imagine you are in a space rocket, about to blast off from the surface of a planet. The planet's gravitational field extends far into space although it becomes weaker with increased distance from the planet. To escape from the planet's pull due to gravity, the rocket must do work against the force of gravity on it due to the planet. If the rocket fuel doesn't provide enough energy to escape, you are doomed to return! The planet's gravitational field is like a trap which the rocket must climb out from to escape. As the rocket rises, its gravitational potential energy (gpe) increases. If it falls back, its gpe decreases. If the rocket carried a 'gpe' meter which was set to zero when it was far away from the planet, the meter reading would be negative when the rocket is on the surface of the planet and would increase towards zero as the rocket moves away from the planet.

Figure 1 *Into space*

Gravitational potential energy is the energy of an object due to its position in a gravitational field. The position for zero gpe is at infinity – in other words, the object would be so far away that the gravitational force on it is negligible. Our rocket climbing out of the planet's field needs to increase its gpe to zero to escape completely. At the surface, its gpe was negative so it needs to do work to escape from the field completely.

The **gravitational potential** at a point in a gravitational field is the gpe per unit mass of a small test mass. This is equal to the work done per unit mass to move a small object from infinity to that point as the gravitational potential at infinity is zero. So we can define gravitational potential at a point as the work done per unit mass to move a small object from infinity to that point.

The gravitational potential, V, at a point is the work done per unit mass to move a small object from infinity to that point.

Therefore, for a small object of mass m at a position where the gravitational potential is V, the work W that must be done on m to enable it to escape completely is given by $W = mV$. Rearranging this gives

$$V = \frac{W}{m}$$

Link

Gravitational fields act on objects due to their mass. Gravitational potential is defined in terms of work done per unit mass. Electric fields act on charged objects. Electric potential is defined in terms of work done per unit positive charge. See Topic 5.3.

Note that the unit of gravitational potential is $J\,kg^{-1}$.

Suppose our rocket has a 'payload' mass of $1000\,kg$ and the gravitational potential at the surface of the planet is $-100\,MJ\,kg^{-1}$. Assume the fuel is used quickly to boost the rocket to high speed. For the rocket to escape completely, the gpe of the $1000\,kg$ payload must increase from $-100 \times 1000\,MJ$ to zero. So the work done on the payload must be at least $100\,000\,MJ$ to escape. If the rocket payload is only given $40\,000\,MJ$ of kinetic energy from the fuel, then it can only increase its gpe by $40\,000\,MJ$. So it can only reach a position in the field where the gravitational potential is $-60\,MJ\,kg^{-1}$.

Note:

In general, if a small object of mass m is moved from gravitational potential V_1 to gravitational potential V_2,

its change of gpe $\Delta E_p = m(V_2 - V_1) = m\Delta V$ where $\Delta V = (V_2 - V_1)$

As the work done ΔW to move it from V_1 to V_2 is equal to the change of its gravitational potential energy, then $\Delta W = m\Delta V$

■ Potential gradients

Equipotentials are lines of constant potential. Hillwalkers ought to know all about equipotentials since a map contour line is a line of constant potential. A contour line joins points of equal height above sea level, so a hillwalker following a contour line has constant potential energy. Sensible hillwalkers take great care where the contour lines are very close to one another. One slip and their gravitational potential energy might fall dramatically!

The equipotentials near the Earth are circles as shown in Figure 2. At increasing distance from the surface, the gravitational field becomes weaker so the gain of gravitational potential energy per metre of height gain becomes less. In other words, away from the Earth's surface, the equipotentials for equal increases of potential are spaced further apart.

However, near the surface over a small region, the equipotentials are horizontal (i.e. parallel to the ground) as shown in Figure 3. This is because the gravitational field over a small region is uniform. A $1\,kg$ mass raised from the surface by $1\,m$ gains $9.8\,J$ of gravitational potential energy; if it is raised another $1\,m$, it gains another $9.8\,J$. So its gpe rises by $9.8\,J$ for every metre of height it gains above the surface.

The **potential gradient** at a point in a gravitational field is the change of potential per metre at that point.

Near the Earth's surface, the potential changes by $9.8\,J\,kg^{-1}$ for every metre of height gained. So the potential gradient near the surface of the Earth is constant and equal to $9.8\,J\,kg^{-1}\,m^{-1}$. However, further from the Earth's surface, the potential gradient becomes less and less.

In general, for a change of potential ΔV over a small distance Δr,

the potential gradient $= \dfrac{\Delta V}{\Delta r}$

Consider a test mass m being moved away from a planet as shown in Figure 3. To move m a small distance Δr in the opposite direction to the gravitational force F_{grav} on it, its gravitational potential energy must be increased

■ by an equal and opposite force F acting through the distance Δr,

■ by an amount of energy equal to the work done by F, $\Delta W = F\Delta r$.

$\mathcal{AQA}$ **Examiner's tip**

$\Delta E_p = mg\Delta h$ can only be applied for values of Δh which are very small compared with the Earth's radius. $\Delta E_p = m\Delta V$ can *always* be applied. Remember that V is a scalar.

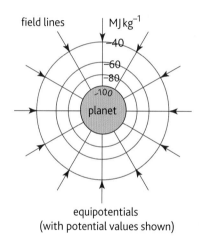

equipotentials
(with potential values shown)

Figure 2 *Equipotentials near a planet*

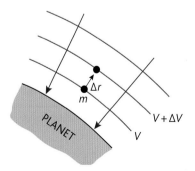

Figure 3 *Potential gradients*

For the test mass, the change of potential ΔV of the test mass $= \dfrac{\Delta W}{m}$

then $\Delta V = \dfrac{F \Delta r}{m}$ so $F = \dfrac{m \Delta V}{\Delta r}$

Hence $F_{grav} = -\dfrac{m \Delta V}{\Delta r}$ as $F_{grav} = -F$

Gravitational field strength, $g = \dfrac{F_{grav}}{m} = -\dfrac{\Delta V}{\Delta r} = -$ the potential gradient

Gravitational field strength, g, is the negative of the potential gradient.

$$g = -\dfrac{\Delta V}{\Delta r}$$

where the minus sign signifies that g acts in the opposite direction to the potential gradient

Potential gradients are like contour gradients on a map. The closer the contours are on a map, the steeper the hill. Likewise, the closer the equipotentials are, the greater the potential gradient is and the stronger the field is. Where the equipotentials show equal changes of potential for equal changes of spacing, the potential gradient is constant. Hence the gravitational field strength is constant and the field is uniform. Notice also that the gradient is always at right angles to the equipotentials, so the direction of the lines of force of the gravitational field are always perpendicular to the equipotentials.

Summary questions

$g = 9.8 \, \text{N kg}^{-1}$

1
a Calculate the gain of gravitational potential energy of an object of mass 12 kg when its centre of mass is raised through a height of 2.0 m.

b Show that the gravitational potential difference between the Earth's surface and a point 2.0 m above the surface is 19.6 J kg^{-1}.

2 A rocket of mass 35 kg launched from the Earth's surface gains 70 MJ of gravitational potential energy when it reaches its maximum height.

a Calculate the gravitational potential difference between the Earth's surface and the highest point reached by the rocket.

b The gravitational potential of the Earth's gravitational field at the surface of the Earth is −63 MJ kg^{-1}. Calculate:

 i the gravitational potential at the highest point reached by the rocket,

 ii the work that would need to have been done by the rocket to escape from the Earth's gravitational field.

3 Figure 4 shows the equipotentials near a non-spherical object.

a Calculate the gravitational potential energy of a 0.1 kg object at:

 i P,

 ii Q,

 iii R.

b How much work must be done on the object to move it from:

 i P to Q,

 ii Q to R.

4 Figure 5 shows equipotentials at a spacing of 1.0 km near a planet. The point labelled X is on the −500 kJ kg^{-1} equipotential.

a Show that the potential gradient at X is 5.0 J kg^{-1} m^{-1},

b Hence calculate the gravitational field strength at X.

c Calculate the work that would need to be done to remove an object of mass 50 kg from X to infinity.

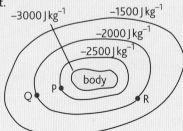

Figure 4

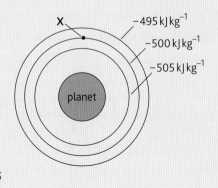

Figure 5

4.3 Newton's law of gravitation

Learning objectives:

■ How does gravitational attraction vary with distance?

■ What do we mean by an inverse-square law?

■ Can we treat spherical objects, such as planets, as point masses?

Specification reference: 3.4.2

We owe our understanding of gravitation to Isaac Newton. 'The notion of gravity was occasioned by the fall of an apple!', said Newton when asked what made him develop the idea of gravity. Newton's theory of gravitation was an enormous leap forward because it explains events from the 'down-to-earth' falling apple to the motion of the planets. Like any good theory, it can be used to make predictions; for example, the return of a comet and its exact path can be calculated using Newton's theory of gravitation. So successful was his theory that it became known as Newton's law of gravitation.

How science works

How Newton established his theory of gravitation

Newton realised that gravity is universal. Any two masses exert a force of attraction on each other. He knew about the careful measurements of planetary motion made by astronomers like Johannes Kepler. Forty or more years before Newton established the theory of gravitation, Kepler had shown that the motion of the planets was governed by a set of laws. Kepler used his own and other astronomers' measurements of motion of each planet, to show that each planet orbits the Sun. The measurements that he made for each planet were its time period T (i.e. the time for one complete orbit of the Sun) and the average radius r of its orbit. He used his measurements to show that the value of r^3/T^2 was the same for all the planets. This is known as **Kepler's third law**.

Table 1 Kepler's third law

	Mercury	Venus	Earth	Mars	Jupiter	Saturn
Average radius r of orbit/10^{10} m	6	11	15	23	78	143
Time T for one orbit/10^7 s	0.8	1.95	3.2	5.9	37.4	93.0
r^3/T^2 /10^{16} m^3 s^{-2}	337	350	330	349	340	338

To explain Kepler's third law, Newton started by assuming that the planets and the Sun were point masses. A scale model of the Solar System with the Sun represented by a 1 p piece would put the Earth about a metre away, represented by a grain of sand! Newton realised that there is a force of gravitational attraction between any planet and the Sun and it caused the planet to orbit the Sun. He assumed that the force of gravitation between a planet and the Sun varies inversely with the square of their distance apart. In other words, if the force is F at distance d apart, then

■ at distance $2d$ apart, the force is $F/4$,

■ at distance $3d$ apart, the force is $F/9$,

■ at distance $4d$ apart, the force is $F/16$.

Using this inverse-square law of force, Newton was able to prove that r^3/T^2 was the same for all the planets. The actual proof is not required for the A2 course but it is outlined in Topic 4.4. Newton then went on to use the inverse-square law of force to explain and make predictions for many other events involving gravity.

Newton's law of gravitation assumes that the gravitational force between any two point objects is

■ always an attractive force,

■ proportional to the mass of each object,

■ proportional to $\dfrac{1}{r^2}$, where r is their distance apart.

These last two requirements can be summarised as

$$\text{gravitational force } F = \frac{Gm_1m_2}{r^2}$$

where m_1 and m_2 are masses of the two objects.

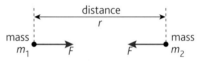

Figure 1 *Newton's law of gravitation*

The constant of proportionality, G, in the above equation, is called the **universal constant of gravitation**. The unit of G can be worked out from the

equation above; rearranged, the equation gives $G = \dfrac{Fr^2}{m_1m_2}$.

So G can be given units of $\text{N m}^2\,\text{kg}^{-2}$. The value of G is $6.67 \times 10^{-11}\,\text{N m}^2\,\text{kg}^{-2}$.

Worked example:

$G = 6.67 \times 10^{-11}\,\text{N m}^2\,\text{kg}^{-2}$.

The distance from the centre of the Sun to the centre of the Earth is $1.5 \times 10^{11}\,\text{m}$. The mass of the Sun is $2.0 \times 10^{30}\,\text{kg}$ and the mass of the Earth is $6.0 \times 10^{24}\,\text{kg}$.

a The Earth has a diameter of $1.3 \times 10^7\,\text{m}$. The Sun has a diameter of about $1.4 \times 10^9\,\text{m}$. Why is it reasonable to consider the Sun and the Earth at a distance of $1.5 \times 10^{11}\,\text{m}$ apart as point masses on this distance scale?

b Calculate the force of gravitational attraction between the Sun and the Earth.

Solution

a On a scale model where the centre of the Sun was 1 m away from the centre of the Earth, the Sun would be a sphere of diameter about 1 cm and the Earth would be a sphere of diameter about 0.1 mm, no larger than a dot. The distance from the Earth to any part of the Sun is therefore the same to within 1%. Therefore this shows that they can be treated as point objects.

b $F = \dfrac{6.67 \times 10^{-11} \times 2.0 \times 10^{30} \times 6.0 \times 10^{24}}{(1.5 \times 10^{11})^2} = 3.6 \times 10^{22}\,\text{N}$

■ **Notes**

1 Work out for yourself the gravitational force between two point masses, each of mass 10 kg apart at 0.1 m apart. The values of m_1, m_2 and r must be put into the equation in units of kilograms and metres. The force of gravitational attraction works out at $6.7 \times 10^{-7}\,\text{N}$ which is far too small to notice except with extremely sensitive equipment. Only if one of the masses is very large does the force become noticeable, unless special techniques are used, as described later.

2 The equation for Newton's law of gravitation can be applied to any two objects provided r is the distance between their centres of mass.

AQA Examiner's tip

Think carefully before writing about the 'separation' of two objects: distance between centres, or distance between surfaces?

How science works

Cavendish's measurement of *G*

The first accurate measurement of *G* was made by Henry Cavendish in 1798. He devised a torsion balance made of two small lead balls at either end of a rod. The rod was suspended horizontally by a torsion wire, as in Figure 2. The wire was calibrated by measuring the couple required to twist it per degree. Then, with the rod at rest in equilibrium, two massive lead balls were brought near the torsion balance to make the wire twist. By measuring the angle which it twisted through, the force of attraction between each massive lead ball and the small ball nearest to it was calculated. The distance between the centres of the small and large masses was also measured. Then *G* was calculated using the equation for the law of gravitation.

Link

Newton's law of gravitation and Coulomb's law of force between point charges are both inverse-square laws. For example, doubling the separation of two point masses or two point charges causes the force to reduce to a quarter. See Topic 5.2.

Figure 2 *Cavendish's measurement of* G

Summary questions

$G = 6.67 \times 10^{-11} \, \text{N} \, \text{m}^2 \, \text{kg}^{-2}$

1 a Calculate the force of gravitational attraction between two 'point objects' of masses 60 kg and 80 kg at a distance of 0.5 m apart.

  b Calculate the distance between two identical point objects, each of mass 0.20 kg, that exert a force of 9.0×10^{-8} N on each other.

2 a Calculate the force of gravitational attraction between the Earth and an object of mass 80 kg on the surface of the Earth where $g = 9.8 \, \text{N} \, \text{kg}^{-1}$.

  b Use the result of your calculation in a to estimate the mass of the Earth. Assume that the mass of the Earth is concentrated at its centre.

  The radius of the Earth = 6.4×10^6 m.

3 The Sun exerted a force of 6.0 N on a 1000 kg comet when it was at a distance of 1.5×10^{11} m from the Sun. Calculate the force due to the Sun on the comet when it was at a distance of:

  a 0.5×10^{11} m from the Sun,

  b 7.5×10^{11} m from the Sun.

4 A space rocket of mass 1500 kg travelled from the Earth to the Moon, a distance of 3.8×10^8 m.

  a When the space rocket was mid-way between the Earth and the Moon, calculate the force of gravitational attraction on it

   i due to the Earth,

   ii due to the Moon.

  b Calculate the magnitude and direction of the force of gravity of the Earth and the Moon on the space rocket when it was mid-way between the Earth and the Moon.

  The mass of the Earth = 6.0×10^{24} kg; the mass of the Moon = 7.4×10^{22} kg

4.4 Planetary fields

Learning objectives:

- What is the shape of the graph of *g* against *r* for points outside the surface of a planet?

- How does the graph of *V* against *r* compare with this?

- What is the significance of the gradient of the *V–r* graph?

Specification reference: 3.4.2

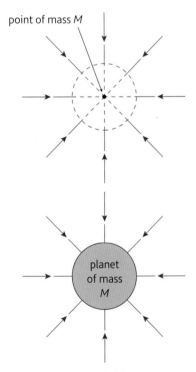

point of mass *M*

planet of mass *M*

Figure 1 *Comparing fields*

Gravitational field strength

The law of gravitation can be used to determine the **gravitational field strength** at any point in the field of a planet or any other spherical mass. Newton showed that the field of a spherical mass is the same as if the mass were concentrated at its centre. The field lines of a spherical mass are always directed towards the centre, so the field pattern is just the same as for a point mass, as shown in Figure 1.

- **For a point mass *M*,** the magnitude of the force of attraction on a 'test mass' *m* (where *m* << *M*) at distance *r* from *M* is given by Newton's law of gravitation $F = \dfrac{GMm}{r^2}$

  Therefore, the magnitude of the gravitational field strength at distance *r* is given by
  $$g = \frac{F}{m} = \frac{GM}{r^2}$$

- **For a spherical mass *M* of radius *R*,** the force of attraction on a 'test mass' *m* at distance *r* **from the centre of *M*** is the same as if mass *M* was concentrated at its centre. Therefore, the force of attraction between *m* and *M*,
  $$F = \frac{GMm}{r^2}$$

Therefore, the magnitude of the gravitational field strength at distance *r* is given by $g = F/m = GMm/r^2$, provided distance *r* is greater than or equal to the radius *R* of the sphere.

Magnitude of the gravitational field strength, $g = \dfrac{GM}{r^2}$ at distance *r* from a point object or from the centre of a sphere of mass *M*.

Note:
The gravitational field strength at the surface of a sphere of radius *R* and mass *M* is given by $g_s = GM/R^2$ as the distance from the centre *r* = *R* at the surface.

Worked example:

$G = 6.67 \times 10^{-11}\,\mathrm{N\,m^2\,kg^{-2}}$

The gravitational field strength at the surface of the Earth is $9.8\,\mathrm{N\,kg^{-1}}$. Calculate:

a the mass of the Earth,

b the gravitational field strength of the Earth at a height of 1000 km above the surface.

The radius of the Earth = 6400 km.

Solution

a Rearranging $g_s = \dfrac{GM}{R^2}$ gives $M = \dfrac{g_s R^2}{G}$

$$= \frac{9.8 \times (6400 \times 10^3)^2}{6.67 \times 10^{-11}} = 6.0 \times 10^{24}\,\mathrm{kg}$$

b At height $h = 1000\,\mathrm{km}, r = R + h = 7400\,\mathrm{km}$

$$\therefore g = \frac{GM}{r^2} = \frac{6.67 \times 10^{-11} \times 6.0 \times 10^{24}}{(7400 \times 10^3)^2} = 7.3\,\mathrm{N\,kg^{-1}}$$

The variation of g with distance from the centre of a spherical planet (or star)

Consider the gravitational field beyond the surface of a spherical planet of mass M and radius R. As we saw on the previous page, for any position at or beyond the surface, the magnitude of the gravitational field strength is given by $g = \dfrac{GM}{r^2}$, where r is the distance from the position to the centre of the sphere.

Because the surface gravitational field strength, $g_s = \dfrac{GM}{r^2}$, then $GM = g_s R^2$

Therefore, $g = \dfrac{g_s R^2}{r^2}$

The equation shows how g changes with increase of distance r from the centre of the planet.

- At distance $r = 2R$, $g = \dfrac{g_s R^2}{(2R)^2} = \dfrac{g_s}{4}$

- At distance $r = 3R$, $g = \dfrac{g_s R^2}{(3R)^2} = \dfrac{g_s}{9}$

- At distance $r = 4R$, $g = \dfrac{g_s R^2}{(4R)^2} = \dfrac{g_s}{16}$

Figure 2 shows how g varies with distance r. The shape of the curve beyond $r = R$ is an 'inverse square law' curve because g decreases in inverse proportion to r^2.

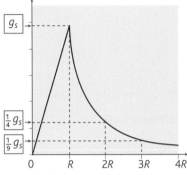

Figure 2 *Gravitational field strength*

Application

Inside a planet

From the equation $g = GM/r^2$, you might think that the magnitude of g inside the Earth becomes ever larger and larger as r becomes smaller and smaller. However, inside the planet, only the mass in the sphere of radius r contributes to g. The rest of the mass outside r up to the surface gives no resultant force. So as r becomes smaller, the mass M which contributes to g becomes smaller too. At the centre, the mass that contributes to g is zero. So g is zero at the centre. Figure 2 also shows how g inside the planet varies with distance from the centre. For a spherical planet of density ρ, prove that $g = 4\pi G\rho r/3$ inside the planet.

Gravitational potential near a spherical planet

At or beyond the surface of a spherical planet, the gravitational potential V at distance r from the centre of the planet of mass M is given by

$$V = \frac{-GM}{r}$$

Applying this formula to the surface of the Earth with $M = 6.0 \times 10^{24}\,\text{kg}$ and $r = 6.4 \times 10^6\,\text{m}$ gives a value of $-63\,\text{MJ kg}^{-1}$. This means that $63\,\text{MJ}$ of work needs to be done to remove a 1 kg mass from the surface of the Earth to infinity.

Figure 3 shows how the force of gravity on a 1 kg mass varies with distance r from the centre of the Earth. As explained previously, the mathematical equation for this curve is $g = \dfrac{g_s R^2}{r^2}$.

The area under the curve represents the work done to move the 1 kg mass from infinity to the surface.

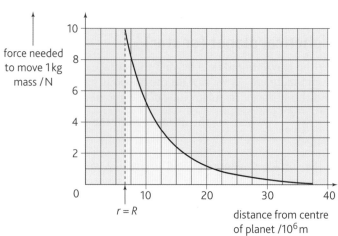

Figure 3 *Work done*

How science works

Multistage rockets

The Russian physicist Konstantin Tsiolovski predicted in 1895 that space rockets would need to be multistage. The reason is that rocket fuel releases no more than about 30 MJ kg⁻¹ when it burns and this is insufficient to enable a single-stage rocket to climb into space from the Earth's surface. A multistage rocket jettisons the lowest 'stage' when the fuel contained in that part has all been burned and only the top stage (the 'payload') escapes from the Earth's gravitational pull.

Each grid square in Figure 3 represents a 1 N force acting for a distance of 2.5×10^6 m and therefore represents 2.5 MJ ($= 1$ N $\times 2.5 \times 10^6$ m) of work done.

The work done to move the 1 kg mass from infinity to the surface can therefore be estimated by counting the number of grid squares under the curve and multiplying this number by 2.5 MJ.

Counting part-filled squares that are half-filled or more as wholly-filled squares, and neglecting part-filled squares that are less than half-filled, show for yourself that this method gives an estimate for the work done which is very close to the value of 63 MJ determined above.

In effect, the area method used above is an application of 'work done = force × distance moved' with a variable force $F = GMm/r^2$ and $m = 1$ kg.

Consider one small step in moving the 1 kg mass from infinity to the surface. Suppose the distance from the centre of the Earth decreases from r_1 to r_2 in making this small step of distance Δr.

The work done, ΔW, to make this small step is given by

$$\Delta W = F\Delta r = \frac{GMm}{r^2} \Delta r$$

In Figure 3, the work done ΔW in making each small step $\Delta r = 2.5 \times 10^6$ m is represented by each column of grid squares under the curve. Thus the total work done to move from infinity to the surface is given by the total area under the curve.

Where does the formula for gravitational potential V = −GM/r come from?

Although the 'proof' below is not required in the specification, it is provided to give some further insight into the use of maths in physics.

The change of potential ΔV for the small step (from $r_1 = r$ to $r_2 = r - \Delta r$) $= V_2 - V_1$, where V_2 is the potential at r_2 and V_1 is the potential at r_1

$$\Delta V = \frac{\Delta W}{m} = F\frac{\Delta r}{m} = -\frac{GM}{r^2} \Delta r \text{ where the minus sign indicates a}$$

decrease in r.

As $\dfrac{1}{r_1} - \dfrac{1}{r_2} = \dfrac{r_2 - r_1}{r_1 r_2} = \dfrac{(r - \Delta r) - r}{r(r + \Delta r)} = \dfrac{-\Delta r}{r^2}$ provided $\Delta r << r$

then $\Delta V = V_2 - V_1 = GM\left|\dfrac{1}{r_1} - \dfrac{1}{r_2}\right|$

Link

The gravitational potential at distance r from the centre of a spherical mass is proportional to $1/r$; the electric potential at distance r from a point charge is also proportional to $1/r$. See Topic 5.3.

Hence $V_2 = -\dfrac{GM}{r_2}$ and $V_1 = -\dfrac{GM}{r_1}$

Therefore, in general, the potential V at distance r from the centre of a planet is given by $V = -\dfrac{GM}{r}$

Potential gradients near a spherical planet

The gravitational potential V near a spherical planet is inversely proportional to the distance r from the centre of the planet as $V = -GM/r$. Figure 4 shows how the gravitational potential of the Earth varies with distance. Note the potential curve is a $1/r$ curve not an inverse-square (i.e. $1/r^2$) curve like the field strength curve in Figure 2. So the potential:

- at distance $2R$ from the centre is $0.50 \times$ the potential at distance R from the centre,
- at distance $3R$ from the centre is $0.33 \times$ the potential at distance R from the centre,
- at distance $4R$ from the centre is $0.25 \times$ the potential at distance R from the centre, etc.

AQA Examiner's tip

Know how to draw $(1/r^2)$ and $-(1/r)$ graphs, and note how g changes much more sharply with distance than V does.

Note

The gradient of the potential curve at any point is equal to $-g$, where g is the gravitational field strength at the point. This is because $g = -$ the potential gradient as explained in Topic 4.2. The potential curve becomes less steep as the distance from the centre decreases. At any point on the curve, the gradient of the curve can be found by drawing a tangent to the curve at that point and measuring the gradient of the tangent.

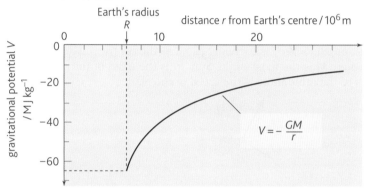

Figure 4 *Gravitational potential near the Earth*

Summary questions

$G = 6.67 \times 10^{-11}\,\text{N}\,\text{m}^2\,\text{kg}^{-2}$

1 The Moon has a radius of 1740 km and its surface gravitational field strength is $1.62\,\text{N}\,\text{kg}^{-1}$ to 3 significant figures.

a Calculate the mass of the Moon.

b The Moon's gravitational pull on the Earth causes the ocean tides. Show that the gravitational pull of the Moon on the Earth's oceans is approximately 3 millionths of the gravitational pull of the Earth on its oceans. Assume that the distance from the Earth to the Moon is 380 000 km.

2 The Sun has a mass of 2.0×10^{30} kg and a mean diameter of 1.4×10^9 m. Calculate:

a its gravitational field strength at

   i its surface,

   ii the Earth's orbit which is at a distance of 1.5×10^{11} m from the Sun.

b The Earth has a mass of 6.0×10^{24} kg. Show that the gravitational field strength of the Earth is equal and opposite to the gravitational field strength of the Sun at a distance of 260 000 km from the centre of the Earth.

3 The tip of the tallest mountain on the Earth, Mount Everest, is 9 km above sea level. The mean radius of the Earth to the nearest kilometre is 6378 km.

a Calculate the difference between the gravitational field strength of the Earth at sea level and the top of Mount Everest.

b Discuss if it is reasonable to assume that the Earth's gravitational field is uniform between the surface and a height of 10 km above the surface.

c Calculate the gain of potential energy of a mountaineer of mass 80 kg who travels to the top of the mountain from sea level.

4 Use the data in Q1 to calculate the gravitational potential at the surface of the Moon and hence calculate the work done to launch a 500 kg rocket from the surface so it escapes from the Moon's gravitational field.

4.5 Satellite motion

- Under what condition is a satellite in a stable orbit?

- What happens to the speed of a satellite if it moves closer to the Earth?

- Why must a geosynchronous satellite be in an orbit above the Equator?

Specification reference: 3.4.2

Figure 1 *Space station in orbit*

Link

By assuming the satellite is in uniform circular motion, we can equate mv^2/r to the gravitational force on the satellite. See Topic 2.2.

How science works

The mass of the Sun

Newton's theory not only explains Kepler's laws, but it also allows the mass M to be calculated if the value of G is known. The Earth orbits the Sun once per year on a circular orbit of radius 1.5×10^{11} m so you can prove for yourself that the value of r^3/T^2 for any planet is 3.4×10^{18} m^3 s^{-2}. Given $G = 6.67 \times 10^{-11}$ N m^2 kg^{-2}, show that the mass of the Sun is 2.0×10^{30} kg.

On any clear night you ought to be able to see satellites passing overhead in the night sky. Although they are pinpoints of light, they are noticeable because they move steadily through the constellations. Newspapers supply information to enable you to identify some of them from their directions. However, satellite motion is not confined to artificial satellites orbiting the Earth. Any small mass which orbits a larger mass is a satellite. The Moon is the Earth's only natural satellite. Mars has two moons, Phobos and Deimos. Jupiter has at least 14 satellites including the four innermost satellites, Io, Callisto, Ganymede and Europa, first observed by Galileo four centuries ago.

Newton knew that the time period, T, of a planet orbiting the Sun depends on the mean radius, r, of the orbit in accordance with Kepler's third law, $r^3/T^2 =$ constant.

He realised that the force of gravitational attraction between each planet and the Sun is the centripetal force that keeps the planet on its orbit. By assuming the gravitational force is given by GMm/r^2, the gravitational field strength, GM/r^2, is therefore equal to the centripetal acceleration v^2/r, where M is the mass of the Sun, m is the mass of the planet, r is the radius of the orbit and v is the speed of the planet.

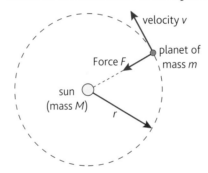

Figure 2 *Explanation of planetary motion*

Therefore, the speed of the planet is given by $v^2 = \dfrac{GM}{r}$

Because speed, $v = \dfrac{\text{circumference of the orbit}}{\text{time period}} = \dfrac{2\pi r}{T}$

then $\dfrac{(2\pi r)^2}{T^2} = \dfrac{GM}{r}$

Rearranging this equation gives $\dfrac{r^3}{T^2} = \dfrac{GM}{4\pi^2}$

As $\dfrac{GM}{4\pi^2}$ is the same for all the planets, then $\dfrac{r^3}{T^2}$ is the same for all the planets.

So, by assuming the force of attraction F varies with distance according to the inverse-square law (i.e. $F \propto 1/r^2$), Newton was able to prove Kepler's third law.

Geostationary satellites

A geostationary satellite orbits the Earth directly above the equator and has a time period of exactly 24 h. It therefore remains in a fixed position above the equator because it has exactly the same time period as the

Earth's rotation. The radius of orbit of a geostationary satellite can be calculated as follows using the equation $r^3/T^2 = GM/4\pi^2$

Hence $T = 24\,h = 24 \times 3600\,s = 86\,400\,s$

$$r^3 = \frac{GMT^2}{4\pi^2} = \frac{6.67 \times 10^{-11} \times 6.0 \times 10^{24} \times (86\,400)^2}{4\pi^2} = 7.6 \times 10^{22}\,m^3$$

$\therefore r = 4.2 \times 10^7\,m = 42\,000\,km$

The radius of the Earth is 6400 km. Therefore, the height of a geostationary satellite above the Earth is 36 000 km (= 42 000 – 6400 km).

Application and How science works

SATNAV at work

Figure 3 *SATNAV at work*

Vehicle satellite navigation (SATNAV) units receive 'time' signals from a system of global positioning satellites (GPS) that orbit the Earth at a height of just over 22 000 km. The signals are synchronised and the receiver in each unit is programmed to measure the time differences between the signals and use the differences to pinpoint its position. The software in the unit is designed to display the local road map showing the vehicle's position and route ahead to the destination supplied by the driver. However, beware as SATNAVs have been known to send heavy goods vehicles down unsuitable narrow roads!

Summary questions

$G = 6.67 \times 10^{-11}\,N\,m^2\,kg^{-2}$

The radius of the Earth = 6400 km, $g = 9.8\,N\,kg^{-1}$ at the Earth's surface.

1 a Two satellites X and Y are seen from the ground crossing the night sky at the same time. Satellite X crosses the sky faster than Y. State with a reason which satellite is higher.

b Explain why satellite TV dishes must be aligned carefully so they always point to the same position above the equator.

2 A space probe moving at a speed of 3.2 km s⁻¹ is in a circular orbit about a spherical planet. The time period of the satellite is 110 min. Calculate:

a the radius of the orbit,

b the centripetal acceleration of the satellite,

c the mass of the planet.

3 a A satellite moves at speed v in a circular orbit of radius r.

i Write down an expression for the centripetal acceleration of the satellite.

ii Show that the speed of the satellite is given by the equation $v^2 = gr$, where g is the gravitational field strength at the orbit.

b A satellite orbits the Earth in a circular orbit at a height of 100 km. Calculate:

i the gravitational field strength of the Earth at this distance,

ii the speed of the satellite,

iii the time period of the satellite.

4 a Show that the speed, v, of a satellite in a circular orbit of radius r about a planet of mass M is given by the equation $v^2 = GM/r$.

b A weather satellite is in a polar orbit above the Earth at a height of 1600 km.

i Show that its speed is 7.1 km s⁻¹.

ii Calculate its time period.

iii Explain why such a satellite can survey global weather patterns every day.

1 **Black holes**

A black hole is an astronomical body which is so massive that nothing can escape from it. Anything that falls into a black hole would never be seen again. The radius of a black hole is defined by its **event horizon**, an imaginary spherical surface surrounding the body. Nothing inside the event horizon can escape, not even light. Radiation can be detected from matter drawn into a black hole before it is trapped inside the event horizon. Astronomers reckon there might be a black hole at the centre of our own galaxy, the Milky Way.

Figure 1 A black hole in space?

The idea of a black hole was first thought up by John Michell in 1783 although the term itself was first used much later by the American physicist, John Wheeler. Michell's idea was not tested until after Einstein published his *General Theory of Relativity* in 1916 in which he predicted mathematically that a strong gravitational field distorts space and time and bends light. He calculated that light grazing the Sun from a star would be deflected by 0.0005° due to the Sun's gravity. The prediction was confirmed by Sir Arthur Eddington in 1919 who led a scientific expedition to South America to test the prediction by photographing stars close to the Sun during a total solar eclipse. The eclipse photographs revealed that the star images were displaced relative to each other just as Einstein had predicted.

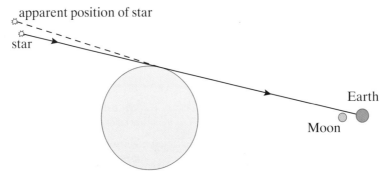

Figure 2 Bending starlight

The modern theory of black holes was started by Karl Schwarzschild who used Einstein's theory to prove light could not escape from an object with a sufficiently strong gravitational field. He showed that such an object is surrounded by an 'event horizon' which nothing inside can pass through and that radius, R, of the event horizon is given by

$R = \dfrac{2GM}{c^2}$, where M is the mass of the black hole and c is the speed of light in free space.

Evidence for black holes has been obtained by astronomers. The central region of the galaxy *M87* is rotating so fast that there must be a massive black hole at its centre. The X-ray source, Cygnus X1, is a binary system consisting of supergiant star accompanied by a very dense invisible star thought to be a black hole pulling matter from its companion.

Questions

$c = 3.0 \times 10^8\,\mathrm{m\,s^{-1}}$, $G = 6.7 \times 10^{-11}\,\mathrm{N\,m^2\,kg^{-2}}$,

(a) (i) The mass of the Earth is $6.0 \times 10^{24}\,\mathrm{kg}$. Show that the radius of the event horizon of a black hole that has the same mass as the Earth would be 8.9 mm.

(ii) Calculate the density of an object with the same mass as the Earth and a radius of 9.0 mm. The mass of the Earth = $6.0 \times 10^{24}\,\mathrm{kg}$.

(5 marks)

(b) (i) Use the scientific examples described above to explain what is meant by a scientific hypothesis.

(ii) What key discovery was made by Eddington in 1919 and what was the significance of this discovery? *(5 marks)*

(c) The Hubble Space Telescope has led to many new astronomical discoveries. Suppose your Government commits itself to establishing a manned space observatory on the Moon by 2025. Some people take the view this project could lead to many new discoveries. Other people take the view that the money for the project would be better spent helping to improve living conditions in poorer countries. Discuss **one** argument in support of each of these views and use your arguments to decide whether or not you would welcome such a project. *(5 marks)*

2 (a) (i) Explain what is meant by the *gravitational field strength* at a point in a gravitational field.

(ii) State the SI unit of gravitational field strength. *(2 marks)*

(b) Planet P has mass M and radius R. Planet Q has a radius $3R$. The values of the gravitational field strengths at the surfaces of P and Q are the same.

(i) Determine the mass of Q in terms of M.

(ii) **Figure 3** shows how the gravitational field strength above the surface of planet P varies with distance from its centre.

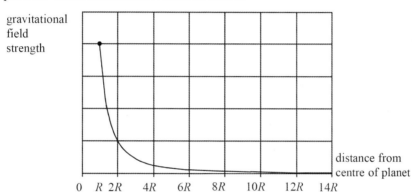

Figure 3

Copy the diagram and draw the variation of the gravitational field strength above the surface of Q over the range shown. *(6 marks)*

AQA, 2006

3 (a) Artificial satellites are used to monitor weather conditions on Earth, for surveillance and for communications. Such satellites may be placed in a *geo-synchronous* orbit or in a low polar orbit.

Describe the properties of the geo-synchronous orbit and the advantages it offers when a satellite is used for communications. *(3 marks)*

(b) A satellite of mass m travels at angular speed ω in a circular orbit at a height h above the surface of a planet of mass M and radius R.

(i) Using these symbols, give an equation that relates the gravitational force on the satellite to the centripetal force.

(ii) Use your equation from part (b)(i) to show that the orbital period, T, of the satellite is given by

$$T^2 = \frac{4\pi^2(R+h)^3}{GM}$$

(iii) Explain why the period of a satellite in orbit around the Earth cannot be less than 85 minutes. Your answer should include a calculation to justify this value. *(6 marks)*

(c) Describe and explain what happens to the speed of a satellite when it moves to an orbit that is closer to the Earth. *(2 marks)*

AQA, 2006

4 (a) (i) Show that the gravitational field strength of the Earth at height h above the surface is given by

$$g = g_s\left(\frac{R}{R+h}\right)^2$$

where g_s is the gravitational field strength at the surface and R is the radius of the Earth.

(ii) Calculate the gravitational field strength of the Earth at a height of 200 km above its surface. *(5 marks)*

(b) An astronaut floats in a spacecraft which is in a circular orbit around the Earth.

Discuss whether or not the astronaut is weightless in this situation. *(3 marks)*

AQA, 2007

5 NASA wishes to recover a satellite, at present stranded on the Moon's surface, and to place it in orbit around the Moon.

(a) (i) **Figure 4** shows a graph of how gravitational field strength due to the Moon varies with distance from the centre of the Moon. Mark on the figure the area that corresponds to the energy needed to move 1 kg from the surface of the Moon to a vertical height of 4000 km above the surface.

radius of the Moon = 1700 km

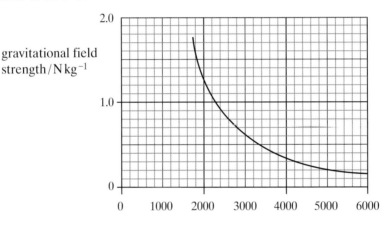

distance from centre of Moon/km

Figure 4

(ii) The satellite has a mass of 450 kg. Estimate the change in gravitational potential energy of the satellite when it is moved from the surface of the Moon to a vertical height of 4000 km above the surface. *(6 marks)*

(b) NASA now decides to bring the satellite back to Earth. Explain why the amount of fuel required to return the satellite to Earth will be *much* less than the amount required to send it to the Moon originally. *(5 marks)*

AQA, 2004

6 (a) Explain what is meant by the *gravitational potential* at a point in a gravitational field. *(2 marks)*

(b) Use the following data to calculate the gravitational potential at the surface of the Moon.

mass of Earth = 81 × mass of Moon

radius of Earth = 3.7 × radius of Moon

gravitational potential at surface of the Earth = −63 MJ kg⁻¹ *(3 marks)*

(c) Sketch a graph using axes as in Figure 5 to indicate how the gravitational potential due to the Moon varies with distance along a line outwards from the surface of the Earth to the surface of the Moon. *(3 marks)*

AQA, 2005

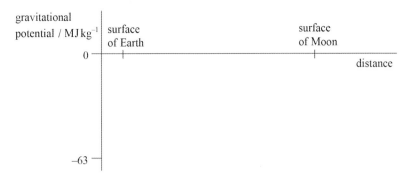

Figure 5

7   (a) State the law that governs the magnitude of the force between two point masses.

(2 marks)

(b) Table 1 shows how the gravitational potential varies for three points above the centre of the Sun.

Table 1

distance from centre of Sun/10^8 m	gravitational potential/10^{10} J kg^{-1}
7.0 (surface of Sun)	−19
16	−8.3
35	−3.8

(i)   Show that the data suggest that the potential is inversely proportional to the distance from the centre of the Sun. *(2 marks)*

(ii) Use the data to determine the gravitational field strength near the surface of the Sun. *(3 marks)*

(iii) Calculate the change in gravitational potential energy needed for the Earth to escape from the gravitational attraction of the Sun.

mass of the Earth = 6.0×10^{24} kg

distance of Earth from centre of Sun = 1.5×10^{11} m *(3 marks)*

(iv) Calculate the kinetic energy of the Earth due to its orbital speed around the Sun and hence find the minimum energy that would be needed for the Earth to escape from its orbit.

Assume that the Earth moves in a circular orbit. *(3 marks)*

AQA, 2005

8   For an object, such as a space rocket, to escape from the gravitational attraction of the Earth it must be given an amount of energy equal to the gravitational potential energy that it has on the Earth's surface. The minimum initial vertical velocity at the surface of the Earth that it requires to achieve this is known as the escape velocity.

(a) (i)   Write down the equation for the gravitational potential energy of a rocket when it is on the Earth's surface. Take the mass of the Earth to be M, that of the rocket to be m and the radius of the Earth to be R.

(ii) Show that the escape velocity, v, of the rocket is given by the equation

$$v = \sqrt{\frac{2GM}{R}}$$ *(3 marks)*

(b) The nominal escape velocity from the Earth is 11.2 km s^{-1}. Calculate a value for the escape velocity from a planet of mass four times that of the Earth and radius twice that of the Earth. *(2 marks)*

(c) Explain why the actual escape velocity from the Earth would be greater than the nominal value calculated from the equation given in part (a)(ii). *(2 marks)*

AQA, 2004

5.1 Field patterns

Learning objectives:

- How can we charge a metal object?

- What does the direction of an electric field line show concerning a test charge?

- How is the strength of an electric field represented by field lines?

Specification reference: 3.4.3

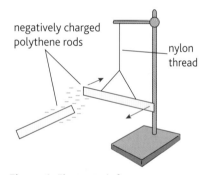

Figure 1 *Electrostatic forces*

negatively charged polythene rods

nylon thread

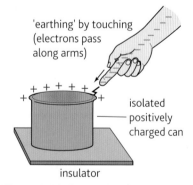

'earthing' by touching (electrons pass along arms)

isolated positively charged can

insulator

Figure 2 *Discharge to Earth*

■ Static electricity

Most plastic materials can be charged quite easily by rubbing with a dry cloth. When charged, they can usually pick up small bits of paper. The bits of paper are attracted to the charged piece of plastic. Do charged pieces of plastic material attract one another? Figure 1 shows an arrangement to test for attraction. A charged perspex ruler will attract a charged polythene comb, but two charged rods of the same material always repel one another.

Like charges repel, unlike charges attract.

Electrons are responsible for charging in most situations. An uncharged atom contains equal numbers of protons and electrons. Add one or more electrons to an uncharged atom and it becomes negatively charged. Remove one or more electrons from an uncharged atom and it becomes positively charged. An uncharged solid contains equal numbers of electrons and protons. To make it negatively charged, electrons must be added to it. To make it positively charged, electrons must be removed from it. When an uncharged perspex rod is rubbed with an uncharged dry cloth, electrons transfer from the rod to the cloth so the rod becomes positively charged and the cloth becomes negatively charged.

- **Electrical conductors** such as metals contain lots of **free electrons**. These are electrons which move about inside the metal and are not attached to any one atom. To charge a metal, it must be first isolated from the Earth. Otherwise, any charge given to it is neutralised by electrons transferring between the conductor and the Earth. Then the isolated conductor can be charged by direct contact with any charged object. If an isolated conductor is charged positively then 'earthed', electrons transfer from the Earth to the conductor to neutralise or discharge it (see Figure 2).

- **Insulating materials** do not contain free electrons. All the electrons in an insulator are attached to individual atoms. Some insulators, such as perspex or polythene, are easy to charge because their surface atoms easily gain or lose electrons.

The shuttling ball experiment shows that an electric current is a flow of charge. A conducting ball is suspended by an insulating thread between two vertical plates, as in Figure 3. When a high voltage is applied across the two plates, the ball bounces back and forth between the two plates. Each time it touches the negative plate, the ball gains some electrons and becomes negatively charged. It is then repelled by the negative plate and pulled across to the positive plate. When contact is made, electrons on the ball transfer to the positive plate so the ball now becomes positively charged and is repelled back to the negative plate to repeat the cycle. Therefore, the electrons from the high voltage supply pass along the wire to the negative plate. There, they are ferried across to the other plate by the ball. Then they pass along the wire back to the supply. A microammeter in series with the plates shows that the shuttling ball causes a current round the circuit. If the plates are brought closer together, the ball shuttles back and forth even more rapidly. As a result, the microammeter reading increases because charge is ferried across at a faster rate.

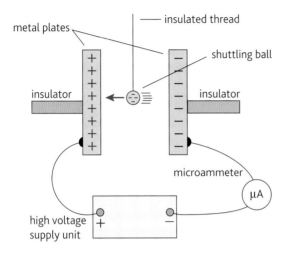

Figure 3 *The shuttling ball experiment*

Suppose the ball shuttles back and forth at frequency f. The time taken for each cycle is therefore $1/f$. The amount and type of charge on the ball depends on the voltage of the plate it last made contact with. Therefore, if the charge ferried across the gap each cycle is Q, the average current round the circuit,

$$I = Qf \left(= \frac{\text{charge } Q}{\text{time for 1 cycle}}\right)$$

Worked example:

$e = 1.6 \times 10^{-19}\,\text{C}$

In a shuttling ball experiment, the microammeter reading was 20 nA when the frequency of the shuttling ball was 4.0 Hz. Calculate:

a the charge carried by the ball,

b the number of electrons needed for the charge calculated in a.

Solution

a $Q = \dfrac{I}{f} = \dfrac{20 \times 10^{-9}}{4.0} = 5.0 \times 10^{-9}\,\text{C}$

b number of electrons $= \dfrac{Q}{e} = \dfrac{5.0 \times 10^{-9}}{1.6 \times 10^{-19}} = 3.1 \times 10^{10}$

The gold leaf electroscope is used to detect charge. If a charged object is in contact with the metal cap of the electroscope, some of the charge on the object transfers to the electroscope. As a result, the gold leaf and the metal stem which is attached to the cap gain the same type of charge and the leaf rises because it is repelled by the stem.

If another object with the same type of charge is brought near the electroscope, the leaf rises further because the object forces some charge on the cap to transfer to the leaf and stem.

Figure 4 *The charged gold leaf electroscope*

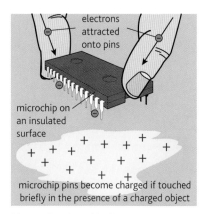

microchip pins become charged if touched
briefly in the presence of a charged object

Figure 5 *Microchip damage*

Link

A line of force, or field line, in an
electric field is a line which a small
positive charge moves along if
free to do so. A line of force in a
gravitational field is a line which a
free point mass moves along if free
to do so. See Topic 4.1.

Application and How science works

Chips and charge

People handling microchips wear antistatic clothing and they work
in rooms fitted with antistatic floors. This is because a tiny amount
of charge on the pins of an electronic chip can be enough to destroy
circuits inside the chip. This can happen if the pins are touched
in the presence of a charged body. The pins are earthed when they
are touched. As a result, electrons transfer between the pins and
Earth. If the connection to Earth is removed, the pins remain
charged when the charged body is removed. Microchips are stored
in antistatic packets and handled with special tools. Antistatic
materials allow charge to flow across the surface.

Field lines and patterns

Any two charged objects exert equal and opposite forces on each other
without being directly in contact. An electric field is said to surround
each charge. Suppose a small positive charge is placed as a test charge
near a body with a much bigger charge which is also positive. If the test
charge is free to move, it will follow a path away from the body with the
bigger charge. The path a free positive 'test' charge follows is called a **line
of force** or a **field line**.

The field lines of an electric field are the lines which positive test charges
follow. The direction of an electric field line is the direction a positive test
charge would move along. Figure 6 shows the patterns of fields around
different charged objects. Each pattern is produced by semolina grains
sprinkled on oil. An electric field is set up across the surface of the oil by
connecting two metal conductors in the oil, to the output terminals of
a high voltage supply unit. The grains line up along the field lines, like
plotting compasses in a magnetic field.

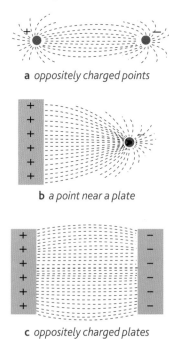

a *oppositely charged points*

b *a point near a plate*

c *oppositely charged plates*

Figure 6 *Electric field patterns*

Oppositely charged objects create a field as shown in Figure 6a. The field lines become concentrated at the points. A positive test charge released from an off-centre position would follow a curved path to the negative point charge.

A point object near an oppositely charged flat plate produces a field as shown in Figure 6b. The field lines are concentrated at the point object but they are at right angles to the plate where they meet. The field is strongest where the lines are most concentrated.

Two oppositely charged plates create a field as shown in Figure 6c. The field lines run parallel from one plate to the other, meeting the plates at right angles. The field is **uniform** between the plates as the field lines are parallel to each other.

Summary questions

$e = 1.6 \times 10^{-19}\,C$

1 Explain each of the following observations in terms of transfer of electrons:

a An insulated metal can is given a positive charge by touching it with a positively charged rod.

b A negatively charged metal sphere suspended on a thread is discharged by connecting it to the ground using a wire.

2 a In the shuttling ball experiment, explain why the ball shuttles faster if:

i the potential difference between the plates is increased,

ii the plates are brought closer together.

b A ball shuttles between two oppositely charged metal plates at a frequency of 2.5 Hz. The ball carries a charge of 30 nC each time it shuttles from one plate to the other. Calculate:

i the average current in the circuit,

ii the number of electrons transferred each time the ball makes contact with a metal plate.

3 An insulated metal conductor is earthed before a negatively charged object is brought near to it.

a Explain why the free electrons in the conductor move as far away from the charged object as they can.

b The conductor is then briefly earthed. The charged object is then removed from the vicinity of the conductor. Explain why the conductor is left with an overall positive charge.

4 a A positively charged point object is placed near an earthed metal plate, as shown in Figure 7.

i Explain why electrons gather at the surface of the metal plate near the object.

ii Explain why there is a force of attraction between the object and the metal plate.

b Sketch the pattern of the field lines of the electric field:

i between two oppositely charged parallel plates,

ii between a positively charged point object and an earthed metal plate.

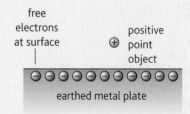

Figure 7

5.2 Electric field strength

Learning objectives:

- How, in principle, can we measure the strength of an electric field?

- Is electric field strength, *E*, a scalar or a vector, and does this affect the sign of a test charge we should use?

- Why should *E* be described as the force per unit charge, rather than the force that acts on one coulomb of charge?

Specification reference: 3.4.3

A charged object in an electric field experiences a force due to the field. Provided the object's size and charge are both sufficiently small, the object may be used as a 'test' charge to measure the strength of the field at any position in the field.

The electric field strength, *E*, at a point in the field is defined as the force per unit charge on a positive test charge placed at that point.

The unit of *E* is the newton per coulomb (NC^{-1}).

If a positive test charge *Q* at a certain point in an electric field is acted on by force *F* due to the electric field, the electric field strength, *E*, at that point is given by the equation

$$E = \frac{F}{Q}$$

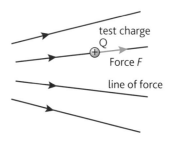

electric field strength, $E = \frac{F}{Q}$ (at Q)

Figure 1 *Electric field strength*

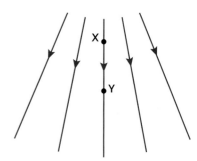

Figure 2 *A non-uniform field*

Notes

1 Rearranging this equation gives $F = QE$ for the force *F* on a test charge *Q* at a point in the electric field where the electric field strength is *E*.

2 Electric field strength is a **vector** in the same direction as the force on a positive test charge. In other words the direction of a field line at any point is the direction of the electric field strength at that point. The force on a small charge in an electric field is:

- in the same direction as the electric field if the charge is positive,

- in the opposite direction to the electric field if the charge is negative.

3 The charge of a 'test charge' needs to be very much less than 1 coulomb as this amount of charge would affect the charges that cause the field so altering the electric field strength.

Worked example:

$e = 1.6 \times 10^{-19} C$

Figure 2 shows the field lines of an electric field.

a Calculate the magnitude of electric field strength at X if a $+3.5\,\mu C$ 'test' charge at X experiences a force of 70 mN.

b At a second position Y in the field, the electric field strength is $15\,000\,NC^{-1}$ in a direction downwards. Calculate the force on an electron at Y and state the direction of the force.

Solution

a $F = 70 \times 10^{-3} N$, $Q = 3.5 \times 10^{-6} C$, $E = \dfrac{F}{Q} = \dfrac{70 \times 10^{-3}}{3.5 \times 10^{-6}} = 2.0 \times 10^{4}\,NC^{-1}$

b $F = QE = 1.6 \times 10^{-19} \times 15\,000 = 2.4 \times 10^{-15}\,N$

The direction of the force on an electron at Y is directly upwards because the field line at Y is directly downwards and the charge on an electron is negative.

Application and How science works

The lightning conductor

Air is an insulator provided it is not subjected to an electric field that is too strong. Such a field ionises the air molecules by pulling electrons out of the molecules. In a thunderstorm, a lightning strike to the ground occurs when a cloud becomes more and more charged and the electric field in the air becomes stronger and stronger. The insulating property of air suddenly breaks down and a massive discharge of electric charge occurs between the cloud and the ground. A lightning conductor is a metal rod at the top of a tall building. The rod is connected to the ground by means of a thick metal conductor. When a charged cloud is overhead, it creates a very strong electric field near the tip of the conductor. Air molecules near the tip are ionised by this very strong field. The ions discharge the thundercloud making a lightning stroke less likely.

Figure 3 *Lightning*

The electric field between two parallel plates

Figure 6c in Topic 5.1 shows that the field lines between two oppositely charged flat conductors are parallel to each other and at right angles to the plates. The field pattern for two oppositely charged flat plates is similar, as shown in Figure 4. The field lines are:

- parallel to each other,
- at right angles to the plates,
- from the positive plate to the negative plate.

The field between the plates is uniform. This is because the electric field strength has the same magnitude and direction everywhere between the plates. The electric field strength E can be calculated from the potential difference V between the plates and their separation d using the equation

$$E = \frac{V}{d}$$

To prove this equation, consider a small charge Q between the plates, as in Figure 4.

1 The force F on a small charge Q in the field is given by $F = QE$, where E is the electric field strength between the plates.

2 If the charge is moved from the positive to the negative plate, the work done W by the field on Q is given by $W =$ force $F \times$ distance moved $d = QEd$

3 By definition, the potential difference between the plates, V is the work done per unit charge when a small charge is moved through potential difference V.

Therefore, $V = \dfrac{W}{Q} = \dfrac{QEd}{Q} = Ed$

Rearranging, $V = Ed$ gives $E = \dfrac{V}{d}$

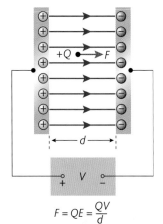

$$F = QE = \frac{QV}{d}$$

Figure 4 *The electric field strength between two parallel plates*

Hint

The unit of E may be written as the newton per coulomb ($N\,C^{-1}$) or the volt per metre ($V\,m^{-1}$).

The link between the two can be seen by combining $F = QE$ and $E = \dfrac{V}{d}$ to give $F = \dfrac{QV}{d}$.

Rearranging this equation gives

$$\frac{F}{Q} = \frac{V}{d} (= E)$$

Therefore, the newton per coulomb and the volt per metre are both acceptable as the unit of E.

Worked example:

A pair of parallel plates at a separation of 80 mm are connected to a high-voltage supply unit which maintains a constant pd of 6000 V between the plates. Calculate:

a the electric field strength between the plates,

b the magnitude and direction of the electrostatic force on an ion of charge 4.8×10^{-19} C when it is between the plates.

Solution

a $E = \dfrac{V}{d} = \dfrac{6000}{80 \times 10^{-3}} = 7.5 \times 10^4 \, \text{V m}^{-1}$

b $F = QE = 4.8 \times 10^{-19} \times 7.5 \times 10^4 = 3.6 \times 10^{-14} \, \text{N}$

The force on the ion is directly towards the negative plate.

■ **Link**

E is the same everywhere in a uniform electric field; *g* is the same everywhere in a uniform gravitational field. See Topic 4.2.

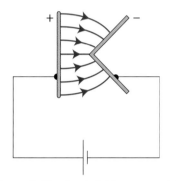

Figure 5 *The electric field near a metal tip*

AQA **Examiner's tip**

Field lines should have arrows (+ to −) and, when not straight, they are smooth curves

■ Field factors

An electric field exists near any charged body. The greater the charge on the body, the stronger the electric field is. For a charged metal conductor, the charge on it is spread across its surface. The more concentrated the charge is on the surface, the greater the strength of the electric field is above the surface.

▨ Figure 5 shows the electric field pattern between a V-shaped conductor opposite a flat plate when a constant pd is applied between the plate and the conductor. The field lines are concentrated at the tip of the V because that is where charge on the V-shaped conductor is most concentrated.

▨ The electric field between two oppositely charged parallel plates depends on the concentration of charge on the surface of the plates. The charge on each plate is spread evenly across the surface of the plate facing the other plate. Measurements show that the electric field strength between the plates is proportional to the charge per unit area on the facing surfaces.

Therefore, for charge *Q* on a plate of surface area *A*, the electric field strength *E* between the plates is proportional to *Q/A*.

Introducing a constant of proportionality, ε_0 (referred to as 'epsilon nought'), into this equation gives $Q/A = \varepsilon_0 E$. The value of ε_0 is 8.85×10^{-12} farads per metre (F m^{-1}), where the farad (the unit of capacitance; see Topic 6.1) is 1 coulomb per volt. It is referred to as the permittivity of free space. It represents that charge per unit area on a surface in a vacuum that produces an electric field of strength 1 volt per metre between the plates. The formula $Q/A = \varepsilon_0 E$ is not required for the A2 specification but ε_0 is and we will meet ε_0 in Topic 5.4.

Summary questions

$e = 1.6 \times 10^{-19}$ C

1 A +40 nC point charge Q_1 is placed in an electric field.

a Calculate the magnitude of the force on Q_1 if the electric field strength where Q_1 is placed is 3.5×10^4 V m^{-1}.

b Q_1 is moved to a different position in the electric field. The force on Q_1 at this position is 1.6×10^{-3} N. Calculate the magnitude of the electric field strength at this position.

2 Figure 6 shows the path of a charged dust particle in an electric field.

a The electric field strength at X is 65 kV m^{-1}. The force due to the field on the particle when it is at X is 8.2×10^{-3} N towards the metal surface.

   i What type of charge does X carry?

   ii Calculate the charge carried by the particle.

b i Calculate the magnitude of the force on the particle when it is at Y where the electric field strength is 58 kV m^{-1},

   ii State the direction of the force on the particle when it is at Y.

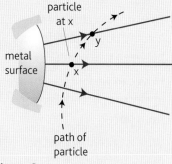

Figure 6

3 A high voltage supply unit is connected across a pair of parallel plates which are at a separation of 50 mm.

a The voltage is adjusted to 4.5 kV. Calculate:

   i the electric field strength between the plates,

   ii the electric force on a droplet in the field that carries a charge of 8.0×10^{-19} C.

b The separation between the plates is altered without changing the pd between the plates. The droplet in **a** is now acted on by a force of 4.5×10^{-14} N. Calculate the new separation between the plates.

4 A certain gas in a tube is subjected to an electric field of increasing strength. The gas becomes conducting when the electric field reaches a strength of 35 kV m^{-1}.

a The electrodes in the tube are at a spacing of 84 mm. Assuming the field between the electrodes is uniform before the gas conducts, calculate the potential difference between the electrodes that is necessary to produce an electric field of strength 35 kV m^{-1} in the tube.

b i Calculate the force on an electron in the tube when the electric field strength is 35 kV m^{-1}.

   ii Explain why the gas becomes conducting only when the electric field strength in the tube reaches a certain value.

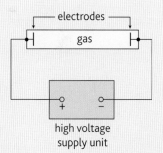

Figure 7

5.3 Electric potential

Learning objectives:

▇ Why is potential defined in terms of the work done per unit + charge?

▇ How do we calculate the electric potential difference between two points?

▇ How can we find the change in electric potential energy from pd?

▇ Why is potential (and pd) measured in V?

Specification reference 3.4.3

The Van de Graaff generator

A Van de Graaff generator can easily produce sparks in air several centimetres in length. Figure 1 shows how a Van de Graaff generator works. Charge created when the rubber belt rubs against a pad is carried by the belt up to the metal dome of the generator. As charge gathers on the dome, the potential difference between the dome and Earth increases until sparking occurs.

A spark suddenly transfers energy from the dome. Work must be done to charge the dome because a force is needed to move the charge on the belt up to the dome. So the electric potential energy of the dome increases as it charges up. Some or all of this energy is transferred from the dome when a spark is created.

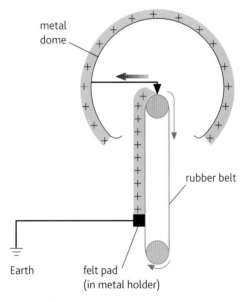

Figure 1 *The Van de Graaff generator*

In general work must be done to move a charged object X towards another object Y that has the same type of charge. Their electric potential energy increases as X moves towards Y.

The electric potential energy of X increases from zero if it is moved from infinity towards Y. The electric field of Y causes a force of repulsion to act on X and this force must be overcome to move X closer to Y.

The **electric potential** at a certain position in any electric field is defined as the work done per unit positive charge on a 'positive test charge' (i.e. a small positively charged object) when it is moved from infinity to that position. By definition, the position of zero potential energy is infinity. Thus the electric potential at a certain position is the potential energy per unit positive charge of a 'positive test charge' at that position.

The unit of electric potential is the volt (V), equal to $1\,\mathrm{J\,C^{-1}}$.

For a positive test charge Q placed at a position in an electric field where its electric potential energy is E_p, the electric potential V at this position is given by

$$V = \frac{E_p}{Q}$$

Note that rearranging this equation gives $E_p = QV$

Suppose a $+1\,\mu C$ test charge is moved into an electric field from infinity to reach a certain position P where the electric potential is $-1000\,V$. The electric potential energy of the test charge at P is therefore $-1.0 \times 10^{-3}\,J$ $(= QV = 1.0 \times 10^{-6}\,C \times -1000\,V)$. In other words, $1.0 \times 10^{-3}\,J$ of work must be done by the test charge to move it from infinity to P.

Note:

If a test charge $+Q$ is moved in an electric field from one position where the electric potential is V_1 to another where the electric potential is V_2, the work done ΔW on it is given by $\Delta W = Q(V_2 - V_1)$

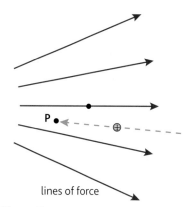

Figure 2

Potential gradients

Equipotentials are lines of constant potential. A test charge moving along an equipotential has constant potential energy. No work is done by the electric field on the test charge because the force due to the field is at right angles to the equipotential. In other words, the lines of force of the electric field cross the equipotential lines at right angles.

The equipotentials for an electric field are like equipotentials for a gravitational field; both are lines of constant potential energy for the appropriate test object, in one case a test charge and in the other case a test mass.

Figure 3 shows the equipotentials of the electric field due to two positively charged objects.

Suppose a $+2.0\,\mu C$ test charge is moved from X to Y.

The potential at X, V_X, is $+1000\,V$ so the test charge at X has potential energy equal to $+2.0 \times 10^{-3}\,J$

$\qquad (= QV_X = +2.0 \times 10^{-6}\,C \times +1000\,V)$

The potential at Y, V_Y, is $+400\,V$ so the test charge at Y has potential energy equal to $+8.0 \times 10^{-4}\,J$

$\qquad (= QV_Y = +2.0 \times 10^{-6}\,C \times +400\,V)$

Therefore, moving the test charge from X to Y lowers its potential energy by $1.2 \times 10^{-3}\,J$.

Note that if the test charge is moved from Y to Z along the $+400\,V$ equipotential, its potential energy remains constant at $+8.0 \times 10^{-4}\,J$.

The **potential gradient** at any position in an electric field is the change of potential per unit change of distance in a given direction.

1 If the field is non-uniform as in Figure 3, the potential gradient varies according to position and direction. The closer the equipotentials are, the greater the potential gradient is at right angles to the equipotentials.

2 If the field is uniform, such as the field between the two oppositely charged parallel plates shown in Figure 4, the equipotentials **between the plates** are equally spaced lines parallel to the plates. Figure 4 also

Link

Equipotentials in an electric field are like map contours which are lines of constant height and therefore of gravitational equipotentials. See Topic 4.2.

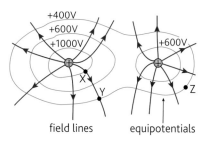

field lines   equipotentials

Figure 3 *Equipotentials*

AQA Examiner's tip

Remember that V is a scalar. Equipotentials always meet field lines at right angles.

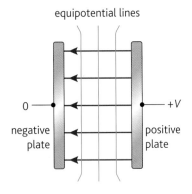

equipotential lines

0 ——•—————————•—— +V

negative plate   positive plate

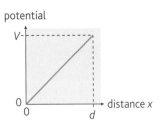

potential

Figure 4 *A uniform potential gradient*

shows how the potential relative to the negative plate changes with perpendicular distance x from the negative plate.

The graph shows that the potential relative to the negative plate is proportional to distance x. In other words, the potential gradient is

■ constant,

■ such that the potential increases in the opposite direction to the electric field,

■ equal to V/d.

As explained in Topic 5.2, the electric field strength E between the plates is equal to V/d and is directed from the + to the – plate. In other words,

the electric field strength is equal to the negative of the potential gradient.

Summary questions

$e = 1.6 \times 10^{-19}\,C$

1 An electron in a beam is accelerated from a potential of −50V to a potential of +450V. Calculate:

a the potential energy of the electron at

   i   −50V,

   ii +450V,

b the change of potential energy of the electron.

2 In Figure 3, a test charge q is moved from X to Z. Calculate the change of potential energy of the test charge

a if $q = +3.0\,\mu C$,

b if $q = −2.0\,\mu C$.

3 An oil droplet carrying a charge of +2e is in air between two parallel metal plates separated by a distance of 20 mm. The pd between the plates is 5.0 V.

a Calculate:

   i   the potential gradient between the two plates,

   ii the force on the droplet.

b Calculate the change of electrical potential energy of the oil droplet if it moves from the midpoint of the plates to the negative plate.

4 a Define electric potential and state its unit.

b Two parallel horizontal metal plates are placed one above the other at a separation of 20 mm. A potential difference of +60V is applied between the plates with the top plate positive.

   i   Calculate the electric field strength between the plates.

   ii Sketch a graph to show how the electric potential V between the plates varies with height h above the lower plate.

5.4 Coulomb's law

Learning objectives:

■ How does the force between two point charges depend on distance?

■ How can we calculate the force between two charged objects?

■ What does the sign of the force (+ or −) indicate?

Specification reference: 3.4.3

■ Coulomb's experiment

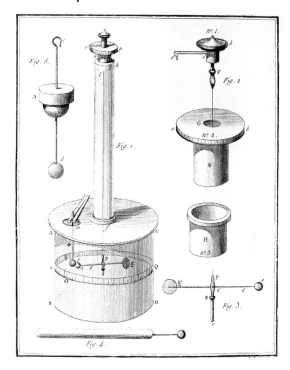

Figure 1 *Coulomb's torsion balance*

Like charges repel and unlike charges attract. The force between two charged objects depends on how close they are to each other. The exact link was first established by Charles Coulomb in France in 1784. He devised a very sensitive torsion balance to measure the force between charged pith balls. Figure 1 shows the arrangement. A needle with a ball made of pith (a substance obtained from plants) at one end and a counterweight at the other end was suspended horizontally by a vertical wire. Another pith ball on the end of a thin vertical rod could be placed in contact with the first ball.

The pith balls were small enough to be considered as point objects. The ball on the rod was charged and then placed in contact with the other ball on the needle. The contact between them charged the second ball which was then repelled by the ball fixed on the rod. This caused the wire to twist until the electrical repulsion was balanced by the twist built up in the wire. By turning the torsion head at the top of the wire, the distance between the two balls could be set at any required value. The amount of turning needed to achieve that distance gave the force. Some of Coulomb's many measurements are below.

Table 1 *Some of Coulomb's results*

distance, r	36	18	8½
force, F	36	144	567

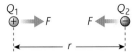

a *unlike charges attract*

b *like charges repel*

$$F = \frac{1}{4\pi\varepsilon_0}\frac{Q_1 Q_2}{r^2}$$

Figure 2 *Coulomb's law*

Measurements for both variables were actually made in degrees, so the above values are in relative units. Can you make out a pattern for these measurements? Halving the distance from 36 to 18 makes the force increase by a factor of 4. Halving the distance from 18 to $8\frac{1}{2}$ (near enough 9) increases the force again by a factor of about 4. The measurements fit the link that the force F is proportional to $1/r^2$. All the other measurements made by Coulomb fitted the same link. Because the force is also proportional to the charge on each ball, Coulomb deduced the following equation, known as **Coulomb's law**, for the force F between two 'point charges' Q_1 and Q_2.

$$F = \frac{kQ_1 Q_2}{r^2}$$

where r is their distance apart.

The constant of proportionality, k, can be shown to be equal to $\frac{1}{4\pi\varepsilon_0}$, where ε_0 is the permittivity of free space. See Topic 5.2.

Coulomb's law is therefore written as

$$F = \frac{1}{4\pi\varepsilon_0}\frac{Q_1 Q_2}{r^2}$$

where r = distance between the two point charges Q_1 and Q_2.

As explained in Topic 5.2, $\varepsilon_0 = 8.85 \times 10^{-12}\,\mathrm{F\,m^{-1}}$ so $\frac{1}{4\pi\varepsilon_0} = 9.0 \times 10^9\,\mathrm{m\,F^{-1}}$

■ Application

Why do salt crystals dissolve in water?

A salt crystal is an ionic crystal. The sodium ions and the chlorine ions in a salt crystal are oppositely charged and the electrostatic forces between them hold them together. Salt crystals dissolve in water because the water weakens the electrostatic forces between the ions at the surface of the crystal so the ions break free from the surface and the crystal gradually dissolves. In fact, the force between two ions in water is about 80 times weaker than the force would be in air for the same distance apart. Note that Coulomb's law as stated above applies strictly to a vacuum. In terms of the force between two point charges in air, the force is effectively the same as it would be in a vacuum.

■ Link

Coulomb's law of force between point charges and Newton's law of gravitation are both inverse square laws. For example, doubling the separation of two point masses or two point charges causes the force to reduce to a quarter. See Topic 4.3.

AQA Examiner's tip

Remember to square r when calculating F.

When substituting charges, get the powers of 10 correct: $\mu = 10^{-6}$, $n = 10^{-9}$, $p = 10^{-12}$

Worked example:

$e = 1.60 \times 10^{-19}\,\mathrm{C}$, $\varepsilon_0 = 8.85 \times 10^{-12}\,\mathrm{F\,m^{-1}}$

Calculate the magnitude of the force between a proton and an electron at a separation of $3.0 \times 10^{-10}\,\mathrm{m}$.

Solution

$$F = \frac{1}{4\pi\varepsilon_0}\frac{Q_1 Q_2}{r^2} = \frac{1.60 \times 10^{-19} \times 1.60 \times 10^{-19}}{4\pi \times 8.85 \times 10^{-12} \times (3.0 \times 10^{-10})^2} = 2.56 \times 10^{-9}\,\mathrm{N}$$

■ Application and How science works

Note on $k = \frac{1}{4\pi\varepsilon_0}$

In Topic 5.2, ε_0 was introduced as the constant of proportionality in the equation $Q/A = \varepsilon_0 E$ linking the electric field strength E at the surface of a flat conductor where the charge Q is evenly distributed over a surface area A.

As explained in Topic 5.5, overleaf, if Coulomb's law is applied to the force on a 'test' charge q at distance r from a point charge Q, the force on

the test charge $F = \dfrac{kQq}{r^2}$ so the electric field strength at distance r is given by

$$E = \frac{F}{q} = \frac{kQ}{r^2}$$

By introducing $\dfrac{1}{4\pi\varepsilon_0}$ as k, the equation $E = \dfrac{kQ}{r^2}$ may be written as

$$\frac{Q}{4\pi r^2} = \varepsilon_0 E \text{ or } \frac{Q}{A} = \varepsilon_0 E$$

where $A = 4\pi r^2 =$ the surface area of a sphere of radius r.

Thus the general equation $Q/A = \varepsilon_0 E$ gives the surface charge density Q/A needed on the surface of a conducting sphere in air to produce an electric field of strength E at the surface. The explanation here is not part of the A2 specification and is provided to give a better understanding of Coulomb's law.

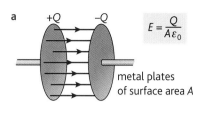

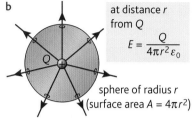

Figure 3 *Comparison of surface electric field strengths*

Summary questions

$\varepsilon_0 = 8.85 \times 10^{-12}\,\text{F m}^{-1}$,

$e = 1.6 \times 10^{-19}\,\text{C}$

1 Calculate the force between an electron and
a a proton at a distance of $2.5 \times 10^{-9}\,\text{m}$,
b a nucleus of a nitrogen atom (charge $+7e$) at a distance of $2.5 \times 10^{-9}\,\text{m}$

2 **a** Two point charges $Q_1 = +6.3\,\text{nC}$ and $Q_2 = -2.7\,\text{nC}$ exert a force of $3.2 \times 10^{-5}\,\text{N}$ on each other when they are at a certain distance, d, apart. Calculate:
  i the distance d, between the two charges,
  ii the force between the two charges if they are moved to distance $3d$ apart.
b A charge of $+4.0\,\text{nC}$ is added to each charge in Q_2. Calculate the force between Q_1 and Q_2 when they are at separation d.

3 A $+30\,\text{nC}$ point charge is at a fixed distance of $6.2\,\text{mm}$ from a point charge Q. The charges attract each other with a force of $4.3 \times 10^{-2}\,\text{N}$.
a Calculate the magnitude of charge Q and state whether Q is a positive or a negative charge.
b The two charges are moved $2.5\,\text{mm}$ further part. Calculate the force between them in this new position.

4 Two point objects, X and Y, carry equal and opposite amounts of charge at a fixed separation of $3.6 \times 10^{-2}\,\text{m}$. The two objects exert a force on each other of $5.1 \times 10^{-5}\,\text{N}$.
a Calculate the magnitude, Q, of each charge and state whether the charges attract or repel each other.
b The charge of each object is increased by adding a positive charge of $+2Q$ to each object. Calculate the separation at which the two objects would exert a force of $5.1 \times 10^{-5}\,\text{N}$ on each other and state whether the objects attract or repel each other.

5.5 Point charges

Learning objectives:

■ What equation gives the electric field strength near a point charge?

■ What equation gives the potential associated with a point charge?

■ Why does $E = 0$ inside a charged sphere?

Specification reference: 3.4.3

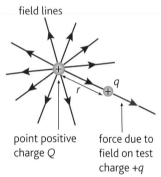

field lines

point positive charge Q

force due to field on test charge +q

Figure 1 *Force near a point charge Q*

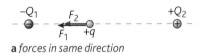

a *forces in same direction*

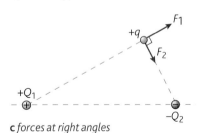

b *forces in opposite direction*

c *forces at right angles*

Figure 2 *Combined electric fields*

A point charge is a convenient expression for a charged object in a situation where distances under consideration are much greater than the size of the object. The same idea applies to a distant star which is considered as a point object because its diameter is much smaller that the distance to it from the Earth. A 'test' charge in an electric field is a point charge that does not alter the electric field in which it is placed. Such an alteration would happen if an object with a sufficiently large charge is placed in an electric field and it causes a change in the distribution of charge that creates the field.

Consider the electric field due to a point charge $+Q$, as shown in Figure 1. The field lines radiate from Q because a test charge $+q$ in the field would experience a force directly away from Q wherever the test charge was placed. Coulomb's law gives the force F on the test charge q at distance r from Q as

$$F = \frac{1}{4\pi\varepsilon_0} \frac{Qq}{r^2}$$

Therefore, as electric field strength $E = F/q$ by definition, the electric field strength at distance r from Q is given by

$$E = \frac{Q}{4\pi\varepsilon_0 r^2}$$

Note that if Q is negative, the above formula gives a negative value of E corresponding to the field lines pointing inwards towards Q.

Worked example:

$\varepsilon_0 = 8.85 \times 10^{-12}\,F\,m^{-1}, e = 1.6 \times 10^{-19}\,C$

Calculate the electric field strength due to a nucleus of charge $+82e$ at a distance of 0.35 nm.

Solution

$$E = \frac{Q}{4\pi\varepsilon_0 r^2} = \frac{+82 \times 1.6 \times 10^{-19}}{4\pi \times 8.85 \times 10^{-12} \times (0.35 \times 10^{-9})^2} = 9.6 \times 10^{11}\,V\,m^{-1}$$

Electric field strength as a vector

If a test charge is in an electric field due to several point charges, each charge exerts a force on the test charge. The resultant force per unit charge F/q on the test charge gives the resultant electric field strength at the position of the test charge. Consider the following situations:

■ **Forces in the same direction**: Figure 2a shows a test charge $+q$ on the line between a negative point charge Q_1 and a positive point charge Q_2 The test charge experiences a force $F_1 = qE_1$ where E_1 is the electric field strength due to Q_1 and a force $F_2 = qE_2$ where E_2 is the electric field strength due to Q_2. The two forces act in the same direction because Q_1 attracts q and Q_2 repels q. So the resultant force $F = F_1 + F_2 = qE_1 + qE_2$

■ Therefore, the resultant electric field strength $E = \dfrac{F}{q} = \dfrac{qE_1 + qE_2}{q} = E_1 + E_2$

- **Forces in opposite directions**: Figure 2b shows a test charge $+q$ on the line between two positive point charges Q_1 and Q_2. The forces on the test charge are the same in magnitude as in Figure 2a but opposite in direction because Q_1 attracts q and Q_2 attracts q. So the resultant force $F = F_1 - F_2 = qE_1 - qE_2$.
- Therefore the resultant electric field strength $E = \dfrac{F}{q} = \dfrac{qE_1 - qE_2}{q}$ $= E_1 - E_2$.
- **Forces at right angles to each other**: Figure 2c shows a test charge $+q$ on perpendicular lines from two positive point charges Q_1 and Q_2. The forces on the test charge are smaller in magnitude than in Figures 2a and b (as the distances to Q_1 and Q_2 are larger) and are perpendicular to each other. The magnitude of the resultant force F is given by Pythagoras' formula $F^2 = F_1^2 + F_2^2$

Therefore, as the resultant electric field strength $E = F/q$, then $E^2 = E_1^2 + E_2^2$ can be used to calculate the resultant electric field strength.

In general, the resultant electric field strength is the vector sum of the individual electric field strengths.

More about radial fields

The electric field lines of force surrounding a point charge Q are radial. The equipotentials are therefore concentric circles centred on Q.

At distance r from Q, **the electric field strength**, $E = \dfrac{Q}{4\pi\varepsilon_0 r^2}$

The equation was derived at the start of Topic 5.5. It shows that the electric field strength E is inversely proportional to the square of the distance r. Figure 3 shows how E varies with distance r from Q from a position which is at distance r_0 from Q. The curve is an 'inverse square law' curve as E is proportional to $1/r^2$.

Notice that the equation is of the same form as the gravitational field strength formula $g = GM/r^2$ for the gravitational field strength at distance r from the centre of a spherical planet. See Topic 4.2 if necessary. The field strength equations are both inverse square relationships because the force between two point charges (Coulomb's law) and the force between two point masses (Newton's law of gravitation) varies with distance according to the inverse square law.

The electric potential $V = \dfrac{Q}{4\pi\varepsilon_0 r}$ at distance r from Q.

Because Coulomb's law $F = \dfrac{1}{4\pi\varepsilon_0} \dfrac{Q_1 Q_2}{r^2}$ and Newton's law $F = \dfrac{Gm_1 m_2}{r^2}$ are both 'inverse square' relationships, the forces vary with distance in the same way. Therefore the formula for electrical potential near a point charge $V = \dfrac{Q}{4\pi\varepsilon_0 r}$ is of the same form as the gravitational potential near a point mass (or spherical mass) i.e. $V = -\dfrac{GM}{r}$ which we derived in Topic 4.4. The equation shows that the electric potential V is inversely proportional to the distance r. Figure 3 also shows how V varies with distance r from Q. The curve is not an 'inverse square law' curve as V is proportional to $1/r$.

However, the gravitational potential in a gravitational field is always negative as the force is always attractive whereas the electric potential in the electric field near a point charge Q can be positive or negative according to whether Q is a positive or a negative charge.

Link

Remember how to calculate the resultant force of two perpendicular forces. See *AS Physics* Topic 7.1.

lines of force

Q

equipotentials

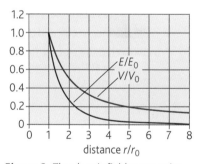

Figure 3 *The electric field near a point charge*

AQA Examiner's tip

A negative E means a field that acts towards a negative charge, whereas a negative V means a value less than 0. Note that E varies with distance more sharply than V does.

Sparks and shocks

When a spherical metal conductor insulated from the ground is charged, the charge spreads out across the surface with the greatest concentration where the surface is most curved. This is why charge gathers at the tip of a lightning conductor when a charged cloud is overhead. As explained in Topic 5.2, the electric field at the tip then becomes so strong that air molecules near the tip become ionised and the air conducts. This effect also explains why a fatal accident can happen if a conducting rod is held near an overhead high voltage cable. An angler walking along a footpath near a railway line was electrocuted because the end of his carbon fibre fishing rod was inadvertently too close to the overhead cable along the track.

Summary questions

$\varepsilon_0 = 8.85 \times 10^{-12}\,\mathrm{F\,m^{-1}}$

1 a Calculate the electric field strength at a distance of 3.2 mm from a + 6.0 nC point charge.

b Calculate the distance from the point charge in a at which the electric field strength is $5.4 \times 10^5\,\mathrm{V\,m^{-1}}$.

2 A +25 μC point charge Q_1 is at a distance of 60 mm from a +100 μC charge Q_2.

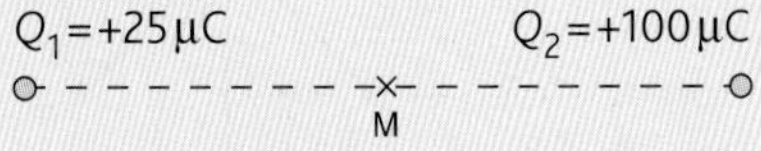

$Q_1 = +25\,\mu C$ $\qquad\qquad Q_2 = +100\,\mu C$

○- - - - - - - - -×- - - - - - - - -○
                  M

Figure 4

a A +15 pC charge q is placed at M, 25 mm from Q_1 and 35 mm from Q_2. Calculate:

i the resultant electric field strength at M,

ii the magnitude and direction of the force on q.

b Show that the electric field strength due to Q_1 and Q_2 is zero at the point which is 20 mm from Q_1 and 40 mm from Q_2.

3 A +15 μC point charge Q_1 is at a distance of 20 mm from a +10 μC charge Q_2.

a Calculate the resultant electric field strength:

i at M, the midpoint between the two charges,

ii at the point P along the line between Q_1 and Q_2 which is 25 mm from Q_1 and 45 mm from Q_2.

b i Explain why there is a point along the line between the two charges at which the electric field strength is zero.

ii Calculate the distance from this point to Q_1 and to Q_2.

4 A +15 μC point charge Q_1 is at a distance of 30 mm from a –30 μC charge Q_2.

a Calculate electric potential at the midpoint of the two charges.

b i Show that the electric potential is zero at a point between the two charges which is 10 mm from Q_1 and 20 mm from Q_2.

ii Calculate the electric field strength at this position and state its direction.

5.6 Comparison between electric and gravitational fields

Learning objectives:

▨ Which electrical quantity is analogous to mass?

▨ What are the main similarities between electric and gravitational fields?

▨ What are the principal differences between electric and gravitational fields?

Specification reference: 3.4.3

The similarities and differences between the two types of field are listed in Table 1. In the mid-nineteenth century, James Maxwell showed that electric and magnetic forces are different manifestations of the electromagnetic force. About two decades ago, physicists proved that the electromagnetic force and the nuclear force responsible for radioactive decay are different manifestations of a more fundamental force, the electroweak force. At the present time, the force of gravity remains outside this theoretical framework, despite repeated attempts to establish a unified theory. The fundamental nature of the force of gravity remains mysterious even though we use it in everyday situations more than any other force.

Table 1 summarises the conceptual links between electric and gravitational fields.

Table 1 *Similarities and differences between gravitational and electric fields*

	Gravitational force	Electric force
Similarities		
line of force or a field line	path of a free 'test' mass in the field	path of a free 'test' charge in the field
Inverse square law of force	Newton's law of gravitation $$F = \frac{Gm_1m_2}{r^2}$$	Coulomb's law of force $$F = \frac{Q_1Q_2}{4\pi\varepsilon_0 r^2}$$
field strength	force per unit mass, $g = \dfrac{F}{m}$	force per unit + charge, $E = \dfrac{F}{q}$
unit of field strength	$N\,kg^{-1}$ or $m\,s^{-2}$	$N\,C^{-1}$ or $V\,m^{-1}$
uniform fields	g is the same everywhere, field lines parallel and equally spaced	E is the same everywhere, field lines are parallel and equally spaced
potential	gravitational potential energy per unit mass	electric potential energy per unit + charge
unit of potential	$J\,kg^{-1}$	$V\ (= J\,C^{-1})$
potential energy between two point mass or charges	$E_P = \dfrac{-Gm_1m_2}{r}$	$E_P = \dfrac{Q_1Q_2}{4\pi\varepsilon_0 r}$
radial fields	due to a point mass or a uniform spherical mass M, $$g = \frac{GM}{r^2}$$ $$V = \frac{-GM}{r}$$	due to a point charge Q, $$E = \frac{Q}{4\pi\varepsilon_0 r^2}$$ $$V = \frac{Q}{4\pi\varepsilon_0 r}$$
Differences		
action at a distance	between any two masses	between any two charged objects
force	attracts only	unlike charges attract, like charges repel
constant of proportionality in force law	G	$\dfrac{1}{4\pi\varepsilon_0}$

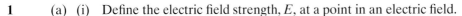

1 (a) (i) Define the electric field strength, E, at a point in an electric field.
    (ii) State whether E is a scalar or a vector quantity. *(3 marks)*

(b) Point charges of $+4.0$ nC and -8.0 nC are placed 80 mm apart, as shown in **Figure 1**.

Figure 1

    (i) Calculate the magnitude of the force exerted on the $+4.0$ nC charge by the -8.0 nC charge.

    (ii) Determine the distance from the $+4.0$ nC charge to the point, along the straight line between the charges, where the electric potential is zero. *(4 marks)*

(c) Point P in the diagram is equidistant from the two charges.

    (i) Draw two arrows on a copy of the diagram at P to represent the directions and relative magnitudes of the components of the electric field at P due to each of the charges.

    (ii) Hence draw an arrow, labelled R, on your diagram at P to represent the direction of the resultant electric field at P. *(3 marks)*

AQA, 2006

2 A small charged sphere of mass 2.1×10^{-4} kg, suspended from a thread of insulating material, was placed between two vertical parallel plates 60 mm apart. When a potential difference of 4200 V was applied to the plates, the sphere moved until the thread made an angle of $6.0°$ to the vertical, as shown in **Figure 2**.

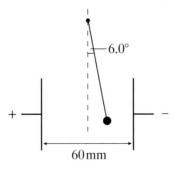

Figure 2

(a) Show that the electrostatic force F on the sphere is given by $F = mg\tan 6.0°$ where m is the mass of the sphere. *(3 marks)*

(b) Calculate:

    (i) the electric field strength between the plates,

    (ii) the charge on the sphere. *(3 marks)*

AQA, 2003

3   **Figure 3** shows some of the equipotential lines that are associated with a point
     negative charge Q.

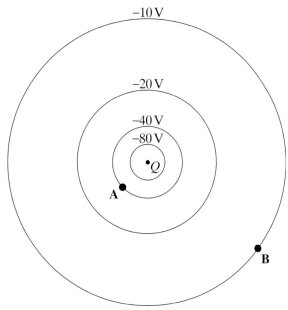

     Figure 3

(a) (i)   Explain why the potentials have a negative sign.
     (ii) Draw on a copy of the diagram three electric field lines. Use arrows to show
           the direction of the field.   *(4 marks)*
(b) (i)   Use data from the diagram, which is full size, to show that the charge Q is
           about -4.5×10^{-11} C.
     (ii) Calculate the electric field strength at B.   *(4 marks)*
(c) (i)   Calculate the energy, in J, transferred when an electron moves from A to B
           in the field.
     (ii) State and explain
           • why the kinetic energy of the electron increases as it moves from A to B,
           • how the de Broglie wavelength of the electron changes as it moves from A to B.
                                                                                  (6 marks)

AQA, 2003

4   **Figure 4** shows the parallel deflecting plates with some dimensions of the ink-jet
     cartridge. In order to land in the centre of the gutter the ink droplet must leave the
     plates at an angle of 35°. On entering the electric field the ink droplet carries a charge
     of -2×10^{-10} C and travels with a horizontal velocity of $20\,\mathrm{m\,s^{-1}}$.

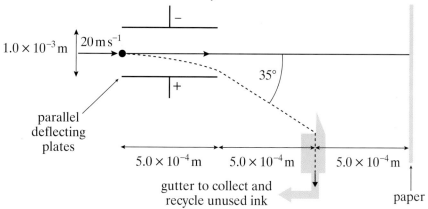

     Figure 4

(a) (i) Draw a vector diagram to show the components and the resultant of the velocity of the charged ink droplet as it leaves the deflecting field. Determine the size of the vertical component.

   (ii) Find the time for which the ink droplet is between the deflecting plates and hence calculate its vertical acceleration during this time.

   (iii) For an ink droplet of mass 2.9×10^{-10} kg, calculate the electric force acting on the ink droplet whilst it is between the deflecting plates.

   (iv) Calculate the electric field strength between the deflecting plates.

   (v) Calculate the potential difference between the deflecting plates. *(12 marks)*

(b) The uncharged, undeflected ink droplets travel beyond the deflecting plates towards the paper. With the aid of a suitable calculation, discuss whether or not the printer manufacturer needs to take into consideration the droplet falling under gravity. *(4 marks)*

AQA, 2003

5 Dry air ceases to be an insulator if it is subjected to an electric field strength of 3.3 kV mm^{-1} or more.

(a) (i) Show that the electric field strength E and the potential V at the surface of a charged sphere of radius R are related by

$$E = \frac{V}{R}$$

   (ii) The dome of a Van de Graaff generator has a radius of 0.20 m. Calculate the maximum potential of this dome in dry air. *(5 marks)*

(b) Two high-voltage conductors are joined together using a small sphere, as shown in **Figure 5**.

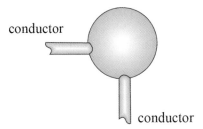

conductor

conductor

Figure 5

The conductors are used to transmit alternating current at an rms potential of 100 kV.

   (i) Calculate the peak potential of the conductor,

   (ii) Calculate the minimum diameter of the sphere necessary to ensure the surrounding air does not conduct. *(3 marks)*

AQA, 2004

6 (a) **Figure 6** shows a small charged metal sphere carrying a charge Q. The potential of the sphere is 8000 V. Copy Figure 6.

Figure 6

   (i) Draw on your diagram at least six lines to show the direction of the electric field in the region around the charged sphere.

   (ii) Draw on your diagram the equipotential lines for potentials of 4000 V and 2000 V.

   (iii) The equation for the field strength at a distance r from the sphere is $\dfrac{Q}{4\pi\varepsilon_0 r^2}$ State the name of the quantity represented by ε_0. *(5 marks)*

(b) **Figure 7** shows an arrangement for determining the charge on a small sphere.

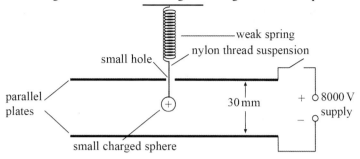

Figure 7

The sphere is suspended from a spring of spring constant $0.18\,\mathrm{N\,m^{-1}}$. It hangs between two parallel plates which can be connected to a high voltage supply.

(i) Explain why nylon thread is used for the suspension.

(ii) Calculate the extension of the spring when a sphere of mass 1.5 g is suspended from it.

(iii) Calculate the magnitude of the electric field strength between the plates when the 8000 V supply is switched on.

(iv) When the 8000 V supply is switched on, the sphere moves down a further 4.5 mm. Calculate the charge on the sphere. *(8 marks)*

(c) One problem with this arrangement is the oscillations of the sphere that occur when the switch is closed.

(i) Show that the period of the oscillations produced is about 0.6 s.

(ii) In practice the oscillations are damped. Sketch a graph showing how the amplitude of the oscillations changes with time for the damped oscillation. *(5 marks)*

AQA, 2007

7 The Earth has an electric charge. The electric field strength outside the Earth varies in the same way as if this charge were concentrated at the centre of the Earth. The axes in **Figure 8** represent the electric field strength, E, and the distance from the centre of the Earth, r. The electric field strength at **A** has been plotted.

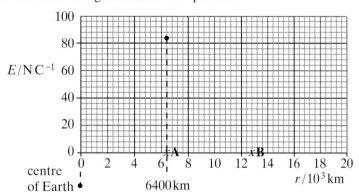

Figure 8

(a) (i) Determine the electric field strength at **B** and then complete the graph to show how the electric field strength varies with distance from the centre of the Earth for distances greater than 6400 km.

(ii) State how you would use the graph to find the electric potential difference between the points **A** and **B**. *(4 marks)*

(b) (i) Calculate the total charge on the Earth.

(ii) The charge is distributed uniformly over the Earth's surface. Calculate the charge per square metre on the Earth's surface. *(4 marks)*

AQA, 2002

6.1 Capacitance

A capacitor is a device designed to store charge. Two parallel metal plates placed near each other form a capacitor. When the plates are connected to a battery, electrons from the negative terminal of the battery flow onto one of the plates. An equal number of electrons leave the other plate to return to the battery via its positive terminal. So each plate gains an equal and opposite charge.

A capacitor consists of two conductors insulated from each other. The symbol for a capacitor is shown in Figure 1. As explained above, when a capacitor is connected to a battery, one of the two conductors gains electrons from the battery and the other conductor loses electrons to the battery. When we say that the charge stored by the capacitor is Q, we mean that one conductor stores charge $+Q$ and the other conductor stores charge $-Q$.

Charging a capacitor at constant current

Figure 2 shows how this can be achieved using a variable resistor, a switch, a microammeter and a cell in series with the capacitor. When the switch is closed, the variable resistor is continually adjusted to keep the microammeter reading constant. At any given time, t, after the switch is closed, the charge Q on the capacitor can be calculated using the equation $Q = It$, where I is the current.

A high-resistance voltmeter connected in parallel with the capacitor enables the capacitor pd to be measured. To investigate how the capacitor pd changes with time for constant current, use the variable resistor to keep the current constant and either

- use a stopwatch and measure the voltmeter reading at measured times, or
- use a data logger as shown in Figure 2.

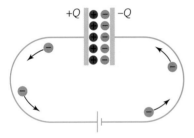

a *Storing charge*

b *Capacitor symbol*

Figure 1

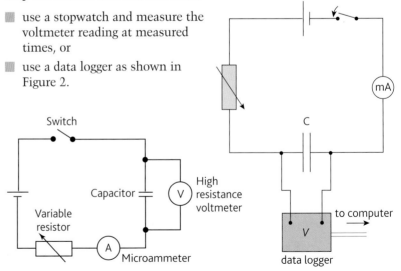

a *Circuit diagram*   **b** *Using a data logger*

Figure 2 *Investigating capacitors*

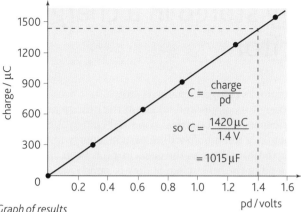

Figure 3 *Graph of results*

Typical readings for a current of 15 μA are shown in the following table. The charge Q has been calculated using $Q = It$.

Table 1 *Current = 15 μA*

time, t/s	0	20	40	60	80	100
pd, V/volts	0	0.29	0.62	0.90	1.22	1.50
charge, Q/μC	0	300	600	900	1200	1500

The graph of charge stored Q against pd V for these measurements is shown in Figure 3. The measurements define a straight line passing through the origin. Therefore, the charge stored Q is proportional to the pd V. In other words, the charge stored per volt is constant.

The capacitance C of a capacitor is defined as the charge stored per unit pd.

The unit of capacitance is the farad (F), equal to 1 coulomb per volt. Note that $1 \mu F = 10^{-6} F$.

For a capacitor which stores charge Q at pd V, its capacitance can be calculated using the equation

$$C = \frac{Q}{V}$$

Note:

Rearranging this equation gives $Q = CV$ or $V = \frac{Q}{C}$.

Application

Capacitor uses

Capacitors are used in:

- ▨ smoothing circuits (i.e. circuits that smooth out unwanted variations in voltage),
- ▨ back-up power supplies (i.e. circuits that take over when the mains supply is interrupted),
- ▨ timing circuits, (i.e. circuits that switch on or off automatically after a preset delay),
- ▨ pulse producing circuits (i.e. circuits that switch on and off repeatedly),
- ▨ tuning circuits, (i.e. circuits that are used to select radios and TV channels),
- ▨ filter circuits (i.e. circuits that remove unwanted frequencies).

Summary questions

1 Complete the following table.

	(a)	(b)	(c)	(d)
charge/μC	60	330		6.30
pd/V	12		9.0	4.5
capacitance /μF		150	1100	

2 A 22 μF capacitor is charged by means of a constant current of 2.5 μA to a pd of 12.0 V. Calculate:

a the charge stored on the capacitor at 12.0 V,

b the time taken.

3 A capacitor is charged by means of a constant current of 0.5 μA to a pd of 5.0 V in 55 s. Calculate:

a the charge stored,

b the capacitance of the capacitor.

4 A capacitor is charged by means of a constant current of 24 μA to a pd of 4.2 V in 38 s. The capacitor is then charged from 4.2 V by means of a current of 14 μA in 50 s. Calculate:

a charge stored at a pd of 4.2 V,

b the capacitance of the capacitor,

c the extra charge stored at a current of 14 μA,

d the pd after the extra charge was stored.

6.2 Energy stored in a charged capacitor

Learning objectives:

■ Why does a capacitor store energy as it is being charged?

■ What form of energy is stored by a capacitor?

■ If the charge stored is doubled, what happens to the amount of energy stored?

Specification reference: 3.4.4

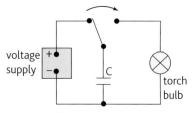

voltage supply
C
torch bulb

Figure 1 *Releasing stored energy*

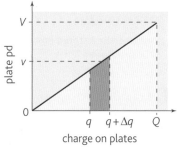

plate pd

q $q+\Delta q$ Q

charge on plates

Figure 2 *Energy stored in a capacitor*

When a capacitor is charged, energy is stored in it because electrons are forced onto one of its plates and taken off the other plate. The energy is stored in the capacitor as electrical potential energy. A charged capacitor discharged across a torch bulb will release its energy in a brief flash of light from the bulb, as long as the capacitor has been charged initially to the operating pd of the bulb. Charge flow is rapid enough to give a large enough current to light the bulb, but only for a brief time. The bulb could be replaced by a miniature electric motor which would spin briefly when the capacitor is discharged through it.

How much energy is stored in a charged capacitor? The charge is forced onto the plates by the battery. In the charging process, the pd across the plates increases in proportion to the charge stored, as shown in Figure 2.

Consider one step in the process of charging a capacitor of capacitance C when the charge on the plates increases by a small amount Δq from q to $q +\Delta q$. The energy stored ΔE in the capacitor is equal to the work done to force the extra charge Δq on to the plates and is given by $\Delta E = v\Delta q$, where v is the average pd during this step. $v\Delta q$ is represented in Figure 2 by the area of the vertical strip of width Δq and height v under the line. Therefore, the area of this strip represents the work done ΔE in this small step.

Now consider all the small steps from zero pd to the final pd V. The total energy stored E is obtained by adding up the energy stored in each small step. In other words, E is represented by the total area under the line from zero pd to pd V. As this area is a triangle of height V and base length Q $(= CV)$, the total energy stored E = triangle area = $\frac{1}{2}$ × height × base = $\frac{1}{2}VQ$

Energy stored by the capacitor, $E = \frac{1}{2}QV$

Notes:

1 Using $Q = CV$ or $V = Q/C$, the above equation may be written as $E = \frac{1}{2}CV^2$ or $E = \frac{1}{2}Q^2/C$

2 In the charging process, the battery supplies charge Q at pd V to the circuit and therefore transfers energy QV to the circuit. Thus 50% of the energy supplied by the battery $(= \frac{1}{2}QV)$ is stored in the capacitor. The other 50% is wasted due to resistance in the circuit as it is transferred to the surroundings when the charge flows in the circuit.

■ Measuring the energy stored in a charged capacitor

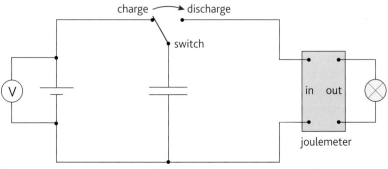

Figure 3 *Measuring energy stored*

A joulemeter is used to measure the energy transfer from a charged capacitor to a light bulb when the capacitor discharges. The capacitor pd V is measured and the joulemeter reading recorded before the discharge starts. When the capacitor has discharged, the joulemeter reading is recorded again. The difference of the two joulemeter readings is the energy transferred from the capacitor during the discharge process. This is the total energy stored in the capacitor before it discharged. This can be compared with the calculation of the energy stored using $E = \frac{1}{2}CV^2$.

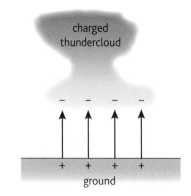

Figure 4 *Energy in a thundercloud*

The energy stored in a thundercloud

Imagine a thundercloud and the Earth below like a pair of charged parallel plates. Because the thundercloud is charged, a strong electric field exists between the thundercloud and the ground. The potential difference between the thundercloud and the ground, $V = Ed$, where E is therefore the electric field strength and d is the height of the thundercloud above the ground.

- For a thundercloud carrying a constant charge Q, the energy stored $= \frac{1}{2}QV = \frac{1}{2}QEd$.
- If the thundercloud is forced by winds to rise to a new height d', the energy stored $= \frac{1}{2}QEd'$.
- As the electric field strength is unchanged (since it depends on the charge per unit area; see Topic 5.2), the increase in the energy stored $= \frac{1}{2}QEd' - \frac{1}{2}QEd = \frac{1}{2}QE\Delta d$, where $\Delta d = d' - d$.

This increase in the energy stored is because work is done by the force of the wind to overcome the electrical attraction between the thundercloud and the ground and make the charged thundercloud move away from ground.

The insulating property of air breaks down if it is subjected to an electric field of strength more than about $300\,\text{kV m}^{-1}$. Prove for yourself that, for every metre rise of the thundercloud carrying a charge of $20\,\text{C}$, the energy stored would increase by $3\,\text{MJ}$. At a height of $500\,\text{m}$, the energy stored would be $1500\,\text{MJ}$.

Summary questions

1 Calculate the charge and energy stored in a $10\,\mu\text{F}$ capacitor charged to a pd of
  a $3.0\,\text{V}$,
  b $6.0\,\text{V}$

2 A $50\,000\,\mu\text{F}$ capacitor is charged from a $9\,\text{V}$ battery then discharged through a light bulb in a flash of light lasting $0.2\,\text{s}$. Calculate:
  a the charge and energy stored in the capacitor before discharge,
  b the average power supplied to the light bulb.

3 An uncharged $2.2\,\mu\text{F}$ capacitor is connected to a $3.0\,\text{V}$ battery. Calculate:
  a the charge and energy
    i stored in the capacitor,
    ii supplied by the battery.
  b Account for the difference between the energy supplied by the battery and the energy stored in the capacitor.

4 In Figure 5, a $4.7\,\mu\text{F}$ capacitor is charged from a $12.0\,\text{V}$ battery by connecting the switch S to X. The switch is then reconnected to Y to charge a $2.2\,\mu\text{F}$ capacitor from the first capacitor, causing the charge to be shared in proportion to the capacitance of each capacitor.

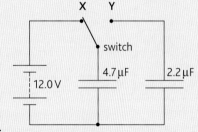

Figure 5

Calculate:
  a the initial charge and energy stored in the $4.7\,\mu\text{F}$ capacitor,
  b i the final charge stored by each capacitor,
    ii the final pd across the two capacitors,
  c the final energy stored in each capacitor.

Account for the loss of energy stored.

Charging and discharging a capacitor through a fixed resistor

Learning objectives:

- What is the shape of the Q–t charging curves? And the Q–t discharging curves?

- Which circuit components could be changed to make the charge/discharge slower?

- What is meant by the time constant of a capacitor–resistor circuit?

Specification reference: 3.4.4

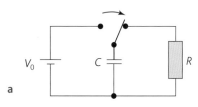

a

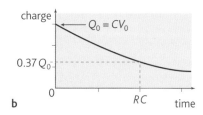

b

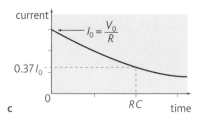

c

Figure 1 *Capacitor discharge*

Capacitor discharge through a fixed resistor

When a capacitor discharges through a fixed resistor, the discharge current decreases gradually to zero. Figure 1a shows a circuit in which a capacitor is discharged through a resistor when the switch is changed over. The reason why the current decreases gradually is that the pd across the capacitor decreases as it loses charge. Because the resistor is connected directly to the capacitor, the resistor current (= pd/resistance) decreases as the pd decreases.

The situation is not unlike water emptying through a pipe at the bottom of a container. When the container is full, the flow rate out of the pipe is high because the water pressure at the pipe is high. As the container empties, the water level falls so the water pressure at the pipe falls and the flow rate decreases.

The graphs in Figure 1 show how the current and the charge decrease with time. Both curves have the same shape as both the current and charge (and pd) decrease exponentially. This means that any of these quantities decreases by the same factor in equal intervals of time. For example, for initial charge Q_0, if the charge is $0.9Q_0$ after a certain time t_1, the charge will be

- $0.9 \times 0.9 \, Q_0$ after time $2 \, t_1$,
- $0.9 \times 0.9 \times 0.9 \, Q_0$ after time $3 \, t_1$ ...
- $0.9^n Q_0$ after time $n t_1$

To understand why the decrease is exponential, consider one small step in the discharge process of a capacitor C through a resistor R when the charge decreases from Q to $Q - \Delta Q$ in time Δt.

At this stage, the current $I = \dfrac{\text{pd across the plates, } V}{\text{resistance, } R} = \dfrac{Q}{CR}$ as $V = \dfrac{Q}{C}$.

Note:

The current is proportional to the charge which is proportional to the pd. So the curves all have the same shape.

Assuming Δt is sufficiently small, the decrease of charge $\Delta Q = -I \Delta t$ (– as Q decreases).

Therefore, $\Delta Q = \dfrac{-Q}{CR} \Delta t$, which gives

$$\frac{\Delta Q}{Q} = -\frac{\Delta t}{CR}$$

The equation tells us that the fractional drop of charge $\Delta Q / Q$ is the same in any short interval of time Δt during the discharge process. For example, suppose $\Delta t = 10 \, \text{s}$ and $CR = 100$. Therefore $\Delta Q / Q = -0.1$ ($= -\Delta t / CR$). So the charge decreases to 0.9 of its value at the start of the 10 s interval. So if the initial charge is Q_0, then the charge still on the plates will be

- $0.9Q_0$ after 10 s,
- $0.9 \times 0.9Q_0$ after a further 10 s,
- $0.9 \times 0.9 \times 0.9Q_0$ after a further 10 s, etc.

In theory, the charge on the plates never becomes zero.

Exponential changes occur whenever the rate of change of a quantity is proportional to the quantity itself.

Rearranging the equation $\frac{\Delta Q}{Q} = -\frac{\Delta t}{CR}$ gives

$$\frac{\Delta Q}{\Delta t} = -\frac{Q}{CR}$$

For very short intervals of time (i.e. $\Delta t \longrightarrow 0$), $\frac{\Delta Q}{\Delta t}$ represents the rate of change of charge and is written $\frac{dQ}{dt}$

Therefore, $\frac{dQ}{dt} = -\frac{Q}{CR}$

The graphical solution to this equation is shown in Figure 1b. The mathematical solution is

$$Q = Q_0 e^{-t/RC}$$

where Q_0 = initial charge, and e = the exponential function (sometimes written 'exp').

The quantity RC is called the **time constant** for the circuit. At time $t = RC$ after the start of the discharge, the charge falls to 0.37 (= e^{-1}) of its initial value.

$$\text{Time constant} = RC$$

where R = circuit resistance, and C = capacitance.

The unit of RC is the second. This is because 1 ohm = 1 volt/ampere and 1 farad = 1 coulomb/volt so the unit of RC = volt/ampere × coulomb/volt = coulomb/ampere = the second.

*Worked example:*_____

A 2200 µF capacitor is charged to a pd of 9.0 V then discharged through a 100 kΩ resistor using a circuit as shown in Figure 1.

a Calculate;

  i the initial charge stored by the capacitor,

  ii the time constant of the circuit,

b Calculate the pd after a time

  i equal to the time constant,

  ii 300 s.

Solution

a i $Q_0 = CV_0 = 2200 \times 10^{-6} \times 9.0 = 2.0 \times 10^{-2}$ C,

  ii Time constant = $RC = 100 \times 10^3 \times 2.2 \times 10^{-3} = 220$ s

b i When $t = RC$, $V = V_0 e^{-1} = 0.37 \times 9.0 = 3.3$ V

  ii When $t = 300$ s, $\frac{t}{RC} = \frac{300}{220} = 1.36$

    $\therefore V = V_0 e^{-t/RC} = 9.0 \, e^{-1.36} = 2.3$ V

Notes

1 The current, the pd and the charge are all proportional to one another. All three quantities decrease exponentially in capacitor discharge in accordance with the equation $x = x_0 e^{-t/CR}$, where x represents either the current or the charge or the pd.

2 The inverse function of e^x is $\ln x$, where ln is the natural logarithm. To calculate t, given x, x_0, R and C, use of the inverse function of e^x gives $\ln x = \ln x_0 - (t/RC)$

3 The exponential function $e^z = 1 + z + \frac{z^2}{2 \times 1} + \frac{z^3}{3 \times 2 \times 1} + \dots$, etc.

It can be shown mathematically that the rate of change of this function with respect to z is the same function. This is why the function appears whenever the rate of change of a quantity is proportional to the quantity itself.

Note that $z = 1$ gives

$e = 1 + 1 + \frac{1}{2} + \frac{1}{6} + \frac{1}{24}$, etc = 2.718 .

You can check this on your calculator by keying in 'e^x' then pressing 1 to give 2.718. Keying in –1 instead of 1 gives 0.37 for e^{-1}.

Note The explanation of why $Q = Q_0 e^{-t/RC}$ is the solution of the equation

$$\frac{dQ}{dt} = -\frac{Q}{CR}$$

is not required in the A2 physics specification.

Link

Wherever a quantity decreases at a rate that is proportional to the quantity, the decrease is exponential. You will meet exponential decrease again in radioactive decay in Unit 5A. See Topic 9.6.

The significance of the time constant

The time constant RC is the time taken, in seconds, for the capacitor to discharge to 37% of its initial charge. Given values of R and C, the time constant can be quickly calculated and used as an approximate measure of how quickly the capacitor discharges. However, as $5RC$ is the time taken to discharge by over 99%, $5RC$ is a better 'rule of thumb' estimate of the time taken for the capacitor to effectively discharge. Prove for yourself that $t = 5RC$ gives a value which is less than 1% of the initial value.

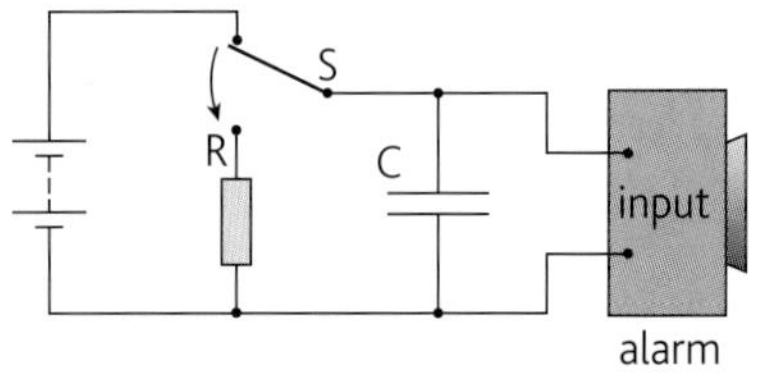

■ Investigating capacitor discharge

Figure 2 shows how to measure the pd across a capacitor as it discharges through a fixed resistor. An oscilloscope is used as it has a very high resistance so the discharge current from the capacitor passes only through the fixed resistor. The oscilloscope is used to measure the capacitor pd at regular intervals. A data logger or a digital voltmeter could be used instead of the oscilloscope.

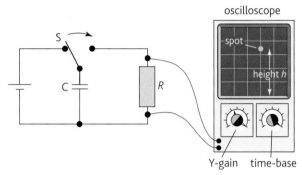

Figure 2 *Measuring capacitor discharge*

The measurements may be used to plot a graph of voltage against time. The time taken for the voltage to decrease to 37% (= 1/e) of the initial value can be measured from the graph and compared with the calculated value of RC.

Applications of capacitor discharge

1 Any electronic timing circuit or time delay circuit makes use of capacitor discharge through a fixed resistor.

   Figure 3 shows an alarm circuit where the alarm rings if the input voltage to the electronic circuit drops below a certain value after the switch is reset. The time delay between resetting the switch and the alarm ringing can be increased by increasing the resistance R or the capacitance C. Such a change to the circuit would make the discharge of C through R slower so increasing the time for the capacitor voltage to decrease sufficiently to make the alarm ring.

2 Capacitor smoothing is used in applications where sudden voltage variations or 'glitches' can have undesirable effects. For example, mains appliances being switched on or off in a building could affect computers connected to the mains supply in the building. A large capacitor in a computer supplies current if the mains supply is interrupted, so the computer circuits continue to function normally.

Figure 3 *A time-delayed alarm circuit*

■ Charging a capacitor through a fixed resistor

When a capacitor is charged by connecting it to a source of constant pd, the charging current decreases as the capacitor charge and pd increases. When the capacitor is fully charged, its pd is equal to the source pd and the current is zero as no more charge flows in the circuit. Figure 4a shows how the capacitor charge and current change with time.

The capacitor charge 'builds up' until the capacitor pd V is equal to the source pd V_0, as shown in Figure 4b. The charge Q_0 on the capacitor is then equal to CV_0. The charge curve is an 'inverted' exponential decrease curve which flattens out at $Q_0 = CV_0$.

The time constant for the circuit, RC, is the time taken for the charge to reach 63% of the final charge (i.e. 37% more charge needed to be fully charged). A graph of the capacitor pd V against time has exactly the same shape as the charge curve because $V = Q/C$.

The capacitor current I decreases exponentially to zero from its initial value I_0, as shown in Figure 4c. The current at any stage is equal to the rate of change of charge. Therefore the current is given by the gradient of the charge–time graph and so it decreases exponentially.

Note:

1 At any instant during the charging process, the source pd
V_0 = the resistor pd + the capacitor pd

Hence $V_0 = IR + \dfrac{Q}{C}$ at any instant.

2 The initial current $I_0 = \dfrac{V_0}{R}$, assuming the capacitor is initially uncharged.

3 At time t after charging starts, $I = I_0 e^{-t/RC}$.

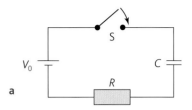

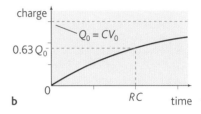

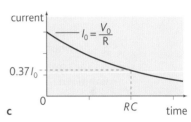

Figure 4 *Capacitor charging*

Summary questions

1 A 50 μF capacitor is charged by connecting it to a 6.0 V battery then discharged through a 100 kΩ resistor.

Calculate:

a i   the charge stored in the capacitor immediately after it has been charged,

ii the time constant of the circuit.

b i   Estimate how long the capacitor would take to discharge to about 2 V.

ii Estimate the resistance of the resistor that you would use in place of the 100 kΩ resistor if the discharge is to be 99% completed within about 5 s.

2 A 68 μF capacitor is charged to a pd of 9.0 V then discharged through a 20 kΩ resistor.

a Calculate:

i   the charge stored by the capacitor at a pd of 9.0 V,

ii the initial discharge current

b Calculate the pd and the discharge current 5.0 s after the discharge started.

3 A 2.2 μF capacitor is charged to a pd of 6.0 V and then discharged through a 100 kΩ resistor. Calculate:

a the charge and energy stored in this capacitor at 6.0 V,

b the pd across the capacitor 0.5 s after the discharge started,

c the energy stored at this time.

4 An uncharged 4.7 μF capacitor is charged to a pd of 12.0 V through a 200 Ω resistor and then discharged through a 220 kΩ resistor. Calculate:

a i   initial charging current,

ii the energy stored in the capacitor at 12.0 V,

b the time taken for the pd to fall from 12.0 V to 3.0 V,

c the energy lost by the capacitor in this time.

1   In an experiment to measure the capacitance C of a capacitor, the circuit in **Figure 1** was used to charge the capacitor then discharge it through a resistor of known resistance R.

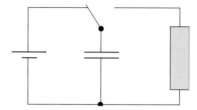

Figure 1

(a) The capacitor pd V at time t after the discharge commenced is given by $V = V_0 e^{-t/CR}$.
Show that this equation can be rearranged into an equation of the form $\ln V = a - bt$, where a and b are constants, and determine expressions for a and b.   *(4 marks)*

(b) As the capacitor discharged, its pd was measured every 30 seconds using a digital voltmeter. The measurements were repeated twice as shown in Table 1.

Table 1

t/s	0	30	60	90	120	150	180	210	240	270	300
V/V	4.50	3.82	3.26	2.78	2.33	2.00	1.70	1.43	1.23	1.04	0.89
	4.51	3.81	3.25	2.77	2.35	2.10	1.72	1.43	1.25	1.02	0.90
	4.50	3.83	3.25	2.76	2.34	1.98	1.69	1.42	1.22	1.04	0.87
mean V/V	4.503	3.820	3.253	2.760	2.340	2.027	1.703				
ln V	1.505	1.340	1.180	1.017	0.850	0.707	0.532				

(i) Complete the missing entries in Table 1.

(ii) Use the measurements to plot a graph of $\ln V$ on the y-axis against t on the x-axis.

(iii) Use your graph to determine the time constant of the discharge circuit.

(iv) The resistance R of the resistor was $68\,k\Omega$. Determine the capacitance C of the capacitor.   *(10 marks)*

(c) (i) Discuss the reliability of the measurements.

(ii) Estimate the accuracy of your value of capacitance, given the resistor value is accurate to within 1%.   *(4 marks)*

2   **Figure 2** shows a $2.0\,\mu F$ capacitor connected to $150\,V$ supply.

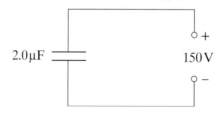

Figure 2

(a) Calculate the charge on the capacitor.   *(2 marks)*

(b) (i) Suggest a graph that could be drawn in order to calculate the energy stored in the capacitor by finding the area under the graph.

(ii) Calculate the energy stored by the capacitor when it has a pd of $150\,V$ across it.   *(3 marks)*

(c) The charged capacitor is removed from the power supply and discharged by connecting a $220\,k\Omega$ resistor across it.

    (i) Calculate the maximum discharge current.

    (ii) Show that the current will have fallen to 10% of its maximum value in a time of approximately 1 s.   *(5 marks)*

AQA, 2002

3   A capacitor of capacitance $330\,\mu F$ is charged to a potential difference of 9.0 V. It is then discharged through a resistor of resistance $470\,k\Omega$.

Calculate:

(a) the energy stored by the capacitor when it is fully charged,   *(2 marks)*

(b) the time constant of the discharging circuit,   *(1 mark)*

(c) the pd across the capacitor 60 s after the discharge has begun.   *(3 marks)*

AQA, 2004

4   A student used a voltage sensor connected to a data logger to plot the discharge curve for a $4.7\,\mu F$ capacitor. **Figure 3** shows the graph she obtained.

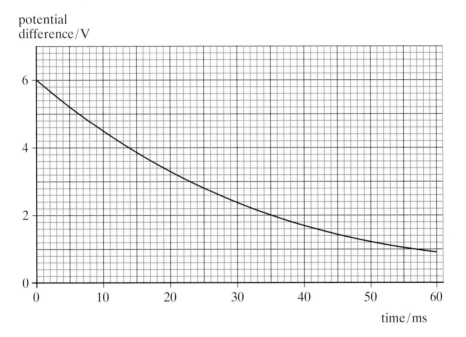

Figure 3

Use data from the graph to calculate:

(a) the initial charge stored,   *(2 marks)*

(b) the energy stored when the capacitor had been discharging for 35 ms,   *(3 marks)*

(c) the time constant for the circuit,   *(3 marks)*

(d) the resistance of the circuit through which the capacitor was discharging.   *(2 marks)*

AQA, 2002

5   **Figure 4** shows a circuit that may be used to investigate the capacitance of a capacitor. The switch moves rapidly between **X** and **Y**, making contact with each terminal 400 times per second. When it makes contact with **X** the capacitor **C** charges, when it makes contact with **Y** the capacitor discharges through the resistor **R**.

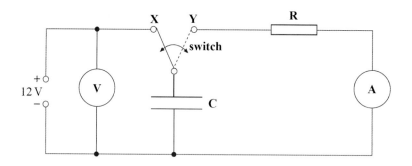

Figure 4

(a) **R** has a value of $220\,\Omega$. The time constant for the circuit is $2.2 \times 10^{-4}\,$s. Calculate the value of capacitor **C**.
(1 mark)

(b) Calculate the periodic time, T, for the oscillation of the switch.
(2 marks)

(c) The switch makes contact with **Y** for time $^T\!/_2$. The capacitor discharges from $12\,$V during this time.

 (i) Calculate the voltage across the charged capacitor after a time $^T\!/_2$.

 (ii) Explain whether or not it is reasonable to assume that the capacitor has completely discharged in the time $^T\!/_2$.
(4 marks)

AQA, 2007

6 (a) Explain what is meant by a capacitance of 1 farad (F).
(1 mark)

(b) The capacitance of a capacitor is $2.3 \times 10^{-11}\,$F. When the potential difference across it is $6.0\,$V, calculate:

 (i) the charge it stores,

 (ii) the energy it stores.
(4 marks)

(c) A student charged the capacitor and then tried to measure the potential difference between the plates using an oscilloscope. The student observed the trace shown in **Figure 5** and concluded that the capacitor was discharging through the oscilloscope.

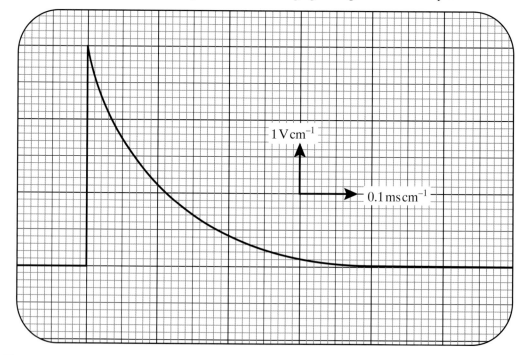

Figure 5

Calculate the resistance of the oscilloscope.
(3 marks)

AQA, 2003

7   A torch bulb produces a flash of light when a 270 μF capacitor is discharged across it.

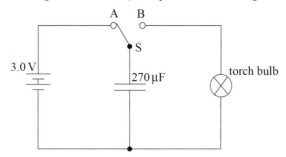

Figure 6

(a) The capacitor is charged to a pd of 3.0 V from the battery, as shown in **Figure 6**.
     Calculate:
     (i)   the energy stored in the capacitor,
     (ii) the work done by the battery.   *(3 marks)*
(b) The capacitor is discharged by moving switch **S** in the diagram from **A** to **B**. The
     discharge circuit has a total resistance of 1.5 Ω.
     (i)   Show that almost all of the energy stored in the capacitor is released when
           the capacitor pd has decreased from 3.0 V to 0.3 V.
     (ii) Emission of light from the torch bulb ceases when the pd falls below 2.0 V.
           Calculate the duration of the light flash.
     (iii) Assuming that the torch bulb produces photons of average wavelength
           500 nm, estimate the number of photons released during the light flash.   *(8 marks)*

AQA, 2006

8   A student uses a system shown in **Figure 7** to measure the contact time of a metal ball
     when it bounces on a metal block.

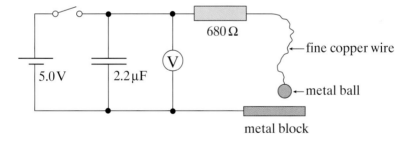

Figure 7

The student charges the capacitor by closing the switch, records the voltmeter reading
and then opens the switch. The student then releases the ball and measures the
voltage after the ball has rebounded from the metal block.

In one test the student records an initial voltage of 5.0 V and a final voltage of 2.2 V.

(a) Calculate the time for which the ball is in contact with the block.   *(3 marks)*
(b) (i)   Calculate the energy lost by the capacitor during the discharge.
     (ii) State where this energy is dissipated and the form it will take.   *(4 marks)*

AQA, 2002

7 Magnetic fields

7.1 Current-carrying conductors in a magnetic field

Learning objectives:

- How can we measure the strength of a magnetic field?

- Upon what factors does the magnitude of the force on a current-carrying wire depend?

- How is the direction of the force found for a current-carrying wire in a magnetic field?

Specification reference: 3.4.5

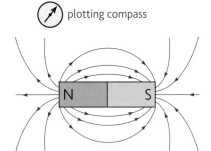

Figure 1 *The magnetic field near a bar magnet*

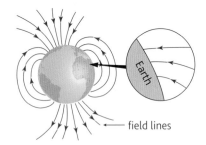

Figure 2 *The Earth's magnetic field*

Magnetic field patterns

Magnetism is a topic with a long scientific history stretching back thousands of years when lodestone was used by explorers as a navigational aid. Scientific research over the past 50 years or so has led to many applications such as accelerators, powerful microwave transmitters, magnetic discs and tape, superconducting magnets and magnetic resonance scanners. Magnetism is a valuable scientific tool used by archaeologists, astronomers and geologists. In short, magnetism has always been a fascinating topic and continues to be so.

A magnetic field is a force field surrounding a magnet or current-carrying wire which acts on any other magnet or current-carrying wire placed in the field. The magnetic field of a bar magnet is strongest at its ends which are referred to as **north-seeking** and **south-seeking** 'poles' according to which direction, north or south, each end points when the magnet is free to align itself with the horizontal component of the Earth's magnetic field. A **line of force** (or magnetic field line) of a magnetic field is a line along which a 'free' north pole would move in the field.

How science works

The Earth's magnetism

The Earth's magnetic field is not unlike the field of a giant bar magnet inside the Earth. It is caused by circulation currents in the molten iron in the Earth's core. The Earth's magnetic poles are known to drift gradually and a magnetic compass points to the Earth's magnetic north pole. At the present time, the Earth's north magnetic pole is in Northern Canada. As a result of studying the magnetism of rocks, scientists discovered that the continents are drifting across the Earth's surface on giant 'tectonic plates' and that the Earth's magnetic field can reverse quite suddenly!

The force on a current-carrying wire in a magnetic field

A current-carrying wire placed at a non-zero angle to the lines of force of an external magnetic field experiences a force due to the field. This effect is known as **motor effect**. The force is perpendicular to the wire and to the lines of force.

The motor effect can be tested using the simple arrangement shown in Figure 3. The wire is placed between opposite poles of a U-shaped magnet so it is at right angles to the lines of force of the magnetic field. When the

(plotting compass)

switch is closed, the section of the wire in the magnetic field experiences a force that pushes it out of the field.

The magnitude of the force depends on the current, the strength of the magnetic field, the length of the wire and on the angle between the lines of force of the field and the current direction.
The force is:

- greatest when the wire is at right angles to the magnetic field,
- zero when the wire is parallel to the magnetic field.

The direction of the force can be related to the direction of the field and to the direction of the current using **Fleming's left-hand rule** shown in Figure 4. If the current is reversed or if the magnetic field is reversed, the direction of the force is reversed.

The magnitude of the force on a current-carrying wire in a magnetic field can be investigated using the arrangement shown in Figure 5. The stiff wire frame is connected in series with a switch, an ammeter, a variable resistor and a battery. When the switch is closed, the magnet exerts a force on the wire which can be measured from the change of the top pan balance reading.

The tests above show that the force F on the wire is proportional to:

1 the current I,
2 the length l of the wire.

The **magnetic flux density** B of the magnetic field, sometimes referred to as the strength of the magnetic field, is defined as the force per unit length per unit current on a current-carrying conductor at right angles to the magnetic field lines.

Therefore, for a wire of length l carrying a current I in a uniform magnetic field B **at 90° to the field lines**, the force F on the wire is given by

$$F = BIl$$

1 The unit of B is the tesla (T), equal to $1\,\text{N}\,\text{m}^{-1}\,\text{A}^{-1}$
2 The direction of the force is given by **Fleming's left-hand rule**. See Figure 4.

Worked example:

A straight horizontal wire XY of length 5.0 m is in a uniform horizontal magnetic field of magnetic flux density 120 mT. The wire is at an angle of 90° to the field lines which are due north in direction. When the wire conducts a current of 14 A from east to west, calculate the magnitude of the force on the wire and state its direction.

Solution

$B = 120\,\text{mT} = 0.12\,\text{T}$

$F = BIl = 0.12 \times 14 \times 5.0 = 8.4\,\text{N}$

The force on the wire is vertically downwards.

Note:

For a straight wire at angle θ to the magnetic field lines, the force on the wire is due to the component of the magnetic field perpendicular to the wire, $B\sin\theta$. Therefore the magnitude of the force on the wire $F = BIl\sin\theta$. This extension of $F = BIl$ is not required for this specification.

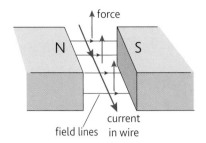

Figure 3 *The motor effect*

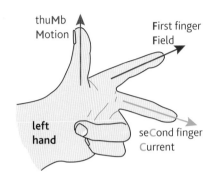

Figure 4 *Fleming's left-hand rule*

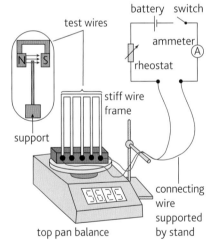

Figure 5 *Measuring the force on a current-carrying wire in a magnetic field*

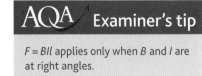

AQA **Examiner's tip**

$F = BIl$ applies only when B and I are at right angles.

■ The couple on a coil in a magnetic field

Consider a rectangular current-carrying coil in a uniform horizontal magnetic field, as shown in Figure 6. The coil has n turns of wire and can rotate about a vertical axis.

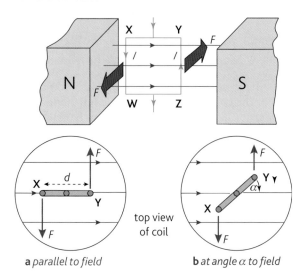

a *parallel to field*   **b** *at angle α to field*

Figure 6 *Couple on a coil*

■ The long sides of the coil are vertical. Each wire down each long side experiences a force BIl. Each long side therefore experiences a horizontal force $F = (BIl)n$ in opposite directions at right angles to the field lines.

■ The pair of forces acting on the long sides form a couple as the forces are not directed along the same line. The torque of the couple $= Fd$, where d is the perpendicular distance between the line of action of the forces on each side. See *AS Physics A* Topic 7.4. If the plane of the coil is at angle α to the field lines, then $d = w\cos\alpha$ where w is the width of the coil.

■ Therefore, the torque $= Fw\cos\alpha = BIlnw\cos\alpha = BIAn\cos\alpha$, where the coil area $A = lw$. If $\alpha = 0$ (i.e. the coil is parallel to the field, the torque $= BIAn$ as $\cos 0 = 1$).

■ If $\alpha = 90°$ (i.e. the coil is perpendicular to the field, the torque $= 0$ as $\cos 90° = 0$.

Application

The electric motor

The **simple electric motor** consists of a coil of insulated wire which spins between the poles of a U-shaped magnet.

When a direct current passes round the coil,

■ the wires at opposite edges of the coil are acted on by forces in opposite directions,

■ the force on each edge makes the coil spin about its axis,

Current is supplied to the coil via a split-ring commutator. The direction of the current round the coil is reversed by the split-ring commutator each time the coil rotates through half a turn. This ensures the current along an edge changes direction when it moves from one pole face to the other. As shown in Figure 7, the result is that the force on each edge continues to turn the coil in the same direction.

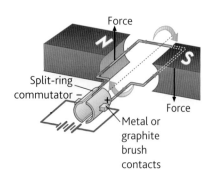

Figure 7 *In an electric motor*

In a practical electric motor, several evenly spaced 'armature' coils are wound on an iron core. Each coil is connected to its own section of the commutator. The result is that each coil in sequence experiences a torque when it is connected to the voltage supply so the armature is repeatedly pushed round. Because the iron core makes the field radial, each coil is in the plane of the field (i.e. $\alpha = 0$) for most of the time. As a result, the torque is steady and the motor runs more smoothly. In addition, the iron core makes the field much stronger so the torque of the motor is much greater.

By using an electromagnet connected to the same voltage supply as the coils, an electric motor can operate with alternating current or with direct current. This is because the magnetic field reverses each time the armature current reverses when an ac supply is used. So the turning effect on the armature is unchanged in direction.

Figure 8 *A practical electric motor*

Summary questions

1 The table below relates the force on a current-carrying wire which is at right angles to the lines of force of a magnetic field and the current. Complete the table below by working out the missing data in each column.

Table 1

	(a)	(b)	(c)	(d)
B/T	0.20 T vertically down	0.20 T vertically down	?	0.1 T horizontal due?
I/A	3.0 A horizontal due North	?	3.0 A horizontal due North	2.0 A vertically up
l/m	0.040 m	0.040 m	0.040 m	0.040 m
F/N	?	0.036 N horizontal due South	0.024 N horizontal due West	? horizontal due East

2 a A straight vertical wire of length 0.10 m carries a downward current of 4.0 A in a uniform horizontal magnetic field of flux density 55 mT that acts due North. Determine the magnitude and direction of the force on the wire.

b A straight horizontal wire of length 50 mm carrying a constant current is in a uniform magnetic field of flux density 140 mT which acts vertically downwards. The wire experiences a force of 28 mN in a direction which is due North. Determine the magnitude and the direction of the current in the wire.

3 A rectangular coil of width 60 mm and of length 80 mm has 50 turns. The coil was placed horizontally in a uniform horizontal magnetic field of flux density 85 mT with its shorter side parallel to the field lines. A current of 8.0 A was passed through the coil. Sketch the arrangement and determine the force on each side of the coil.

4 The Earth's magnetic field at a certain position on the Earth's surface has a horizontal component of 18 μT due North and a downwards vertical component of 55 μT. Calculate:

a the magnitude of the Earth's magnetic field at this position,

b the magnitude and direction of the force on a vertical wire of length 0.80 m carrying a current of 4.5 A downwards.

7.2 Moving charges in a magnetic field

Learning objectives:

▨ What happens to charged particles in a magnetic field?

▨ Why does a force act on a wire in a magnetic field when a current flows along the wire?

▨ What equation can we use to find the force on a moving charge?

Specification reference: 3.4.5

Electron beams

The picture on the screen of a colour television tube is formed as a result of three electron beams in the tube scanning the screen inside the tube. The beams are controlled by magnetic fields produced by coils outside the tube. Changing the current through a coil changes the strength of the magnetic field it produces which changes the direction of the electron beams.

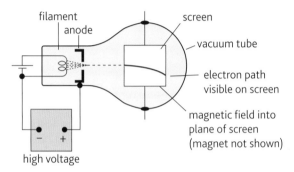

Figure 1 *An electron deflection tube*

Figure 1 shows a vacuum tube designed to show the effect of a magnetic field on an electron beam. The production of the electron beam is explained in Topic 7.3. The path of the beam can be seen where it passes over the fluorescent screen in the tube. The beam is deflected downwards when a magnetic field is directed into the plane of the screen. Each electron in the beam experiences a force due to the magnetic field. The beam follows a circular path because the direction of the force on each electron is perpendicular to the direction of motion of the electron (and to the field direction). The direction of the force on an electron in the beam can also be worked out using Fleming's left-hand rule, provided we remember the convention that the current direction is opposite to the direction in which the electrons move.

The reason why a current-carrying wire in a magnetic field experiences a force is that the electrons moving along the wire are pushed to one side by the force of the field. If the electrons in Figure 1 had been confined to a wire, the whole wire would have been pushed downwards.

Link

The positron was the first antimatter particle to be discovered when a β particle track in a magnetic field was found that curved in the opposite direction to the β– tracks. See *AS Physics*, Topic 1.4.

Figure 2 *Charged particles in a magnetic field*

How science works

A high-energy collision

Magnetic fields are used in particle physics detectors to separate different charged particles out and, as explained in Topic 7.3, to measure their momentum from the curvature of the tracks they create. All charged particles moving across the lines of a magnetic field are acted on by a force due to the field. Positively charged particles such as protons are pushed in the opposite direction to negatively charged particles such as electrons.

Figure 2 shows charged particles curving across a magnetic field. The positively charged particles curve in the opposite direction to the negatively charged particles. The particles were created by a collision between a fast-moving incoming particle and the nucleus of an atom.

▓ Force on a moving charge in a magnetic field

A beam of charged particles crossing a vacuum tube is an electric current across the tube. Suppose each charged particle has a charge Q and moves at speed v. In a time interval t, each particle travels a distance vt. Its passage is equivalent to current $I = Q/t$ along a wire of length $l = vt$.

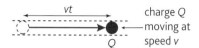

Figure 3 *Force on a moving charge*

If the particles pass through a uniform magnetic field in a direction at right angles to the field lines, each particle experiences a force F due to the field. If the particles were confined to a wire, the force would be given by $F = BIl$. For moving charges, the same equation applies where $I = \dfrac{Q}{t}$ and $l = vt$.

Therefore, for a charged particle moving across a uniform magnetic field in a direction at right angles to the field, $F = BIl = B\left(\dfrac{Q}{t}\right)(vt) = BQv$

For a particle of charge Q moving through a uniform magnetic field at speed v in a perpendicular direction to the field, the force on the particle is given by

$$F = BQv$$

If the direction of motion of a charged particle in a magnetic field is at angle θ to the lines of the field, then the component of B perpendicular to the direction of motion of the charged particle, $B\sin\theta$, is used to give $F = BQv\sin\theta$.

- ▓ If the velocity of the charged particle is perpendicular to the direction of the magnetic field, $\theta = 90°$ so the equation becomes $F = BQv$ because $\sin 90° = 1$.

- ▓ If the velocity of the charged particle is parallel to the direction of the magnetic field, $\theta = 0$ so $F = 0$ because $\sin 0 = 0$.

Note:

The equation $F = BQv\sin\theta$ is not required for this specification.

Application

The Hall probe

Hall probes are used to measure magnetic field strength. A Hall probe contains a slice of semiconducting material. Figure 4 shows the slice in a magnetic field with the field lines perpendicular to the flat side of the slice. A constant current passes through the slice as shown. The charge carriers (which are electrons in an n-type semiconductor) are deflected by the field. As a result, a potential difference is created between the top and bottom edges of the slice. This effect is known as the Hall effect after its discoverer.

The pd, referred to as the Hall voltage, is proportional to the magnetic flux density, provided the current is constant. This is because each charge carrier passing through the slice is subjected to a magnetic force $F_{\text{mag}} = BQv$, where v is the speed of the charge

AQA Examiner's tip

Stationary charges in a magnetic field experience no **magnetic force**. Also when applying Fleming's left-hand rule to charged particles, the current direction for negative particles is in the opposite direction to the direction of motion of the particles.

▓ Note

The Hall probe is not on the specification and is presented here as an application of the equations for the electric and magnetic form on a charged particle.

initially

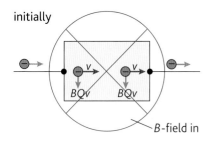

finally

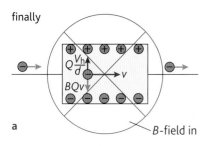

a

Figure 4 *The Hall effect*
a *The Hall voltage*

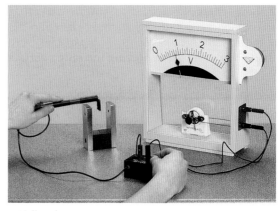

b *Using a Hall probe*

carrier. Once the Hall voltage has been created, the magnetic deflection of a charge carrier entering the slice is opposed by the force on it due to the electric field created by the Hall voltage. The electric field force $F_{elec} = QV_h/d$, where V_h represents the Hall voltage. See Topic 5.2. Therefore, $QV_h/d = BQv$ gives $V_h = Bvd$. For constant current, v is constant so V_h is proportional to B.

Summary questions

$e = 1.6 \times 10^{-19}\,C$

1 **a** In Figure 1, how would the force on the electrons in the magnetic field differ if:

   i the magnetic field was reversed in direction,

   ii the magnetic field was reduced in strength,

   iii the speed of the electrons was increased.

  b Calculate the force on an electron that enters a uniform magnetic field of flux density 150 mT at a velocity of $8.0 \times 10^6\,m\,s^{-1}$ at an angle of

   i 90°,

   ii 0° to the field.

2 Electrons in a vertical wire move upwards at a speed of $2.5 \times 10^{-3}\,m\,s^{-1}$ into a uniform horizontal magnetic field of magnetic flux density 95 mT. The field is directed along a line from South to North as shown in Figure 5. Calculate the force on each electron and determine its direction.

3 A beam of protons and π^+ mesons moving at the same speed is directed into a uniform magnetic field in the same direction as the field.

  a Explain why the beam is not deflected by the field.

  b If the particles had been directed into the field in a direction at right angles to the field lines at the same speed, state and explain what effect this would have had on the beam.

4 In a Hall probe, electrons passing through the semiconductor experience a force due to a magnetic field.

  a Explain why a potential difference is created across the semiconductor as a result of the application of the magnetic field.

  b When the magnetic flux density was 90 mT, each electron moving through the slice experiences a force of $6.4 \times 10^{-20}\,N$ due to the magnetic field. Calculate:

   i the mean speed of the electrons passing through the slice,

   ii the magnetic force on each electron if the magnetic flux density is increased to 120 mT.

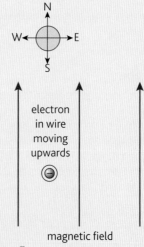

Figure 5

7.3 Charged particles in circular orbits

Learning objectives:

▦ What happens to the direction of the magnetic force when electrons are deflected by a magnetic field?

▦ Why do the moving charges move in a path that is circular?

▦ What factors affect the radius of the circular path?

Specification reference: 3.4.5

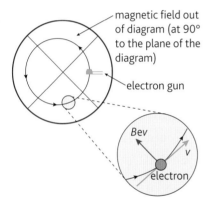

Figure 1 *A circular orbit in a magnetic field*

Link

We can apply the centripetal acceleration formula $a = v^2/r$ because the particle is in uniform circular motion. See Topic 2.2.

AQA Examiner's tip

Check whether a question refers to radius or diameter. Remember that equipment must be evacuated to prevent loss of speed.

Magnetic fields are used to control beams of charged particles in many devices, from television tubes to high energy accelerators. The force of the magnetic field on a moving charged particle is at right angles to the direction of motion of the particle.

▦ No work is done by the magnetic field on the particle as the force always acts at right angles to the velocity of the particle. Its direction of motion is changed by the force but not its speed. The kinetic energy of the particle is unchanged by the magnetic field.

▦ In accordance with Fleming's left-hand rule, the magnetic force is always perpendicular to the velocity at any point along the path. The particle therefore moves on a circular path with the force always acting towards the centre of curvature of the circular path. See Topic 2.2.

▦ The force causes a centripetal acceleration because it is perpendicular to the velocity. Figure 1 shows the deflection of a beam of electrons in a uniform magnetic field. The path is a complete circle because the magnetic field is uniform and the particle remains in the field.

The radius, r, of the circular orbit in Figure 1 depends on the speed v of the particles and the magnetic flux density B.

At any point on the orbit, the particle is acted on by a magnetic force $F = BQv$ and it experiences a centripetal acceleration, $a = \dfrac{v^2}{r}$ towards the centre of the circle.

Applying Newton's second law in the form $F = ma$ gives

$$BQv = \frac{mv^2}{r}$$

Rearranging this equation gives

$$r = \frac{mv}{BQ}$$

This equation shows that r decreases (so the path is more curved):

1 if B is increased or if v is decreased,
2 if particles with a larger specific charge, Q/m, are used.

Thermionic devices

In Figure 1, the beam of electrons is produced by an 'electron gun'. This consists of an electrically heated filament wire near a positively charged metal anode which attracts electrons emitted by the hot filament wire. This emission process is called thermionic emission. The electrons pass through a small hole in the anode to form the beam. The greater the potential difference between the anode and the filament wire, the higher the speed of the electrons when they reach the anode so the faster they are in the beam. The oscilloscope, the cathode ray television tube and the magnetron valve used in microwave cookers and radar systems all rely on thermionic emission.

Application

The cyclotron

The cyclotron is used in hospitals to produce high energy beams for radiation therapy. It consists of two hollow D-shaped electrodes (referred to as 'dees') in a vacuum chamber. With a uniform magnetic

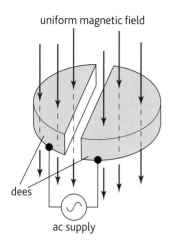

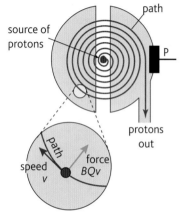

Figure 2 *The cyclotron*

field applied perpendicular to the plane of the dees, a high-frequency alternating voltage is applied between the dees.

Charged particles are directed into the one of the dees near the centre of the cyclotron. The charged particles are forced on a circular path by the magnetic field, causing them to emerge from the dee they were directed into. As they cross into the other dee, the alternating voltage reverses so they are accelerated into the other dee where they are once again forced on a circular path by the magnetic field. On emerging from this dee, the voltage reverses again and accelerates the particles into the first dee where the process is repeated. This occurs because the time taken by a particle to move round its semi-circular path in each dee does not depend on the particle speed (provided the speed stays much less than the speed of light c). This is because $r = \dfrac{mv}{BQ}$ so the time taken to complete the semi-circle $= \dfrac{\pi r}{v} = \dfrac{m\pi}{BQ}$ which is independent of the particle's speed.

Note:

1   Each time a particle crosses from one dee to the other it gains speed and its radius of orbit increases. The particles emerge from the cyclotron when the radius of orbit is equal to the dee radius R.

Using the equation $r = \dfrac{mv}{BQ}$, it follows that the speed v of the particles on exit from the cyclotron is given by

$$v = \frac{BQR}{m}, \text{ where } R \text{ is the dee radius.}$$

2   The time T for one full cycle of the alternating voltage must be equal to the time taken by a particle to complete one full circle. Hence $T = \dfrac{2m\pi}{BQ}$. Therefore the frequency f of the alternating voltage must be set at a value given by the equation

$$f = \frac{1}{T} = \frac{BQ}{2\pi m}.$$

Application and How science works

The mass spectrometer

The mass spectrometer is used to analyse the type of atoms present in a sample. The atoms of the sample are ionised and directed in a narrow beam at the same velocity into a uniform magnetic field. Each ion is deflected in a semi-circle by the magnetic field onto a detector, as shown in Figure 3. The radius of curvature of the path of each ion depends on the specific charge Q/m of the ion in accordance with the equation $r = mv/BQ$. Each type of ion is deflected by a different amount onto the detector. The detector is linked to a computer which is programmed to show the relative abundance of each type of ion in the sample.

The ions in the beam enter the magnetic field at the same velocity because they pass through a velocity selector, as shown in Figure 3. The velocity selector consists of a magnet and a pair of parallel plates at spacing d and voltage V_p due to a high voltage supply. The magnet and the plates are aligned so each ion passing through the velocity selector is acted on by an electric field force, $F_{elec} = QV_p/d$, in the opposite direction to a magnetic field force $F_{mag} = B_sQv$ where B_s is the magnetic flux density of the magnet in the velocity

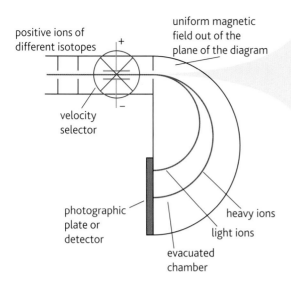

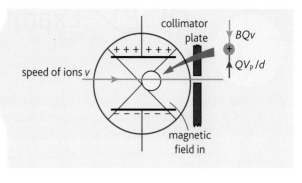

Figure 3 *The mass spectrometer*

selector. Ions moving at a certain velocity such that $B_sQv = QV_p/d$ experience equal and opposite forces so pass through undeflected. All other ions are deflected and do not pass through the collimator slit. So although the beam emerging from the collimator consists of different types of ions, they all have the same speed $v = V_p/B_sd$.

Link

The magnetic field force is cancelled out by the electric field force. See Topic 5.2 for the force on a charged particle in a uniform electric field.

Summary questions

$e = 1.6 \times 10^{-19}\,C$, e/m for the electron $= 1.76 \times 10^{11}\,C\,kg^{-1}$

1 A beam of electrons at a speed of $3.2 \times 10^7\,m\,s^{-1}$ is directed into a uniform magnetic field of flux density 8.5 mT in a direction perpendicular to the field lines. The electrons move on a circular orbit in the field.

  a i Explain why the electrons move on a circular orbit.

  ii Calculate the radius of the orbit.

  b The flux density is adjusted until the radius of orbit is 65 mm. Calculate the flux density for this new radius.

2 A narrow beam of electrons was directed at a speed of $2.9 \times 10^7\,m\,s^{-1}$ into a uniform magnetic field.

  a The beam followed a circular path of radius 35 mm in the magnetic field. Calculate the flux density of the magnetic field.

  b The speed of the electrons in the beam was halved by reducing the anode voltage. Calculate the new radius of curvature of the beam in the field.

3 The first cyclotron, used to accelerate protons, was 0.28 m in diameter and was in a magnetic field of flux density 1.1 T.

  a Show that protons emerged from this cyclotron at a maximum speed of $1.5 \times 10^7\,m\,s^{-1}$.

  b Calculate the maximum kinetic energy, in MeV, of a proton from this accelerator.

  The mass of a proton
  $= 1.67 \times 10^{-27}\,kg$, 1 MeV $= 1.6 \times 10^{-13}\,J$

4 In a mass spectrometer, a beam of ions at a speed of $7.6 \times 10^4\,m\,s^{-1}$ was directed into a uniform magnetic field of flux density 680 mT.

  a An ion was deflected in a semi-circular path of diameter 28 mm on to the detector. Calculate the specific charge of the ion.

  b A different type of ion was deflected onto the same detector when the magnetic flux density was changed to 400 mT. Calculate the specific charge of this ion.

1   (a)   The equation $F = BIl$, where the symbols have their usual meanings, gives the
          magnetic force that acts on a conductor in a magnetic field.

          Give the unit of each of the quantities in the equation: F, B, I, l.

          State the condition under which the equation applies.   *(2 marks)*

    (b)   **Figure 1** shows a horizontal copper bar of 25 mm × 25 mm square cross-section
          and length l carrying a current of 65 A.

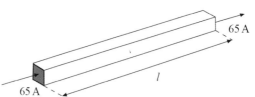

Figure 1

          (i)   Calculate the minimum value of the flux density of the magnetic field in
                which it should be placed if its weight is to be supported by the magnetic
                force that acts on it.

                density of copper = $8.9 \times 10^3 \, \text{kg m}^{-3}$

          (ii) Copy the diagram and draw an arrow to show the direction in which the
                magnetic field should be applied if your calculation in part (i) is to be valid.
                Label this arrow M.   *(5 marks)*

AQA, 2003

2   A 'bus bar' is a metal bar which can be used to conduct a large electric current. In a
    test, two bus bars, **X** and **Y**, of length 0.83 m are clamped at either end parallel to each
    other, as shown in **Figure 2**.

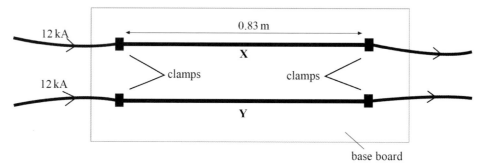

Figure 2

    (a)   When a constant current of 12 kA is carried by each bus bar, they exert a force of
          180 N on each other. This force is due to the magnetic field created by the current
          carried by each bus bar.

          (i)   Calculate the magnetic flux density due to the current in one bus bar at the
                position of the other bus bar.

          (ii) The magnetic flux density at any given distance from a straight conductor is
                proportional to the current through the conductor. Calculate the force on
                each bus bar if X carried a current of 6 kA and Y carried a current of 12 kA
                in the same direction.   *(6 marks)*

    (b)   When the same alternating current is passed through the two bus bars, both
          vibrate strongly.

(i) Explain why the bars vibrate.

(ii) State **one** way the amplitude of the vibrations could be reduced without reducing the current.

(4 marks)

AQA, 2007

3   (a)

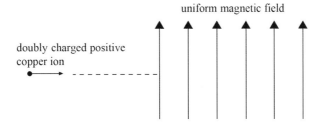

uniform magnetic field

doubly charged positive copper ion

Figure 3

Figure 3 shows a doubly charged positive ion of the copper isotope $^{63}_{29}Cu$ that is projected into a vertical magnetic field of flux density 0.28 T, with the field directed upwards. The ion enters the field at a speed of $7.8 \times 10^5 \, m \, s^{-1}$.

(i) State the initial direction of the magnetic force that acts on the ion.

(ii) Describe the subsequent path of the ion as fully as you can. Your answer should include both a qualitative description and a calculation.

mass of $^{63}_{29}Cu$ ion = $1.05 \times 10^{-25} \, kg$

(5 marks)

(b) State the effect on the path in part (a) if the following changes are made separately.

(i) The strength of the magnetic field is doubled.

(ii) A singly charged positive Cu ion replaces the original one.

(3 marks)

AQA, 2004

4   **Figure 4** shows a diagram of a mass spectrometer.

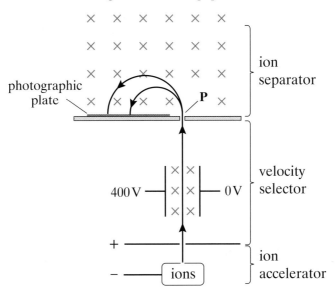

magnetic field into paper

photographic plate

P

ion separator

velocity selector

400 V   0 V

ion accelerator

ions

+

–

Figure 4

(a) The magnetic field strength in the velocity selector is 0.14 T and the electric field strength is $20\,000 \, V \, m^{-1}$.

(i) Define the unit for magnetic flux density, the tesla.

(ii) Show that the velocity selected is independent of the charge on an ion.

(iii) Show that the velocity selected is about $140 \, km \, s^{-1}$.

(5 marks)

(b) A sample of nickel is analysed in the spectrometer. The two most abundant isotopes of nickel are $^{58}_{28}Ni$ and $^{60}_{28}Ni$. Each ion carries a single charge of $+1.6 \times 10^{-19} \, C$.

The $^{58}_{28}$Ni ion strikes the photographic plate 0.28 m from the point **P** at which the ion beam enters the ion separator.

Calculate:

(i) the magnetic flux density of the field in the ion separator,

(ii) the separation of the positions where the two isotopes hit the photographic plate. *(5 marks)*

AQA, 2003

5 The protons in an accelerator were directed at a solid target, causing antiprotons and negative pions, as well as other particles and antiparticles, to emerge at high speed from the target. A uniform magnetic field was used to separate the negative particles from the uncharged and positive particles, as shown in **Figure 5**.

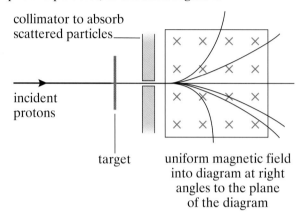

collimator to absorb scattered particles

incident protons

target

uniform magnetic field into diagram at right angles to the plane of the diagram

Figure 5

(a) Show that the speed, v, of a charged particle moving in a circular path of radius r in a uniform magnetic field B is given by

$$v = \frac{BQr}{m}$$

where m is the mass of the particle and Q is its charge. *(1 mark)*

(b) An antiproton and a negative pion follow the same path in the magnetic field. Explain why they have the same momentum but different speeds. *(3 marks)*

(c) State, in terms of quarks and antiquarks, the composition of each of the following: antiproton, negative pion. *(3 marks)*

AQA, 2004

6 **Figure 6** shows the arrangement of an apparatus for determining the masses of ions. In an evacuated chamber, positive ions from an ion source pass through the slit at **P** with the same velocity v. After passing **P**, the ions enter a region over which a uniform magnetic field is applied. The ions travel in a semi-circular path of diameter d and are detected at points such as **R**.

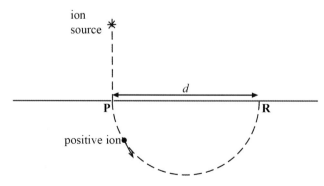

ion source

positive ions

Figure 6

(a) (i) State the direction of the applied magnetic field.

(ii) Explain why the ions travel in a semi-circular path whilst in the magnetic field.

(iii) By considering the force that acts on an ion of mass m and charge Q, having velocity v, show that the diameter d of the path of the ions is given by

$$d = \frac{2mv}{BQ}$$

where B is the flux density of the magnetic field. *(7 marks)*

(b) In an experiment using singly ionised magnesium ions travelling at a velocity of $7.5 \times 10^4\,\mathrm{m\,s^{-1}}$, d was $110\,\mathrm{mm}$ when B was $0.34\,\mathrm{T}$. Use this result to calculate the charge to mass ratio of these ions. *(2 marks)*

(c) (i) Some ions of the same element, whilst travelling at the same velocity as each other at **P**, may arrive at a point that is close to, but slightly different from, **R**. Explain why this might happen.

(ii) Other ions of the same element, also travelling at the same velocity at **P** as all of the others, may travel in a path whose diameter is half that of the others. Explain why this might happen. *(3 marks)*

AQA, 2007

7 **Figure 7** shows the path of protons in a proton synchrotron.

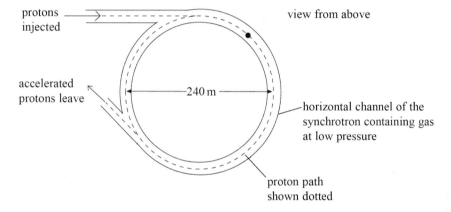

Figure 7

The protons are injected at a speed of $1.2 \times 10^5\,\mathrm{m\,s^{-1}}$ and a magnetic field is applied to make them move in a circular path.

(a) Calculate the magnetic flux density of the field required for protons to move in the circular path when their speed is $1.2 \times 10^5\,\mathrm{m\,s^{-1}}$.

(b) Explain how the magnetic flux density required to maintain the circular path has to change as the kinetic energy of the protons increases. *(5 marks)*

AQA, 2007

8 Electromagnetic induction

8.1 Generating electricity

Learning objectives:

▦ What must happen to a conductor (or to the magnetic field in which it's placed) for electricity to be generated?

▦ What factors would cause the induced emf to be greater?

▦ Does an induced emf always cause a current to flow?

Specification reference: 3.4.5

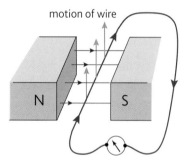

Figure 1 *Generating an electric current*

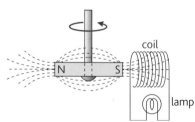

Figure 2 *A motor as a generator*

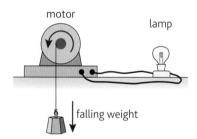

Figure 3 *A simple dynamo*

▦ Investigating electromagnetic induction

To generate electricity, all you need is a magnet and some wire connected to a sensitive meter, as shown in Figure 1. When the magnet is moved near the wire, a small current passes through the meter. This happens because an electromotive force (emf) is **induced** in the wire. This effect, known as **electromagnetic induction,** occurs whenever a wire cuts across the lines of a magnetic field. If the wire is part of a complete circuit, the **induced emf** forces electrons round the circuit. The induced emf can be increased by:

▦ moving the wire faster,

▦ using a stronger magnet,

▦ making the wire into a coil, as in Figure 3, and pushing the magnet in or out of the coil.

No emf is induced in the wire if the wire is parallel to the magnetic field lines as it moves through the field. The wire must cut across the lines of the magnetic field for an emf to be induced in the wire.

Other methods of generating an induced emf include:

1 **Using an electric motor in reverse,** as in Figure 2. The falling weight makes the motor coil turn between the poles of the magnet in the motor. The emf induced in the coil forces a current round the circuit and so causes the lamp to light. The faster the coil turns, the brighter the lamp is.

2 **Using a cycle dynamo,** as in Figure 3. When the magnet in the dynamo spins, an emf is induced in the coil. If the coil is connected to a lamp, the lamp lights because the emf forces a current round the circuit.

In both examples above, an emf is induced because there is relative motion between coil and the magnet. In the electric motor in reverse, the coil spins and the magnet is fixed. In the dynamo, the magnet spins and the coil is fixed.

▦ Energy changes

When a magnet is moved relative to a conductor (e.g. a wire or a coil), an emf is induced in the circuit. If the conductor is part of a complete circuit which has no other sources of emf, a current passes round the circuit just as if the circuit included a battery. However, unlike the emf of a battery which is constant, the induced emf becomes zero when the relative motion between the magnet and the wires ceases.

An electric current transfers energy from the source of the emf in a circuit to the other components in the circuit. For example, when a dynamo is used to light a lamp, energy is transferred from the dynamo to the lamp. The current through the dynamo coil causes a reaction force on the coil due to the magnet. Work must therefore be done to keep the magnet spinning. The energy transferred from the coil to the lamp is equal to the work done on the coil to keep it spinning, assuming no energy is wasted as sound or due to friction or internal resistance.

The rate of transfer of energy from the source of emf to the other components of the circuit is equal to the product of the induced emf and the current. This is because:

- the induced emf is the energy transferred from the source per unit charge that passes through the source,
- the current is the charge flow per second.

So the induced emf × the current = energy transferred per unit charge from the source × the charge flow per second = energy transferred per second from the source.

How science works

Michael Faraday 1791–1861

Electromagnetic induction was discovered by Michael Faraday in 1831 at the Royal Institution, London. Faraday knew that a current passing along a wire produces a magnetic field near the wire and he wanted to know if a magnet could be used to produce a current. Using a magnetic compass near a loop of wire as a detector of current, he showed that the compass deflected whenever the magnet was moved in or out of the wire. He used the term 'electromotive force' (emf) to describe the voltage induced in a wire. When he demonstrated his discoveries to an invited audience at the Royal Institution, he was asked the question 'What use is electricity, Mr Faraday?' He replied with another question 'What use is a new baby?' No one can tell what can grow from a new discovery.

Figure 4 *Michael Faraday*

Understanding electromagnetic induction

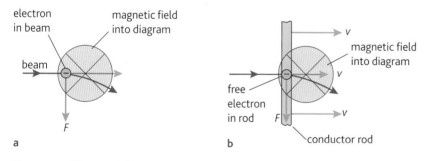

Figure 5 *Deflection of electrons in a magnetic field*

When a beam of electrons is directed across a magnetic field, each electron experiences a force at right angles to its direction of motion and to the field direction. A metal rod is a tube containing lots of free electrons. If the rod is moved across a magnetic field, as shown in Figure 5, the magnetic field forces the free electrons in the rod to one end away from the other end. So one end of the rod becomes negative and the other end positive. In this way, an emf is induced in the rod. The same effect happens if the magnetic field is moved and the rod is stationary. As long as there is relative motion between the rod and the magnetic field, an emf is induced in the rod. If the relative motion ceases, the induced

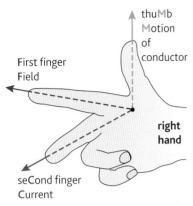

First finger
Field

thuMb
Motion
of
conductor

right
hand

seCond finger
Current

Figure 6 *Fleming's right-hand rule*

emf becomes zero because the magnetic field no longer exerts a force on
the electrons in the rod. Note that when the rod is part of a complete
circuit, the electrons are forced round the circuit. In other words, the
induced emf drives a current round the circuit.

■ The dynamo rule

In Figure 5, the magnetic field is into the plane of the diagram and the
motion of the conductor relative to the rod is rightwards. The electrons
in the rod are forced downwards. The direction of the induced current
can also be worked out using **Fleming's right-hand rule**, also referred to
as the **dynamo rule**, as shown in Figure 6. The direction of the induced
current is, in accordance with the current convention, opposite to the
direction of the flow of electrons in the conductor.

■ Summary questions

1 A coil of wire is connected to a sensitive meter.

  a Explain why the meter shows a brief reading when a magnet is pushed
into the coil.

  b State two ways in which the meter reading could be made larger.

2 An electric motor consists of a coil of wire between the poles of a
magnet. The motor is connected to a lamp. A thread wrapped round the
motor spindle is used to support a weight, as shown in Figure 2, p.120.

  a Explain why the lamp lights when the weight descends.

  b What difference would have been made if the magnet had been much
stronger?

  c Explain why a lamp connected to a dynamo lights when the dynamo
turns.

  d Why is the dynamo easier to turn when the lamp is disconnected?

3 A horizontal rod aligned along a line from east to west is dropped
through a horizontal magnetic field which is directed from south to
north.

  a i What is the direction of the velocity of the rod?

    ii Determine which end of the rod is positive. Explain your answer.

  b Explain why no emf is induced in the rod if it is aligned from north to
south then dropped in the field.

8.2 The laws of electromagnetic induction

Learning objectives:

- What is magnetic flux, and magnetic flux linkage?

- How is the induced emf in a coil related to the magnetic flux linkage through it?

- What is Lenz's law and which conservation law explains it?

Specification reference: 3.4.5

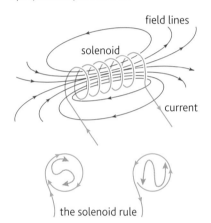

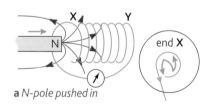

the solenoid rule

Figure 1 *The magnetic field near a solenoid*

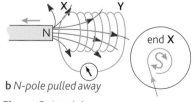

a *N-pole pushed in*

b *N-pole pulled away*

Figure 2 *Lenz's law*

Coils, currents and fields

A magnetic field is produced in and around a coil when it is connected to a battery and a current is passed through it. A magnetic compass near the coil is deflected when current passes through it. For a long coil or solenoid, the pattern of the magnetic field lines is like the pattern for a bar magnet – except the magnetic field lines near a bar magnet loop round from the north pole to the south pole of the magnet. Figure 1 shows the magnetic field pattern of a current-carrying solenoid. The field lines pass through the solenoid and loop round outside the solenoid from one end (the north pole) to the other end (the south pole). If each end in turn is viewed from outside the solenoid:

- current passes a**N**ticlockwise (or cou**N**terclockwise) round the '**N**orth pole' end,
- current passes clockwise round the 'south pole' end.

Lenz's law

When a bar magnet is pushed into a coil connected to a meter, the meter deflects. If the bar magnet is pulled out of the coil, the meter deflects in the opposite direction. What determines the direction of the induced current? Consider the North pole of a bar magnet approaching end X of a coil, as shown in Figure 2.

The induced current passing round the circuit creates a magnetic field due to the coil. The coil field must act against the incoming North pole, otherwise it would pull the N-pole in faster, making the induced current bigger, pulling the N-pole in even faster still, etc. Clearly, conservation of energy forbids this creation of kinetic and electrical energy from nowhere. So the induced current creates a magnetic field in the coil which opposes the incoming N-pole. The induced polarity of end X must therefore be a N-pole so as to repel the incoming N-pole. Therefore, the current must go round end X of the coil in an anticlockwise direction, as shown.

If the magnet is removed from inside the coil, the induced current passes round end X of the coil in a clockwise direction. This corresponds to an induced S-pole at end X which therefore opposes the magnet moving away.

Lenz's law states that the direction of the induced current is always such as to oppose the change that causes the current.

The explanation of Lenz's law is that energy is never created or destroyed. The induced current could never be in a direction to help the change that causes it; that would mean producing electrical energy from nowhere, which is forbidden!

Application

Regenerative braking

A battery-powered or hybrid electric vehicle contains an alternator that can be used as an electric motor or as a generator. When the alternator is used as an electric motor, it is driven by the batteries.

Figure 3 *An electric car*

When the brakes are applied, the alternator is used to generate electricity which is used to recharge the battery. Some of the kinetic energy is transferred to electrical energy in the battery. The induced current through the alternator coil creates a magnetic field that acts against the magnetic field of the alternator. So the alternator experiences a braking force which helps to slow the vehicle down.

The fuel consumption of a hybrid vehicle (i.e. a vehicle with a petrol engine and an electric motor) is significantly less than that of a petrol-only vehicle. This is because some of the hybrid vehicle's kinetic energy is converted to chemical energy in its battery when the vehicle brakes. The battery supplies this energy to the electric motor when it takes over from the petrol engine at low speeds.

■■■ Faraday's law of electromagnetic induction

Consider a conductor of length, l, which is part of a complete circuit cutting through the lines of a magnetic field of flux density B.

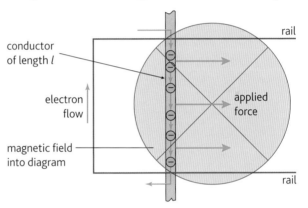

Figure 4 *Induced emf in a conductor*

> ■ **Note**
>
> Think carefully about the energy changes here. The energy transferred by the applied force (i.e. the work done) is transformed to electric energy. The circuit needs to be complete otherwise no induced current flows, no electrical energy is transferred and the applied force would make the rod move faster and faster.

An emf, E, is induced in the conductor and an induced current I passes round the circuit.

The conductor experiences a force $F = BIl$ due to carrying a current in a magnetic field. The force opposes the motion of the conductor and so an equal and opposite force must be applied to the conductor to keep it moving in the field. If the conductor moves a distance Δs in time Δt,

■ the work done W by the applied force is given by $W = F\Delta s = BIl\,\Delta s$.

■ the charge transfer along the conductor in this time $Q = I\Delta t$.

Therefore, the induced emf $\quad \varepsilon = \dfrac{W}{Q} = \dfrac{BIl\,\Delta s}{I\Delta t} = \dfrac{Bl\,\Delta s}{\Delta t}$

As $l\Delta s$ is the area A 'swept out' by the conductor in time Δt,

the induced emf, $\quad\quad\quad \varepsilon = \dfrac{BA}{\Delta t}$

The product of the **magnetic flux density**, B, and the area, A, swept out (= BA), is called the **magnetic flux**. The concept of magnetic flux is very useful for calculating induced emfs. The example of the conductor cutting across the field lines shows that the induced emf is equal to the magnetic flux swept out by the conductor each second. Michael Faraday was the first person to show how induced emfs could be calculated from magnetic flux changes.

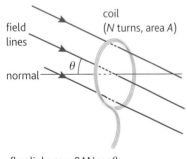

flux linkage = $BAN\cos\theta$

Figure 5 *Flux linkage*

▓ **Magnetic flux**, $\Phi = BA$.

▓ **Magnetic flux linkage** through a coil of N turns $= N\Phi = NBA$ where B is the magnetic flux density perpendicular to area A.

▓ The unit of magnetic flux is the **weber** (Wb), equal to $1\,\mathrm{T\,m^2}$.

Note that flux density B (in teslas) is the flux per unit area passing at right angles (i.e. normally) through the area. Therefore 1 tesla = 1 weber per square metre.

More about flux linkage

1 When the magnetic field is along the normal (i.e. perpendicular) to the coil face, the flux linkage $= N\Phi = BAN$.

2 When the coil is turned through $180°$, the flux linkage $= -BAN$.

3 When the magnetic field is parallel to the coil area, the flux linkage $= 0$ as no field lines pass through the coil area.

In general, when the magnetic field is at angle θ to the normal at the coil face, the flux linkage through the coil $N\Phi = BAN\cos\theta$

Faraday's law of electromagnetic induction states that the induced emf in a circuit is equal to the rate of change of flux linkage through the circuit.

Induced emf $\varepsilon = -N\dfrac{\Delta\Phi}{\Delta t}$

where $N\dfrac{\Delta\Phi}{\Delta t}$ is the change of flux linkage per second.

The minus sign represents the fact that the induced emf acts in such a direction as to opposite the change that causes it.

Examples

1 A moving conductor in a magnetic field

An emf is induced in the conductor provided the conductor cuts across the lines of the magnetic field. The direction of motion of the conductor in Figure 4 is at right angles to the field lines.

As explained earlier, the magnitude of the induced emf $\varepsilon = Bl\,\Delta s/\Delta t$, where l is the length of the conductor and Δs is the distance it moves in time Δt. Note that the change of flux in this time, $\Delta\Phi = Bl\,\Delta s$ so the change of flux per second, $\Delta\Phi/\Delta t$, is equal to the magnitude of the induced emf.

Because the speed of the conductor, $v = \Delta s/\Delta t$, the induced emf

$$\varepsilon = \frac{Bl\,\Delta s}{\Delta t} = Blv$$

Induced emf $\varepsilon = Blv$

2 A fixed coil in a changing magnetic field

Figure 6 shows a small coil on the axis of a current-carrying solenoid. The magnetic field of the solenoid passes through the small coil. If the current in the solenoid changes, an emf is induced in the small coil. This is because the magnetic field through the coil changes so the flux linkage through it changes, causing an induced emf.

The flux linkage through the coil, $N\Phi = BAN$, where A is the coil area and N is the number of turns of the coil. Suppose the magnetic flux density changes from B to $B + \Delta B$ in time Δt so the flux linkage changes by an amount $N\Delta\Phi$ $(= \Delta BAN)$.

The magnitude of the induced emf $= \dfrac{N\Delta\Phi}{\Delta t} = \dfrac{AN\Delta B}{\Delta t}$

Notes

1 The unit of flux change per second, the weber per second, is the same as the volt. Therefore, the weber is equal to 1 volt second.

2 Whenever the flux linkage through a circuit changes, an emf is induced in the circuit. The flux can be due to a permanent magnet or due to a current-carrying wire.

 a If the flux is due to a permanent magnet, motion of the magnet relative to the circuit is necessary to cause an induced emf. This is how an emf is generated in an ac generator or a dynamo.

 b If the flux is due to a current-carrying wire, changing the current in the wire causes an induced emf in the circuit. This is how an emf is generated in a **transformer** or an induction coil.

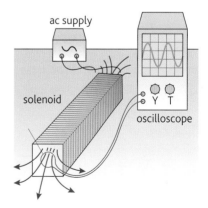

Figure 6 *A changing magnetic field*

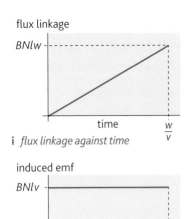

i *flux linkage against time*

ii *induced emf against time*

Figure 7 *Flux changes*

Because B is proportional to the current I in the solenoid, the magnitude of the induced emf is therefore proportional to the rate of change of current in the solenoid.

3 A rectangular coil moving into a uniform magnetic field

Consider a rectangular coil of N turns, length l and width w moving into a uniform magnetic field of flux density B at constant speed v. Figure 8 shows a similar situation. Suppose the coil enters the field at time $t = 0$.

▐ The time taken by the coil to enter the field completely $= \dfrac{\text{coil width}}{\text{speed}} = \dfrac{w}{v}$.

During this time, the flux linkage $N\Phi$ increases steadily from 0 to $BNlw$. Therefore, the change of flux linkage per second,

$$N\frac{\Delta \Phi}{\Delta t} = \frac{BNlw}{w/v} = BNlv$$

▐ When the coil is completely in the field, the flux linkage through it $(= BNlw)$ does not change so the induced emf is zero. In other words, the emf induced in the leading side is cancelled by the emf induced in the trailing side once the trailing side has entered the field. Figure 7 shows how the flux linkage and the induced emf change with time.

Summary questions

1 A uniform magnetic field of flux density 72 mT is confined to a region of width 60 mm, as shown in Figure 8. A rectangular coil of length 50 mm and width 20 mm has 15 turns. The coil is moved into the magnetic field at a speed of 10 mm s^{-1} with its longer edge parallel to the edge of the magnetic field.

a Calculate:

   i the flux linkage through the coil when it is completely in the field,

   ii the time taken for the flux linkage to increase from zero to its maximum value,

   iii the induced emf in the coil as it enters the field.

b i Sketch a graph to show how the flux linkage through the coil changes with time from the instant the coil enters the field to when it leaves the field completely.

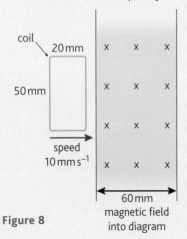

Figure 8

ii Sketch a graph to show how the induced emf in the coil varies with time.

2 A rectangular coil of length 40 mm and width 25 mm has 20 turns. The coil is in a uniform magnetic field of flux density 68 mT.

a Calculate the flux linkage through the coil when the coil is at right angles to the field lines.

b The coil is removed from the field in 60 ms. Calculate the mean value of the induced emf.

3 A circular coil of diameter 24 mm has 40 turns. The coil is placed in a uniform magnetic field of flux density 85 mT with its plane perpendicular to the field lines.

a Calculate:

   i the area of the coil in m^2,

   ii the flux linkage through the coil.

b The coil was reversed in a time of 95 ms. Calculate:

   i the change of flux linkage through the coil,

   ii the magnitude of the induced emf.

4 A small circular coil of diameter 15 mm and 25 turns is placed in a fixed position on the axis of a solenoid, as shown in Figure 7. The magnetic flux density of the solenoid at this position varies with current according to the equation $B = kI$, where $k = 1.2 \times 10^{-3}$ T A^{-1}.

a Calculate the flux linkage through the coil when the current in the solenoid is 1.5 A.

b The current in the solenoid was reduced from 1.5 A to zero in 0.20 s. Calculate the magnitude of the induced emf in the small coil.

8.3 The alternating current generator

Learning objectives:

- Which two features of the output voltage waveform change if the coil is turned faster?

- Why is the output alternating?

- Why is it preferable for practical generators to have fixed coils and a rotating (electro)magnet?

Specification reference: 3.4.5

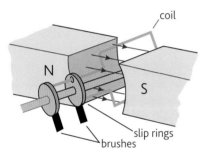

Figure 1 *The ac generator*

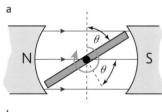

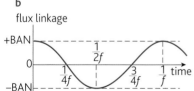

Figure 2 *Flux linkage in a spinning coil*

Link

Remember the peak value of an alternating pd = √2 × the rms value. See *AS Physics* Topic 6.1.

The alternating current generator

The simple ac generator consists of a rectangular coil that spins in a uniform magnetic field, as shown in Figure 1. When the coil spins at a steady rate, the flux linkage changes continuously. At an instant when the normal to the plane of the coil is at angle θ to the field lines, the flux linkage through the coil, $N\Phi = BAN\cos\theta$, where B is the magnetic flux density, A is the coil area and N is the number of turns on the coil.

For a coil spinning at a steady frequency, f, $\theta = 2\pi ft$ at time t after $\theta = 0$. So the flux linkage $N\Phi$ ($= BAN \cos 2\pi ft$) changes with time as shown in Figure 2.

- The gradient of the graph is the change of flux linkage per second, $\dfrac{N\Delta\Phi}{\Delta t}$, so it represents the induced emf. It can be shown mathematically that the induced emf alternates according to the equation

$$\varepsilon = \varepsilon_0 \sin 2\pi ft$$

where f is the frequency of rotation of the coil and ε_0 is the peak emf. The above equation may be written as $\varepsilon = \varepsilon_0 \sin\omega t$ as the angular frequency of the coil, $\omega = 2\pi f$

- The induced emf is zero when the sides of the coil move parallel to the field lines. At this position, the rate of change of flux is zero and the sides of the coil do not cut the field lines.

- The induced emf is a maximum when the sides of the coil cut at right angles across the field lines. At this position, the emf induced in each wire of each side $= Blv$, where v is the speed of each wire and l is its length. So for N turns and two sides, the induced emf at this position $\varepsilon_0 = 2NBlv$. The equation shows that the peak emf can be increased by increasing the speed (i.e. the frequency of rotation) or using a stronger magnet or a bigger coil or a coil with more turns.

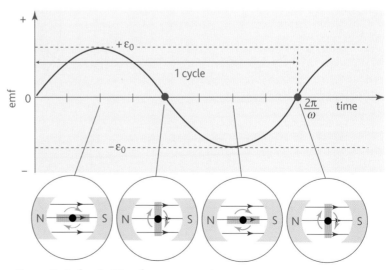

Figure 3 *Emf against time for an ac generator*

Notes

1 As the speed of each side, $v =$ circumference × frequency = πwf, where w is the width of the coil, then $\varepsilon_0 = 2NBlv = 2\pi fNBA$ where the coil area $A = lw$.

Substituting $\omega = 2\pi f$
gives $\varepsilon_0 = BAN\omega$
hence $\varepsilon = BAN\omega \sin \omega t$

2 A dc generator can be made by replacing the two slip rings of the ac generator with a split-ring, as shown in Figure 4. The emf does not reverse its polarity because the connections between the split-ring and the brushes reverse every half cycle.

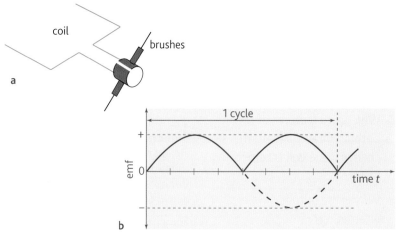

Figure 4 *The dc generator a The split-ring commutator b emf against time*

Application

Power station alternators

A power station alternator has three sets of coils at 120° to one another. Each set of coils produces an alternating emf 120° out of phase with each of the other two emfs. The coils are called the 'stators' because they are stationary, so they don't need slip ring connectors and an electromagnet called the 'rotor' spins between them.

The electromagnet is supplied with current from a dc generator. So the turning of the rotor induces an alternating emf in each set of stator coils. The three phases are distributed via transformers and power lines to factories and local sub-stations. A local sub-station supplies mains electricity to local premises, a third on each of the three phases. This is why your home can sometimes suffer a blackout when other homes nearby still have electricity. This happens when a fault in the local sub-station cuts out one phase but not the others.

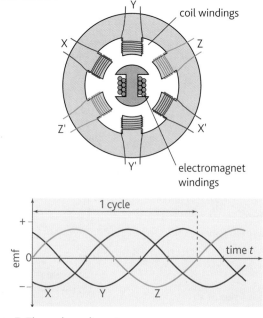

Figure 5 *Three-phase alternator*

Back emf

An emf is induced in the spinning coil of an electric motor because the flux linkage through the coil changes. The induced emf ε is referred to as a **back emf** because it acts against the pd. V applied to the motor in accordance with Lenz's law. At any instant, $V - \varepsilon = IR$, where I is the current through the motor coil and R is the circuit resistance.

Because the induced emf is proportional to the speed of rotation of the motor, the current changes as the motor speed changes.

- At low speed, the current is high because the induced emf is small.
- At high speed, the current is low because the induced emf is high.

Note:

Multiplying the equation $V - \varepsilon = IR$ by I throughout gives $IV - I\varepsilon = I^2R$

Rearranging this equation gives:

electrical power supplied by the source IV	=	electrical power transferred to mechanical power $I\varepsilon$	+	electrical power wasted due to circuit resistance I^2R

Application

When the motor spins without driving a load, it spins at high speed so the current is very small because the back emf is large. Its speed is limited by friction in the bearings and by air resistance. So it uses very little power.

When the motor is used to drive a load, its speed is much less than when off-load so the back emf is smaller and the current is larger. The power it uses from the voltage source that is not transferred as mechanical power to the load is wasted due to the resistance heating effect of the electrical current.

Summary questions

1. a An ac generator produces an alternating emf with a peak value of 8.0V and a frequency of 20 Hz. Sketch a graph to show how the emf varies with time.

    b The frequency of rotation of the ac generator in a is increased to 30 Hz. On the same axes, sketch a graph to show how the emf varies with time at 30 Hz.

2. A rectangular coil of N turns and area A spins at a constant frequency f in a uniform magnetic field of flux density B. Complete the table to show how the flux linkage and induced emf relate to the orientation of the coil during one cycle of rotation.

time	orientation of coil	flux linkage	induced emf
0	parallel to field	?	$+\varepsilon_0$
0.25/f	perpendicular to field	$+ BAN$	?
0.50/f	parallel to field	?	?
0.75/f	perpendicular to field	?	?

3. The coil of an ac generator has 80 turns, a length of 65 mm and a width of 38 mm. It spins in a uniform magnetic field of flux density 130 mT at a constant frequency of 50 Hz.

    a Calculate the maximum flux linkage through the coil.

    b i Show each side of the coil moves at a speed of 6.0 m s^{-1},

    ii Show that the peak voltage is 8.1V.

4. An electric motor is to be used to move a variable load. The motor is connected in series with a battery and an ammeter.

    a Explain why the motor current is very small when the load is zero.

    b Explain why the motor current increases when the load is increased.

8.4 Transformers

Learning objectives:

- What is the purpose of transformers?

- What energy changes take place in a transformer?

- How is the efficiency of transformers improved by better design?

Specification reference: 3.4.5

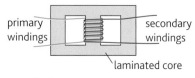

a *practical arrangement*

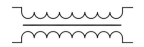

b *transformer symbol*

Figure 1 *The transformer*

The transformer rule

A transformer changes an alternating pd to a different peak value. Any transformer consists of two coils: the primary coil and the secondary coil. The two coils have the same iron core. When the primary coil is connected to a source of alternating pd, an alternating magnetic field is produced in the core. The field passes through the secondary coil. So an alternating emf is induced in the secondary coil by the changing magnetic field. The symbol for the transformer is shown in Figure 1.

A transformer is designed so that all the magnetic flux produced by the primary coil passes through the secondary coil.

Let Φ = the flux in the core passing through each turn at an instant when an alternating pd V_P is applied to the primary coil.

- The flux linkage in the secondary coil = $N_S\Phi$, where N_S is the number of turns on the secondary coil. From Faraday's law, the induced emf in the secondary coil, $V_S = N_S \dfrac{\Delta\Phi}{\Delta t}$

- The flux linkage in the primary coil = $N_P\Phi$, where N_P is the number of turns on the primary coil. From Faraday's law, the induced emf in the primary coil = $N_P \dfrac{\Delta\Phi}{\Delta t}$

The induced emf in the primary coil opposes the pd applied to the primary coil, V_P. Assuming the resistance of the primary coil is negligible, so all the applied pd acts against the induced emf in the primary coil, the applied pd

$$V_P = N_P \frac{\Delta\Phi}{\Delta t}$$

Dividing the equation for V_S by the equation for V_P gives

$$\frac{V_S}{V_P} = N_S \frac{\Delta\Phi}{\Delta t} \Big/ N_P \frac{\Delta\Phi}{\Delta t}$$

Cancelling $\dfrac{\Delta\Phi}{\Delta t}$ from this equation gives the **transformer rule**:

$$\frac{V_S}{V_P} = \frac{N_S}{N_P}$$

- A **step-up transformer** has more turns on the secondary coil than on the primary coil. So the secondary voltage is stepped up compared with the primary voltage (i.e. $N_S > N_P$ so $V_S > V_P$).

- A **step-down transformer** has fewer turns on the secondary coil than on the primary coil. So the secondary voltage is stepped down compared with the primary voltage (i.e. $N_S < N_P$ so $V_S < V_P$).

Transformer efficiency

Transformers are almost 100% efficient because they are designed with:

1 low-resistance windings to reduce power wasted due to the heating effect of the current.

2 a laminated core which consists of layers of iron separated by layers of insulator. Induced currents in the core itself, referred to as **eddy currents**,

are reduced in this way so the magnetic flux is as high as possible. Also, the heating effect of the induced currents in the core is reduced.

3 a core of '**soft iron**' which is easily magnetised and demagnetised. This reduces power wasted through repeated magnetisation and demagnetisation of the core.

$$\text{The efficiency of a transformer } = \frac{\text{power delivered by the secondary coil}}{\text{power supplied to the primary coil}}$$

$$= \frac{I_s V_s}{I_p V_p} \times 100\%$$

When a device (e.g. a lamp) is connected to the secondary coil, because the efficiency of a transformer is almost equal to 100%,

$$\begin{array}{c} \text{the electrical power supplied} \\ \text{to the primary coil} \end{array} = \begin{array}{c} \text{the electrical power supplied} \\ \text{by the secondary coil} \end{array}$$

Therefore, the current ratio $\dfrac{I_s}{I_p} = \dfrac{V_p}{V_s} = \dfrac{N_p}{N_s}$

▦ In a step-up transformer, the voltage is stepped up and the current is stepped down.

▦ In a step-down transformer, the voltage is stepped down and the current is stepped up.

*Worked example:*_____

A transformer is used to step down 230V mains to 12V. When a 12V 48W lamp is connected to the transformer's secondary coil, the lamp lights normally.

a The transformer has 1150 turns on its primary coil. Calculate the number of turns on its secondary coil.

b When the lamp is on, the primary current in the transformer is 0.22A. Calculate:

   i the current in the secondary coil,

   ii the efficiency of the transformer.

Solution

a Rearranging $\dfrac{V_s}{V_p} = \dfrac{N_s}{N_p}$ gives $N_s = N_p \dfrac{V_s}{V_p} = \dfrac{1150 \times 12}{230} = 60$ turns

b i The power supplied to the lamp $= I_s V_s = 48\,\text{W}$

   therefore $I_s = \dfrac{48}{V_s} = \dfrac{48}{12} = 4.0\,\text{A}$

   ii Efficiency $= \dfrac{I_s V_s}{I_p V_p} = \dfrac{48}{230 \times 0.22} = 0.95\ (= 95\%)$

▦ The Grid System

Electricity from power stations in the United Kingdom is fed into **The National Grid System** which supplies electricity to most parts of the country. The National Grid is a network of transformers and cables, underground and on pylons, which covers all regions of the U.K. Each power station generates alternating current at a precise frequency of 50 Hz at about 25 kV.

▮ Note

The changing magnetic flux in the core induces a **back emf** in the primary coil as well as an emf in the secondary coil. The back emf acts against the primary voltage, making the primary current very small when the secondary current is 'off'.

When the secondary current is on, the magnetic field it creates is in the opposite direction to the magnetic field of the primary current. In this situation, the back emf in the primary coil is reduced so the primary current is larger than when the secondary current is off.

AQA **Examiner's tip**

Transformers only work if the magnetic flux through them is changing; they won't work with steady dc.

A *step-down* transformer steps down the voltage but *increases* the current.

Summary questions

1 a Explain why an alternating emf is induced in the secondary coil of a transformer when the primary coil is connected to an alternating voltage supply.

b In terms of electrical power, explain why the current through the primary coil of a transformer increases when a device is connected to the secondary coil.

2 a Explain why a transformer is designed so that as much of the magnetic flux produced by the primary coil of a transformer passes through the secondary coil.

b Explain why a transformer works using alternating current but not using direct current.

3 A transformer has a primary coil with 120 turns and a secondary coil with 2400 turns.

a Calculate the primary voltage needed for a secondary voltage of 230V.

b A 230 V 60 W lamp is connected to its secondary coil. Calculate the current through

i the secondary coil,

ii the primary coil.

State any assumptions made in this calculation.

4 a Explain why transmission of electrical power over a long distance is more efficient at high voltage than at low voltage.

b A power cable of resistance 200 Ω is to be used to deliver 2.0 MW of electrical power at 120 kV from a power station to an industrial estate. Calculate:

i the current through the cable,

ii the power wasted in the cable.

Step-up transformers at the power station increase the alternating voltage to 400 kV or more for long-distance transmission via the grid system. Step-down transformers operate in stages, as shown in Figure 2. Factories are supplied with all three phases at either 33 kV or 11 kV. Homes are supplied via a local transformer sub-station with single-phase ac at 230 V.

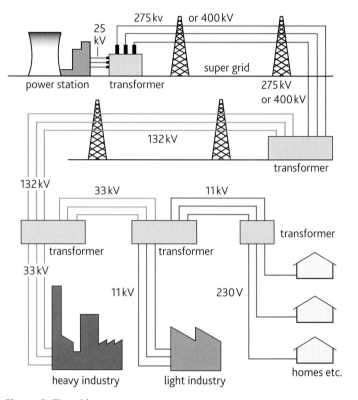

Figure 2 *The grid system*

Transmission of electrical power over long distances is much more efficient at high voltage than at low voltage. The reason is that the current needed to deliver a certain amount of power is reduced if the voltage is increased. So power wasted due to the heating effect of the current through the cables is reduced. To deliver power P at voltage V, the current required $I = P/V$. If the resistance of the cables is R, the power wasted through heating the cables is $I^2R = P^2R/V^2$. Therefore, the higher the voltage is, the smaller the ratio of the wasted power to the power transmitted is.

For example, for transmission of 1 MW of power through cables of resistance 500 Ω at 25 kV, the current necessary would be 40 A (= 1 MW/25 kV) so the power wasted would be 0.8 MW (= I^2R = 40² × 500 W). Prove for yourself that at 400 kV, the power wasted would be about 3 kW. Check your answer using the equation derived above.

Link

Superconducting cables would be even more efficient. At present, materials that are superconducting at sufficiently high temperatures do not exist. See *AS Physics* Topic 4.3.

AQA Examination-style questions

1 A coil is connected to a centre zero ammeter, as shown in **Figure 1**. A student drops a magnet so that it falls vertically and completely through the coil.

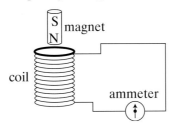

Figure 1

(a) Describe what the student would observe on the ammeter as the magnet falls through the coil. *(2 marks)*

(b) If the coil were not present the magnet would accelerate downwards at the acceleration due to gravity. State and explain how its acceleration in the student's experiment would be affected, if at all,

    (i) as it entered the coil,

    (ii) as it left the coil. *(4 marks)*

(c) Suppose the student forgot to connect the ammeter to the coil, therefore leaving the circuit incomplete, before carrying out the experiment. Describe and explain what difference this would make to your conclusions in part (b). *(3 marks)*

AQA, 2004

2 Faraday's law of electromagnetic induction predicts that the induced emf, E, in a coil is given by

$$\frac{\Delta(N\Phi)}{t}.$$

(a) (i) What quantity does the symbol Φ represent?

    (ii) State the SI unit for Φ. *(2 marks)*

(b) In **Figure 2** the magnet forms the bob of a simple pendulum. The magnet oscillates with a small amplitude along the axis of a 240 turn coil that has a cross-sectional area of $2.5 \times 10^{-4} \, \text{m}^2$.

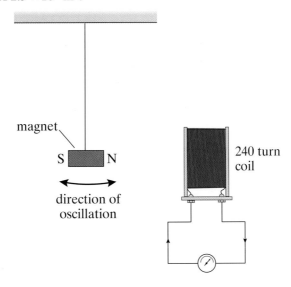

Figure 2

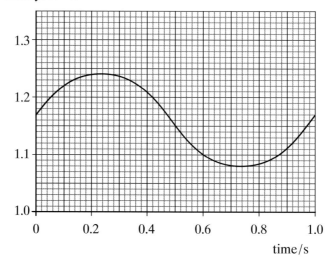

magnetic flux density/10^{-2} T

time/s

Figure 3

Figure 3 shows how the magnetic flux density, B, through the coil varies with time, t, for one complete oscillation of the magnet. The magnetic flux density through the coil can be assumed to be uniform.

(i) Calculate the maximum emf induced in the coil.

(ii) Sketch a graph to show how the induced emf in the coil varies during the same time interval.

(iii) Explain how the pendulum may be modified to double the frequency of oscillation of the magnet.

(iv) The frequency of oscillation of the magnet is increased without changing the amplitude. Explain why this increases the maximum induced emf.

(v) State **two** other ways of increasing the maximum induced emf. *(11 marks)*

AQA, 2003

3 **Figure 4** shows a system used by an engineer to determine the rate of revolution of a rotating axle.

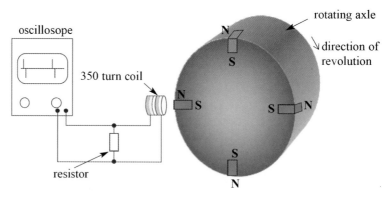

Figure 4

Four small bar magnets are embedded in the axle as shown. The N pole of each magnet is towards the outside of the axle. A voltage is produced between the terminals of a coil placed close to the rotating axle. The voltage produced is monitored using an oscilloscope. The waveform produced is shown in **Figure 5**.

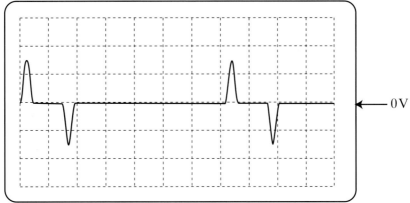

Oscilloscope grid marked in cm
The Y amplifier setting = 5 mV cm⁻¹
The time-base setting   = 10 ms cm⁻¹

Figure 5

(a) Determine the number of revolutions made by the axle in one minute. *(3 marks)*

(b) (i) Use Faraday's law to explain how the voltage pulses are produced.

  (ii) The coil has 350 turns. Determine the maximum rate of change of flux through the coil. *(6 marks)*

(c) Use Lenz's law to explain the production of positive and negative voltage pulses. *(3 marks)*

(d) Draw on a copy of **Figure 5** the waveform that shows the changes you would expect to see when the rate of revolution of the axle increases. *(3 marks)*

AQA, 2007

4 (a) Copy and complete the diagram in **Figure 6** to show a current balance, which may be used to measure the magnetic flux density between the poles of the ceramic magnets. Clearly label the directions of the current and the magnetic force acting on the conductor in the field.

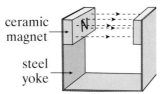

ceramic
magnet

steel
yoke

Figure 6 *(3 marks)*

(b) (i) The armature of a simple motor consists of a square coil of 20 turns and carries a current of 0.55 A just before it starts to move. The lengths of the sides of the coil are 0.15 m and they are positioned perpendicular to a magnetic field of flux density 40 mT. Calculate the force on each side of the coil.

  (ii) Explain why the current falls below 0.55 A once the coil of the motor is rotating.

  (iii) The resistance of the coil is 0.50 Ω. When the coil is rotating at a constant rate the minimum current in the coil is found to be 0.14 A. Calculate the maximum rate at which the flux is cut by the coil. *(8 marks)*

AQA, 2003

5 (a) Explain what is meant by the term *magnetic flux linkage*. State its unit. *(2 marks)*

(b) Explain, in terms of electromagnetic induction, how a transformer may be used to step down voltage. *(4 marks)*

(c) A minidisc player is provided with a mains adapter. The adapter uses a transformer with a turns ratio of 15 : 1 to step down the mains voltage from 230 V.

  (i) Calculate the output voltage of the transformer.

  (ii) State **two** reasons why the transformer may be less than 100% efficient. *(4 marks)*

AQA, 2004

6 (a) A transformer, operating from 230 V, supplies a 12 V garden lighting system consisting of 8 lamps. Each lamp is rated at 30 W and they are connected in parallel.

   (i) The primary coil of the transformer has 3000 turns. Calculate the number of turns on the secondary coil.

   (ii) Show that the total resistance of the lamps when they are working at normal brightness is 0.60 Ω.

   (iii) Calculate the power input to the transformer, assuming that the transformer is perfectly efficient. *(8 marks)*

(b) **Figure 7** shows a brass pendulum bob swinging through the magnetic field above a strong magnet. Its oscillations are observed to be quite heavily damped.

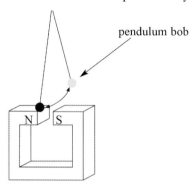

pendulum bob

Figure 7

Explain, using the principles of electromagnetic induction, why this pendulum is heavily damped. *(4 marks)*

AQA, 2006

7 (a) Electrical power is transmitted through cables of total resistance 1.8 Ω, operated with alternating current at an rms voltage of 11 kV. The power supplied to the input of the cables is 960 kW. Calculate

   (i) the peak value of the current in the cables,

   (ii) the percentage of the input power that is available at the output end of the cables. *(7 marks)*

(b) When public electricity supplies were first introduced, many of the power stations generated direct current. This meant that premises that were a large distance from the power station could not be supplied economically with electricity.

   Discuss this by reference to the physical principles involved, stating why ac is now preferred for distributing electrical power. *(5 marks)*

AQA✓ Examination-style questions

Unit 4: Fields and further mechanics

1   The pile-driver crane in **Figure 1** is used on a construction
    site to drive a steel girder vertically into the ground.
    The hammer of the pile-driver is raised and dropped
    repeatedly onto the upper end of the girder.

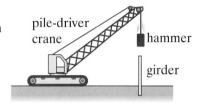

Figure 1

   (a) The hammer is a steel cylinder of length 1.50 m
        and diameter 0.60 m.
        (i)   Calculate the mass of the cylinder.
              density of steel = $7800\,\text{kg}\,\text{m}^{-3}$
        (ii) The hammer is released from a height of 0.80 m above the top end of the girder.
              Calculate the velocity of the hammer just before it hits the girder.   *(4 marks)*
   (b) (i)   The girder has a mass of 1600 kg. Calculate its velocity immediately after the
              impact, assuming the hammer does not rebound after the impact.
        (ii) The impact causes the girder to penetrate 25 mm into the ground. Estimate
              the average force of friction on the girder during this movement.   *(6 marks)*

AQA, 2007

2   In a football match, a player kicks a stationary football of mass 0.44 kg and gives it a
    speed of $32\,\text{m}\,\text{s}^{-1}$.
   (a) (i)   Calculate the change of momentum of the football.
        (ii) The contact time between the football and the footballer's boot was 9.2 ms.
              Calculate the average force of impact on the football.   *(3 marks)*
   (b) A video recording showed that the toe of the boot was moving on a circular arc of
        radius 0.62 m centred on the knee joint when the football was struck. The force of
        the impact slowed the boot down from a speed of $24\,\text{m}\,\text{s}^{-1}$ to a speed of $15\,\text{m}\,\text{s}^{-1}$.
        (i)   Calculate the deceleration of the boot along the line of the impact force
              when it struck the football.
        (ii) Calculate the centripetal acceleration of the boot just before impact.
        (iii) Discuss briefly the radial force on the knee joint before impact and during
              the impact.   *(4 marks)*

AQA, 2005

3   When the wheels of a car rotate at 6.5 revolutions per second the external rear view
    mirror vibrates violently. This is because the centre of mass of one of the wheels is not
    at the centre of the wheel. To correct this, a mass of 0.015 kg is attached to the rim of
    the wheel 0.25 m from the centre of the wheel as shown in **Figure 2**.

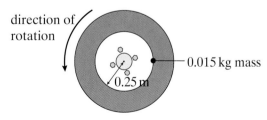

Figure 2

   (a) (i)   Calculate the force exerted by the wheel on the 0.015 kg mass due to the
              rotation of the wheel.
        (ii) Copy **Figure 2** and draw an arrow to show the direction the 0.015 kg mass would
              move if it became detached when in the position shown in **Figure 2** while the
              wheel is rotating.   *(4 marks)*

(b) Sketch a graph to show how the vertical component of the force acting on the 0.015 kg mass due to the rotation of the wheel varies with time, *t*, during one complete rotation of the wheel. At *t* = 0 the 0.015 kg mass is in the position shown in **Figure 2**. Show upwards force as positive and downwards force as negative, and include a suitable time scale. *(2 marks)*

(c) Without the mass in place, the rotation of the wheel makes the external rear-view mirror of the car undergo forced vibrations.

Explain what is meant by *forced vibrations* and state and explain how these vibrations will vary as the car increases in speed from rest. *(7 marks)*

AQA 2004

4   The rotor of a model helicopter has four blades. Each of the blades is 0.55 m long with a uniform cross-sectional area of 3.5×10^{-4} m² and negligible mass. An end-cap of mass 1.5 kg is attached to the outer end of each blade.

(a) (i) Show that there is a force of about 7 kN acting on each end-cap when the blades rotate at 15 revolutions per second.

   (ii) State the direction in which the force acts on the end-cap.

   (iii) Show that this force leads to a longitudinal stress in the blade of about 20 MPa.

   (iv) Calculate the change in length of the blade as a result of its rotation.
      Young modulus of the blade material = 6.0×10^{10} Pa

   (v) Calculate the total strain energy stored in **one** of the blades due to its extension. *(10 marks)*

(b) The model helicopter can be made to hover above a point on the ground by directing the air from the rotors vertically downwards at speed *v*.

   (i) Show that the change in momentum of the air each second is $A\rho v^2$, where *A* is the area swept out by the blades in one revolution and ρ is the density of air.

   (ii) The model helicopter has a weight of 900 N. Calculate the speed of the air downwards when the helicopter has no vertical motion.
      Density of air = 1.3 kg m⁻³ *(5 marks)*

AQA 2003

5   When the pump of a central heating system reaches a certain speed after being switched on, a straight section of a pipe vibrates strongly.

(a) Explain why the pipe vibrates strongly at a certain pump speed.

(b) State and explain **one** way to reduce these vibrations of the pipe. *(5 marks)*

AQA 2006

6   The International Space Station (ISS) moves in a circular orbit around the Earth at a speed of 7.68 km s⁻¹ and at a height of 380 km above the Earth's surface.

(a) Calculate the centripetal acceleration of the ISS. *(3 marks)*

(b) Explain why a scientist working on board the ISS experiences 'apparent weightlessness'. *(2 marks)*

This state of apparent weightlessness makes the space station an ideal laboratory for experiments in 'zero gravity', conditions such as the study of lattice vibrations in solids.

(c) **Figure 3** shows a mass–spring system which, in zero gravity, provides a good model of forces acting on an atom in a solid lattice.

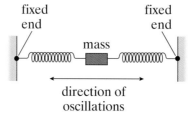

Figure 3

When the mass is displaced and released it oscillates as shown. The motion is very similar to the motion in one dimension of an atom in a crystalline solid. The springs behave like the bonds between adjacent atoms.

(i) The mass in the model system is 2.0 kg and it oscillates with a period of 1.2 s. Show that the stiffness of the spring system is about 55 N m⁻¹.

(ii) The bonds between the atoms in a particular solid have the same stiffness as the model system and the mass of the oscillating atom is 4.7×10^{-26} kg. Calculate the frequency of oscillation of the atom. *(4 marks)*

AQA 2005

7   **Figure 4** shows a way to measure the mass of a lorry. The vehicle and its contents are driven onto a platform mounted on a spring. The platform is then made to oscillate vertically and the mass is found from a measurement of the natural frequency of oscillation.

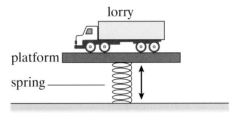

Figure 4

(a) (i) State whether the period of oscillation increases, decreases or remains unchanged when the amplitude of oscillation of the platform is reduced.

(ii) The spring constant k of the supporting spring is increased to four times its original value.

State the value of the ratio

$$\frac{\text{new oscillation period}}{\text{old oscillation period}}$$

(iii) The time period of oscillation is T when a lorry is on the platform. The spring constant of the spring is k. Show that the total mass M of lorry and platform is given by

$$M = \frac{kT^2}{4\pi^2}$$

(iv) A lorry and its contents have a total mass of 5300 kg. The spring constant of the supporting spring k is 1.9×10^5 N m⁻¹. The frequency of oscillation of the platform with the lorry resting on it is 0.91 Hz.

Calculate the mass of the platform. *(7 marks)*

(b) The driver is required to turn off the vehicle engine whilst the measurement is taking place.

The driver of the lorry in part (a)(iv) fails to do this and slowly increases the frequency of vibration of his vehicle from 0.5 Hz to about 4 Hz whilst the measurement is in progress and the platform is free to move. Describe and explain how the amplitude and frequency of the platform vary as this frequency increase occurs. You should use a sketch graph to support your answer. *(4 marks)*

AQA 2003

8   Whilst investigating the oscillations of a helical spring, a student carried out measurements when various masses were suspended from the spring. For each mass, the length l of the spring was measured and 50 vertical oscillations were timed. The results are shown in the table. *(2 marks)*

length l/mm	time for 50 oscillations/s	time period T/s	T^2/s²
316	12.5	0.25	0.063
333	17.5		
349	22.0		
364	25.5		
381	28.5		
397	31.0		

(a) Copy and complete the table.

(b) (i) Assuming that the spring obeys Hooke's law, show that

$$T^2 = 4\pi^2 \frac{(l - l_0)}{g}$$

where l_0 is the length of the unloaded spring and T is the time period of vertical oscillations.

    (ii) Plot a graph of T^2 against l.

    (iii) Use the graph to determine values for g and l_0. *(9 marks)*

(c) Estimate the value of l which would give a time period of 1.00 s. State and explain **one** reason why the behaviour of the spring may cause your estimated value to be incorrect. *(4 marks)*

AQA 2005

9 (a) (i) State **one** similarity of electric and gravitational fields.

    (ii) State **one** difference between electric and gravitational fields. *(2 marks)*

(b) A satellite of mass 165 kg has the radius of its orbit reduced from 4.24×10^7 m to 8.08×10^6 m.

Calculate the change in potential energy of the satellite and state whether it is an increase or a decrease. *(3 marks)*

(c) The orbital change mentioned in part (b) reduces the period of the orbit from 24 hours to 2 hours. State and explain why each of these orbits is useful for information collection or transfer. *(3 marks)*

AQA 2005

10 (a) State the factors that affect the gravitational field strength at the surface of a planet. *(2 marks)*

(b) **Figure 5** shows the variation, called an anomaly, of gravitational field strength at the Earth's surface in a region where there is a large spherical granite rock buried in the Earth's crust.

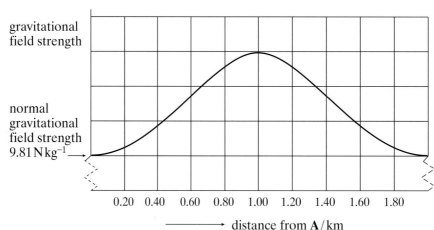

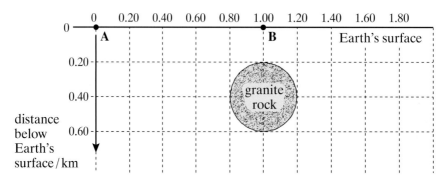

Figure 5

The density of the granite rock is $3700\,\text{kg}\,\text{m}^{-3}$ and the mean density of the surrounding material is $2200\,\text{kg}\,\text{m}^{-3}$.

  (i) Show that the difference between the mass of the granite rock and the mass of an equivalent volume of the surrounding material is $5.0 \times 10^{10}\,\text{kg}$.

  (ii) Calculate the difference between the gravitational field strength at B and that at point A on the Earth's surface that is a long way from the granite rock.

  (iii) Describe how the graph of gravitational field strength would change if the granite rock were buried deeper in the Earth's crust.

(9 marks)

AQA 2003

11 A dish on a communications satellite is used to transmit a beam of microwaves of wavelength λ. The beam spreads with an angular width $\dfrac{\lambda}{d}$, in radians, where d is the diameter of the dish.

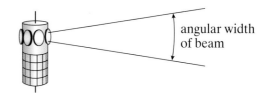

Figure 6

  (a) (i) Calculate the angular width, in degrees, of a beam of frequency $1200\,\text{MHz}$ transmitted using a dish of diameter $1.8\,\text{m}$.

    (ii) Show that the beam has a width of $2100\,\text{km}$ at a distance of $15\,000\,\text{km}$ from the satellite.

(4 marks)

  (b) (i) Show that the speed, v, of a satellite in a circular orbit at height h above the Earth is given by

$$v = \sqrt{\frac{GM}{R + h}}$$

    where R is the radius of the Earth and M is the mass of the Earth.

    (ii) Calculate the speed and the time period of a satellite at a height of $15\,000\,\text{km}$ in a circular orbit about the Earth.

    (iii) The satellite passes directly over a stationary receiver at the North Pole. Show that the beam moves at a speed of $1.3\,\text{km}\,\text{s}^{-1}$ across the Earth's surface and that the receiver can remain in contact with the satellite for no more than 27 minutes each orbit.

(9 marks)

AQA 2005

12 The hydrogen atom may be represented as a central proton with an electron moving in a circular orbit around it as shown in **Figure 7**. When the atom is in the ground state, the radius of the electron's orbit is $5.3 \times 10^{-11}\,\text{m}$.

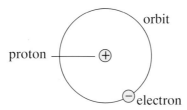

Figure 7

  (a) By applying this model to the hydrogen atom in the ground state, calculate:

    (i) the force of electrostatic attraction between the electron and the proton,

    (ii) the speed of the electron,

    (iii) the ratio of the de Broglie wavelength of the electron to the circumference of the orbit.

(6 marks)

(b) The total energy of the electron in a hydrogen atom may be shown to have discrete values given, in J, by

$$E = \frac{2.2 \times 10^{-18}}{n^2}$$

where $n = 1$ for the ground state, $n = 2$ for the first excited state, and so on.

(i) Calculate the wavelength of the light emitted when the electron returns to the ground state from the first excited state.

(ii) Explain why visible light will not be produced by any transition in which the electron returns to the ground state.

(5 marks)

AQA 2005

13 (a) An α particle emitted from a certain isotope has a kinetic energy of 2.8 MeV.

(i) Show that the speed of the α particle immediately after it is emitted is $1.2 \times 10^7 \, \text{m s}^{-1}$.

(ii) Calculate the de Broglie wavelength of the α particle immediately after it is emitted.

(4 marks)

(b) In a Rutherford scattering experiment, a beam of 2.8 MeV α particles is directed normally at a thin gold foil. An α particle in the beam approaches the nucleus of an atom of the gold isotope head on as shown in **Figure 8**.

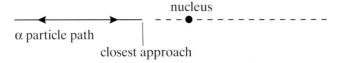

Figure 8

(i) Calculate the least distance of approach of the α particle from the centre of the gold nucleus.

(ii) By comparing your answers to part (a)(ii) and part (b)(i), explain why diffraction of α particles by the gold nuclei is not significant.

(5 marks)

AQA 2004

14 Two capacitors **A** and **B** are separately charged to a pd of 40.0 V before being discharged through the same resistor of value 10.0 kΩ. The discharge curves are shown in **Figure 9**.

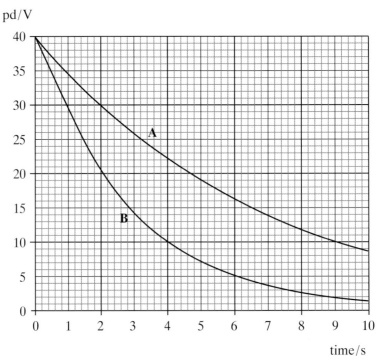

Figure 9

(a) Show that the time for the pd across capacitor **A** to halve is always approximately 4.5 s.

(b) Calculate the capacitance of **A**.

(c) Calculate the energy dissipated in the resistor in the interval between $t = 0$ and $t = 4.0$ s as capacitor **B** discharges. *(8 marks)*

AQA 2007

15 **Figure 10** shows a motor lifting a small mass. The energy required comes from a charged capacitor.

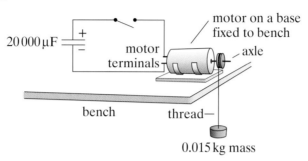

Figure 10

The capacitor was charged to a potential difference of 4.5 V and then discharged through the motor.

(a) (i) The motor only operates when the voltage at its terminals is at least 2.5 V.

Calculate the energy delivered to the motor when the potential difference across the capacitor falls from 4.5 V to 2.5 V.

(ii) The motor lifted the mass through a distance of 0.35 m. Calculate the efficiency of the transfer of energy from the capacitor to gravitational potential energy of the mass. Give your answer as a percentage.

(iii) Give **two** reasons why the transfer is inefficient. *(7 marks)*

(b) The motor operated for 1.3 s as the capacitor discharged from 4.5 V to 2.5 V.

Calculate:

(i) the average useful power developed in lifting the mass,

(ii) the effective resistance of the motor, assuming that it remained constant. *(5 marks)*

AQA 2004

16 A steel wire of diameter 0.24 mm is stretched between two fixed points 0.71 m apart. A U-shaped magnet is placed at the centre of the wire so that the wire passes between its poles, as shown in **Figure 11**.

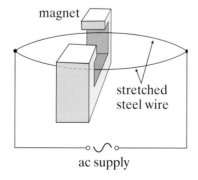

Figure 11

(a) (i) Explain why the wire vibrates when an alternating current is passed through it.

(ii) Explain why the wire vibrates strongly in its fundamental mode when the frequency of the alternating current is 290 Hz.

(iii) Show that the speed of the waves on the wire is 410 m s^{-1}. *(6 marks)*

(b) The speed, c, of waves on a wire of mass per unit length, μ, is related to the tension, T, in the wire by

$$c = \sqrt{\frac{T}{\mu}}$$

    (i)   The wire in **Figure 11** is at a tension of 60 N. Calculate its mass per unit length.

    (ii) Hence calculate the density of the metal. *(5 marks)*

AQA 2005

17   **Figure 12** shows a particle **P** with charge $+6.4 \times 10^{-19}$ C about to enter a region where there is a uniform electric field of strength 2.0×10^4 N C^{-1}. **Figure 13** shows the same charged particle about to enter a region where there is a uniform magnetic field of flux density 0.17 T directed into the paper.

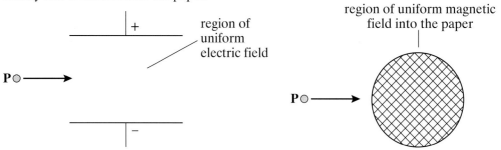

       Figure 12   **Figure 13**

(a) Sketch the paths taken by the particle when in each field. *(2 marks)*

(b) (i)   State what is meant by *uniform electric field strength*.

      (ii) The separation of the plates in **Figure 12** is 0.045 m. Calculate the potential difference between the plates. *(4 marks)*

(c) (i)   Calculate the magnitude of the force on the particle when it is in the electric field.

      (ii) Calculate the initial velocity of the charged particle for which the magnitude of the force on the particle is the same in each field. *(4 marks)*

(d) Explain why the speed of the particle changes in one of the above situations but remains constant in the other. *(6 marks)*

AQA 2005

18   (a) A satellite moves in a circular orbit at constant speed. Explain why its speed does not change even though it is acted on by a force. *(3 marks)*

    (b) At a certain point along the orbit of a satellite in uniform circular motion, the Earth's magnetic flux density has a component of 56 μT towards the centre of the Earth and a component of 17 μT in a direction perpendicular to the plane of the orbit.

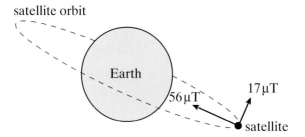

    Figure 14

    (i)   Calculate the magnitude of the resultant magnetic flux density at this point.

    (ii) The satellite has an external metal rod pointing towards the centre of the Earth. Calculate the angle between the direction of the resultant magnetic field and the rod.

    (iii) Explain why an emf is induced in the rod in this position. *(4 marks)*

AQA 2002

19 In a television cathode ray tube, electrons are accelerated through a potential difference of 12 kV in a vacuum before striking the screen.

(a) (i) Calculate the speed of an electron accelerated through this potential difference.

   (ii) The beam current is 25 mA. Calculate the number of electrons that strike the screen in one second. *(4 marks)*

(b) The electron beam is deflected in the television tube by a changing magnetic field produced by currents in coils placed around the tube.

   (i) Explain how this changing magnetic field can lead to induction effects in other electrical circuits in the television.

   (ii) Explain how this changing magnetic field could lead to faults in these other electrical television circuits.

   (iii) The electron beam is moved from the left-hand side of the screen to the right-hand side by uniformly varying the field from -3.5×10^{-4} T to $+3.5 \times 10^{-4}$ T in a time of 50 μs. Each turn of a 250-turn coil of wire in this changing field has an area of 4.0×10^{-3} m^2

   Calculate the **maximum** emf that can appear in the 250-turn coil.

   (iv) Explain why the answer to part (b)(iii) is a maximum value. *(8 marks)*

AQA 2004

20 (a) Eddy currents in the cores of transformers are one cause of inefficiency in transformers.

   (i) Explain what is meant by an eddy current, how eddy currents are produced in transformer cores and why they lead to inefficient operation of the transformer.

   (ii) Explain how the design of a transformer minimises the inefficiency due to eddy currents. *(6 marks)*

(b) **Figure 15** shows a laboratory arrangement for demonstrating the operation of a transformer.

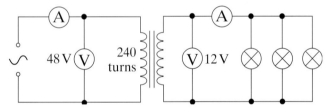

Figure 15

The supply voltage was adjusted until the three 12 V, 36 W lamps operated normally. The voltmeter readings are shown on **Figure 15**. The efficiency of the transformer was 100%.

Calculate:

(i) the reading of the ammeter in the secondary circuit,

(ii) the reading of the ammeter in the primary circuit,

(iii) the number of turns on the secondary coil of the transformer. *(5 marks)*

AQA 2005

Nuclear physics, therma physics plus an optional topic

Chapters in this unit

9 Radioactivity

10 Nuclear energy

11 Thermal physics

12 Gases

Section A Nuclear and thermal physics

Introduction

Section A consists of two main topic areas: nuclear physics and thermal physics. Both areas depend on a good understanding of AS studies on the structure of the atom and mechanics.

Nuclear physics

This area develops work from AS Unit 1 on the nucleus by first looking in depth at Rutherford's landmark α-scattering experiment that established the nuclear model of the atom. The properties of α, β and γ radiation including ionisation, absorption and range in air are then considered including the experimental verification of the inverse square law for γ radiation. The properties of each type of radiation are also considered in terms of relative hazards to humans of exposure and the safe handling and storage of radioactive sources. The random nature of radioactive decay is considered in detail, including the theory of radioactive decay and half-life calculations such as those involved in radioactive dating and the safe storage of radioactive material.

Nuclear instability is considered in terms of equations representing the changes that take place when α, β^-, β^+ and electron capture occur in relation to stable nuclei plotted on an N–Z graph. In addition, the evidence from γ radiation studies for nuclear excited states is considered and the use of γ radiation from such states is studied. The study of the nucleus then moves on to consider how its density can be calculated from experimental measurements of the radius of different nuclides.

The last part of this topic area considers why energy is released in nuclear fission and fusion, how we can calculate the energy released in such changes, how the release of fission energy is controlled in a thermal nuclear reactor and how safety is ensured in the operation of nuclear reactors and in the storage of nuclear waste.

Thermal physics

This is the study of the thermal properties of materials, including how much energy is needed to change the temperature or the physical state of a given mass of substance and the properties and nature of ideal gases which are gases that obey the experimental gas laws. The properties of an ideal gas are then explained by applying the kinetic theory of matter and the laws of mechanics to a simple molecular model of a gas. The success of this model is a classic example of the successful application of a theory to explain an experimental law, thereby gaining a deep understanding in this instance of the nature and properties of an ideal gas.

Section B An optional topic

Section B consists of four options: Astrophysics, Medical physics, Applied physics, Turning points in physics. You are expected to study one option only. Each option builds on and develops the knowledge and understanding gained in specific parts of the AS course.

An outline of the content of each option is given in the introduction to this book. Full student course notes, examination support and learning activities for each option are provided in *AQA A2 Physics A Online* on *Kerboodle!*

What you already know before starting Unit 5 section A:

From your AS studies on particle physics, you should know that:

- [ ] every atom has a positively charged nucleus surrounded by electrons. The nucleus is composed of protons and neutrons except for the $^1_1$H nucleus which is a single proton.

- [ ] an unstable nucleus becomes stable or less unstable by emitting an α particle or a β⁻ particle or a β⁺ particle or a γ photon or capturing an inner shell electron.

- [ ] α emission occurs from nuclei with too many neutrons and protons, β⁻ emission occurs from nuclei with too many neutrons and β⁺ emission or electron capture takes place from nuclei with too many protons.

- [ ] an α particle consists of two neutrons and two protons, a β⁻ particle is an electron created and emitted by a nucleus and a β⁺ particle is a positron created and emitted by a nucleus.

- [ ] ionisation is the process of creating charged atoms from uncharged atoms; the radiation from unstable nuclei is ionising radiation and is therefore harmful.

- [ ] energy can be changed into mass and mass into energy on a scale given by $E = mc^2$

From your AS studies on mechanics and materials, you should know that:

- [ ] $\text{speed} = \dfrac{\text{distance}}{\text{time}}$ for constant speed.

- [ ] for an object of mass m moving at speed v, its kinetic energy $= \frac{1}{2}mv^2$ (provided $v \ll c$, the speed of light in free space).

- [ ] $\text{density} = \dfrac{\text{mass}}{\text{volume}}$

Radioactivity

9.1 The discovery of the nucleus

How science works

What made Rutherford originate the nuclear model of the atom?

Rutherford had previously investigated the scattering of alpha particles by gas atoms and noted on rare occasions an α particle was scattered through a very large angle when most particles were hardly scattered, if at all. He realised there could be a 'nucleus' of positively charged matter inside the atom which could explain these rare events.

Notes

1   The α particles must have the same speed otherwise slow α particles would be deflected more than faster α particles on the same initial path.

2   The container must be evacuated or else the α particles would be stopped by air molecules.

3   The source of the α particles must have a long half-life otherwise later readings would be lower than earlier readings due to radioactive decay of the source nuclei.

The nuclear model of the atom was proposed by Ernest Rutherford in 1911. He knew from the work of J.J. Thomson that every atom contains one or more electrons. Thomson had shown that the electron is a negatively charged particle inside every atom but no-one knew until Rutherford's theory was confirmed experimentally in 1913 how the positive charge in the atom was distributed. Thomson thought the atom could be like a 'currant bun' – with electrons dotted in the atom like currants in a bun. In this model, the positive charge was supposedly spread throughout the atom like the dough of the bun.

Rutherford knew that the atoms of certain elements were unstable and emitted radiation. It had been shown that there were three types of such radiation, referred to as **alpha radiation** (symbol α), **beta radiation** (symbol β) and **gamma radiation** (symbol γ). Rutherford knew that α radiation consisted of fast-moving positively charged particles. He and his co-workers used this type of radiation to probe the atom. He reckoned that a beam of α particles directed at a thin metal foil might be scattered slightly by the atoms of the foil if the positive charge was spread out throughout each atom. He was astonished when he discovered that some of the particles bounced back from the foil – in his own words 'as incredible as if you fired a 15 inch naval shell at tissue paper and it came back'.

Let's consider Rutherford's experiment in more detail. Rutherford used a narrow beam of α particles, all of the same kinetic energy, in an evacuated container to probe the structure of the atom. Figure 1 shows an outline of the arrangement he used. A thin metal foil was placed in the path of the beam. α particles scattered by the metal foil were detected by a detector which could be moved round at a constant distance from the point of impact of the beam on the metal foil.

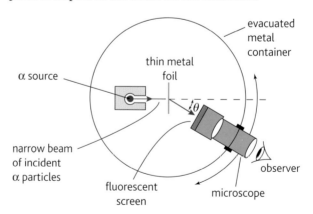

Figure 1 *Rutherford's α-scattering apparatus*

Rutherford used a microscope to observe the pinpoints of light emitted by α particles hitting a fluorescent screen. He measured the number of α particles reaching the detector per minute for different angles of deflection from zero to almost 180°. His measurements showed that:

1 most α particles passed straight through the foil with little or no deflection; about 1 in 2000 were deflected,

2 a small percentage of α particles (about 1 in 10 000) were deflected through angles of more than 90°.

Imagine throwing tennis balls at a row of vertical posts separated by wide gaps. Most of the balls would pass between the posts and therefore would not be deflected much. However, some would rebound as a result of hitting a post. Rutherford realised the α-scattering measurements could be explained in a similar way by assuming every atom has a 'hard centre' much smaller than the atom. His interpretation of each result was that

- most of the atom's mass is concentrated in a small region, the **nucleus**, at the centre of the atom,
- the nucleus is positively charged because it repels α particles (which carry positive charge) that approach it too closely.

Figure 2 shows the paths of some α particles which pass near a fixed nucleus.

- α particle C collides 'head-on' with the nucleus and rebounds back so its angle of deflection is 180°.
- α particles A, B and D are deflected through different angles. The closer the initial direction of an α particle is to the 'head-on' direction,
  - the greater its deflection is because the electrostatic force of repulsion between the α particle and the nucleus increases with decreased separation between them,
  - the smaller the least distance of approach of the α particle to the nucleus is.
- α particle E does not approach the nucleus closely enough to be significantly deflected.

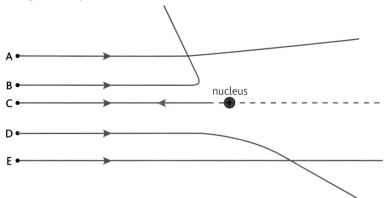

Figure 2 *α-scattering paths*

Using Coulomb's law of force (i.e. the law of force between charged objects) and Newton's laws of motion, Rutherford used his nuclear model to explain the exact pattern of the results. By testing foils of different metal elements, he also showed that the magnitude of the charge of a nucleus is $+Ze$, where e is the charge of the electron and Z is the **atomic number** of the element.

Estimate of the size of the nucleus

About 1 in 10 000 α particles are deflected by more than 90° when they pass through a metal foil. The foil must be very thin otherwise α particles are scattered more than once. For such single scattering by a foil that has n layers of atoms, the probability of an α particle being deflected by a given

Figure 3 *Ernest Rutherford*

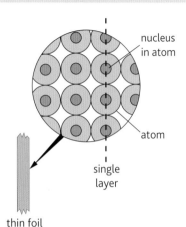

Nuclear diameter is of the order of 10^{-15} m.

nucleus in atom

atom

single layer

thin foil

Figure 4 *Estimating nuclear size*

Notes

We can also estimate the diameter of a nucleus from the least distance of approach in a head-on collision between an α particle of known kinetic energy and a nucleus. In such an impact, the α particle stops momentarily at the least distance of approach. At this point, the potential energy of the α particle in the electric field of the nucleus is equal to the initial kinetic energy, E_K, of the α particle.

Hence, using the formula in Topic 5.5 for the potential energy of two point charges gives:

$E_K = \dfrac{Q_\alpha Q_N}{4\pi\varepsilon_0 d}$, where Q_α is the charge of the α particle ($+2e$), Q_N is the charge of the nucleus ($= +Ze$) and d is the least distance of approach. Prove for yourself that the least distance of approach of an α particle with kinetic energy of 8×10^{-13} J to an aluminium nucleus ($Z = 13$) is about 7×10^{-15} m which is about 10^5 times smaller than the diameter of a typical atom. A more accurate method of determining the radius of a nucleus is explained in Topic 9.9.

atom is therefore about 1 in $10\,000n$. This probability depends on the effective area of cross-section of the nucleus to that of the atom. Therefore, for a nucleus of diameter d in an atom of diameter D, the area ratio is equal to $\dfrac{\frac{1}{4}\pi d^2}{\frac{1}{4}\pi D^2}$. So $d^2 = \dfrac{D^2}{10\,000n}$. A typical value of $n = 10^4$ gives $d = \dfrac{D}{10\,000}$.

In other words, the size of a nucleus relative to an atom is about the same as a football to a football stadium!

Summary questions

1　a In the Rutherford α particle scattering experiment, most of the α particles passed straight through the metal foil. What did Rutherford deduce about the atom from this discovery?

　b A small fraction of the α particles were deflected through large angles. What did Rutherford deduce about the atom from this discovery?

2　In Rutherford's α particle scattering experiment, why was it essential that:

　a the apparatus was in an evacuated chamber

　b the foil was very thin

　c the α particles in the beam all had the same speed

　d the beam was narrow?

3　An α particle collided with a nucleus and was deflected by it, as shown in Figure 5.

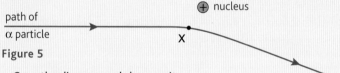

path of α particle

X

⊕ nucleus

Figure 5

　a Copy the diagram and show on it

　　i the direction of motion of the α particle,

　　ii the direction of the force on the α particle when it was at the position marked X.

　b Describe how

　　i the kinetic energy of the α particle,

　　ii the potential energy of the α particle changed during this interaction.

4　In the α particle scattering experiment, about 1 in 10 000 α particles are deflected by more than 90°.

　a For a metal foil which has n layers of atoms, explain why the probability of an α particle being deflected by a given atom is therefore about 1 in $10\,000n$.

　b Assuming this probability is equal to the ratio of the cross-sectional area of the nucleus to that of the atom, estimate the diameter of a nucleus for atoms of diameter 0.5 nm in a metal foil of thickness 10 μm.

　c Calculate the least distance of approach of an α particle to a gold nucleus ($Z = 79$) if the initial kinetic energy of the α particle is 8.0×10^{-13} J.

$\varepsilon_0 = 8.85 \times 10^{-12}$ F m^{-1}, $e = 1.6 \times 10^{-19}$ C

9.2 The properties of α, β and γ radiation

Learning objectives:

▥ What are α, β and γ radiation?

▥ Why is it dangerous?

▥ What are the properties of α, β and γ radiation?

Specification reference: 3.5A.1

Figure 1 *Marie Curie (1867–1934)*

▥ **Application and How science works**

The discovery of radioactivity

Marie Curie established the nature of radioactive materials. She showed how radioactive compounds could be separated and identified. She and her husband and Henri Becquerel won the 1903 Nobel prize for physics for their discovery of radioactivity. After Pierre's death in 1906, she continued her painstaking research and was awarded a second Nobel Prize in 1911 – an unprecedented honour.

In 1896, Henri Becquerel was investigating materials that glow when placed in an X-ray beam. He wanted to find out if strong sunlight could make uranium salts glow. He prepared a sample and placed it in a drawer on a wrapped photographic plate, ready to test the salts on the next sunny day. When he developed the film, he was amazed to see the image of a key. He had put the key on the plate in the drawer and then put the uranium salts on top of the key. He realised that uranium salts emit radiation which can penetrate paper and blacken a photographic film. The uranium salts were described as being radioactive. The task of investigating radioactivity was passed on by Becquerel to one of his students, Marie Curie. Within a few years, Marie Curie discovered other elements which are radioactive. One of these elements, radium, was found to be over a million times more radioactive than uranium.

▥ Rutherford's investigations on radioactivity

Rutherford wanted to find out what the radiation emitted by radioactive substances was and what caused it. He found that the radiation:

▥ ionised air, making it conduct electricity. He made a detector which could measure the radiation from its ionising effect.

▥ was of two types. One type which he called alpha (α) radiation was easily absorbed. The other type which he called beta (β) radiation was more penetrating. A third type of radiation, called gamma (γ) radiation, even more penetrating than β radiation, was discovered a year later.

AQA **Examiner's tip**

Don't confuse the radiation with the source; the source is radioactive not the radiation.

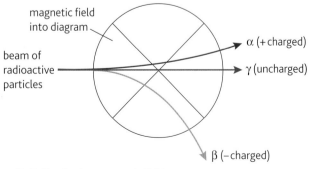

Figure 2 *Deflection by a magnetic field*

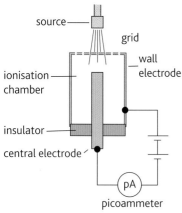

source

grid

wall
electrode

ionisation
chamber

insulator

central electrode

pA

picoammeter

Figure 3 *Investigating ionisation*

■ Link

α particles from a given source
have the same range in air as each
other whereas β particles do not.
The α particles from a given **isotope**
are always emitted with the same
kinetic energy. This is because each
α particle and the nucleus that
emits it move apart with equal and
opposite amounts of momentum.
This isn't the case with β particles
because a neutrino or antineutrino
is emitted as well. In β emission, the
nucleus, the β particle and a neutrino
or antineutrino share the energy
released in variable proportions.
See *AS Physics* Topic 1.2.

Further tests showed that a magnetic field deflects α and β radiation in
opposite directions and has no effect on γ radiation. From the deflection
direction, it was concluded that α radiation consists of positively charged
particles and β radiation consists of negatively charged particles. γ
radiation was later shown to consist of high energy **photons**.

■ Radioactivity experiments

Ionisation

The ionising effect of each type of radiation can be investigated using
an ionisation chamber and a picoammeter, as shown in Figure 3. The
chamber contains air at atmospheric pressure. Ions created in the
chamber are attracted to the oppositely charged electrode where they
are discharged. Electrons pass through the picoammeter as a result of
ionisation in the chamber. The current is proportional to the number of
ions per second created in the chamber.

■ α radiation causes strong ionisation. However, if the source is moved
away from the top of the chamber, ionisation ceases beyond a certain
distance. This is because α radiation has a range in air of no more
than a few centimetres.

■ β radiation has a much weaker ionising effect than α radiation.
Its range in air varies up to a metre or more. A β particle therefore
produces fewer ions per millimetre along its path than an α particle
does.

■ γ radiation has a much weaker ionising effect than either α or β
radiation. This is because photons carry no charge so they have less
effect than α or β particles do.

Cloud chamber observations

A cloud chamber contains air saturated with a vapour at a very low
temperature. Due to ionisation of the air, an α or a β particle passing
through the cloud chamber leaves a visible track of minute condensed
vapour droplets. This is because the air space is supersaturated. When
an ionising particle passes through the supersaturated vapour, the ions
produced trigger the formation of droplets.

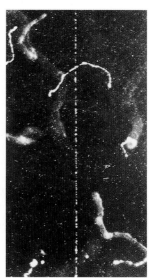

a *α particle tracks*   **b** *β particle tracks*

Figure 4 *Cloud chamber photographs*

- α particles produce straight tracks that radiate from the source and are easily visible. The tracks from a given isotope are all of the same length, indicating that the α particles have the same range.
- β particles produce wispy tracks that are easily deflected as a result of collisions with air molecules. The tracks are not as easy to see as α particle tracks because β particles are less ionising than α particles.

Absorption tests

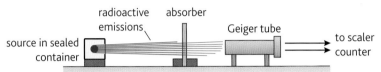

Figure 5 *Investigating absorption*

Figure 5 shows how a Geiger tube and a counter may be used to investigate absorption by different materials. Each particle of radiation that enters the tube is registered by the counter as a single count.

The number of counts in a given time is measured and used to work out the **count rate** which is the number of counts divided by the time taken. Before the source is tested, the count rate due to background radioactivity must be measured. This is the count rate without the source present.

- The count rate is then measured with the source at a fixed distance from the tube without any absorber present. The background count rate is then subtracted from the count rate with the source present to give the corrected (i.e. true) count rate from the source.
- The count rate is then measured with the absorber in a fixed position between the source and the tube. The corrected count rates with and without the absorber present can then be compared.

By using absorbers of different thickness of the same material, the effect of the absorber thickness can be investigated. Figure 6 shows a typical set of measurements for the absorption of β radiation by aluminium. Note that the count rate scale is a logarithmic scale (see Topic 15.3).

Absorption summary

- α **radiation** is absorbed completely by paper and thin metal foil.
- β **radiation** is absorbed completely by about 5 mm of metal.
- γ **radiation** is absorbed completely by several centimetres of lead.

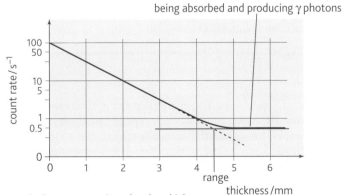

Figure 6 *Count rate against absorber thickness*

■ How science works

The Geiger tube

The Geiger tube is a sealed metal tube that contains argon gas at low pressure. The thin mica window at the end of the tube allows α and β particles to enter the tube. γ photons can enter the tube through the tube wall as well. A metal rod down the middle of the tube is at a positive potential as shown in Figure 7. The tube wall is connected to the negative terminal of the power supply and is earthed.

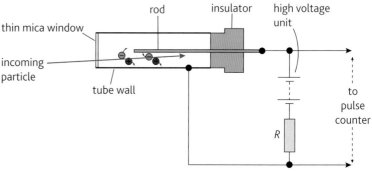

Figure 7 *A Geiger tube*

When a particle of **ionising radiation** enters the tube, the particle ionises the gas atoms along its track. The negative ions are attracted to the rod and the positive ions to the wall. The ions accelerate and collide with other gas atoms, producing more ions. These ions produce further ions in the same way so that within a very short time, many ions are created and discharged at the electrodes. A pulse of charge passes round the circuit through resistor R, causing a voltage pulse across R which is recorded as a single count by the pulse counter.

The **dead time** of the tube, the time taken to regain its non-conducting state after an ionising particle enters it, is typically of the order of 0.2 ms. Another particle that enters the tube in this time will not cause a voltage pulse. Therefore, the count rate should be no greater than about $5000\,\text{s}^{-1}$ (= 1/0.2 ms)

Range in air

The arrangement in Figure 5, on the previous page, without the absorbers may be used to investigate the range of each type of radiation in air. The count rate is measured for different distances between the source and the tube, starting with the source close to the tube. The background count rate must also be measured in the absence of the source so the corrected count rate can be calculated for each distance.

■ α radiation has a range of only a few centimetres in air. The count rate decreases sharply once the tube is beyond the range of the α particles. This can be seen in Figure 4 as the tracks from the source are the same length indicating that the particles from a given source have the same range and therefore the same initial kinetic energy. The range differs from one source to another indicating that the initial kinetic energy differs from one source to another.

■ β radiation has a range in air of up to about a metre. The count rate gradually decreases with increasing distance until it is the same as the background count rate at a distance of about 1 m. The reason for the gradual decrease of count rate as the distance increases is that the β particles from any given source have a range of initial kinetic energies up to a maximum. Faster β particles travel further in air than slower β particles as they have greater initial kinetic energy.

■ γ radiation has an unlimited range in air. The count rate gradually decreases with increasing distance because the radiation spreads out in all directions, as shown in Figure 2, page 151. The proportion of the γ photons from the source entering the tube decreases according the inverse square law, as explained in Topic 9.3. See Topic 9.3 for a summary of the properties of α, β and γ radiation.

Summary questions

1 A beam of radiation from a radioactive substance passes through paper and is then stopped by an aluminium plate of thickness 5 mm.

   a What type of particles are in this beam?

   b Describe a further test you could do to check your answer in a.

2 What type of radioactivity was responsible for the image of the key seen by Becquerel in the effect described at the beginning of this topic?

   a Explain why an image of the key was produced on the photographic plate.

   b Which type of radiation from a radioactive source is

   ■ least ionising,

   ■ most ionising?

   c When an α-emitting source above an ionisation chamber grid was moved gradually away from the grid, the ionisation current suddenly dropped to zero. Explain why the current suddenly dropped to zero.

3 In an absorption test as shown in Figure 5 using a β-emitting source and a Geiger counter, a count rate of 8.2 counts per second was obtained without the absorber present and a count rate of 3.7 counts per second was obtained with the absorber present. The background count rate was 0.4 counts per second. What percentage of the β particles hitting the absorber

   a pass through it,

   b are stopped by the absorber?

4 In an investigation to find out the type of radiation emitted by a radioactive source, a Geiger tube was placed near the source and its count rate was significantly more than the background count rate. When an aluminium plate was placed between the source and the tube, the count rate was reduced but it was still significantly more than the background count rate.

   a What can be concluded from these observations?

   b When the distance from the source to the tube was doubled with the aluminium plate still present, the corrected count rate decreased to about 25%. What conclusion can be drawn from this observation?

9.3 More about α, β and γ radiation

Learning objectives:

- What happens to the nucleus in a radioactive change?

- How does the intensity of γ radiation change as it spreads out?

- How do we represent the change in a nucleus when it emits α, β or γ radiation?

Specification reference: 3.5A.1

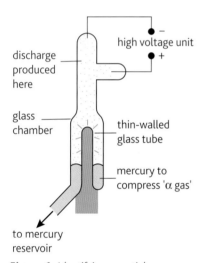

discharge produced here

glass chamber

high voltage unit

thin-walled glass tube

mercury to compress 'α gas'

to mercury reservoir

Figure 1 *Identifying α particles*

Link

γ photons are emitted from 'excited' nuclei with energies of the order of MeV (where $1\,MeV = 1.6 \times 10^{-13}\,J$) which means their wavelength is of the order of $10^{-11}\,m$ or less. See *AS Physics* Topic 1.3.

The nature of α, β and γ radiation

α radiation consists of positively charged particles. Each α particle is composed of two protons and two neutrons, the same as the nucleus of a helium atom. Rutherford devised an experiment in which α particles were collected as a gas in a glass tube fitted with two electrodes. When a voltage was applied to the electrodes, the gas conducted electricity and emitted light. Using a spectrometer, he proved that the spectrum of light from the tube was the same as from a tube filled with helium gas.

Rutherford made the discovery that neutralised α particles are the same as helium some years before his discovery that every atom contains a nucleus. After he established the nuclear model of the atom, it was realised that the nucleus of the hydrogen atom, the lightest known atom, was a single positively charged particle which became known as the **proton**. Rutherford realised that other nuclei contain protons and he predicted the existence of neutral particles of similar mass, **neutrons**, in the nucleus. For example, the helium nucleus carries twice the charge of the hydrogen nucleus and therefore contains two protons. However, its mass is four times the mass of the hydrogen nucleus so Rutherford predicted that it contained two neutrons as well as two protons. The existence of the neutron was established in 1932 by James Chadwick, one of Rutherford's former students.

β radiation from naturally occurring radioactive substances consists of fast-moving electrons. This was proved by measuring the deflection of a beam of β particles using electric and magnetic fields. The measurements were used to work out the specific charge (which is the charge/mass) of the particles. This was shown to be the same as the specific charge of the electron. An electron is created and emitted from a nucleus with too many neutrons as a result of a neutron suddenly changing into a proton.

A nucleus with too many protons is also unstable and emits a **positron**, the antiparticle of the electron, when a proton changes to a neutron. Such unstable nuclei are not present in naturally occurring radioactive substances. They are created when high energy protons collide with nuclei. As outlined in Unit 1, the theory that for every type of particle there is a corresponding antiparticle was put forward by Paul Dirac in 1928. The first antiparticle to be discovered, the positron, was discovered by Carl Anderson four years later.

γ radiation consists of photons with a wavelength of the order of $10^{-11}\,m$ or less. This discovery was made by using a crystal to diffract a beam of γ radiation in a similar way to the diffraction of light by a diffraction grating.

The inverse square law for γ radiation

The **intensity** I of the radiation is the radiation energy per second passing normally through unit area.

- For a point source that emits n γ photons per second, each of energy hf, the radiation energy per second from the source $= nhf$

- At distance r from the source, all the photons emitted from the source pass through a total area $= 4\pi r^2$ (the surface area of a sphere of radius r)

So the intensity I of the radiation at this distance =

$$\frac{\text{radiation energy per second}}{\text{total area}} = \frac{nhf}{4\pi r^2}$$

Therefore $I = \frac{k}{r^2}$, where the constant $k = \frac{nhf}{4\pi}$

Thus I varies with the inverse square of distance r.

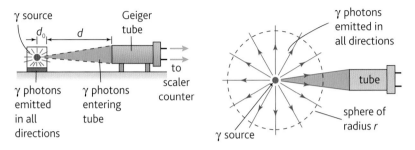

Figure 2 *Verifying the inverse square law for γ radiation*

Table 1 *Nature and properties of α, β and γ radiation*

	α radiation	**β radiation**	**γ radiation**
nature	2 protons + 2 neutrons	β^- = electron (β^+ = positron)	photon of energy of the order of MeV
range in air	fixed range, depends on energy, can be up to 100 mm	range up to about 1 m	follows the inverse square law
deflection in a magnetic field	deflected	opposite direction to α particles, and more easily deflected	not deflected
absorption	stopped by paper or thin metal foil	stopped by approx 5 mm of aluminium	stopped by several centimetres of lead
ionisation	produces about 10^4 ions per mm in air at standard pressure	produces about 100 ions per mm in air at standard pressure	very weak ionising effect
energy of each particle/photon	constant for a given source	varies up to a maximum for a given source	constant for a given source

The equations for radioactive change

A **nuclide** $^A_Z X$ contains Z protons and $A - Z$ neutrons.

▪ Its charge = $+Ze$, where e is the charge of the proton
▪ Its mass, in **atomic mass units** $\approx A$

α emission

An α particle consists of 2 neutrons and 2 protons so is represented by the symbol $^4_2\alpha$. As explained in Unit 1 of *AS Physics*, Topic 1.2, the equation below represents the change that takes place when a nuclide $^A_Z X$ emits an α particle to form a new nuclide $^{A-4}_{Z-2} Y$.

$$^A_Z X \longrightarrow {}^4_2\alpha + {}^{A-4}_{Z-2} Y$$

β⁻ emission

A negative β particle (i.e. electron) is represented by the symbol $^{0}_{-1}\beta$ (or β⁻) as its charge $= -e$ and it is not a neutron or a proton.

The equation below represents the changes that take place when a nucleus $^{A}_{Z}X$ emits a β⁻ particle. In effect, a neutron in a neutron-rich nucleus changes into a proton and an (electron) antineutrino $\bar{v}_e$ is emitted at the same time as the β⁻ particle is created.

$$^{A}_{Z}X \longrightarrow {}^{0}_{-1}\beta + {}^{A}_{Z+1}Y + \bar{v}_e$$

β⁺ emission

A positive β particle (i.e. positron) is represented by the symbol $^{0}_{+1}\beta$ (or β⁺) as its charge $= +e$ and it is not a neutron or a proton.

The equation below represents the changes that take place when a nucleus $^{A}_{Z}X$ emits a positron. In effect, a proton in a proton-rich nucleus changes into a neutron and an electron neutrino v_e is emitted at the same time as the β⁺ particle is created.

$$^{A}_{Z}X \longrightarrow {}^{0}_{+1}\beta + {}^{A}_{Z-1}Y + v_e$$

Electron capture

Some proton-rich nuclides can capture an inner-shell electron. This causes a proton in the nucleus to change into a neutron with the emission of an electron neutrino v_e at the same time.

$$^{A}_{Z}X + {}^{0}_{-1}e \longrightarrow {}^{A}_{Z-1}Y + v_e$$

The inner-shell vacancy is filled by an outer-shell electron, as a result causing an X-ray photon to be emitted by the atom.

γ emission

No change occurs in the number of protons or neutrons of a nucleus when it emits a γ photon.

A γ photon is emitted if a nucleus has excess energy after it has emitted an α or a β⁻ particle.

Summary questions

1 Copy and complete each of the following equations representing α emission.

a $^{238}_{92}U \longrightarrow {}_{90}Th + $

b $_{90}Th \longrightarrow {}^{224}_{88}Ra + $

2 Copy and complete each of the following equations representing β⁻ emission.

a $^{64}_{29}Cu \longrightarrow {}_{30}Zn + {}^{0}\beta + $

b $_{15}P \longrightarrow {}^{32}S + {}^{0}\beta + $

3 The bismuth isotope $^{213}_{83}Bi$ decays by emitting a β⁻ particle to form an unstable isotope of polonium (Po) which then decays by emitting an α particle to form an unstable isotope of lead (Pb). This isotope then decays by emitting a β⁻ particle to form a stable isotope of bismuth.

a Write down the symbol for each of the three product nuclides in this sequence.

b Write down the number of protons and the number of neutrons in a nucleus of

  i the bismuth isotope $^{213}_{83}Bi$,

  ii the stable bismuth isotope.

4 A point source of γ radiation is placed 200 mm from the end of a Geiger tube. The corrected count rate was measured at 12.7 counts per second. Calculate:

a the corrected count rate if the source was moved to a distance of 400 mm from the tube,

b the distance between the source and the tube for a corrected count rate of 20 counts per second.

9.4 The dangers of radioactivity

Learning objectives:

■ Why is ionising radiation harmful?

■ What factors determine whether α, β, or γ are the most dangerous?

■ How can exposure to ionising radiation be reduced?

Specification reference: 3.5A.1

Figure 1 *A radioactive warning sign*

■ The hazards of ionising radiation

Ionising radiation is hazardous because it damages living cells. Such radiation includes **X-rays**, protons and neutrons as well as α, β, and γ radiation. **Ionising radiation** affects living cells because:

■ it can destroy cell membranes which causes cells to die, or

■ it can damage vital molecules such as DNA directly or indirectly by creating 'free radical' ions which react with vital molecules. Normal cell division is affected and nuclei become damaged. Damaged DNA may cause cells to divide and grow uncontrollably, causing a tumour which may be cancerous. Damaged DNA in a sex cell (i.e. an egg or a sperm) may cause a mutation which may be passed on to future generations.

As a result of exposure to ionising radiation, living cells die or grow uncontrollably or mutate, affecting the health of the affected person (somatic effects) and possibly affecting future generations (genetic effects). High doses of ionising radiation kill living cells. Cell mutation and cancerous growth occurs at low doses as well as at high doses. There is no evidence of the existence of a threshold level of ionising radiation below which living cells would not be damaged.

■ Radiation monitoring

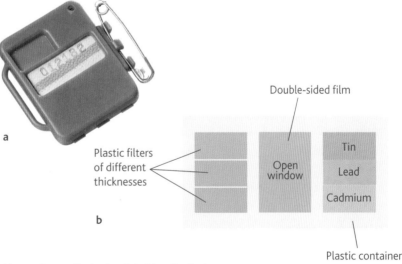

Figure 2 a *a film badge* **b** *inside a film badge*

Anyone using equipment that produces ionising radiation must wear a **film badge** to monitor his or her exposure to ionising radiation. The badge contains a strip of photographic film in a light-proof wrapper. Different areas of the film are covered by absorbers of different materials and different thicknesses. When the film is developed, the amount of exposure to each form of ionising radiation can be estimated from the blackening of the film. If the badge is overexposed, the wearer is not allowed to continue working with the equipment.

The biological effect of ionising radiation depends on the dose received and the type of radiation. The dose is measured in terms of the energy absorbed per unit mass of matter from the radiation. The same dose of different types of ionising radiation has different effects. For example, α radiation produces far more ions per millimetre than γ radiation in the same substance so it is far more damaging. However, α radiation from a source outside the body cannot penetrate the skin's outer layer of dead cells so is much less damaging than if the source were inside the body.

Application

Radiation dose limits

For any dose of ionising radiation, its **dose equivalent**, measured in sieverts (Sv), is the dose due to 250 kV X-rays that would have the same effect. For example, 1 millisievert of α radiation has the same biological effect as 10 millisieverts of 250 kV X-rays.

Maximum permissible exposure limits are recommended safety limits for the annual dose equivalent which a radiation worker should not exceed. The recommended limit is 15 mSv per year, although the average dose due to occupation is much lower at 2 mSv per year. This is based on the death rates of survivors of the atomic bombs dropped on Hiroshima and Nagasaki which is estimated at 3 deaths per 100 000 survivors for each millisievert of radiation. Thus the risk to a radiation worker exposed to 2 mSv per year for 5 years would be 3 in 10 000.

Background radiation

We are all subject to **background radiation** which occurs naturally due to cosmic radiation and from radioactive materials in rocks, soil and in the air. Background radiation does vary with location due to local geological features. For example, radon gas which is radioactive can accumulate in poorly ventilated areas of buildings in certain locations. Figure 3 shows the sources of background radiation in the UK.

Safe use of radioactive materials

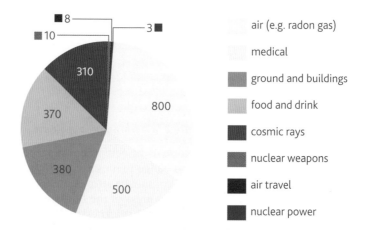

Figure 3 *Sources of background radiation in the UK in terms of the average radiation dose per person per year in μSv*

Because radioactive materials produce ionising radiation, they must be stored and used with care. In addition, disposal of a radioactive substance must be carried out in accordance with specific regulations. Only approved institutions are allowed to use radioactive materials. Approval is subject to regular checks and approved institutions are categorised according to purpose.

1 **Storage of radioactive materials** should be in lead-lined containers. Most radioactive sources produce γ radiation as well as α or β radiation so the lead lining of a container must be thick enough to reduce the γ radiation from the sources in the container to about the background level. In addition, regulations require that the containers are under 'lock and key' and a record of the sources is kept.

2 **When using radioactive materials**, established rules and regulations must be followed. No source should be allowed to come into contact with the skin.

   ▓ Solid sources should be transferred using handling tools such as tongs or a glove-box or using robots. The handling tools ensure the material is as far from the user as practicable so the intensity of the γ radiation from the source at the user is as low as possible and the user is beyond the range of α or β radiation from the source.

   ▓ Liquid and gas sources and solids in powder form should be in sealed containers. This is to ensure radioactive gas cannot be breathed in and radioactive liquid cannot be splashed on the skin or drunk.

   ▓ Radioactive sources should not be used for longer than is necessary. The longer a person is exposed to ionising radiation, the greater is the dose of radiation received.

Link

The intensity of a γ beam that passes through an absorber decreases exponentially with the thickness of the absorber. If a certain thickness of a material cuts the intensity of a γ beam to half, twice the thickness will cut the intensity to a quarter, etc. See Topic 9.5.

Hint

A typical radioactive source used in a school might produce of the order of 10^5 radioactive particles per second, each typically of energy of the order of MeV ($1\,MeV = 1.6 \times 10^{-13}\,J$). Show for yourself that the energy transfer per second from such a source is of the order of $10^{-8}\,J\,s^{-1}$. In 15 minutes or so, the source would transfer $10^{-5}\,J$ to its surroundings. If this amount of energy were to be absorbed by about 10 kg of living tissue, the dose would be about $10^{-6}\,Sv$ ($= 1\,\mu Sv$) which is not insignificant.

AQA Examiner's tip

ALARA stands for 'as low as reasonably achievable'. Risks are always reduced by increasing the distance from sources and shortening the time exposure.

Summary questions

1 What is meant by ionisation?

   a Explain why a source of α-radiation is not as dangerous as a source of β radiation provided the sources are outside the body.

2 a Discuss the reasons why ionising radiation is hazardous to a person exposed to the radiation.

   b i What is the purpose of a film badge worn by a radiation worker?

   ii With the aid of a diagram, describe what is in a film badge and how the film badge is tested.

3 a Explain why a radioactive source should be

   i kept in a lead-lined storage box when not in use,

   ii transferred using a pair of tongs with long handles.

   b Discuss the precautions you would take when carrying out an experiment using a source of γ radiation.

4 a State **four** sources of ionising radiation which we are all exposed to.

   b State **two** sources of ionising radiation which are likely to affect people in certain occupations more than the general public.

   c Radon gas is a source of α radiation that can seep into buildings from the ground. Explain why the presence of this gas in the air in a building is a serious health hazard.

9.5 Radioactive decay

- What do we mean by the activity of a radioactive isotope?

- What is the half-life of a radioactive isotope?

- Does anything affect radioactive decay?

Specification reference: 3.5A.1

Half-life

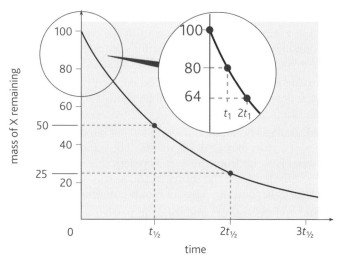

Figure 1 *A radioactive decay curve*

Link

Although in theory a radioactive decay curve never falls to zero, in practice it eventually falls to a level which is indistinguishable from background radiation. See Topic 9.4.

When a nucleus of a radioactive isotope emits an α or a β particle, it becomes a nucleus of a different element because its proton number changes. The number of nuclei of the initial radioactive isotope therefore decreases. The mass of the initial isotope decreases gradually as the number of nuclei of the isotope decreases. Figure 1 shows how the mass decreases with time. The curve is referred to as a **decay curve**. The mass of the isotope decreases with time at a slower and slower rate. Measurements show that the mass decreases exponentially which means that the mass drops by a constant factor (e.g. ×0.8) in equal intervals of time. For example, if the initial mass of the radioactive isotope is 100 g and the mass decreases to a factor of ×0.8 every 1000 s, then

- after 1000 s, the mass remaining = 80 g (= 0.8 × 100 g),
- after 2000 s, the mass remaining = 64 g (= 0.8 × 0.8 × 100 g),
- after 3000 s, the mass remaining = 51 g (= 0.8 × 0.8 × 0.8 × 100 g)

A convenient measure for the rate of decrease is the time taken for a decrease by half. This is the half-life of the process.

The half-life, $T_{1/2}$, of a radioactive isotope is the time taken for the mass of the isotope to decrease to half the initial mass. This is the same as the time taken for the number of nuclei of the isotope to decrease to half the initial number.

Consider a sample of a radioactive isotope X which initially contains 100 g of the isotope.

- After 1 half-life, the mass of X remaining = 0.5 × 100 = 50 g
- After 2 half-lives from the start, the mass of X remaining
  = 0.5^2 × 100 = 25 g
- After 3 half-lives from the start, the mass of X remaining
  = 0.5^3 × 100 = 12.5 g

After n half-lives from the start, the mass of X remaining
= $0.5^n m_0$, where m_0 = the initial mass

The mass of X decreases exponentially. This is because radioactive decay is a **random** process and the number of nuclei that decay in a certain time is in proportion to the number of nuclei of X remaining. To understand this idea, consider a game of dice where there are 1000 dice, each representing a nucleus of X. The throw of a dice is a random process in which each face has an equal chance of being uppermost.

- 1st throw; when the dice are all thrown, you would expect $\frac{1}{6}$ of the dice to show the same figure on the upper surface. Let all the dice that show '1' uppermost represent nuclei that have disintegrated, an expected total of 167 ($= \frac{1000}{6}$). If these are removed, then 833 dice remain.
- 2nd throw; the remaining dice are thrown to give $\frac{1}{6}$ of 833 as the expected number of '1' s. So 694 dice ($= 833 - \frac{833}{6}$) remain.
- 3rd throw; the remaining dice are thrown to give $\frac{1}{6}$ of 694 as the expected number of '1' s. So 578 dice ($= 694 - \frac{694}{6}$) remain.
- 4th throw; the remaining dice are thrown to give $\frac{1}{6}$ of 578 as the expected number of '1' s. So 482 dice ($= 578 - \frac{578}{6}$) remain.

The analysis shows that 4 throws are needed to reduce the number of dice to less than half the initial number. Prove for yourself that a further 4 throws would reduce the number of dice to 25% of the initial number. Figure 2 shows how the number of dice remaining decreases with time. The curve has the same shape as Figure 1. The half-life of the process is 3.8 'throws'.

Activity

The activity A of a radioactive isotope is the number of nuclei of the isotope that disintegrate per second. In other words, it is the rate of change of the number of nuclei of the isotope. The unit of activity is the **becquerel (Bq)**, where 1 Bq = 1 disintegration per second.

The activity of a radioactive isotope is proportional to the mass of the isotope. Because the mass of a radioactive isotope decreases with time due to radioactive decay, the activity decreases with time. Figure 3 shows an experiment in which the activity of a radioactive isotope of protactinium $^{234}_{91}$Pa is measured and recorded using a Geiger tube and a counter. This isotope is a β-emitter produced by the decay of the radioactive isotope of thorium $^{234}_{90}$Th. In this experiment, an organic solvent in a sealed bottle is used to separate protactinium from thorium to enable the activity of the protactinium to be monitored.

Before the experiment is carried out, the background count rate is measured without the bottle present. The bottle is then shaken to mix the aqueous and solvent layers and then placed near the end of the Geiger tube. The layers are allowed to separate as shown in Figure 3. The protactinium is collected by the solvent and the thorium by the aqueous layer. The Geiger tube detects β particles emitted by the decay of the protactinium nuclei in the solvent layer.

The counter is used to measure the number of counts every 10 s. The count rate is the number of counts in each ten second interval divided by 10 s. The background count rate is subtracted to give the corrected count rate. Since the activity is proportional to the corrected count rate, a graph of the corrected count rate against time, as in Figure 4 on the next page, shows how the activity of the protactinium decreases with time.

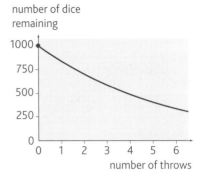

Figure 2 *Exponential decrease*

Note

Reminder about molar mass and the Avogadro constant.

For an element with a mass number A,

- its molar mass M is its mass number in grams,
- one mole of the element contains N_A atoms where N_A is the Avogadro constant,
- mass m of the element contains $(m/M)N_A$ atoms.

See Topic 12.2 for more information.

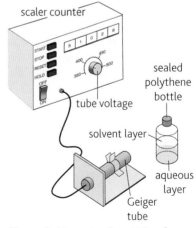

Figure 3 *Measuring the activity of protactinium*

corrected
count rate/s^{-1}

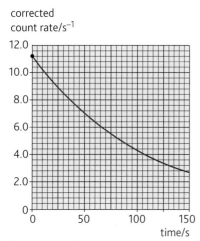

Figure 4 *A radioactive decay curve*

Activity and power

For a radioactive source of activity A that emits particles (or photons) of the same energy E, the energy per second released by radioactive decay in the source by the radiation is the product of its activity and the energy of each particle. In other words, the power of the source $= AE$.

The energy transfer per second from a radioactive source $= AE$

If the source is in a sealed container and emits only α particles which are all absorbed by the container, the container gains thermal energy from the absorbed radiation equal to the energy transferred from the source. For example, for a source that has an activity of 30 MBq and emits particles of energy 2.5 MeV, the energy transfer per second from the source $= 30 \times 10^6$ Bq $\times 2.5$ MeV $= 7.5 \times 10^7$ MeV s$^{-1} = 1.2 \times 10^{-5}$ J s^{-1}.

Summary questions

$N_A = 6.02 \times 10^{23}$ mol^{-1}, 1 MeV $= 1.6 \times 10^{-13}$ J

1 Figure 5 shows how the mass of a certain radioactive isotope decreases with time. Use the graph to work out

a the half-life of this isotope,

b the mass of the isotope remaining after 120 s.

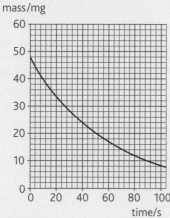

mass/mg

Figure 5

2 A freshly-prepared sample of a radioactive isotope X contains 1.8×10^{15} atoms of the isotope. The half-life of the isotope is 8.0 hours. Calculate:

a the number of atoms of this isotope remaining after

i 8 h,

ii 24 h.

b the number of atoms of X that would have decayed after

i 8 h,

ii 24 h.

c the energy transfer from the sample in 24 h if the isotope emits α particles of energy 5 MeV .

3 $^{131}_{53}$I is a radioactive isotope of iodine which has a half-life of 8.0 days. A sample of this isotope has an initial activity of 38 kBq. Calculate the activity of this sample

a 8.0 days later,

b 32 days later.

4 $^{137}_{55}$Cs is a radioactive isotope of caesium which has a half-life of 35 years. A sample of this isotope has a mass of 1.0×10^{-3} kg.

a Calculate the number of atoms in 1.0×10^{-3} kg of this isotope.

b Calculate the number of atoms of the isotope remaining in the sample after 70 years.

9.6 The theory of radioactive decay

Specification reference: 3.5A.1

Learning objectives:

- Can a radioactive source decay completely?
- What is exponential decrease?
- Why is radioactive decay a random process?

The random nature of radioactive decay

An unstable nucleus becomes stable by emitting an α or a β particle or a γ photon. This is an unpredictable event. Every nucleus of a radioactive isotope has an equal probability of undergoing radioactive decay in any given time interval. Therefore, for a large number of nuclei of a radioactive isotope, the number of nuclei that disintegrate in a certain time interval depends only on the total number of nuclei present.

Consider a sample of a radioactive isotope X that initially contains N_0 nuclei of the isotope.

Let N represent the number of nuclei of X remaining at time t after the start.

Suppose in time Δt, the number of nuclei that disintegrate is ΔN.

Because radioactive disintegration is a random process, ΔN is proportional to:

1 N, the number of nuclei of X remaining at time t,

2 the duration of the time interval Δt.

Therefore $\Delta N = -\lambda N \Delta t$, where λ is a constant referred to as the **decay constant**. The minus sign is necessary because ΔN is a decrease.

So the rate of disintegration, $\dfrac{\Delta N}{\Delta t} = -\lambda N$

For a given radioactive isotope, its **activity, A**, is the rate of disintegration $\dfrac{\Delta N}{\Delta t}$

Therefore, the activity A of N atoms of a radioactive isotope is given by

$$A = \lambda N$$

The solution of the equation $\dfrac{\Delta N}{\Delta t} = -\lambda N$ is $N = N_0 e^{-\lambda t}$, where e^x is the exponential function. See below.

Figure 1 shows that a graph of N against t gives a decay curve. The number of nuclei N decreases exponentially with time. In other words,

- in one half-life, the remaining number of nuclei $N_1 = 0.5 N_0$
- in two half-lives, the remaining number of nuclei $N_2 = 0.25 N_0$
- in n half-lives, the remaining number of nuclei $N = 0.5^n N_0$

The graph of the number of nuclei N against time t as represented by the equation $N = N_0 e^{-\lambda t}$ is shown in Figure 1. It is a curve with exactly the same shape as Figure 1 in Topic 9.5.

The mass, m, of a radioactive isotope decreases from initial mass m_0 in accordance with the equation $m = m_0 e^{-\lambda t}$ because the mass m is proportional to the number of nuclei, N, of the isotope.

The activity A of a sample of N nuclei of an isotope decays in accordance with the equation

$$A = A_0 e^{-\lambda t}$$

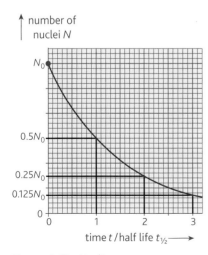

Figure 1 $N = N_0 e^{-\lambda t}$

Notes

The following notes are not part of the A2 specification and are provided to help students gain a deeper understanding of the topic.

1   The exponential function appears in any situation where the rate of change of a quantity is in proportion to the quantity itself. This is because the rate of change of each term in the function sequence is equal to the previous term in the sequence.

2   The exponential function,
$$e^x = 1 + x + \frac{x^2}{2!} + \frac{x^3}{3!} + \dots$$
Differentiating e^x with respect to x gives e^x (i.e. $\frac{d(e^x)}{dx} = e^x$) because differentiating each term in the expression for e^x gives the previous term.

The exponential function is indicated on a calculator as 'e^x' or 'inv ln'. See Topic 15.3.

3   The natural logarithm function, $\ln x$, is the inverse exponential function. In other words, if $y = e^x$, then $\ln y = x$.

Therefore, $N = N_0 e^{-\lambda t}$ may be written $\ln N = \ln N_0 - \lambda t$

The graph of $\ln N$ against t is therefore a straight line with:

■   a gradient $= -\lambda$, and

■   a y-intercept $= \ln N_0$

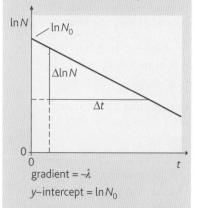

gradient $= -\lambda$

y–intercept $= \ln N_0$

Figure 2 $\ln N$ against t

4   The exponential decrease formula is also used in the theory of capacitor discharge. See Topic 6.3.

This is because the activity A = the number of disintegrations per second $= \lambda N$

Hence $A = \lambda N_0 e^{-\lambda t} = A_0 e^{-\lambda t}$ where $A_0 = \lambda N_0$.

The corrected count rate C due to a sample of a radioactive isotope at a fixed distance from a Geiger tube is proportional to the activity of the source. Therefore, the count rate decreases with time in accordance with the equation $C = C_0 e^{-\lambda t}$, where C_0 is the count rate at time $t = 0$.

The above equations for the number of nuclei N, the activity A and the count rate C are all of the same general form, namely $x = x_0 e^{-\lambda t}$, where x represents N or A or C and x_0 represents the initial value.

Worked example:

A sample of a radioactive material initially contains 1.2×10^{20} atoms of the isotope. The decay constant for the isotope is $3.6 \times 10^{-3}\,s^{-1}$. Calculate:

a   the number of atoms of the isotope remaining after 1000 s,

b   the activity of the sample after 1000 s.

Solution

a $N_0 = 1.2 \times 10^{20}, \lambda = 3.6 \times 10^{-3}\,s^{-1}, t = 1000\,s,$

$\lambda t = 3.6 \times 10^{-3} \times 1000 = 3.6$

$\therefore N = N_0 e^{-\lambda t} = 1.2 \times 10^{20}\, e^{-3.6} = 1.2 \times 10^{20} \times 2.7 \times 10^{-2} = 3.2 \times 10^{18}$

b   Activity $A = \lambda N = 3.6 \times 10^{-3} \times 3.2 \times 10^{18} = 1.2 \times 10^{16}\,Bq$

■ The decay constant

The decay constant λ is the probability of an individual nucleus decaying per second. If there are 10 000 nuclei present and 300 decay in 20 s, the decay constant is $0.0015\,s^{-1}$ $(= (300/10\,000)/20\,s)$.

In general, if the change of the number of nuclei ΔN in time Δt is given by $\Delta N = -\lambda N \Delta t$ then the probability of decay, $\frac{\Delta N}{N} = \lambda \Delta t$ (the minus sign is not needed here as reference is made to decay).

So the probability per unit time $= \frac{\Delta N}{N/\Delta t} = \lambda$

As explained in Topic 9.5, **the half-life, $T_{1/2}$** of a radioactive isotope is the time taken for half the initial number of nuclei to decay. The longer the half-life, the smaller the decay constant because the probability of decay per second is smaller.

The half-life $T_{1/2}$ is related to the decay constant λ according to the equation

$$T_{1/2} = \frac{\ln 2}{\lambda}$$

As $\ln 2 = 0.693$, this equation may be written as $T_{1/2} = \frac{0.693}{\lambda}$.

Proof of $T_{\frac{1}{2}} = \dfrac{\ln 2}{\lambda}$

The proof of this equation is not part of the A2 specification. It is provided below to help students develop a better understanding of the topic.

Let the number of nuclei $N = N_0$ at time $t = 0$

Therefore at time $t = T_{\frac{1}{2}}$, $N = 0.5N_0$

Inserting $t = T_{\frac{1}{2}}$, $N = 0.5N_0$ into $N = N_0 e^{-\lambda t}$ gives $0.5\,N_0 = N_0 e^{-\lambda T_{\frac{1}{2}}}$

Cancelling N_0 therefore gives $0.5 = e^{-\lambda T_{\frac{1}{2}}}$

Taking the natural logarithm (ln) of each side gives $\ln 0.5 = -\lambda T_{\frac{1}{2}}$

Because $\ln 0.5 = -\ln 2$, then $\ln 2 = \lambda T_{\frac{1}{2}}$

Rearranging this equation gives $T_{\frac{1}{2}} = \dfrac{\ln 2}{\lambda}$

Summary questions

$N_A = 6.02 \times 10^{23}\ \text{mol}^{-1}$, $1\,\text{MeV} = 1.6 \times 10^{-13}\,\text{J}$

1 $^{131}_{53}\text{I}$ is a radioactive isotope of iodine which has a half-life of 8.0 days. A fresh sample of this isotope contains 4.2×10^{16} atoms of this isotope. Calculate:

  a the decay constant of this isotope,

  b the number of atoms of this isotope remaining after 24 h.

2 A radioactive isotope has a half-life of 35 years. A fresh sample of this isotope has an activity of 25 kBq. Calculate:

  a the decay constant in s^{-1},

  b the activity of the sample after 10 years.

3 a Calculate the number of atoms present in 1.0 kg of $^{226}_{88}\text{Ra}$.

  b The isotope $^{226}_{88}\text{Ra}$ has a half-life of 1620 years. For an initial mass of 1.0 kg of this isotope, calculate:

  i the mass of this isotope remaining after 1000 years,

  ii how many atoms of the isotope will remain after 1000 years.

4 A fresh sample of a radioactive isotope has an initial activity of 40 kBq. After 48 h, its activity has decreased to 32 kBq. Calculate:

  a the decay constant of this isotope,

  b its half-life.

Hint

To calculate N at time t, given values of N_0 and $T_{\frac{1}{2}}$,

■ **either** calculate λ using $\lambda = \dfrac{\ln 2}{T_{\frac{1}{2}}}$

  then use the equation $N = N_0 e^{-\lambda t}$,

■ **or** calculate the number of half-lives, n, using $n = \dfrac{t}{T_{\frac{1}{2}}}$ then use

  $N = 0.5^n N_0$.

Link

Radioactive waste from a nuclear reactor contains a range of unstable isotopes with different half-lives. The waste products must be stored for many years until their activity is no more than background. See Topic 10.4.

9.7 Radioactive isotopes in use

Learning objectives:

- How do we do radioactive dating?

- What are radioactive tracers?

- What do we use radioactivity for in hospitals?

Specification reference: 3.5A.1

Radioactive isotopes are used for many purposes. The choice of an isotope for a particular purpose depends on its half-life and on the type of radiation it emits. For some uses, the choice also depends on how the isotope is obtained and on whether or not it produces a stable decay product. In addition, the toxicity and biochemical suitability of the pharmaceuticals to which it is attached need to be considered in medical and related applications. The following examples are intended to provide a wider awareness of important uses of radioactive substances and to set contexts in which knowledge and understanding of radioactivity is developed further.

Radioactive dating

Carbon dating

Living plants and trees contain a small percentage of the radioactive isotope of carbon, $^{14}_{6}C$, which is formed in the atmosphere as a result of cosmic rays knocking out neutrons from nuclei. These neutrons then collide with nitrogen nuclei to form carbon-14 nuclei.

$$^{1}_{0}n + ^{14}_{7}N \longrightarrow ^{14}_{6}C + ^{1}_{1}p$$

Carbon dioxide from the atmosphere is taken up by living plants as a result of photosynthesis. So a small percentage of the carbon content of any plant is carbon-14. This isotope has a half-life of 5570 years so there is negligible decay during the lifetime of a plant. Once a tree has died, no further carbon is taken in so the proportion of carbon-14 in the dead tree decreases as the carbon-14 nuclei decay. Because activity is proportional to the number of atoms still to decay, measuring the activity of the dead sample enables its age to be calculated, provided the activity of the same mass of living wood is known.

Worked example:

A certain sample of dead wood is found to have an activity of 0.28 Bq. An equal mass of living wood is found to have an activity of 1.3 Bq. Calculate the age of the sample. Give your answer in years to 3 significant figures.

The half-life of carbon-14 is 5570 years.

Solution

The half-life, $T_{1/2}$, in seconds $= 5570 \times 365 \times 24 \times 3600\,s = 1.76 \times 10^{11}\,s$

$\therefore$ the decay constant of carbon-14, $\lambda = \dfrac{0.693}{T_{1/2}} = \dfrac{0.693}{1.76 \times 10^{11}}$

$= 3.95 \times 10^{-12}\,s^{-1}$

Using activity $A = A_0 e^{-\lambda t}$ where $A = 0.28$ Bq and $A_0 = 1.30$ Bq gives

$0.28 = 1.3\,e^{-\lambda t}$ so $e^{-\lambda t} = \left(\dfrac{0.28}{1.30}\right) = 0.215$

$\therefore \lambda t = 1.535$

$t = \dfrac{1.535}{\lambda} = \dfrac{1.535}{3.95 \times 10^{-12}}\,s = 3.88 \times 10^{11}\,s = 12\,300$ years

Hint

A useful check is to estimate the number of half-lives needed for the activity to decrease from 1.30 Bq to 0.28 Bq. You should find that just over 2 half-lives are needed, corresponding to about 11 000 years.

Argon dating

Ancient rocks contain trapped argon gas as a result of the decay of the radioactive isotope of potassium, $^{40}_{19}K$, into the argon isotope $^{40}_{18}Ar$. This happens when its nucleus captures an inner shell electron. As a result, a proton in the nucleus changes into a neutron and a neutrino is emitted.

The equation for the change is

$$^{40}_{19}K + ^{0}_{-1}e \longrightarrow ^{40}_{18}Ar + \nu_e$$

The potassium isotope $^{40}_{19}K$ also decays by β^- emission to form the calcium isotope $^{40}_{20}Ca$. This process is 8 times more probable than electron capture.

$$^{40}_{19}K \longrightarrow ^{0}_{-1}\beta + ^{40}_{20}Ca + \bar{\nu}_e$$

The effective half-life of the decay of $^{40}_{19}K$ is 1250 million years. The age of the rock (i.e. the time from when it solidified) can be calculated by measuring the proportion of argon-40 to potassium-40.

For every N potassium-40 atoms now present, if there is 1 argon-40 atom present, there must have originally been $N + 9$ potassium atoms. (i.e. 1 that decayed into argon-40 + 8 that decayed into calcium-40 + N remaining). The radioactive decay equation $N = N_0 e^{-\lambda t}$ can then be used to find the age of the sample.

For example, suppose for every 4 potassium-40 atoms now present, a certain rock now has 1 argon-40 atom. Therefore, $N = 4$ and $N_0 = 13$. Substituting these values into the equation $N = N_0 e^{-\lambda t}$ gives $4 = 13e^{-\lambda t}$. Therefore $e^{-\lambda t} = 4/13 = 0.308$ which gives $t = -\ln 0.308/\lambda$.

Substituting $0.693/T_{1/2}$ for λ into this equation gives $t = (-\ln 0.308/0.693) \, T_{1/2} = 1.70 \, T_{1/2}$. The age of the sample is therefore 2120 million years.

Hint

A useful check is to estimate the number of half-lives needed for n to decrease 13 to 4. You should find that between 1 and 2 half-lives are needed, corresponding to an age of between 1250 and 2500 million years.

Radioactive tracers

A radioactive tracer is used to follow the path of a substance through a system. Table 1, overleaf, gives some examples. In general, the radioactive isotope(s) in the tracer should:

- have a half-life which is stable enough for the necessary measurements to be made and short enough to decay quickly after use,
- emit β radiation or γ radiation so it can be detected outside the flow path.

Link

The metastable isotope of technetium $^{99}_{43}Tc^m$ is widely used in medical diagnosis because it is a γ emitter with a half-life of 6 hours and it can be prepared 'on site'. See Topic 9.8.

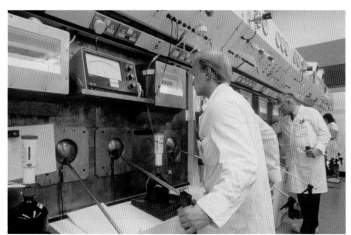

Figure 1 *Using tracers*

Table 1 *Examples of radioactive tracers*

application	method	tracer
detecting underground pipe leaks	radioactive tracer injected into the flow. A detector on the surface above the pipeline is used to detect leakage	injected fluid contains a β-emitter or a γ– emitter (depending on factors such as depth, soil density) as α-radiation would be absorbed by the pipes
modelling oil reservoirs mathematically to improve oil recovery	water containing a radioactive tracer is injected into an oil reservoir at high pressure, forcing some of the oil out. Detectors at the production wells monitor breakthrough of the radioactive isotope	'tritiated' water ^3H_2O, a β-emitter with a half-life of 12 years
investigating the uptake of fertilisers by plants	plant watered with a solution containing a fertiliser. By measuring the radioactivity of the leaves, the amount of fertiliser reaching them can be determined	fertiliser contains phosphorus, $^{32}_{15}P$, a β-emitter with a half-life of 14 days
monitoring the uptake of iodine by the thyroid gland	patient is given a solution containing sodium iodide which contains a small quantity of radioactive iodine, $^{131}_{53}I$. The activity of the patient's thyroid and the activity of an identical sample prepared at the same time is measured 24 h later	solution of sodium iodide contains iodine $^{131}_{53}I$, a β-emitter with a half-life of 8 days

Figure 2 *Measuring engine wear*

■ **Application and How science works**

Industrial uses of radioactivity

The examples below are just three of a wide range of applications of radioactivity in industry and technology.

Engine wear

The rate of wear of a piston ring in an engine can be measured by fitting a ring that is radioactive. As the ring slides along the piston compartment, radioactive atoms transfer from the ring to the engine oil. By measuring the radioactivity of the oil, the mass of radioactive metal transferred from the ring can be determined and the rate of wear calculated. A metal ring can be made radioactive by exposing it to neutron radiation in a nuclear reactor. Each nucleus that absorbs a neutron becomes unstable and disintegrates by β⁻ emission.

Thickness monitoring

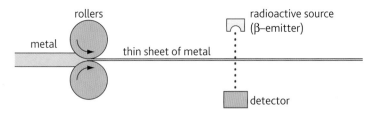

if the radiation reaching the detector changes the detector makes the rollers move further apart or closer together

Figure 3 *The manufacture of metal foil*

Metal foil is manufactured by using rollers to squeeze plate metal on a continuous production line. A detector measures the amount of radiation passing through the foil. If the foil is too thick, the detector reading drops. A signal from the detector is fed back to the control system to make the rollers move closer together and so make the foil thinner. The source used is a β⁻ emitter with a long half-life. α radiation would be absorbed completely by the foil and γ radiation would pass straight through without absorption.

Power sources for remote devices

Satellites, weather sensors and other remote devices can be powered using a radioactive isotope in a thermally-insulated sealed container which absorbs all the radiation emitted by the isotope. A thermocouple attached to the container produces electricity as a result of the container becoming warm through absorbing radiation.

For mass m of the isotope, its activity $A = \lambda N$ where N is the number of radioactive atoms present in mass m. If each disintegration of a nucleus releases energy E, the energy transfer per second from the source $= \lambda NE$. The source needs to have a reasonably long half-life so it does not need to be replaced frequently but a very long half-life may require too much mass to generate the necessary power.

Summary questions

$N_A = 6.02 \times 10^{23}$ mol⁻¹, 1 MeV $= 1.6 \times 10^{-13}$ J

1
a Explain why living wood is slightly radioactive.

b A sample of ancient wood of mass 0.50 g is found to have an activity of 0.11 Bq. A sample of living wood of the same mass has an activity of 0.13 Bq. Calculate the age of the sample of wood.

The half-life of radioactive carbon $_6^{14}$C is 5570 years.

2 The radioactive isotope of iodine, $_{53}^{131}$I, is used for medical diagnosis of the kidneys. The isotope has a half-life of 8 days. A sample of the isotope is to be given to a patient in a glass of water. The passage of the isotope through each kidney is then monitored using two detectors outside the body. The isotope is required to have an activity of 800 kBq at the time it is given to the patient.

a Calculate:

i   the activity of the sample 24 hours after it was given to the patient,

ii the activity of the sample when it was prepared 24 hours before it was given to the patient,

iii the mass of $_{53}^{131}$I in the sample when it was prepared.

b The reading from the detector near one of the patient's kidneys rises then falls. The reading from the other detector which is near the other kidney rises and does not fall. Discuss the conclusions that can be drawn from these observations.

3
a In the manufacture of metal foil, describe how the thickness of the foil is monitored using a radioactive source and a detector.

b Explain why the source needs to:

i   be a β-emitter, not an α-emitter or a γ-emitter,

ii have a long half-life.

4 A cardiac pacemaker is a device used to ensure that a faulty heart beats at a suitable rate. The required electrical energy in one type of pacemaker is obtained from the energy released by a radioactive isotope. The radiation is absorbed inside the pacemaker. As a result, the absorbing material gains thermal energy and heats a thermocouple attached to the absorbing material. The voltage from the thermocouple provides the source of electrical energy for the pacemaker.

a i   Discuss whether the radioactive source should be an α–emitter or a β-emitter or a γ-emitter.

ii The radioactive source needs to have a reasonably long half-life, otherwise it would need to be replaced frequently. Discuss the disadvantages of using a radioactive source with a very long half-life.

b The energy source for a remote weather station is the radioactive isotope of strontium, $_{38}^{90}$Sr which has a half-life of 28 years. It emits β particles of energy 0.40 MeV . For a mass of 10 g of this isotope, calculate:

i   its activity,

ii the energy released per second.

9.8 More about decay modes

Learning objectives:

▨ What can we tell about radioactive isotopes from an N–Z chart?

▨ Why don't naturally occurring isotopes emit β⁺ radiation?

▨ What happens to an unstable nucleus that emits γ radiation?

Specification reference: 3.5A.1

The N–Z graph

A useful way to survey nuclear stability is to plot a graph of the neutron number N against the proton number Z for all known isotopes, as shown in Figure 1. Each isotope is plotted on the graph according to its values of N and Z. The graph shows that stable nuclei lie along a belt curving upwards with an increasing neutron–proton ratio from the origin to $N = 120$, $Z = 80$ approximately.

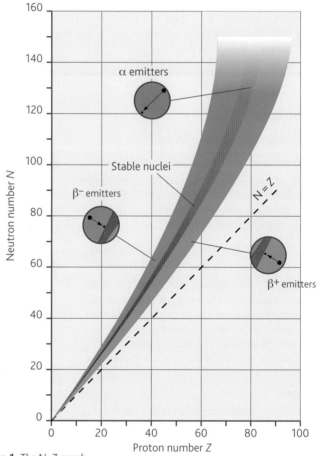

Figure 1 *The N–Z graph*

▨ **For light isotopes** (Z from 0 to no more than 20), the stable nuclei follow the straight line $N = Z$. Such nuclei have equal numbers of protons and neutrons.

▨ **As Z increases beyond about 20**, stable nuclei have more neutrons than protons. The neutron/proton ratio increases. The extra neutrons help to bind the **nucleons** together without introducing repulsive electrostatic forces as more protons would do.

▨ **α-emitters** occur at high values of proton numbers greater than about $Z = 80$. These nuclei have more neutrons than protons but they are too large to be stable. This is because the **strong nuclear force** between the nucleons is unable to overcome the electrostatic force of repulsion between the protons.

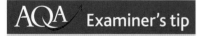

Examiner's tip

Neutron–proton ratio is high for β⁻ and low for β⁺ emitters.

There are no α-emitters for Z < about 60.

β⁻-**emitters** occur to the left of the stability belt where the isotopes are neutron-rich compared to stable isotopes. As explained previously, neutron-rich isotopes become stable or less unstable by 'converting' a neutron into a proton and emitting a β⁻ particle (and an electron antineutrino) at the same time.

β⁺-**emitters** occur to the right of the stability belt where the isotopes are proton-rich compared to stable isotopes. As explained previously, proton-rich isotopes become stable or less unstable by 'converting' a proton into a neutron and emitting a β⁺ particle (and an electron neutrino) at the same time. Electron capture also takes place in this region.

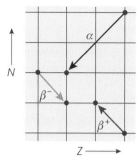

Figure 2 *N–Z changes*

The change that takes place when an unstable nucleus becomes less unstable or stable can be represented on the *N–Z* graph as shown in general in Figure 1 and in detail in Figure 2.

A nucleus that emits an α particle loses two protons and two neutrons so it moves diagonally downwards to the left across two grid squares.

A nucleus that emits a β⁻ particle loses a neutron and gains a proton so it moves diagonally downwards to the right across one grid square.

A nucleus that emits a β⁺ particle (or captures an electron) loses a proton and gains a neutron so it moves diagonally upwards to the left across one grid square.

■ Radioactive series

Many radioactive isotopes decay to form another isotope which might itself be unstable. When an unstable nucleus emits an α particle, its position on the *N–Z* plot moves downwards parallel to the *N = Z* line to a new position with a greater neutron–proton ratio. If the 'daughter' nucleus is also unstable, it will decay to form a nucleus of a different isotope (which may itself be stable or unstable) by either by emitting:

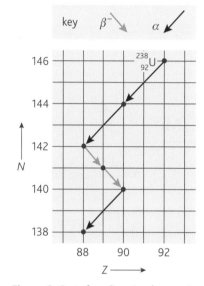

Figure 3 *Part of a radioactive decay series*

a further α particle, or:

a β⁻ particle if its position is to the left of the stability belt, or:

a β⁺ particle or by undergoing electron capture if, in both cases, its position is to the right of the stability belt.

Thus an unstable nucleus, before it becomes stable, may undergo a series of isotopic changes in which each change involves an emission of an α particle or a β particle. Naturally occurring radioactive isotopes decay through a series of such changes with one or more of the changes having a very long half-life – hence the reason why such isotopes have not decayed completely.

For example, the uranium isotope $^{238}_{92}$U has a half-life of 4500 million years and decays through a series of changes outlined below.

$$^{238}_{92}U \xrightarrow{\alpha} {}^{234}_{90}Th \xrightarrow{\alpha} {}^{230}_{88}Ra \xrightarrow{\beta^-} {}^{230}_{89}Ac \xrightarrow{\beta^-} {}^{230}_{90}Th \xrightarrow{\alpha} {}^{226}_{88}Ra \longrightarrow \ldots \longrightarrow {}^{206}_{82}Pb$$

Any radioactive series may be represented on the *N–Z* graph by a sequence of 'decay arrows' as shown in Figure 3, which represents the first five changes above. Notice there are no β⁺ emissions in the sequence because such an emission after an α emission would make the nucleus more neutron-rich, so moving it away from the stability belt. A β⁻ emission after an α emission makes the nucleus less neutron-rich causing it to be more stable and nearer the stability belt.

■ Link

β⁻-emitters can also be manufactured by bombarding stable isotopes with neutrons. β⁺-emitters can only be produced by bombarding stable isotopes with protons. The protons need to have sufficient kinetic energy to overcome coulomb repulsion from the nucleus. See Topic 9.1.

Notes

1 In Figure 4 the presence of two excited states is indicated by the fact that the two smaller γ energies add up to the largest γ energy.

2 In this example, the parent nucleus can also decay by β⁻ emission to the excited state of $^{27}_{13}$Al at 0.83 MeV then by emission of a γ photon of energy 0.83 MeV to the ground state. The β⁻ emission for this change is shown on Figure 4 by the dashed arrow.

Nuclear energy levels

After an unstable nucleus emits an α or a β particle or undergoes electron capture, it might emit a γ photon. Emission of a γ photon does not change the number of protons or the number of neutrons in the nucleus but it does allow the nucleus to lose energy. This happens if the 'daughter' nucleus is formed in an **excited state** after it emits an α or a β particle or undergoes electron capture. The excited state is usually short-lived and the nucleus moves to its lowest energy state, its **ground state**, either directly or via one or more lower-energy excited states. We can represent such changes by means of an energy level diagram, as shown by the example in Figure 4 in which:

■ a magnesium $^{27}_{12}$Mg nucleus decays by β⁻ emission (shown as a blue arrow) to form an aluminium $^{27}_{13}$Al nucleus in an excited state 1.02 MeV above the ground state at zero energy,

■ the aluminium nucleus de-excites by emitting (as shown by the green arrows) either a 1.02 MeV γ photon (1), or a 0.19 MeV γ photon (2) followed by a 0.83 MeV γ photon (3).

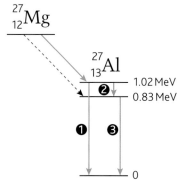

Figure 4 *Nuclear energy states*

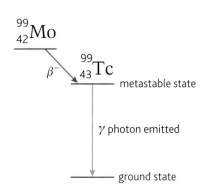

Figure 5 *The metastable state of technetium $^{99}_{43}$Tc*

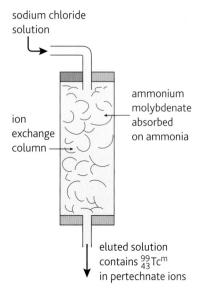

Figure 6 *The technetium generator*

Application and How science works

The technetium generator

The technetium generator is used in hospitals to produce a source which emits γ radiation only. Some radioactive isotopes such as the technetium isotope $^{99}_{43}$Tc form in an excited state after an α emission or a β emission and stay in the excited state long enough to be separated from the parent isotope. Such a long-lived excited state is said to be a **metastable state**. Nuclei of the technetium isotope $^{99}_{43}$Tc form in a metastable state (indicated by the symbol $^{99}_{43}$Tc^m) after β⁻ emission from nuclei of the molybdenum isotope $^{99}_{42}$Mo which has a half-life of 67 h. $^{99}_{43}$Tc^m has a half-life of 6 h and decays to the ground state by γ emission.

Technetium $^{99}_{43}$Tc in the ground state is a β⁻-emitter with a half-life of 500 000 years and it forms a stable product. Therefore, a sample of $^{99}_{43}$Tc^m with no molybdenum present effectively emits only γ photons. Such samples of technetium $^{99}_{43}$Tc^m are used in medical diagnosis applications, as outlined below.

The technetium generator consists of an ion exchange column containing ammonium molybdenate exposed to neutron radiation several days earlier to make a significant number of the molybdenum nuclei unstable. When a solution of sodium chloride is passed through the column, some of the chlorine ions exchange with pertechnate ions but not with molybdenate ions so the solution that emerges contains $^{99}_{43}$Tc^m nuclei.

Examples of diagnostic uses of $^{99}_{43}Tc^m$

■ Monitoring blood flow through the brain using external detectors after a small quantity of sodium pertechnate solution is administered intravenously,

■ The γ camera is designed to 'image' internal organs and bones by detecting γ radiation from sites in the body where a γ-emitting isotope such as $^{99}_{43}Tc^m$ nuclei are located. For example, bone deposits can be located using a phosphate tracer labelled with $^{99}_{43}Tc^m$. The γ camera itself consists of detectors called photomultiplier tubes in a lead shield behind a lead collimator grid which ensures each tube only detects γ photons emitted from nuclei located at a well-defined spot directly in front of the tube.

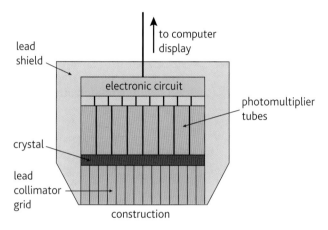

Figure 7 *The γ camera*

Summary questions

1 a Sketch an N–Z graph to show how N varies with Z for the known stable isotopes.

   b Show on your diagram possible locations of an isotope that is

   i an α-emitter,

   ii a β⁻-emitter,

   iii a β⁺-emitter.

2 A nucleus of the polonium isotope $^{216}_{84}Po$ decays to form a stable nucleus X by emitting in succession an α particle, a β⁻ particle, a further β⁻ particle then another α particle.

   a Determine the number of protons and the number of neutrons in X.

   b Show the changes on the grid of an N–Z chart.

3 a Explain what is meant by electron capture.

   b State one similarity and one difference between electron capture and positron emission.

4 The germanium isotope $^{77}_{32}Ge$ has a metastable state which decays to the ground state by emission of a 0.16 MeV γ photon. The isotope decays by β⁻ emission to form the arsenic isotope $^{77}_{33}As$ in an excited state 0.48 MeV above the ground state of $^{77}_{33}As$.

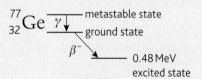

a Copy and complete the energy level diagram above to show these changes.

b The excited state of $^{77}_{33}As$ also decays to the ground state via an excited state which is 0.27 MeV above the ground state. Calculate the energies of the γ photons emitted in this decay.

9.9 Nuclear radius

Learning objectives:

- Are more massive nuclei wider?

- How does the radius of a nucleus depend on its mass number *A*?

- How dense is the nucleus?

Specification reference: 3.5A.1

Notes

The following notes are not required in the A2 specification for this module. They are provided here to help you to gain a better understanding of the topic.

1 The angle θ_{min} depends on the radius *R* of the nucleus in accordance with the equation $R \sin \theta_{min} = 0.61\lambda$, where λ is the de Broglie wavelength of the electrons. The equation is derived by applying wave theory to plane waves passing at normal incidence through a circular gap.

2 The wavelength of high-energy electrons is calculated using the equation $\lambda = hc/E$, where *E* is the energy of the electrons. The speed of a high-energy electron is very close to *c*, the speed of light in a vacuum. Therefore, $\lambda = h/mv = h/mc = hc/E$, as $E = mc^2$. In practice, electrons need to be accelerated through pds greater than about 100 million volts to be diffracted significantly by the nucleus.

3 Prove for yourself that values of $E = 420$ MeV and $\theta_{min} = 44°$ obtained for oxygen nuclei give a de Broglie wavelength of 3.0 fm and a nuclear radius for the oxygen nucleus of 2.6 fm. See Reference data at the end of the book for values of *h* and *c*. Note that 1 MeV $= 1.6 \times 10^{-13}$ J

High-energy electron diffraction

In Topic 9.1, we estimated the diameter of the nucleus to be about a femtometre (1 fm = 10^{-15} m) using two methods. In this topic we will look at a much more accurate method to measure the diameter of different nuclides using high-energy electrons. When a beam of high-energy electrons is directed at a thin solid sample of an element, the incident electrons are diffracted by the nuclei of the atoms in the foil. The beam is produced by accelerating electrons through a potential difference of the order of a hundred million volts. The electrons are diffracted by the nuclei because the **de Broglie wavelength** of such high-energy electrons is of the order of 10^{-15} m which is about the same as the diameter of the nucleus. A detector is used to measure the number of electrons per second diffracted through different angles.

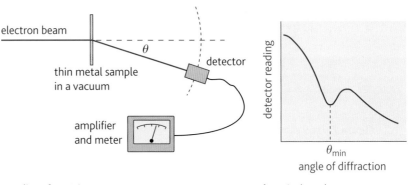

a *outline of experiment*   **b** *typical results*

Figure 1 *High energy electron diffraction*

The measurements show that as the angle θ of the detector to the 'zero order' beam is increased, the number of electrons per second (i.e. the intensity of the beam) diffracted into the detector decreases then increases slightly then decreases again.

- Scattering of the beam electrons by the nuclei occurs due to their charge. This is the same as α-scattering by nuclei except the electrons are attracted not repelled by the nuclei. This effect causes the intensity to decrease as angle θ increases.

- Diffraction of the beam electrons by each nucleus causes intensity maxima and minima to be superimposed on the effect above. This happens provided the de Broglie wavelength of the electrons in the beam is no greater than the dimensions of the nucleus. These superimposed intensity variations are, on a much smaller scale, similar to the concentric bright and dark fringes seen when a parallel beam of monochromatic light is directed at a circular gap or obstacle. The angle of the first minimum from the centre, θ_{min}, is measured and used to calculate the diameter of the nucleus, provided the wavelength of the incident electrons is known. See the notes in the margin.

Dependence of nuclear radius on nucleon number

Using samples of different elements, the radius R of different nuclides can be measured. By plotting a suitable graph as explained below, it can be shown that R depends on mass number A according to $R = r_0 A^{1/3}$, where the constant $r_0 = 1.05\,\text{fm}$.

- A graph of $\ln R$ against $\ln A$ gives a straight line with a gradient of $\frac{1}{3}$ and a y-intercept equal to $\ln r_0$ This is because $\ln R = \ln A^{1/3} + \ln r_0 = \frac{1}{3}\ln A + \ln r_0$. See Topic 15.3. Plotting this graph as shown in Figure 2a therefore confirms the power of A in the equation is $\frac{1}{3}$ and it also gives a value for r_0 as the y-intercept is equal to $\ln r_0$.
- A graph of R against $A^{1/3}$ gives a straight line through the origin with a gradient equal to r_0 as shown in Figure 2b. Plotting this graph gives an accurate value of r_0.
- A graph of R^3 against A gives a straight line through the origin with a gradient equal to r_0^3. Plotting this graph would also give an accurate value of r_0.

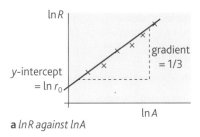
a *ln R against ln A*

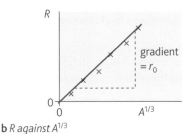
b *R against $A^{1/3}$*

Figure 2 *Nuclear radius graphs*

Nuclear density

Assuming the nucleus is spherical, its volume $V = \frac{4}{3}\pi R^3 = \frac{4}{3}\pi(r_0 A^{1/3})^3 = \frac{4}{3}\pi r_0^3 A$

This means that the nuclear volume V is proportional to the mass of the nucleus. In other words, the density of the nucleus is constant, independent of its radius, and is the same throughout a nucleus. From this, we can conclude that nucleons are separated by the same distance regardless of the size of the nucleus and are therefore evenly separated inside the nucleus.

We can calculate the density of a nucleus using the volume formula above $(V = \frac{4}{3}\pi r_0^3 A)$ and the knowledge that its mass $m = A\text{u}$ where $1\,\text{u} = 1$ atomic mass unit $= 1.661 \times 10^{-27}\,\text{kg}$.

Hence the density of a nucleus $= \dfrac{A\text{u}}{\frac{4}{3}\pi r_0^3 A} = \dfrac{1\,\text{u}}{\frac{4}{3}\pi r_0^3} = \dfrac{1.661 \times 10^{-27}}{\frac{4}{3}\pi(1.05 \times 10^{-15})^3}$
$$= 3.4 \times 10^{17}\,\text{kg m}^{-3}$$

- A cubic millimetre of nuclear matter would have a mass of about 340 million kilograms, about the same as the total body mass of about 4 million adults.
- A neutron star is almost as dense as the nucleus of an atom. For example, a neutron star of diameter 25 km and a mass of about $4 \times 10^{30}\,\text{kg}$ (about 2 solar masses) has a density of $6 \times 10^{16}\,\text{kg m}^{-3}$.

Link
log–log graphs are used to find the power n in a relationship of the form $y = kx^n$. If a graph of $\log y$ against $\log x$ is not straight, the relationship is not of this form. See Topic 15.3.

Hint
density $= \dfrac{\text{mass}}{\text{volume}}$.
See *AS Physics* 11.1.

Summary questions
$r_0 = 1.05\,\text{fm}$

1. a Explain why a beam of high-energy electrons directed at a target is diffracted by the nuclei in the target.
   b Sketch a graph to show how the intensity of the electrons varies with the angle of diffraction.
   c The radius of a nucleus can be determined from high-energy electron diffraction experiments. Explain why it is important that the electrons in the beam have the same kinetic energy.

2. The volume of a $^{28}_{14}\text{Si}$ nucleus is $1.4 \times 10^{-43}\,\text{m}^3$. Use this value to calculate:
   a the radius of the nucleus,
   b the radius of a $^{120}_{50}\text{Sn}$ nucleus.

3. a State the relationship between the radius R of a nucleus and its mass number A.
   b Calculate the radius and the volume of a $^{238}_{92}\text{U}$ nucleus.

4. a Compare, without calculations, the scattering by nuclei of α particles and high-energy electrons.
   b Calculate the radius and density of a $^{14}_{7}\text{N}$ nucleus.

AQA Examiner's tip
Know how to raise a number to any given power; know how to plot and use a log–log graph of $y = kx^n$ to find n.

1   The neutron–proton model of the nucleus was first put forward by Rutherford to explain the general composition of the nucleus. The existence of the neutron was not proved experimentally until some years later.

(a) Give **two** reasons why Rutherford's neutron–proton model was considered more than an untested hypothesis when it was first put forward.   *(3 marks)*

(b) The α particles from any α-emitting isotope have the same initial kinetic energy and a well-defined range in air at atmospheric pressure. The table below shows the range R in air and the initial kinetic energy E of α particles from several α-emitting isotopes.

R/mm	39	48	53	57	66	78
E/MeV	5.3	6.0	6.5	6.8	7.4	8.3

Plot a suitable graph to find out if the relationship between R and E is of the form $R = kE^n$, where k and n are constants, and determine a value for n. Explain your choice of graph.   *(10 marks)*

2   **Figure 1** shows the apparatus in which α particles are directed at a metal foil in order to investigate the structure of the atom.

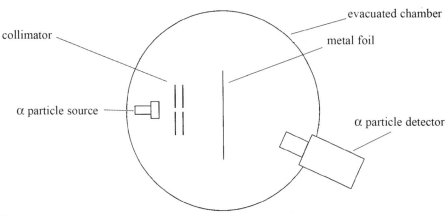

Figure 1

(a) (i)   Give **two** reasons why the metal foil should be thin.

(ii) Explain why the incident beam of α particles should be narrow.   *(3 marks)*

(b) Describe and explain **one** feature of the distribution of the scattered α particles that suggests the nucleus contains most of the mass of an atom.   *(2 marks)*

(c) **Figure 2** shows three α particles with the same constant velocity incident on an atom in the metal foil. They all approach the nucleus close enough to be deflected by at least 10°.

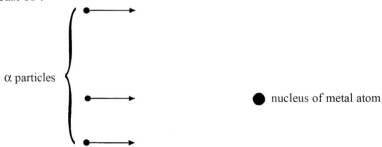

Figure 2

Draw the paths followed by the three α particles whose initial directions are shown by the arrows.

(3 marks)

AQA, 2007

3 A radioactive nucleus decays with the emission of an alpha particle and a gamma-ray photon.

(a) Describe the changes that occur in the proton number and the nucleon number of the nucleus. *(2 marks)*

(b) Comment on the relative penetrating powers of the two types of ionising radiation. *(1 mark)*

(c) Gamma rays from a point source are travelling towards a detector. The distance from the source to the detector is changed from 1.0 m to 3.0 m.

Calculate:

$$\frac{\text{intensity of radiation at 3.0 m}}{\text{intensity of radiation at 1.0 m}}$$

(2 marks)

AQA, 2006

4 (a) A radioactive source gives an initial count rate of 110 counts per second. After 10 minutes the count rate is 84 counts per second.

background radiation = 3 counts per second

(i) Give **three** origins of the radiation that contributes to this background radiation.

(ii) Calculate the decay constant of the radioactive source in s^{-1}.

(iii) Calculate the number of radioactive nuclei in the initial sample assuming that the detector counts all the radiation emitted from the source. *(7 marks)*

(b) Discuss the dangers of exposing the human body to a source of α radiation. In particular compare the dangers when the α source is held outside, but in contact with the body, with those when the source is placed inside the body. *(3 marks)*

AQA, 2004

5 The radioactive isotope of sodium $_{11}^{22}\text{Na}$ has a half-life of 2.6 years. A particular sample of this isotope has an initial activity of 5.5×10^5 Bq.

(a) Explain what is meant by the *random nature* of radioactive decay. *(2 marks)*

(b) Sketch a graph of the activity of the sample of sodium over a period of 6 years. *(2 marks)*

(c) Calculate:

(i) the decay constant, in s^{-1}, of $_{11}^{22}\text{Na}$,

1 year = 3.15×10^7 s

(ii) the number of atoms of $_{11}^{22}\text{Na}$ in the sample initially,

(iii) the time taken, in s, for the activity of the sample to fall from 1.0×10^5 Bq to 0.75×10^5 Bq. *(6 marks)*

AQA, 2003

6 Iodine-123 is a radioisotope used medically as a tracer to monitor thyroid and kidney functions. The decay of an iodine-123 nucleus produces a gamma ray which, when emitted from inside the body of a patient, can be detected externally.

(a) Why are gamma rays the most suitable type of nuclear radiation for this application? *(2 marks)*

(b) In a laboratory experiment on a sample of iodine-123 the following data were collected.

time/h	0	4	8	12	16	20	24	28	32
count rate/counts s^{-1}	512	401	338	279	217	191	143	119	91

Why was it unnecessary to correct these values for background radiation? *(2 marks)*

(c) Draw a graph of count rate against time. *(2 marks)*

(d) Use your graph to find an accurate value for the half-life of iodine-123.

Show clearly the method you use. *(3 marks)*

(e) Give **two** reasons why radioisotopes with short half-lives are particularly suitable for use as a medical tracer. *(2 marks)*

AQA, 2004

7 (a) Sodium-21 ($^{21}_{11}$Na) decays to neon-21 ($^{21}_{10}$Ne). A nucleus of neon-21 is stable.

  (i) State the names of the particles emitted when a sodium-21 nucleus decays.

  (ii) How many neutrons are there in a nucleus of neon-21? *(3 marks)*

  (b) **Figure 2** shows how the activity A of a freshly prepared sample of sodium-21 varies as it decays. **Figure 3** shows how N, the number of sodium-21 nuclei, varies with time t during the same time interval.

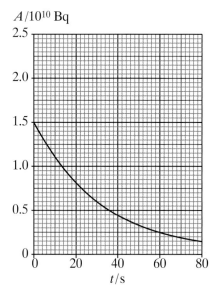

Figure 3   **Figure 4**

  (i) Use the graphs to find the number of active sodium nuclei and the corresponding activity one half-life after $t = 0$. Hence find the probability of decay of a sodium-21 nucleus.

  (ii) The total energy produced when a sodium-21 nucleus decays is 5.7×10^{-13} J. Calculate the number of radioactive atoms in a sample that is producing 2.6 mJ of energy each second. *(6 marks)*

AQA, 2003

8 (a) Calculate the radius of the $^{238}_{92}$U nucleus.

  $r_0 = 1.3 \times 10^{-15}$ m *(2 marks)*

  (b) At a distance of 30 mm from a point source of γ rays the corrected count rate is C.

  Calculate the distance from the source at which the corrected count rate is $0.10\,C$, assuming that there is no absorption. *(2 marks)*

  (c) The activity of a source of β particles falls to 85% of its initial value in 52 s. Calculate the decay constant of the source. *(3 marks)*

  (d) Explain why the isotope of technetium, ^{99}Tc$_m$, is often chosen as a suitable source of radiation for use in medical diagnosis. *(3 marks)*

AQA, 2006

9   The high-energy electron diffraction apparatus represented in **Figure 3** can be used to determine nuclear radii. The intensity of the electron beam received by the detector is measured at various diffraction angles, θ.

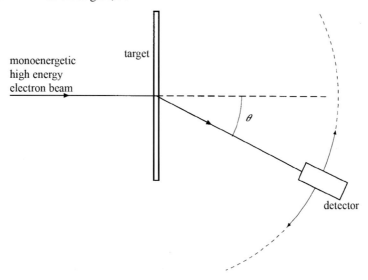

Figure 5

(a) Sketch a graph to show how, in such an electron diffraction experiment, the electron intensity varies with the angle of diffraction, θ.   *(2 marks)*

(b) (i) Use the data in the table to plot a straight line graph that confirms the relationship

$$R = r_0 A^{1/3}$$

element	radius of nucleus, $R/10^{-15}$ m	nucleon number, A
lead	6.66	208
tin	5.49	120
iron	4.35	56
silicon	3.43	28
carbon	2.66	12

(ii) Estimate the value of r_0 from the graph.   *(5 marks)*

(c) Discuss the merits of using high-energy electrons to determine nuclear radii rather than using α particles.   *(3 marks)*

AQA, 2005

10.1 Energy and mass

Learning objectives:

- What does $E = mc^2$ mean?

- What happens to the mass of an object when it gains or loses energy?

- How can we calculate the energy released in a nuclear reaction?

Specification reference: 3.5A.2

In 1905, Einstein published his theory of special relativity. He showed that moving clocks run slower than stationary clocks, fast-moving objects appear shorter than when stationary, the mass of a moving object changes with its speed and no material object can travel as fast as light. He also showed that the mass of an object increases (or decreases) when it gains (or loses) energy, E, in accordance with the equation

$$E = mc^2$$

where m is the change of its mass and c is the speed of light in free space which is $3.0 \times 10^8 \, \text{m s}^{-1}$.

For example,

- a sealed torch that radiates 10 W of light for 10 h (= 36 000 s) would lose 0.36 MJ of energy (= 10 W × 36 000 s). Its mass would therefore decrease by 4.0×10^{-12} kg (= $0.36 \, \text{MJ}/c^2$), an insignificant amount compared with the mass of the torch,

- a car of 1000 kg mass that speeds up from a standstill to 30 m s^{-1} would gain 450 kJ of kinetic energy so its mass when moving at 30 m s^{-1} would be 5.0×10^{-12} kg (= $450 \, \text{kJ}/c^2$) more than when it is at rest.

- an unstable nucleus that releases a 5 MeV γ photon would lose 8.0×10^{-13} J of energy. Its mass would therefore decrease by 8.9×10^{-30} kg (= $8.0 \times 10^{-13} \, \text{J}/c^2$) which is not an insignificant amount compared with the mass of a nucleus.

The equation applies to all energy changes of any object. These two examples show that such changes are important in nuclear reactions but are not usually significant otherwise. A century after Einstein published his theory, the reason why the mass of an object changes when energy is transferred to or from it is still not clearly understood. However, as explained in your AS course, we know that for every type of particle, there is a corresponding antiparticle with the same mass and opposite charge (if charged) and we know that

- when a particle and its corresponding antiparticle meet, they **annihilate** each other and 2 gamma (γ) photons are produced, each of energy mc^2 where m is the mass of the particle or antiparticle.

- a single γ photon of energy in excess of $2 \, mc^2$ can produce a particle and an antiparticle, each of mass m, in a process known as **pair production**.

Energy changes in reactions

Reactions on a nuclear or sub-nuclear scale do involve significant changes of mass. For example, in radioactive decay, if we know the exact rest mass of each particle involved, we can calculate the energy released Q from the difference Δm in the total mass before and after the reaction. In general, for a spontaneous reaction in which no energy is supplied

$$\text{the energy released } Q = \Delta mc^2$$

In any change where energy is released such as radioactive decay, the total mass after the change is always less than the total mass before the change. This is because, in the change, some of the mass is converted to energy which is released.

1 In α **decay**, the nucleus recoils when the α particle is emitted so the energy released is shared between the α particle and the nucleus. Applying conservation of momentum to the recoil, you should be able to show that the energy released is shared between the α particle and the nucleus in inverse proportion to their masses.

2 In β **decay,** the energy released is shared in variable proportions between the β particle, the nucleus and the neutrino or antineutrino released in the decay. When the β particle has maximum kinetic energy, the neutrino or antineutrino has negligible kinetic energy in comparison. The maximum kinetic energy of the β particle is very slightly less than the energy released in the decay because of recoil of the nucleus.

3 In **electron capture**, the nucleus emits a neutrino which carries away the energy released in the decay. The atom also emits an X-ray photon when the inner-shell vacancy due to the electron capture is filled.

Notes

1 To calculate the energy corresponding to a mass difference of 1 atomic mass unit ($1u = 1.661 \times 10^{-27}$ kg), using $E = mc^2$ gives $E = 1.661 \times 10^{-27}$ kg $\times (3.0 \times 10^8 \, \text{m s}^{-1})^2 = 1.49 \times 10^{-10}$ J $= 931.3$ MeV.

2 When calculating Q in beta decay, assume the mass of the neutrino is negligible.

3 If the mass of each atom is given instead of the mass of its nucleus, calculate the mass of each nucleus by subtracting the mass of the electrons ($= Zm_e$) in the atom from the mass of each atom.

Worked example:

The polonium isotope $^{210}_{84}$Po emits α particles and decays to form the stable isotope of lead $^{206}_{82}$Pb. Write down an equation to represent this process and calculate the energy released when a $^{210}_{84}$Po nucleus emits an α particle.

mass of $^{210}_{84}$Po nucleus $= 209.93667 \, u$

mass of $^{206}_{82}$Pb nucleus $= 205.92936 \, u$

mass of α particle $= 4.00150 \, u$

$1u$ is equivalent to 931.3 MeV

Solution

$^{210}_{84}$Po $\longrightarrow$ $^{4}_{2}\alpha + ^{206}_{82}$Pb (+ energy released Q)

mass difference $=$ total initial mass $-$ total final mass

$= 209.93667 - (205.92936 + 4.00150) = 5.81 \times 10^{-3} u$

energy released Q $=$ mass difference in u $\times 931.3 = 5.41$ MeV

Examiner's tip

In an exam question, if the masses of the nuclei and particles involved are given in atomic mass units (u), calculate the difference between the total initial mass and the total final mass in u then multiply by 931.3 to give the energy released in MeV. The conversion factor $1u = 931.3$ MeV is given in the data booklet so you don't have to prove it unless specifically asked to do so.

More about the strong nuclear force

As explained in your AS course, the fact that most nuclei are stable tells us there must be an attractive force, the strong nuclear force, between any two protons or neutrons in the nucleus.

The strength of the strong nuclear force can be estimated by working out the force of repulsion between two protons at a separation of 1 fm ($= 10^{-15}$ m), the approximate size of the nucleus. The strong nuclear force must be greater in magnitude that this force of repulsion. Prove for yourself, using Coulomb's law of force (see 5.4), that the force of repulsion between 2 protons at a separation of 10^{-15} m is of the order of 200 N. So the strong nuclear force is at least 200 N.

■ The range of the strong nuclear force is no more than about 3 to 4 × 10^{-15} m. The diameter of a nucleus can be measured from high-energy electron scattering experiments (see Topic 9.9). The results show that nucleons are evenly spaced at about 10^{-15} m in the nucleus and therefore the strong nuclear force acts only between nearest neighbour nucleons.

■ The energy needed to pull a nucleon out of the nucleus is of the order of millions of electron volts (MeV). This can be deduced because the strong nuclear force is at least about 200 N and it acts over a distance of about 2 to 3 × 10^{-15} m. The work done by the strong nuclear force over this distance is therefore about 7 × 10^{-13} J (= 200 N × 3.5 × 10^{-15} m) which is about 4 MeV, as 1 MeV = 1.6 × 10^{-13} J.

■ The strong nuclear force between two nucleons must become repulsive at separations of about 0.5 fm or less, otherwise nucleons would pull each other closer and closer together and the nucleus would be much smaller than it is.

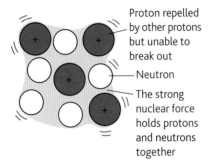

Proton repelled by other protons but unable to break out

Neutron

The strong nuclear force holds protons and neutrons together

Figure 1 *The strong nuclear force*

Summary questions

rest mass of an electron = 9.11×10^{-31} kg

1 u = 931.3 MeV

$g = 9.81$ m s^{-2}

1 Calculate the mass increase of:

a a 10 kg object when it is raised through a height of 2.0 m,

b an electron when it is accelerated from rest through a pd of

   i   5000 V,

   ii 5 MV

2 The bismuth isotope $^{212}_{83}$Bi emits α particles and decays to form the stable isotope of thallium $^{208}_{81}$Tl.

a Write down an equation to represent this process and calculate the energy released.

mass of $^{212}_{83}$Bi nucleus = 211.945 62 u

mass of $^{208}_{81}$Tl nucleus = 207.937 46 u

mass of α particle = 4.001 50 u

b Explain without calculation why the thallium nucleus in the above decay gains a small proportion of the energy released.

3 The strontium isotope $^{90}_{38}$Sr emits β$^-$ particles and decays to form the stable isotope of thallium $^{90}_{39}$Y.

a Write down an equation to represent this process and calculate the energy released.

mass of $^{90}_{38}$Sr nucleus = 89.886 40 u

mass of $^{90}_{39}$Y nucleus = 89.885 25 u

mass of β$^-$ particle = 0.000 55 u

b Explain without calculation why the kinetic energy of the β$^-$ particle released when the strontium nucleus decays varies from zero up to a maximum.

4 The copper isotope $^{64}_{29}$Cu decays through electron capture to form the stable isotope of nickel $^{64}_{28}$Ni.

a Write down an equation to represent this process and calculate the energy released.

mass of $^{64}_{29}$Cu nucleus = 63.913 81 u

mass of $^{64}_{28}$Ni nucleus = 63.912 56 u

mass of electron = 0.000 55 u

b State the name of the particle that takes away the energy released by the nucleus in electron capture.

10.2 Binding energy

Learning objectives:

▥ What is binding energy?

▥ Which nuclei are the most stable?

▥ Why is energy released when a $^{235}_{92}$U nucleus undergoes fission?

Specification reference: 3.5A.2

Suppose all the nucleons in a nucleus were separated from one another, removing each one from the nucleus in turn. Work must be done to overcome the strong nuclear force and separate each nucleon from the others. The potential energy of each nucleon is therefore increased when it is removed from the nucleus.

The binding energy of the nucleus is the work that must be done to separate a nucleus into its constituent neutrons and protons.

When a nucleus **forms** from separate neutrons and protons, energy is released as the strong nuclear force does work pulling the nucleons together, The energy released is equal to the binding energy of the nucleus. Because energy is released when a nucleus forms from separate neutrons and protons, the mass of a nucleus is less than the mass of the separated nucleons.

The mass defect Δm of a nucleus is defined as the difference between the mass of the separated nucleons and the mass of the nucleus.

▥ Calculation of the mass defect of a nucleus of known mass; a nucleus of an isotope $^{A}_{Z}$X is composed of Z protons and $(A-Z)$ neutrons. Therefore, for a nucleus $^{A}_{Z}$X of mass M_{NUC},

its mass defect $\Delta m = Zm_p + (A-Z)m_N - M_{NUC}$

where m_p and m_N represent the masses of the proton and the neutron respectively.

▥ Calculation of the binding energy of a nucleus; The mass defect Δm is due to energy released when the nucleus formed from separate neutrons and protons. The energy released in this process is equal to the binding energy of the nucleus. Therefore,

the binding energy of a nucleus = $\Delta m c^2$

▥ **Link**

Remember $1\,\text{MeV} = 1.6 \times 10^{-13}\,\text{J}$ (and $1\,\text{eV} = 1.6 \times 10^{-19}\,\text{J}$). See *AS Physics* Topic 1.4.

Worked example:

> The mass of a nucleus of the bismuth isotope $^{212}_{83}$Bi is $211.800\,12\,\text{u}$. Calculate the binding energy of this nucleus in MeV.
>
> The mass of a proton, $m_p = 1.007\,28\,\text{u}$; the mass of a neutron, $m_N = 1.008\,67\,\text{u}$.
>
> $1\,\text{u}$ is equivalent to $= 931.3\,\text{MeV}$
>
> *Solution*
>
> Mass defect $\Delta m = 83\,m_p + (212-83)\,m_N - M_{NUC} = 1.922\,55\,\text{u}$
>
> $\therefore$ binding energy $= 1.922\,55\,\text{u} \times 931.3\,\text{MeV/u} = 1790\,\text{MeV}$

▥ How science works

α particle tunnelling

If two protons and two neutrons inside a sufficiently large nucleus bind together as a 'cluster', they may be emitted from the nucleus as an α particle. This is because the binding energy of an α particle is very

1 The mass of an atom of an isotope $^A_Z X$ is measured using a mass spectrometer. The mass of a nucleus can then be calculated by subtracting the mass of Z electrons from the atomic mass.

2 The atomic mass unit, $1u = 1.661 \times 10^{-27}$ kg. This is defined as $\frac{1}{12}$th of the mass of an atom of the carbon isotope $^{12}_6 C$.

3 The energy corresponding to a mass of $1u = 1.661 \times 10^{-27} \times (3.00 \times 10^8)^2 J = 931.3$ MeV. In an exam question, if the mass of the nucleus is given in kilograms, you can convert this to atomic mass units and use the method above to calculate the mass defect. The values of the mass of the proton and the neutron are given in atomic mass units in the data sheet.

large at about 7 MeV per nucleon compared with other neutron and proton clusters that may form. The α particle therefore gains sufficient kinetic energy (= to the binding energy of the cluster) to give it a small probability of 'quantum tunnelling' from the nucleus.

Figure 1 shows how the potential energy of an α particle varies with its distance from outside the nucleus to inside. The 'coulomb' barrier is due to the electrostatic force on the α particle. The 'well' is due to the strong nuclear force. The gain of kinetic energy of the α particle when it forms in the nucleus is sufficient for it to reach the coulomb barrier but not for it to surmount the barrier directly. However, the wave nature of the α particle gives it a small probability of tunnelling through the barrier.

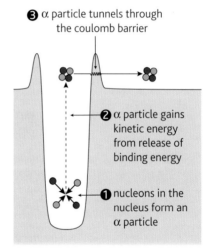

Figure 1 *Quantum tunnelling from the nucleus*

Nuclear stability

The binding energy of each nuclide is different. The **binding energy per nucleon** of a nucleus is the average work done per nucleon to remove all the **nucleons** from a nucleus; it is therefore a measure of the stability of a nucleus. For example, the binding energy per nucleon of the $^{212}_{83}Bi$ nucleus is 8.4 MeV per nucleon (= 1790 MeV/212 nucleons).

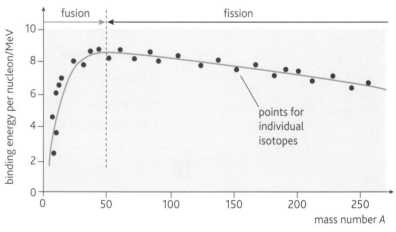

Figure 2 *Binding energy per nucleon for all known nuclides*

If the binding energies per nucleon of two different nuclides are compared, the nucleus with more binding energy per nucleon is the more stable of the two nuclei. Figure 2 shows a graph of the binding energy per nucleon against mass number A for all the known nuclides. This graph is a curve which has a maximum value of 8.7 MeV per nucleon between $A = 50$ and $A = 60$. Nuclei with mass numbers in this range are the most stable nuclei. As explained below, energy is released in:

- **nuclear fission**, the process in which a large unstable nucleus splits into two fragments which are more stable than the original nucleus. The binding energy per nucleon increases in this process, as shown in Figure 2.
- **nuclear fusion**, the process of making small nuclei fuse together to form a larger nucleus. The product nucleus has more binding energy per nucleon than the smaller nuclei. So the binding energy per nucleon also increases in this process, provided the nucleon number of the product nucleus is no greater than about 50.

Note:

The change of binding energy per nucleon is about 0.5 MeV in a fission reaction and can be more than 10 times as much in a fusion reaction.

Summary questions

mass of a proton, $m_p = 1.00728\,u$;

mass of a neutron, $m_N = 1.00867\,u$

$1\,u$ is equivalent to 931.3 MeV

1 a Explain what is meant by the binding energy of a nucleus.

   b Sketch a curve to show how the binding energy per nucleon of a nucleus varies with its mass number A, showing the approximate scale on each axis.

2 Calculate the binding energy per nucleon, in MeV per nucleon, of:

   a a $^{12}_{6}C$ nucleus (mass = 12 u by definition),

   b a $^{56}_{26}Fe$ nucleus (mass = 55.920 67 u)

3 a Calculate the binding energy per nucleon in MeV per nucleon, of
   i an α particle, ii a $^{3}_{2}He$ nucleus.

   Mass of an α particle = 4.001 50 u; mass of a $^{3}_{2}He$ nucleus = 3.014 93 u

   b Use the results of your calculations in a to explain why an α particle rather than a $^{3}_{2}He$ nucleus is emitted by a large unstable nucleus.

4 a Complete the equation below to show the fusion reaction that occurs when two protons fuse together to form a $^{2}_{1}H$ nucleus.

   $$p + p \longrightarrow {}^{2}_{1}H + \beta^{+}$$

   b Calculate the binding energy per nucleon, in MeV, of the $^{2}_{1}H$ nucleus.

   mass of $^{2}_{1}H$ nucleus = 2.013 55 u

10.3 Fission and fusion

Learning objectives:

■ How much energy is released in a fission or a fusion reaction?

■ Why can't small nuclei be split?

■ Why can't large nuclei be fused?

Specification reference: 3.5A.2

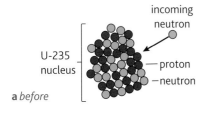

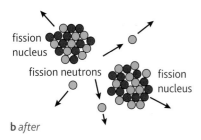

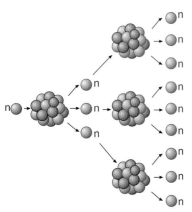

Figure 1 Induced fission

Induced fission

Fission of a nucleus occurs when a nucleus splits into two approximately equal fragments. This happens when the uranium isotope $^{235}_{92}U$ is bombarded with neutrons, a discovery made by Hahn and Strassmann in 1938. The process is known as **induced fission**. The plutonium isotope, $^{239}_{94}Pu$, is the only other isotope that is fissionable. This isotope is an artificial isotope formed by bombarding nuclei of the uranium isotope $^{235}_{92}U$ with neutrons.

Hahn and Strassman knew that bombarding different elements with neutrons produces radioactive isotopes. Uranium is the heaviest of all the naturally occurring elements; scientists thought that neutron bombardment could turn uranium nuclei into even heavier nuclei. Hahn and Strassmann undertook the difficult work of analysing chemically the products of uranium after neutron bombardment to try to discover any new elements heavier than uranium. Instead, they discovered that many lighter elements such as barium were present after bombardment, even though the uranium was pure before. The conclusion could only be that uranium nuclei were split into two approximately equal fragment nuclei as a result of neutron bombardment.

Further investigations showed that each fission event releases energy and two or three neutrons.

■ **Fission neutrons**, the neutrons released in a fission event, are each capable of causing a further fission event as a result of a collision with another $^{235}_{92}U$ nucleus. A **chain reaction** is therefore possible in which fission neutrons produce further fission events which release fission neutrons and cause further fission events and so on. If each fission event releases 2 neutrons on average, after n 'generations' of fission events, the number of fission neutrons would be 2^n. Prove for yourself that fission of 6×10^{23} $^{235}_{92}U$ nuclei (i.e. 235 g of the isotope) would happen in 79 generations. As explained on page 191, each fission event releases about 200 MeV of energy. Because each event takes no more than a fraction of a second, a huge amount of energy is released in a very short time. Using the above figures, complete fission of 235 g of $^{235}_{92}U$ would release about 10^{13} J (= $6 \times 10^{23} \times 200$ MeV). This is about a million times more than the energy released as a result of burning a similar mass of fossil fuel.

■ **Energy is released** when a fission event occurs because the fragments repel each other (as they are both positively charged) with sufficient force to overcome the strong nuclear force trying to hold them together. The fragment nuclei and the fission neutrons therefore gain kinetic energy. The two fragment nuclei are smaller and therefore more tightly bound than the original $^{235}_{92}U$ nucleus. In other words, they have more binding energy so they are more stable than the original nucleus. The energy released is equal to the change of binding energy. The binding energy of each nucleon increases from about 7.5 MeV to about 8.5 MeV as a result of the fission event. As there are about 240 nucleons in the original nucleus, the energy released in a fission event is of the order of 200 MeV (= 240 × about 1 MeV).

■ Many fission products are possible when a fission event occurs. For example, the following equation shows a fission event in which

Figure 2 A chain reaction in a nuclear reactor

a $^{235}_{92}$U nucleus is split into a barium nucleus $^{144}_{56}$Ba nucleus and a krypton $^{90}_{36}$Kr nucleus and two neutrons are released.

$$^{235}_{92}\text{U} + {^1_0}\text{n} \longrightarrow {^{144}_{56}}\text{Ba} + {^{90}_{36}}\text{Kr} + 2\,{^1_0}\text{n} + \text{energy released, } Q$$

■ The energy released, Q, can be calculated using $E = mc^2$ in the form $Q = \Delta mc^2$, where Δm is the difference between the total mass before and after the event.

■ In the above equation, the mass difference

$$\Delta m = M_{\text{U-238}} - M_{\text{Ba-144}} - M_{\text{Kr-90}} - m_{\text{n}'}$$

where M represents the appropriate nuclear mass and m_n is the mass of the neutron.

Nuclear fusion

Fusion takes place when two nuclei combine to form a bigger nucleus. The binding energy curve (see Topic 10.2, Figure 2), shows that if two light nuclei are combined, the individual nucleons become more tightly bound together. The binding energy per nucleon of the product nucleus is greater than of the initial nuclei. In other words, the nucleons become even more trapped in the nucleus when fusion occurs. As a result, energy is released equal to the increase of binding energy.

Nuclear fusion can only take place if the two nuclei that are to be combined collide at high speed. This is necessary to overcome the electrostatic repulsion between the two nuclei so they can become close enough to interact through the strong nuclear force. Some examples of nuclear fusion reactions are given below.

1 The fusion of two protons produces a nucleus of deuterium (the hydrogen isotope $^2_1$H), a β^+ particle and a neutrino, ν.

$$^1_1\text{p} + {^1_1}\text{p} \longrightarrow {^2_1}\text{H} + {^{0}_{+1}}\beta + \nu$$

2 The fusion of a proton and a deuterium nucleus $^2_1$H produces a nucleus of the helium isotope $^3_2$He and 5.5 MeV of energy.

$$^2_1\text{H} + {^1_1}\text{p} \longrightarrow {^3_2}\text{He}$$

3 The fusion of two nuclei of helium isotope, $^3_2$He, produces a nucleus of the helium isotope $^4_2$He, two protons and 12.9 MeV of energy.

$$^3_2\text{He} + {^3_2}\text{He} \longrightarrow {^4_2}\text{He} + 2\,{^1_1}\text{p}$$

In each case, the energy released in the reaction may be calculated using $E = mc^2$ in the form $Q = \Delta mc^2$, where Δm is the difference between the total mass before and after the event.

Solar energy is produced as a result of fusion reactions inside the Sun. The temperature at the centre of the Sun is thought to be 10^8 K or more. At such temperatures, atoms are stripped of their electrons. Matter in this state is referred to as 'plasma'. The nuclei of the plasma move at very high speeds because of the enormous temperature. When two nuclei collide, they fuse together because they overcome the electrostatic repulsion due to their charge and approach each other closely enough to interact through the strong nuclear force. Protons (i.e. hydrogen nuclei) inside the Sun's core fuse together in stages (corresponding to equations 1, 2 and 3 above) to form helium $^4_2$He nuclei. For each helium nucleus formed, 25 MeV of energy is released. This corresponds to 6 MeV per proton, considerably more than the energy released per nucleon in a fission event.

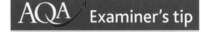

AQA Examiner's tip

Energy released in nuclear fission = change of binding energy. Fission of a given nuclide doesn't have a unique outcome

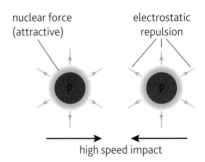

nuclear force (attractive)   electrostatic repulsion

high speed impact

Figure 3 Fusion of two protons

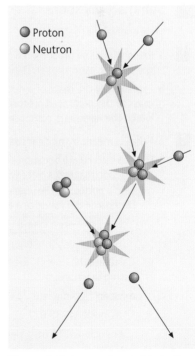

● Proton
● Neutron

Figure 4 Fusion reactions inside the Sun

Figure 5 *The JET fusion reactor*

Application

Fusion power

Fusion reactors are still at the prototype stage even though scientific teams in several countries have been working on fusion research for more than 50 years. Prototype fusion reactors such as JET, the Joint European Torus, in the United Kingdom have produced large amounts of power but only for short periods of time. JET produces less power than it uses but the less powerful International Thermonuclear Experimental Reactor (ITER) due to start up in 2016 is designed to produce several times more power than it uses.

Energy is released in JET by fusing nuclei of deuterium ^2_1H and tritium ^3_1H to produce nuclei of the helium isotope ^4_2He and neutrons, as below.

$$^2_1H + {}^3_1H \longrightarrow {}^4_2He + {}^1_0n + 17.6\,MeV$$

The neutrons are absorbed by a 'blanket' of lithium surrounding the reactor vessel. The reaction between the neutrons and the lithium nuclei, as shown below, produces tritium which is then used in the main reaction. Deuterium occurs naturally in water as it forms 0.01% of naturally occurring hydrogen.

$$^6_3Li + {}^1_0n \longrightarrow {}^4_2He + {}^3_1H + 4.8\,MeV$$

The plasma is contained in a doughnut-shaped steel container and is heated by passing a very large current through it. A magnetic field is used to confine the plasma so it does not touch the sides of its steel container, otherwise it would lose its energy. In theory, the energy released per second should be more than is needed to heat the plasma so the reactor ought to give a continuous output of power. However, at the present time, power can only be produced for a short time as the plasma becomes unstable at such high temperatures.

Summary questions

1 u is equivalent to 931 MeV

1 a Explain why the protons in a nucleus do not leave the nucleus even though they repel each other.

  b Explain why the mass of a nucleus is less than the mass of the separated protons and neutrons from which the nucleus is composed.

2 a What is meant by nuclear fission?

  b i The incomplete equation below represents a reaction that takes place when a neutron collides with a nucleus of the uranium isotope $^{235}_{92}U$. Determine the values of a and b in this equation.

$$^{235}_{92}U + {}^1_0n \longrightarrow {}^{136}_{a}Xe + {}^b_{36}Kr + 2{}^1_0n$$
$$+\ \text{energy released, } Q$$

  ii Calculate the energy, in Mev, released in this fission reaction.

  masses: $^{235}_{92}U$ nucleus 234.993 u,

  $^{136}_{a}Xe$ nucleus 135.877 u,

  $^b_{36}Kr$ nucleus 97.886 u, neutron 1.008 67 u

3 a What is meant by nuclear fusion?

  b Hydrogen nuclei fuse together to form helium nuclei in the Sun. Two stages in this process are represented by the following equations:

$$^1_1p + {}^1_1p \longrightarrow {}^2_1H + {}^0_{-1}\beta$$
$$^2_1H + {}^1_1p \longrightarrow {}^3_2He + {}^0_{-1}\beta$$

  i Describe the reactions that these equations represent.

  ii Calculate the energy released in each reaction.

  masses: β particle 0.000 55 u, proton 1.007 28 u,

  ^2_1H nucleus 2.013 55 u, ^3_2He nucleus 3.014 93 u,

4 a Explain why light nuclei do not fuse when they collide unless they are moving at a sufficiently high speed.

  b Calculate the energy released in the following fusion reaction:

$$^3_2He + {}^3_2He \longrightarrow {}^4_2He + 2{}^1_1p$$

  masses: proton 1.007 28 u,

  ^3_2He nucleus 3.014 93 u,

  α particle 4.00150

  c Show that about 25 MeV of energy is released when a ^4_2He nucleus is formed from 4 protons.

10.4 The thermal nuclear reactor

Learning objectives:

▓ How does a nuclear reactor work?

▓ What is a thermal nuclear reactor?

▓ How is a nuclear reactor controlled?

Specification reference: 3.5A.2

▓ Inside a nuclear reactor

A thermal nuclear reactor in a nuclear power station contains fuel rods spaced evenly in a steel vessel known as the **reactor core**, as shown in Figure 1. The reactor core also contains **control rods** and a **coolant** (water at high pressure in the pressurised water reactor (PWR) shown in Figure 1) as well as the fuel rods and is connected by means of steel pipes to a **heat exchanger**. A pump is used to force the coolant through the reactor core (where it is heated) and through the heat exchanger where it is used to raise steam to drive the turbines that turn the electricity generators in the power station.

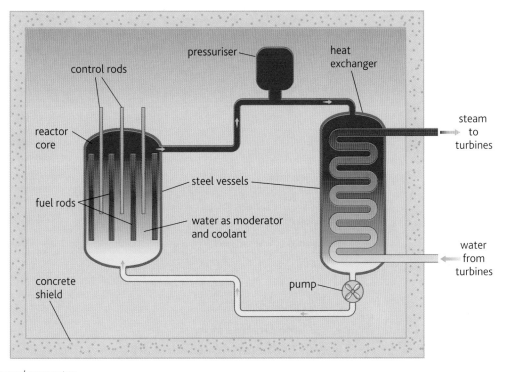

Figure 1 *Inside a nuclear reactor*

▓ The fuel rods contain enriched uranium which consists mostly of U-238, the non-fissionable uranium isotope $^{238}_{92}U$, and about 2–3% U-235, the uranium isotope $^{235}_{92}U$ which is fissionable. In comparison, natural uranium contains 99% U-238.

▓ The function of the control rods is to absorb neutrons. The depth of the control rods in the core is automatically adjusted to keep the number of neutrons in the core constant so that exactly one fission neutron per fission event on average goes on to produce further fission. This condition keeps the rate of release of fission energy constant. If the control rods are pushed in further, they absorb more neutrons so that the number of fission events per second and the rate of release of fission energy is reduced.

▥ Link

Neutron loss depends on the surface area; neutron production depends on the mass of material. Below the critical mass, loss/production is too high. The same idea explains why a small object cools faster than a large object. Energy loss depends on the surface area, so temperature loss depends on surface area/mass. See Topic 11.2.

▥ The fission neutrons need to be slowed down significantly to cause further fission of U-235 nuclei otherwise they would be travelling too fast to cause further fission. For this reason, the fuel rods need to be surrounded by a **moderator** so the neutrons are slowed down by repeated collisions with the moderator atoms. The reactor is described as a **thermal reactor** because the fission neutrons are slowed down to kinetic energies comparable to the kinetic energies of the moderator molecules. In the PWR, the water in the reactor core acts as the moderator as well as acting as a coolant.

▥ For a chain reaction to occur, the mass of the fissile material (e.g. U-235) must be greater than a minimum mass, referred to as the **critical mass.** This is because some fission neutrons escape from the fissile material without causing fission and some are absorbed by other nuclei without fission. If the mass of fissile material is less than the critical mass needed, too many of the fission neutrons escape because the surface area to mass ratio of the material is too high.

▥ Different types of thermal reactors are in operation throughout the world. Table 1 shows some of the features of the PWR reactor which operates in many countries including the UK and the Advanced Gas-cooled Reactor (AGR) which operates only in the UK.

Table 1 *Comparison of thermal reactors*

	AGR	PWR
fuel	uranium oxide in stainless steel cans	uranium oxide in zirconium alloy cans
moderator	graphite	water
coolant	CO_2 gas	water
coolant temperature/K	900	600
typical power output/MW	1300	700

▥ Application

Moderators at work

The atoms of a moderator in a nuclear reactor gain kinetic energy from fission neutrons colliding with them. The transfer of kinetic energy in such a collision is most effective if the mass of the moderator atom is as close as possible to the mass of the neutron. For this reason and taking account of practical considerations such as chemical stability, graphite (which consists of carbon-12 atoms) and water are commonly used as moderators.

Prove for yourself that an elastic 'head-on' collision between a neutron and a carbon atom which is initially stationary would result in the neutron losing about 72% of its kinetic energy to the carbon atom and that 42 such collisions would reduce the neutron's kinetic energy from 1 MeV to 1 eV.

Chernobyl

The Chernobyl disaster in the Ukraine in 1986 released radioactive materials into the atmosphere and led to the permanent evacuation of all the people in the surrounding area. The disaster was caused when the operators were testing reactor no. 4 to find out if the coolant pumps would keep operating in the event of a loss of power until the emergency diesel generators took over. To carry out the test, the safety systems to shut the reactor down in an emergency were switched off. When the reactor was powered down by pushing the control rods further into the core, the power fell much more than expected so the movement of the control rods was reversed. This caused an unexpected surge in the rate of fission events which produced a massive explosion in the reactor core. The fuel rods melted, the reactor cap was blown off and radioactive fission products were thrown up into the atmosphere.

A subsequent inquiry concluded that the main causes of the explosion were design faults in the reactor (e.g. graphite in the cap ignited in the explosion) which are not features of AGR or PWR reactors and human error (too many control rods being moved at once).

Figure 2 *Chernobyl*

Safety features

A nuclear reactor needs to have a range of safety features to protect its workforce , the wider community and the environment.

1 The reactor core is a thick steel vessel designed to withstand the high pressure and temperature in the core. The thick steel vessel absorbs β radiation and some of the γ radiation and neutrons from the core.

2 The core is in a building with very thick concrete walls which absorb the neutrons and γ radiation that escape from the reactor vessel.

3 Every reactor has an emergency shut-down system designed to insert the control rods fully into the core to stop fission completely.

4 The sealed fuel rods are inserted and removed from the reactor by means of remote handling devices. The rods are much more radioactive after removal than before. This is because the fuel cans

   a before use, contain U-235 and U-238 which emit only α radiation and this is absorbed by the fuel cans,

   b after use, emit β and γ radiation due to the many neutron-rich fission products that form.

In addition, the spent fuel rods contain the plutonium isotope $^{239}_{94}$Pu as a result of the absorption of neutrons by U-238 nuclei. This plutonium isotope is a very active α emitter and if inhaled causes lung cancer.

A nuclear future?

A nuclear reactor can produce enough electricity for a large city and it produces far less carbon dioxide emissions than a fossil fuel power station. In 2008, the UK government announced its intention to permit the construction of new nuclear power stations not just to replace the current generation of nuclear reactors but also to

Figure 3 *Spent fuel rods in a cooling pond*

generate significantly more electricity than at present. These new power stations together with more **renewable energy** resources are intended to enable the UK to meet its target for carbon emissions. The new nuclear reactors will be more fuel-efficient and have a longer design life. As well as active safety features such as the control rods, they will include passive safety features such as the use of natural convection which do not require operator intervention.

Radioactive waste

Radioactive waste is categorised as high-, intermediate- or low-level waste according to its activity. Most high-level radioactive waste is from nuclear power stations or from specialist users in universities, and industry or from hospitals that use radioactive isotopes for diagnosis or therapy.

Disposal of any form of radioactive waste must be in accordance with legal regulations and by approved disposal companies to ensure that the radioactive waste is stored safely in secure containers until its activity is insignificant. Disposal by dilution, e.g. diluting radioactive water from nuclear power station cooling systems with large quantities of water and then dispersing it into the sea is no longer acceptable and has been banned.

- **High-level radioactive waste** such as spent fuel rods from a nuclear power station contains many different radioactive isotopes, including fission fragments as well as unused uranium-235 and uranium-238 and plutonium-239. The spent fuel rods must be removed by remote control and stored underwater in cooling ponds for up to a year because they continue to release heat due to radioactive decay. In Britain, the rods are then transferred in large steel casks to the THORP reprocessing plant at Sellafield in Cumbria where the unused uranium and plutonium is then removed and stored in sealed containers for further possible use. The rest of the material (i.e. the fission products and the fuel cans) is radioactive waste and is stored in sealed containers in deep trenches at Sellafield. Such waste must be stored safely for centuries as it contains long-lived radioactive isotopes which must be prevented from contaminating food and water supplies.

In other countries, high-level radioactive waste is stored in the same way or in underground caverns which are geologically stable. In some countries, the waste is vitrified by mixing it with molten glass and then stored as glass blocks in underground caverns.

The long-term safe storage of high-level radioactive waste remains a major issue in Britain because no one wants such storage in their own locality, nor do people want radioactive waste to be carried through their own locality to storage facilities elsewhere.

- **Intermediate-level waste** such as radioactive materials with low activity and containers of radioactive materials are sealed in drums that are encased in concrete and stored in specially constructed buildings with walls of reinforced concrete.
- **Low-level waste** such as laboratory equipment and protective clothing is sealed in metal drums and buried in large trenches.

AQA Examination-style questions

1   (a)   In a nuclear reactor, some of the $^{238}_{92}\text{U}$ nuclei absorb neutrons to become uranium $^{239}_{92}\text{U}$ nuclei. These nuclei decay in two stages to become nuclei of the plutonium isotope $^{239}_{94}\text{Pu}$.

        (i)   Write down an equation to represent the formation of a $^{239}_{92}\text{U}$ nucleus from a $^{238}_{92}\text{U}$ nucleus.

        (ii)   What types of particles are emitted when a $^{239}_{92}\text{U}$ nucleus decays to form a $^{239}_{94}\text{Pu}$ nucleus?   *(3 marks)*

   (b)   The THORP reprocessing plant at Sellafield is used to recover uranium and plutonium from spent fuel rods. In addition to reprocessing nuclear waste from the UK, it also reprocesses waste from nuclear reactors in other countries as well as from the UK. Uranium-238 and plutonium-239 can both be used in a type of nuclear reactor called a *fast breeder* reactor, although this type of reactor has not yet been fully appraised in terms of reliability and safety. By using such reactors in the future, the lifetime of the world's reserves of uranium would be extended from a few hundred years to several thousand years. Plutonium can also be used to make nuclear bombs. Discuss the arguments for and against reprocessing nuclear waste.   *(5 marks)*

2   (a)   In the context of an atomic nucleus,

        (i)   state what is meant by *binding energy*, and explain how it arises,

        (ii)   state what is meant by *mass difference*,

        (iii)   state the relationship between binding energy and mass difference.   *(4 marks)*

   (b)   Calculate the average binding energy per nucleon, in MeV nucleon^{-1}, of the zinc nucleus $^{64}_{30}\text{Zn}$.

      mass of $^{64}_{30}\text{Zn}$ atom = 63.929 15 u   *(5 marks)*

   (c)   Why would you expect the zinc nucleus to be very stable?   *(1 mark)*

                                                                 AQA, 2004

3   (a)   (i)   Describe the physical process of *nuclear fusion*.

        (ii)   Describe the physical process of *nuclear fission*.

        (iii)   Explain why each of these processes releases energy.   *(6 marks)*

   (b)   Energy is also released by radioactive decay, such as the decay of radon-220 as represented by the equation

$$^{220}_{86}\text{Rn} \longrightarrow {}^{216}_{84}\text{Po} + \alpha$$

      Calculate the energy released, in J, by the decay of one nucleus of radon-220.

      mass of ^{220}Rn nucleus = 219.964 10 u

      mass of ^{216}Po nucleus = 215.955 72 u

      mass of α particle = 4.001 50 u   *(3 marks)*

                                                                  AQA, 2007

4   (a)   A solar panel of area 2.5 m^2 is fitted to a satellite in orbit above the Earth. The panel produces a current of 2.4 A at a potential difference of 20 V when solar radiation is incident normally on it.

        (i)   Calculate the electrical power output of the panel.

        (ii)   Solar radiation on the satellite has an intensity of 1.4 kW m^{-2}. Calculate the efficiency of the panel.   *(4 marks)*

   (b)   The back-up power system in the satellite is provided by a radioactive isotope enclosed in a sealed container which absorbs the radiation from the isotope. Energy from the radiation is converted to electrical energy by means of a thermoelectric module.

(i) The isotope has an activity of 1.1×10^{14} Bq and produces α particles of energy 5.1 MeV. Show that the container absorbs energy from the α particles at a rate of $90 \, \text{J s}^{-1}$.

(ii) The isotope has a half-life of 90 years. Calculate the decay constant λ of this isotope.

(iii) The mass number of the isotope is 239.

Calculate the mass of isotope needed for an activity of 1.1×10^{14} Bq. *(7 marks)*

AQA, 2003

5   **Figure 1** shows the general relationship between the nuclear binding energy per nucleon (*B*) and nucleon number (*A*).

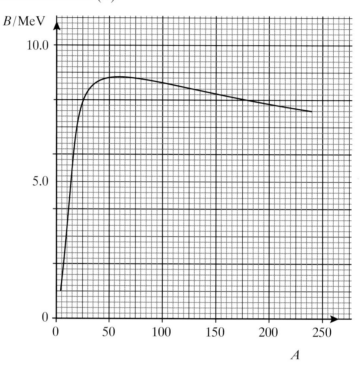

Figure 1

(a) (i) Copy **Figure 1** and mark with the letter S to show the nucleon number and the nuclear binding energy per nucleon for the nuclide with the most stable nuclear structure.

(ii) Write down the nucleon number and the nuclear binding energy per nucleon for this nuclide.

(iii) Calculate the total binding energy of this nuclide. *(3 marks)*

(b) A fusion reaction in which two protons combine to form a deuterium nucleus is summarised by the equation:

$$ {}^{1}_{1}\text{H} + {}^{1}_{1}\text{H} \longrightarrow {}^{2}_{1}\text{H} + {}^{0}_{1}\text{e} + \nu + 1.44 \, \text{MeV} $$

(i) What do the symbols ${}^{0}_{1}\text{e}$ and ν represent?

(ii) By considering charge, baryon number and lepton number for each side of the equation, show that this reaction satisfies the conservation laws for these quantities.

(iii) Subsequently two γ-ray photons are released, each with an energy of 0.51 MeV. Calculate the wavelength of these photons. *(18 marks)*

(c) With reference to **Figure 1** explain why the fission of a heavy nucleus is likely to release more energy than when a pair of light nuclei undergo nuclear fusion.

You may wish to sketch the general shape of **Figure 1** in order to aid your explanation. *(5 marks)*

AQA, 2004

6 (a) With reference to the process of nuclear fusion, explain why energy is released when two small nuclei join together, and why it is difficult to make two nuclei come together. *(3 marks)*

(b) A fusion reaction takes place when two deuterium nuclei join, as represented by

$$_1^2\text{H} + {}_1^2\text{H} \longrightarrow {}_2^3\text{He} + {}_1^0\text{n}$$

mass of ^{2}H nucleus = 2.013 55 u

mass of ^{3}He nucleus = 3.014 93 u

Calculate:

(i) the mass difference produced when two deuterium nuclei undergo fusion,

(ii) the energy released, in J, when this reaction takes place. *(3 marks)*

AQA, 2003

7 (a) In the context of the processes that occur in a nuclear power reactor, explain what is meant by:

(i) thermal neutrons,

(ii) induced fission,

(iii) a self-sustaining chain reaction. *(5 marks)*

(b) (i) Describe the process of moderation that takes place in an operational reactor.

(ii) How is the fission rate controlled in a power reactor? *(7 marks)*

8 (a) When a fuel rod has been in use in a nuclear reactor for several years, it produces less output power and presents a greater hazard than it did when first installed. Explain why this is so. *(3 marks)*

(b) Describe how the spent fuel rods are handled and processed after they have been removed from a nuclear reactor. Indicate how the active wastes are dealt with in order to reduce the hazards they could present to future generations. *(5 marks)*

Thermal physics

11.1 Internal energy and temperature

When you are outdoors in winter, you need to wrap up well otherwise heat transfer from your body to the surroundings takes place and you lose energy. In summer, if you are in a very hot room, you gain energy from the room due to heat transfer.

Energy transfer between two objects takes place if:

- one object exerts a force on the other one and makes it move. In other words, one object does work on the other one.

- one object is hotter than the other so heat transfer takes place by means of conduction, convection or radiation. In other words, heat transfer is energy transfer due to a temperature difference.

Internal energy

The brake pads of a moving vehicle become hot if the brakes are applied for long enough. The work done by the frictional force between the brake pads and the wheel heats the brake pads which gain energy from the kinetic energy of the vehicle. The temperature of the brake pads increases as a result and the internal energy of each brake pad increases.

Figure 1 *Heat transfer in winter*

As explained below, the internal energy of an object is the energy of its molecules due to their individual movements and positions. The internal energy of an object due to its temperature is sometimes referred to as **thermal energy.** However, some of the internal energy of an object might be due to other causes. For example, an iron bar that is magnetised has more internal energy than if it is unmagnetised because of the magnetic interaction between its atoms.

The internal energy of an object changes as a result of:

- heat transfer or energy transfer by radiation to or from the object, or
- work done on or by the object, including work done by electricity.

If the internal energy of an object is constant, either:

- there is no heat transfer or energy transfer due to radiation and no work is done, or
- heat transfer, energy transfer due to radiation and work done 'balance' each other out.

For example, the internal energy of a lamp filament increases when the lamp is switched on because work is done by the electricity supply pushing electrons through the filament. The filament becomes hot as a result. When it reaches its operating temperature, heat transfer to the surroundings takes place and it radiates light. Work done by the electricity supply pushing electrons through the filament is balanced by heat transfer and light radiated from the filament.

About molecules

A molecule is the smallest particle of a pure substance that is characteristic of the substance. For example, a water molecule consists of two hydrogen atoms joined to an oxygen atom.

An atom is the smallest particle of an element that is characteristic of the element. For example, a hydrogen atom consists of a proton and an electron.

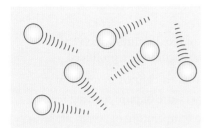

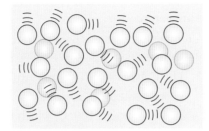

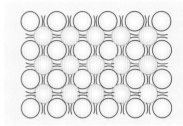

In a gas, the particles are far apart. There are almost no forces of attraction between them. The particles move about at high speed. Because the particles are so far apart, a gas occupies a very much larger volume than the same mass of liquid.

The molecules collide with the container. These collisions are responsible for the pressure which a gas exerts on its container.

In a liquid the particles are free to move around. A liquid therefore flows easily and has no fixed shape. There are still forces of attraction between the particles. When a liquid is heated, some of the particles gain enough energy to break away from the other particles. The particles which escape from the body of the liquid become a gas.

A solid is made up of particles arranged in a regular 3-dimensional structure. There are strong forces of attraction between the particles. Although the particles can vibrate, they cannot move out of their positions in the structure.

When a solid is heated, the particles gain energy and vibrate more and more vigorously. Eventually they may break away from the solid structure and become free to move around. When this happens, the solid has turned into liquid: it has melted.

Figure 2 *Particles in a solid, a liquid and a gas*

- In a solid, the atoms and molecules are held to each other by forces due to the electrical charges of the protons and electrons in the atoms. The molecules in a solid vibrate randomly about fixed positions. The higher the temperature of the solid, the more the molecules vibrate. The energy supplied to raise the temperature of a solid increases the kinetic energy of the molecules. If the temperature is raised sufficiently, the solid melts. This happens because its molecules vibrate so much that they break free from each other and the substance loses its shape. The energy supplied to melt a solid raises the potential energy of the molecules because they break free from each other.

- In a liquid, the molecules move about at random in contact with each other. The forces between the molecules are not strong enough to hold the molecules in fixed positions. The higher the temperature of a liquid, the faster its molecules move. The energy supplied to a liquid to raise its temperature increases the kinetic energy of the liquid molecules. Heating the liquid further causes it to vaporise. The molecules have sufficient kinetic energy to break free and move away from each other.

- In a gas or vapour, the molecules also move about randomly but much further apart on average than in a liquid. Heating a gas or a vapour makes the molecules speed up and so gain kinetic energy.

The internal energy of an object is the sum of the random distribution of the kinetic and potential energies of its molecules.

Increasing the internal energy of a substance increases the kinetic and/or potential energy associated with the random motion and positions of its molecules.

▥ Temperature and temperature scales

The temperature of an object is a measure of the degree of hotness of the object. The hotter an object is, the more internal energy it has. Place your hand in cold water and it loses internal energy due to heat transfer. Place it in warm water and it gains internal energy due to heat transfer. If the water is at the same temperature as your hand, no overall heat transfer takes place. Your hand is then in **thermal equilibrium** with the water. No overall heat transfer takes place between two objects at the same temperature.

A temperature scale is defined in terms of **fixed points** which are standard degrees of hotness which can be accurately reproduced.

▥ The **Celsius scale** of temperature, in °C, is defined in terms of:
1 ice point, 0 °C, which is the temperature of pure melting ice,
2 steam point, 100 °C, which is the temperature of steam at standard atmospheric pressure.

▥ The **absolute scale** of temperature, in kelvins (K) is defined in terms of:
1 **absolute zero**, 0 K, which is the lowest possible temperature,
2 the triple point of water, 273.16 K, which is the temperature at which ice, water and water vapour coexist in thermodynamic equilibrium.

Because ice point on the absolute scale is 273.15 K and steam point is 100 K higher, then

temperature in °C = absolute temperature in kelvins − 273.15

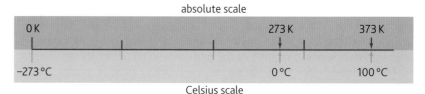

Figure 3 *Temperature scales*

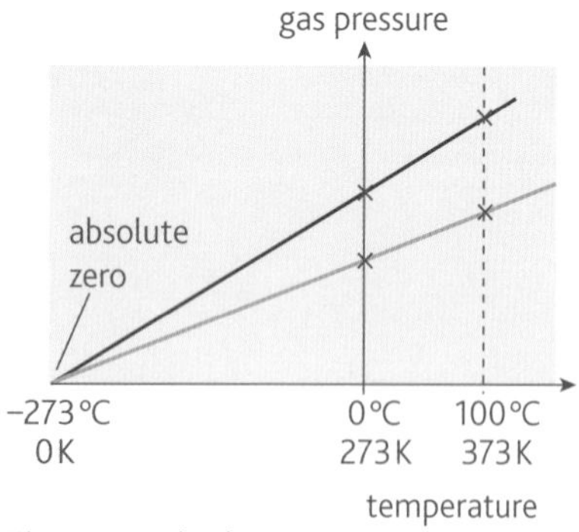

AQA Examiner's tip

Add 273 to change from °C to kelvins. The kelvin scale depends on a fundamental feature of nature, namely the lowest possible temperature. In comparison, the Celsius scale depends on the properties of a substance, water, chosen for convenience rather than for any fundamental reason.

▥ About absolute zero

The absolute scale of temperature, also referred to as the kelvin scale, is based on absolute zero, the lowest possible temperature. No object can have a temperature below absolute zero. **An object at absolute zero has minimum internal energy**, regardless of the substances the object consists of.

The pressure of a fixed mass of an ideal gas in a sealed container of fixed volume decreases as the gas temperature is reduced (see Topic 12.1). If the pressure measured at ice point and at steam point is plotted on a graph as shown in Figure 4, the line between the two points always cuts the temperature axis at −273 °C, regardless of which gas is used or how much gas is used.

Figure 4 *Absolute zero*

How science works

The coldest places in the world

You don't need to travel to the South Pole to find the coldest places in the world. Go to the nearest University physics department that has a low temperature research laboratory. Substances have very strange properties at very low temperatures. For example, metals cooled to a few degrees within absolute zero become superconductors which means they have zero electrical resistance. Superfluids that can empty themselves out of containers have been discovered. Temperatures within a few microkelvins of absolute zero have been reached in these laboratories.

A thermometer test

Use a travelling microscope to measure the interval between adjacent graduations on the scale of an accurate liquid-in glass thermometer. You may be surprised to find that the interval distance is not the same near the middle of the scale as it is near the ends of the scale. This is because the expansion of the liquid is not directly proportional to the change of temperature.

All thermometers are calibrated in terms of the temperature measured by a gas thermometer. This is a thermometer consisting of a dry gas in a sealed container. The pressure of the gas is proportional to the absolute temperature of the gas. By measuring the gas pressure, p_{Tr}, at the triple point of water (273.16 K by definition) and at an unknown temperature T/K, the unknown temperature in kelvins can be calculated using

$$\frac{T}{273.16} = \frac{p}{p_{Tr}},$$ where p is the gas pressure at the unknown temperature.

Although the above formula is not on your A level specification, the above notes are provided to give you a clear understanding of how accuracy is ensured when we use a thermometer.

Figure 5 *A low temperature research laboratory*

Summary questions

1. a Explain why an electric motor becomes warm when it is used.

   b A battery is connected to an electric motor which is used to raise a weight at a steady speed. When in operation, the electric motor is at a constant temperature which is above the temperature of its surroundings. Describe the energy transfers that take place.

2. a State what is meant by internal energy.

   b Describe a situation in which the internal energy of an object is constant even though work is done on the object.

3. a State one difference between the motion of the molecules in a solid and the molecules in a liquid.

   b Describe how the motion of the molecules in a solid changes when the solid is heated.

4. a State each of the following temperatures to the nearest degree on the absolute scale:

   i   the temperature of pure melting ice,

   ii 20 °C,

   iii −196 °C

   b The pressure of a constant-volume gas thermometer was 100 kPa at a temperature of 273 K.

   i   Calculate the temperature, in kelvins, of the gas when its pressure was 120 kPa.

   ii Calculate the pressure of the gas at 100 °C.

11.2 Specific heat capacity

Learning objectives:

- What do we mean by 'heating up' and by 'cooling down'?

- Which materials heat and cool fastest?

- What is specific heat capacity? How do we measure it?

Specification reference: 3.5A.3

Table 1 *Some specific heat capacities*

substance	specific heat capacity /$J\,kg^{-1}\,K^{-1}$
aluminium	900
concrete	850
copper	390
iron	490
lead	130
oil	2100
water	4200

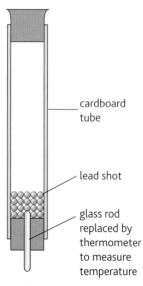

Figure 1 *The inversion tube experiment*

cardboard tube

lead shot

glass rod replaced by thermometer to measure temperature

Heating and cooling

Sunbathers on the hot sandy beaches of the Mediterranean Sea dive into the sea to cool off. Sand heats up much more readily than water does. Even when the sand is almost too hot to walk barefoot across, the sea water is refreshingly cool. The temperature rise of an object when it is heated depends on:

- the mass of the object,

- the amount of energy supplied to it,

- the substance or substances from which the object is made.

The specific heat capacity, c, of a substance is the energy needed to raise the temperature of unit mass of the substance by 1 K without change of state. The unit of c is $J\,kg^{-1}\,K^{-1}$.

Specific heat capacities of some common substances are shown in Table 1.

To raise the temperature of mass m of a substance from temperature T_1 to temperature T_2,

$$\text{the energy needed } \Delta Q = mc(T_2 - T_1)$$

For example, to calculate the energy that must be supplied to raise the temperature of 5.0 kg of water from 20 °C to 100 °C, using the above formula gives $\Delta Q = 5.0 \times 4200 \times 80 = 1.7 \times 10^6\,J$.

The inversion tube experiment

In this experiment, the gravitational potential energy of an object falling in a tube is converted into internal energy when it hits the bottom of a tube. Figure 1 shows the idea. The object is a collection of tiny lead spheres.

The tube is inverted each time the spheres hit the bottom of the tube. The temperature of the lead shot is measured initially and after a certain number of inversions.

Let m represent the mass of the lead shot.

For a tube of length L, the loss of gravitational potential energy for each inversion $= mgL$

Therefore, for n inversions, the loss of gravitational potential energy $= mgLn$

The gain of internal energy of the lead shot $= mc\,\Delta T$, where c is the specific heat capacity of lead and ΔT is the temperature rise of the lead shot.

Assuming all the gravitational potential energy lost is transferred to internal energy of the lead shot,

$$mc\Delta T = mgLn$$

$$\therefore \ c = \frac{gLn}{\Delta T}$$

The experiment can therefore be used to measure the specific heat capacity of lead with no other measurements than the length of the tube, the temperature rise of the lead and the number of inversions.

Specific heat capacity measurements using electrical methods

Measurement of the specific heat capacity of a metal

A block of the metal of known mass m in an insulated container is used. A 12 V electrical heater is inserted into a hole drilled in the metal and used to heat the metal by supplying a measured amount of electrical energy. A thermometer inserted into a second hole drilled in the metal is used to measure the temperature rise ΔT (= its final temperature − its initial temperature). A small amount of water or oil in the thermometer hole will improve the thermal contact between the thermometer and the metal.

The electrical energy supplied
$$= \text{heater current } I \times \text{heater pd } V \times \text{heating time } t$$

∴ assuming no heat loss to the surroundings, $mc\Delta T = IVt$

∴ $c = \dfrac{IVt}{m\Delta T}$

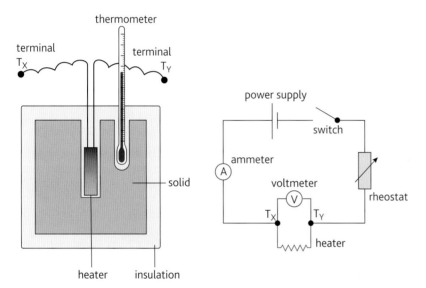

Figure 2 *Measuring c*

Notes

1 Notice that the unit of mass × the unit of c × the unit of temperature change gives the joule. In other words, kg × J kg⁻¹ K⁻¹ × K = J.

2 The **heat capacity, C,** of an object is the heat supplied to raise the temperature of the object by 1 K. Therefore, for an object of mass m made of a single substance of specific heat capacity c, its heat capacity $C = mc$. For example, the heat capacity of 5.0 kg of water is 21 000 J K⁻¹ = 5.0 kg × 4200 J kg⁻¹ K⁻¹.

AQA Examiner's tip

A temperature change is the same in °C as it is in K. If you are given the initial and final temperatures in °C, just calculate the temperature difference in °C.

Measurement of the specific heat capacity of a liquid

A known mass of the liquid is used in an insulated calorimeter of known mass and known specific heat capacity. A 12 V electrical heater is placed in the liquid and used to heat it directly. A thermometer inserted into the liquid is used to measure the temperature rise, ΔT.

▨ The electrical energy supplied = current I × voltage V × heating time t
▨ The energy needed to heat the liquid =
   mass of liquid (m_l) × specific heat capacity of liquid (c_l) × temperature rise (ΔT)
▨ The energy needed to heat the calorimeter =
   mass of calorimeter (m_{cal}) × specific heat capacity of calorimeter (c_{cal}) × temperature rise (ΔT)

Assuming no heat loss to the surroundings,

$$\therefore IVt = m_1 c_1 \Delta T + m_{cal} c_{cal} \Delta T$$

Hence c can be calculated from this equation as all the other quantities are known.

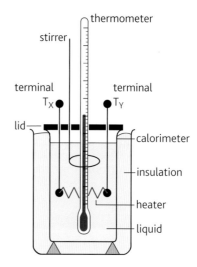

Figure 3 *Measurement of the specific heat capacity of a liquid*

Summary questions

Use the data in Table 1 for the following calculations.

1 Calculate:

a the energy needed to heat an aluminium pan of mass 0.30 kg from 15 °C to 100 °C,

b the energy needed to heat 1.50 kg of water from 15 °C to 100 °C.

2 a Calculate the time taken to heat the water and pan in Q1 from 15 °C to 100 °C using a 2.0 kW electric hot plate, assuming no heat transfer to the surroundings occurs.

b Calculate the energy needed to raise the temperature of 80 kg of water in an insulated copper tank of mass 20 kg from 20 °C to 50 °C.

3 In an inversion tube experiment, 0.50 kg of lead shot at an initial temperature of 18 °C was inverted fifty times in a tube of length 1.30 m. The final temperature of the lead shot was 23 °C. Calculate:

a the total gravitational potential energy released by the lead,

b the specific heat capacity of lead. Assume $g = 9.81\,\mathrm{m\,s^{-2}}$.

4 An electric shower is capable of heating water from 10 °C to 40 °C when the flow rate is 0.025 kg s^{-1}. Calculate the minimum power of the heater.

Application

Continuous flow heating

In an electric shower, water passes steadily through copper coils heated by an electrical heater. The water is hotter at the outlet than at the inlet. This is an example of continuous flow heating. For mass m of fluid passing through the heater in time t at a steady flow rate, assuming no heat loss to the surroundings:

the electrical energy supplied per second $IV = mc\dfrac{\Delta T}{t}$

where ΔT is the temperature rise of the water.

Note that when the outflowing water has attained a steady temperature, the temperature of the copper coils does not change, so no '$mc\Delta T$' term is needed for the copper coils in the above equation.

For a solar heating panel, the heat energy gained per second by the liquid that flows through the panel $= mc\dfrac{\Delta T}{t}$

where m is the of liquid flowing through the panel in time t, c is the specific heat capacity of the liquid and ΔT is its temperature rise.

Note:

If the volume flow rate is given, you need to know the density of the fluid to calculate the rate of flow of mass (m/t). See *AS Physics* Topic 11.1.

11.3 Change of state

Learning objectives:

■ What is latent heat?

■ How do we measure it?

■ Why does the temperature of a substance remain steady when it is changing state?

Specification reference: 3.5A.3

When a solid is heated and heated, its temperature increases until it melts. If it is a pure substance, it melts at a well-defined temperature, its **melting point**. Once all the solid has melted, continued heating causes the temperature of the liquid to increase until the liquid boils. This occurs at a certain temperature, the **boiling point**. The substance turns to a vapour as it boils away.

The three physical states of a substance, solid, liquid and vapour, have different physical properties. For example:

■ the density of a gas is much less than the density of the same substance in the liquid or the solid state. This is because the molecules of a liquid and of a solid are packed together in contact with each other. In contrast, the molecules of a gas are on average separated from each other by relatively large distances.

■ liquids and gases can flow, but solids cannot. This is because the atoms in a solid are locked together by strong force bonds which the atoms are unable to break free from. In a liquid or a gas, the molecules are not locked together because they have too much kinetic energy and the force bonds are not strong enough to keep the molecules fixed to each other.

■ Latent heat

When a solid or a liquid is heated so its temperature increases, its molecules gain kinetic energy. In a solid, the atoms vibrate more about their mean positions. In a liquid, the molecules move about faster, still keeping in contact with each other but free to move about.

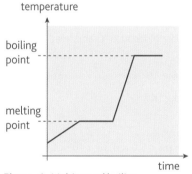

Figure 1 *Melting and boiling*

1 **When a solid is heated at its melting point**, its atoms vibrate so much that they break free from each other. The solid therefore becomes a liquid due to energy being supplied at the melting point. The energy needed to melt a solid at its melting point is referred to as **latent heat of fusion**.

Latent heat is released when a liquid solidifies. This happens because the liquid molecules slow down as the liquid is cooled; at the melting point, the molecules move slowly enough for the force bonds to lock the molecules together. Some of the latent heat released keeps the temperature at the melting point until all the liquid has solidified.

■ 'Latent' means 'hidden': latent heat supplied to melt a solid may be thought of as hidden because no temperature change takes place even though the solid is being heated.

■ Fusion is a term used for the melting of a solid because the solid 'fuses' into a liquid as it melts.

2 **When a liquid is heated at its boiling point**, the molecules gain enough kinetic energy to overcome the bonds that hold them close together. The molecules therefore break away from each other to form bubbles of vapour in the liquid. The energy needed to vaporise a liquid is referred to as **latent heat of vaporisation**.

Latent heat is released when a vapour condenses. This happens because the vapour molecules slow down as the vapour is cooled; the molecules move slowly enough for the force bonds to pull the molecules together to form a liquid.

Some solids vaporise directly when heated. This process is known as **sublimation**.

In general, much more energy is needed to vaporise a substance than to melt it. For example, 2.25 MJ is needed to vaporise 1 kg of water at its boiling point. In comparison, 0.336 MJ is needed to melt 1 kg of ice at its melting point. The energy needed to change the state of unit mass (i.e. 1 kg) of a substance at its melting point (or its boiling point) is referred to as its specific latent heat of fusion (or vaporisation).

The **specific latent heat of fusion, l_f** of a substance is the energy needed to change the state of unit mass of the substance from solid to liquid without change of temperature.

The **specific latent heat of vaporisation** of a substance is the energy needed to change the state of unit mass of the substance from liquid to vapour without change of temperature.

Therefore, the energy Q needed to change the state of mass m of a substance from solid to liquid or liquid to vapour without change of temperature is given by

$$Q = ml$$

where l is the specific latent heat of fusion or vaporisation as appropriate.

The unit of specific latent heat is $\mathrm{J\,kg^{-1}}$.

Hint

Where a substance changes its state and changes its temperature, to calculate the energy transferred,

- use $Q = ml$ to calculate the energy transferred when its state changes,
- use $Q = mc(T_2 - T_1)$ when its temperature changes.

Worked example:

Calculate the energy needed to melt 5.0 kg of ice at 0 °C and heat the melted ice to 50 °C.

specific latent heat of fusion of ice = $3.36 \times 10^5\,\mathrm{J\,kg^{-1}}$

specific heat capacity of water = $4200\,\mathrm{J\,kg^{-1}\,K^{-1}}$

Solution

To melt 5.0 kg of ice, energy needed $Q_1 = ml = 5.0 \times 3.36 \times 10^5 = 1.68 \times 10^6\,\mathrm{J}$

To heat 5.0 kg of melted ice (i.e. water) from 0 °C to 50 °C, energy needed $Q_2 = mc\,(T_2 - T_1) = 5.0 \times 4200 \times (50 - 0) = 1.05 \times 10^6\,\mathrm{J}$

Therefore, the total energy needed $= Q_1 + Q_2 = 2.73 \times 10^6\,\mathrm{J}$

Link

If the volume of a substance is given, you need to know its density to find its mass. See *AS Physics* Topic 11.1.

Temperature–time graphs

If a pure solid is heated to its melting point and beyond, its temperature–time graph will be as shown in Figure 2.

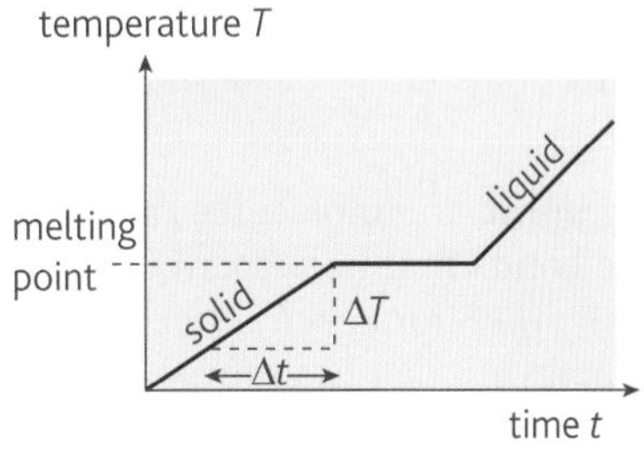

Figure 2 *Temperature against time for a solid being heated*

Assuming no heat loss occurs during heating and energy is transferred to the substance at a constant rate P (i.e. power supplied):

- before the solid melts, $P = mc_S\left(\frac{\Delta T}{\Delta t}\right)_S$ where $\left(\frac{\Delta T}{\Delta t}\right)_S$ is the rise of temperature per second and c_S is the specific heat capacity of the solid. Therefore the rise of temperature per second of the solid, $\left(\frac{\Delta T}{\Delta t}\right)_S = \frac{P}{mc_S}$

- after the solid melts, $P = mc_{L} \left| \frac{\Delta T}{\Delta t} \right|_{L}$ where $\left| \frac{\Delta T}{\Delta t} \right|_{L}$ is the rise of temperature per second and c_{L} is the specific heat capacity of the liquid. Therefore the rise of temperature per second of the liquid, $\left| \frac{\Delta T}{\Delta t} \right|_{L} = \frac{P}{mc_{L}}$

Therefore, if the solid has a larger specific heat capacity than the liquid, the rate of temperature rise of the solid is less than that of the liquid. In other words, the liquid heats up faster than the solid.

Hint

At the melting point, P = energy supplied per second is $\frac{ml}{t}$, where l is the specific latent heat of fusion of the substance and t is the time taken to melt mass m of the substance. Therefore, the time taken to melt the substance $t = \frac{ml}{P}$.

Summary questions

1. a Explain why energy is needed to melt a solid.
   b Explain why the internal energy of the water in a beaker must be reduced to freeze the water.

2. Calculate the mass of water boiled away in a 3 kW electric kettle in 2 min.
   The specific latent heat of vaporisation of water is 2.25 MJ kg⁻¹.

3. A plastic beaker containing 0.080 kg of water at 15 °C was placed in a refrigerator and cooled to 0 °C in 1200 s.
   a Calculate how much energy each second was removed from the water in this process. The specific heat capacity of water = 4200 J kg⁻¹ K⁻¹.
   b Calculate how long the refrigerator would take to freeze the water in a. The specific latent heat of fusion of water = 3.4×10^{5} J kg⁻¹.

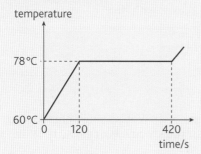

Figure 3

4. The temperature–time graph shown in Figure 3 was obtained by heating 0.12 kg of a substance in an insulated container. The specific heat capacity of the substance in the solid state is 1200 J kg⁻¹ K⁻¹.
   Calculate:
   a the energy per second supplied to the substance in the solid state if its temperature increased from 60 °C to its melting point at 78 °C in 120 s,
   b the energy needed to melt the solid if it took 300 s to melt with energy supplied at the same rate as in a.

AQA Examiner's tip

Change of state for a pure substance is at constant temperature.

AQA Examination-style questions

specific heat capacity of water $= 4200\,\mathrm{J\,kg^{-1}\,K^{-1}}$
specific heat capacity of ice $= 2100\,\mathrm{J\,kg^{-1}\,K^{-1}}$
specific latent heat of fusion of ice $= 3.3 \times 10^5\,\mathrm{J\,kg^{-1}}$
specific latent heat of vaporisation of water $= 2.3 \times 10^6\,\mathrm{J\,kg^{-1}}$

1 A tray containing 0.20 kg of water at 20 °C is placed in a freezer.

    (a) The temperature of the water drops to 0 °C in 10 min.

        Calculate:

        (i) the energy lost by the water as it cools to 0 °C,

        (ii) the average rate at which the water is losing energy, in $\mathrm{J\,s^{-1}}$. *(3 marks)*

    (b) (i) Estimate the time taken for the water at 0 °C to turn completely into ice.

        (ii) State any assumptions you make. *(3 marks)*

                              AQA, 2003

2 (a) Calculate the energy released when 1.5 kg of water at 18 °C cools to 0 °C and then freezes to form ice, also at 0 °C. *(4 marks)*

    (b) Explain why it is more effective to cool cans of drinks by placing them in a bucket full of melting ice rather than in a bucket of water at an initial temperature of 0 °C. *(2 marks)*

                              AQA, 2006

3 An electrical heater is used to heat a 1.0 kg block of metal, which is well lagged. The table shows how the temperature of the block increased with time.

temp/°C	20.1	23.0	26.9	30.0	33.1	36.9
time/s	0	60	120	180	240	300

    (a) Plot a graph of temperature against time. *(3 marks)*

    (b) Determine the gradient of the graph. *(2 marks)*

    (c) The heater provides thermal energy at the rate of 48 W. Use your value for the gradient of the graph to determine a value for the specific heat capacity of the metal in the block. *(2 marks)*

    (d) The heater in part (c) is placed in some crushed ice that has been placed in a funnel as shown in **Figure 1**.

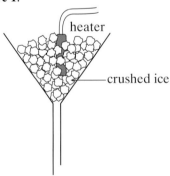

Figure 1

The heater is switched on for 200 s and 32 g of ice are found to have melted during this time.

Use this information to calculate a value for the specific latent heat of fusion for water, stating **one** assumption made. *(3 marks)*

                              AQA, 2002

4 In an experiment to measure the temperature of the flame of a Bunsen burner, a lump of copper of mass $0.12\,kg$ is heated in the flame for several minutes. The copper is then transferred quickly to a beaker, of negligible heat capacity, containing $0.45\,kg$ of water, and the temperature rise of the water measured.

specific heat capacity of copper $= 390\,J\,kg^{-1}\,K^{-1}$

(a) If the temperature of the water rises from $15\,°C$ to $35\,°C$, calculate the thermal energy gained by the water. *(2 marks)*

(b) (i) State the thermal energy lost by the copper, assuming no heat is lost during its transfer.

(ii) Calculate the fall in temperature of the copper.

(iii) Hence calculate the temperature reached by the copper while in the flame. *(4 marks)*

AQA, 2006

5 A bicycle and its rider have a total mass of $95\,kg$. The bicycle is travelling along a horizontal road at a constant speed of $8.0\,m\,s^{-1}$.

(a) Calculate the kinetic energy of the bicycle and rider. *(2 marks)*

(b) The brakes are applied until the bicycle and rider come to rest. During braking, 60% of the kinetic energy of the bicycle and rider is converted to thermal energy in the brake blocks. The brake blocks have a total mass of $0.12\,kg$ and the material from which they are made has a specific heat capacity of $1200\,J\,kg^{-1}\,K^{-1}$.

(i) Calculate the maximum rise in temperature of the brake blocks.

(ii) State an assumption you have made in part (b)(i). *(4 marks)*

AQA, 2004

6 A female runner of mass $60\,kg$ generates thermal energy at a rate of $800\,W$.

(a) Assuming that she loses no energy to the surroundings and that the average specific heat capacity of her body is $3900\,J\,kg^{-1}\,K^{-1}$, calculate:

(i) the thermal energy generated in one minute,

(ii) the temperature rise of her body in one minute. *(3 marks)*

(b) In practice it is desirable for a runner to maintain a constant temperature. This may be achieved partly by the evaporation of sweat. The runner in part (a) loses energy at a rate of $500\,W$ by this process.

Calculate the mass of sweat evaporated in one minute. *(3 marks)*

(c) Explain why, when she stops running, her temperature is likely to fall. *(2 marks)*

AQA, 2005

7 In a geothermal power station, water is pumped through pipes into an underground region of hot rocks. The thermal energy of the rocks heats the water and turns it to steam at high pressure. The steam then drives a turbine at the surface to produce electricity.

(a) Water at $21\,°C$ is pumped into the hot rocks and steam at $100\,°C$ is produced at a rate of $190\,kg\,s^{-1}$.

(i) Show that the energy per second transferred from the hot rocks to the power station in this process is at least $500\,MW$.

(ii) The hot rocks are estimated to have a volume of $4.0 \times 10^6\,m^3$. Estimate the fall of temperature of these rocks in one day if thermal energy is removed from them at the rate calculated in part (i) without any thermal energy gain from deeper underground.

specific heat capacity of the rocks $= 850\,J\,kg^{-1}\,K^{-1}$

density of the rocks $= 3200\,kg\,m^{-3}$ *(7 marks)*

(b) Geothermal energy originates as energy released in the radioactive decay of the uranium isotope deep inside the Earth. Each nucleus that decays releases $4.2\,MeV$.

Calculate the mass of $^{238}_{92}U$ that would release energy at a rate of $500\,MW$.

half-life of $^{238}_{92}U = 4.5 \times 10^9$ years

molar mass of $^{238}_{92}U = 0.238\,kg\,mol^{-1}$ *(5 marks)*

AQA, 2006

12.1   The experimental gas laws

When you use a cycle pump to inflate a tyre, you raise the air pressure in the tyre because the pump pushes air through a valve into the tyre. The valve lets the air in but does not allow it out. The tyre is a buffer between the wheel frame and the ground. If the tyre pressure is too low, the wheel frame will rub on the ground when cycling.

The **pressure** of a gas is the force per unit area that the gas exerts normally (i.e. at right angles to) on a surface. Pressure is measured in pascals (Pa), where $1\,Pa = 1\,N\,m^{-2}$. The pressure of a gas depends on its temperature, the volume of the gas container and on the mass of gas in the container.

▨ Boyle's law

The apparatus shown in Figure 1 may be used to investigate how the pressure of a fixed mass of gas depends on its volume when the temperature remains the same. Measurements using this apparatus show that the gas pressure × its volume is constant for a fixed mass of gas at constant temperature. This is known as Boyle's law, after Robert Boyle who first discovered the law in 1662. Note that a change at constant temperature is called an **isothermal** change.

Boyle's law states that for a fixed mass of gas at constant temperature,

$$pV = \text{constant}$$

where p = gas pressure and V = gas volume.

The measurements plotted as a graph of pressure against 1/volume give a straight line through the origin. This is because Boyle's law may be written as $p = \text{constant} \times \dfrac{1}{V}$ which represents the equation $y = mx$ for a straight-line graph through the origin, if p is plotted on the y-axis and $\dfrac{1}{V}$ on the x-axis.

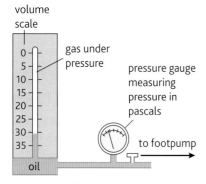

Figure 1 *Testing Boyle's law*

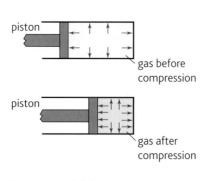

Figure 2 *Boyle's law*

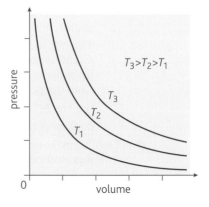

Charles' law

Using a glass tube open at one end containing dry air trapped by a suitable liquid, we can find out how the volume of a fixed mass of gas at constant pressure varies with temperature. Plotting the measurements of the volume of the gas at 0 °C and 100 °C on a graph leads to idea of absolute zero. No matter how much gas is used, provided the gas is an ideal gas, its volume would be zero at absolute zero which is –273.15 °C.

Figure 3 shows how the volume of a fixed mass of gas at constant pressure varies with absolute temperature T in kelvins. In the graph is a straight line through the origin. The relationship, known as **Charles' law**, between the gas volume V and the temperature T in kelvins can therefore be written as:

$$\frac{V}{T} = \text{constant}$$

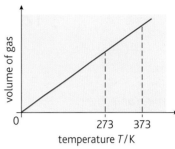

Figure 3 *Charles' law*

AQA Examiner's tip

In gas calculations, the temperature must be in kelvins.

The pressure law

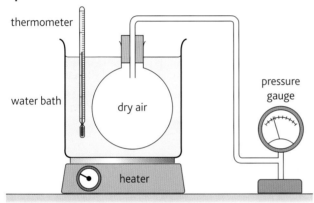

Figure 4 *The pressure law*

Figure 4 shows how the pressure of a fixed mass of gas at constant volume can be measured at different temperatures. If the measurements are plotted on a graph of pressure against temperature in kelvins, they give a straight line through the origin (as shown in Topic 11.1). The relationship between pressure p and temperature T, in kelvins, can therefore be written as

$$\frac{p}{T} = \text{constant}$$

How science works

Deep sea diving

The extra pressure on an underwater swimmer due to a few metres of water is enough to cause breathing difficulties. Special breathing apparatus is used to attain much greater depths. Gases in the lungs are compressed by the high pressure on the body and they pass into the blood system. A sudden ascent under water releases dissolved nitrogen into the blood system causing a life-threatening painful condition known as 'the bends'. Divers have to learn how to work out factors such as safe rates of ascent or descent.

Summary questions

1 A hand pump of volume $2.0 \times 10^{-4} \text{ m}^3$ is used to force air through a valve into a container of volume $8.0 \times 10^{-4} \text{ m}^3$ which contains air at an initial pressure of 101 kPa. Calculate the pressure of the air in the container after one stroke of the pump, assuming the temperature is unchanged.

2 A sealed can of fixed volume contains air at a pressure of 101 kPa at 100 °C. The can is then cooled to a temperature of 20 °C. Calculate the pressure of the air in the can.

3 The volume of a fixed mass of gas at 15 °C was 0.085 m³. The gas was then heated to 55 °C without change of pressure. Calculate the new volume of this gas.

4 A hand pump was used to raise the pressure of the air in a flask of volume $1.20 \times 10^{-4} \text{ m}^3$, without and then with powder in the flask.

■ Without the powder in the flask, the pressure increased from 110 kPa to 135 kPa.

■ With 0.038 kg of powder in the flask, the pressure increased from 110 kPa to 141 kPa.

a Show that the volume of air in the hand pump initially was $2.7 \times 10^{-5} \text{ m}^3$.

b Calculate the volume and the density of the powder.

12.2 The ideal gas law

Learning objectives:

- What is an ideal gas?
- Can we combine the experimental gas laws?
- What is the origin of the Avogadro constant?

Specification reference: 3.5A.3

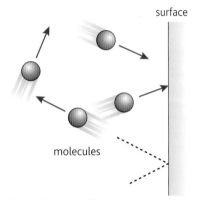

Figure 1 *Molecules in motion*

Link

Randomness occurs in radioactive decay as well as in Brownian motion of molecules. You can't predict when a random event will take place. See Topic 9.5.

Molecules in a gas

The molecules of a gas move at random with different speeds. When a molecule collides with another molecule or with a solid surface, it bounces off without loss of speed. The pressure of a gas on a surface is due to the gas molecules hitting the surface. Each impact causes a tiny force on the surface. Because there are a very large number of impacts each second, the overall result is that the gas exerts a measurable pressure on the surface.

Molecules are too small to see individually. The effect of individual molecules in a gas can be seen if smoke particles are observed using a microscope. If a beam of light is directed through the smoke, the smoke particles are seen as tiny specks of light wriggling about unpredictably. This type of motion is called **Brownian motion** after Robert Brown who first observed it in 1827 with pollen grains in water. The motion of each particle is due to it being bombarded unevenly and at random by individual molecules. The particle therefore experiences forces, due to these impacts, which change its magnitude and direction at random.

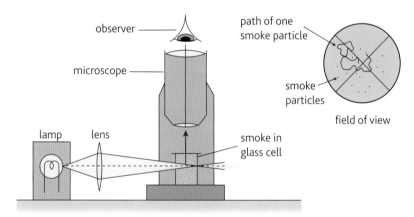

Figure 2 *Brownian motion*

The Avogadro constant

The density of oxygen gas is 16 times that of hydrogen gas at the same temperature. Therefore, the mass of a certain volume of oxygen is 16 times that of the mass of the same volume of hydrogen at the same temperature. When such measurements were first made in the 19th century, Amadeo Avogadro put forward the hypothesis that equal volumes of gases at the same temperature and pressure contain equal number of molecules.

How many molecules are in a certain amount of gas? Avogadro thought of the idea of counting atoms and molecules in terms of the number of atoms in 1 gram of hydrogen. Now we use 12 grams of the carbon isotope $^{12}_{6}C$ as the standard amount as hydrogen gas contains a small proportion of the isotope of hydrogen $^{2}_{1}H$ which cannot easily be removed.

- The **Avogadro constant**, N_A, is defined as the number of atoms in exactly 12 g of the carbon isotope $^{12}_{6}C$. The value of N_A (to 4 significant figures) is 6.023×10^{23}. Therefore the mass of an atom of $^{12}_{6}C$ is 1.993×10^{-23} g ($= 12\,g/6.02 \times 10^{23}$).

One atomic mass unit (u) is $\frac{1}{12}$th of the mass of a $^{12}_{6}C$ atom. The mass of a carbon atom is 1.993×10^{-26} kg, so $1\,u = 1.661 \times 10^{-27}$ kg.

Molar mass

One **mole** of a substance consisting of identical particles is defined as the quantity of substance that contains N_A particles. The number of moles in a certain quantity of a substance is its **molarity.** The unit of molarity is the mol.

The **molar mass** of a substance is the mass of 1 mole of the substance. The unit of molar mass is $kg\,mol^{-1}$. For example, the molar mass of oxygen gas is $0.032\,kg\,mol^{-1}$. So 0.032 kg of oxygen gas contains N_A oxygen molecules.

Therefore,

1 the number of moles in mass M_S of a substance $= M_S/M$, where M is the molar mass of the substance,

2 the number of molecules in mass M_S of a substance $= N_A M_S/M$

For example, because the molar mass of carbon dioxide is 0.044 kg $(= 44\,g)$, then:

■ 2 moles of carbon dioxide has a mass of 88g and contains $2N_A$ molecules,

■ 10 moles of carbon dioxide has a mass of 440 g and contains $10N_A$ molecules,

■ n moles of carbon dioxide has a mass of 88 n g and contains nN_A molecules.

The ideal gas equation

An **ideal gas** is a gas that obeys Boyle's law. The three experimental gas laws can be combined to give the equation:

$$\frac{pV}{T} = \text{constant, for a fixed mass of ideal gas}$$

where p is the pressure, V is the volume and T is the absolute temperature. This equation takes in all situations where the pressure, volume and temperature of a fixed mass of gas changes.

As explained earlier, equal volumes of ideal gases at the same temperature and pressure contain equal numbers of moles. Further measurements show that one mole of any ideal gas at 273 K and a pressure of 101 kPa has a volume of $0.0224\,m^3$. Therefore, for 1 mole of any ideal gas, the value of pV/T for 1 mole is equal to 8.31 J $mol^{-1}\,K^{-1}$

$$\left(= \frac{pV}{T} = \frac{101 \times 10^3\,Pa \times 0.0224\,m^3}{273\,K} \right).$$

This value is known as the **molar gas constant**, R.

Hence the combined gas law may be written as

$$pV_m = RT$$

where V_m = volume of 1 mole of ideal gas at pressure p and temperature T.

Therefore, for n moles of ideal gas,

$$pV = nRT$$

where V = volume of the gas at pressure p and temperature T in kelvins.

This equation is known as the **ideal gas equation**.

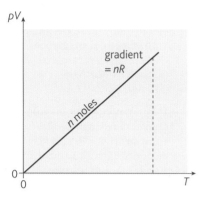

Figure 3 *A graph of pV against T for an ideal gas*

Using the ideal gas equation

■ The **mass** M_s of a substance is equal to its molar mass M × the number of moles n. Since $n = \dfrac{pV}{RT}$ for an ideal gas, then $M_s = M\left(\dfrac{pV}{RT}\right)$ gives the mass of ideal gas in volume V at pressure p and absolute temperature T.

■ The **density of an ideal gas** of molar mass M, $\rho = \dfrac{\text{mass } M_s}{\text{volume } V}$

$$= \frac{nM}{V} = \frac{pM}{RT}.$$

Therefore, for an ideal gas at constant pressure, its density ρ is inversely proportional to its temperature T.

■ In the equation $pV = nRT$, substituting the number of moles $n = \dfrac{N}{N_A}$ gives

$$pV = NkT$$

where the **Boltzmann constant** $k = \dfrac{R}{N_A}$.

Prove for yourself that $k = 1.38 \times 10^{-23}\,\text{J K}^{-1}$. We will meet k again in the next topic when we discuss how much **kinetic energy** a gas molecule has.

Worked example:

$R = 8.31\,\text{J mol}^{-1}\,\text{K}^{-1}$

Calculate the number of moles and the mass of air in a balloon when the air pressure in the balloon is 170 kPa, the volume of the balloon is $8.4 \times 10^{-4}\,\text{m}^3$ and the temperature of the air in the balloon is 17 °C.

molar mass of air = 0.029 kg mol^{-1}

Solution

$T = 273 + 17 = 290\,\text{K}$

Using $pV = nRT$ gives $n = \dfrac{pV}{RT} = \dfrac{170 \times 10^3 \times 8.4 \times 10^{-4}}{8.31 \times 290} = 5.9 \times 10^{-2}\,\text{mol}$

Mass of air = number of moles × molar mass = $5.9 \times 10^{-2} \times 0.029$

$= 1.7 \times 10^{-3}\,\text{kg}$

Summary questions

$N_A = 6.02 \times 10^{23}\,\text{mol}^{-1}$
$R = 8.31\,\text{J mol}^{-1}\,\text{K}^{-1}$

1 A gas cylinder has a volume of 0.024 m³ and is fitted with a valve designed to release the gas if the pressure of the gas reaches 125 kPa. Calculate:

a the maximum number of moles of gas that can be contained by this cylinder at 50 °C,

b the pressure in the cylinder of this amount of gas at 10 °C.

2 In an electrolysis experiment, $2.2 \times 10^{-5}\,\text{m}^3$ of a gas is collected at a pressure of 103 kPa and a temperature of 20 °C. Calculate:

a the number of moles of gas present,

b the volume of this gas at 0 °C and 101 kPa.

3 a Sketch a graph to show how the pressure of 2 moles of gas varies with temperature when the gas is heated from 20 °C to 100 °C in a sealed container of volume 0.050 m³.

b The molar mass of the gas in a is 0.032 kg mol^{-1}. Calculate the density of the gas.

4 The molar mass of air is 0.029 kg mol^{-1}.

a Calculate the density of air at 20 °C and a pressure of 101 kPa.

b Calculate the number of molecules in 0.001 m³ of air at 20 °C and a pressure of 101 kPa.

12.3 The kinetic theory of gases

Learning objectives:

- Can we explain the increase of pressure of a gas when it is compressed or heated?

- How can we model the behaviour of a gas?

- What does the mean kinetic energy of a gas molecule depend on?

Specification reference: 3.5A.3

The gas laws can be explained by assuming a gas consists of point molecules moving about at random, continually colliding with the container walls. Each impact causes a force on the container. The force of many impacts is the cause of the pressure of the gas on the container walls.

Explanation of Boyle's law; the pressure of a gas at constant temperature is increased by reducing its volume because the gas molecules travel less distance between impacts at the walls due to the reduced volume. Hence there are more impacts per second so the pressure is greater.

Explanation of the pressure law; the pressure of a gas at constant volume is increased by raising its temperature. The average speed of the molecules is increased by raising the gas temperature so the impacts of the molecules on the container walls are harder and more frequent. Hence the pressure is raised as a result.

Molecular speeds

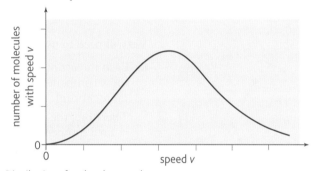

Figure 1 *Distribution of molecular speeds*

The molecules in an ideal gas have a continuous spread of speeds, as shown in Figure 1. The speed of an individual molecule changes when it collides with another gas molecule but the distribution stays the same, provided the temperature does not change.

The **root mean square speed** of the molecules,

$$c_{rms} = \left[\frac{(c_1^2 + c_2^2 + \ldots + c_N^2)}{N} \right]^{1/2},$$

where $c_1, c_2, c_3 \ldots c_N$ represent the speeds of the individual molecules and N is the number of molecules in the gas.

If the temperature of a gas is raised, its molecules move faster on average. The root mean square speed of the molecules increases. The distribution curve becomes flatter and broader as there are molecules at higher speeds.

The kinetic theory equation

For an ideal gas consisting of N identical molecules, each of mass m, in a container of volume V, the pressure p of the gas is given by

$$pV = \tfrac{1}{3} Nmc_{rms}^2$$

where c_{rms} is the root mean square speed of the gas molecules.

Hint

Note that the root mean square speed of the molecules of a gas is not the same as the mean speed which is the sum of the speeds divided by the number of molecules.

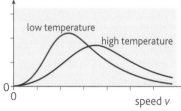

number of molecules with speed *v*

low temperature

high temperature

0

speed *v*

Figure 2 *The effect of temperature on the distribution of speeds*

We need to apply the laws of mechanics and statistics to the molecular model of a gas to derive the **kinetic theory equation**. In doing so, certain assumptions must be made about the molecules in a gas.

1   The molecules are point molecules. The volume of each molecule is negligible compared with the volume of the gas.

2   They do not attract each other. If they did, the effect would be to reduce the force of their impacts on the container surface.

3   They move about in continual random motion.

4   The collisions they undergo with each other and with the container surface are elastic collisions (i.e. there is no overall loss of kinetic energy in a collision).

5   Each collision with the container surface is of much shorter duration than the time between impacts.

Part 1

Consider one molecule of mass m in a rectangular box of dimensions l_x, l_y and l_z as shown in Figure 3. Let u_1, v_1 and w_1 represent its velocity components in the x, y and z directions, respectively.

Note that the speed, c_1, of the molecule is given by the following rule for adding perpendicular components (in this case the three velocity components u_1, v_1 and w_1),

$$c_1^2 = u_1^2 + v_1^2 + w_1^2$$

We will need to use this rule in Part 2.

▓ Each impact of the molecule with the shaded face in Figure 3 reverses the x-component of velocity thus changing the x-component of its momentum from $+mu_1$ to $-mu_1$

Therefore, the change of its momentum due to the impact
= final momentum – initial momentum = $(-mu_1) - (mu_1) = -2mu_1$

▓ The time, t, between successive impacts on this face is given by:

$$t = \frac{\text{the total distance to the opposite face and back}}{x\text{-component of velocity}} = \frac{2l_x}{u_1}$$

Using Newton's second law therefore gives

the force on the molecule $= \dfrac{\text{change of momentum}}{\text{time taken}}$

$$= \frac{-2mu_1}{(2l_x/u_1)} = \frac{-mu_1^2}{l_x}$$

Since the force F_1 of the impact on the surface is equal and opposite to the force on the molecule in accordance with Newton's third law, then

$$F_1 = \frac{+mu_1^2}{l_x}$$

▓ As pressure $= \dfrac{\text{force}}{\text{area}}$, the pressure p_1 of the molecule on the surface is given by

$$p_1 = \frac{\text{force}}{\text{area of the shaded face } (l_y l_z)} = \frac{mu_1^2}{l_x l_y l_z} = \frac{mu_1^2}{V}$$

where V = the volume of the box = $l_x l_y l_z$

Part 2

For N molecules in the box moving at different velocities, the total pressure p is the sum of the individual pressures p_1, p_2, $p_3 \ldots p_N$ where each subscript refers to each molecule.

Hence $p = \dfrac{mu_1^2}{V} + \dfrac{mu_2^2}{V} + \dfrac{mu_3^2}{V} + \ldots + \dfrac{mu_N^2}{V}$

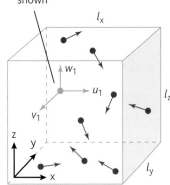

chosen molecule with its velocity components shown

Figure 3 *Molecules in a box*

$$= \frac{m}{V}\left(u_1^2 + u_2^2 + u_3^2 + \dots + u_N^2\right) = \frac{Nm\bar{u}^2}{V}$$

where $\bar{u}^2 = \dfrac{u_1^2 + u_2^2 + u_3^2 + \dots + u_N^2}{N}$

As the motion of the molecules is random, there is no preferred direction of motion. The equation above could equally well have been derived in terms of the y-components of velocity $v_1, v_2, v_3 \dots v_N$ or the z-components of velocity $w_1, w_2, w_3 \dots w_N$.

i.e. $p = \dfrac{Nm\bar{v}^2}{V}$ where $\bar{v}^2 = \dfrac{v_1^2 + v_2^2 + v_3^2 + \dots + v_N^2}{N}$

$p = \dfrac{Nm\bar{w}^2}{V}$ where $\bar{w}^2 = \dfrac{w_1^2 + w_2^2 + w_3^2 + \dots + w_N^2}{N}$

Therefore:

$$p = \frac{Nm}{3V}\left(\bar{u}^2 + \bar{v}^2 + \bar{w}^2\right)$$

The note below shows that, because the motion of the molecules is random, **the root mean square speed** of the gas molecules is given by the equation:

$$c_{rms}^2 = \bar{u}^2 + \bar{v}^2 + \bar{w}^2$$

Hence $p = \dfrac{Nm}{3V}c_{rms}^2$ or $pV = \dfrac{1}{3}Nmc_{rms}^2$

Note

As explained in part 1, the speed c of each molecule is related to its velocity components according to equations of the form:

$c_1^2 = u_1^2 + v_1^2 + w_1^2$

$c_2^2 = u_2^2 + v_2^2 + w_2^2$

$c_3^2 = u_3^2 + v_3^2 + w_3^2$

$c_N^2 = u_N^2 + v_N^2 + w_N^2$

The root mean square speed of the molecules, c_{rms} is defined by:

$c_{rms}^2 = \dfrac{c_1^2 + c_2^2 + c_3^2 + \dots + c_N^2}{N}$

So $c_{rms}^2 = \dfrac{u_1^2 + v_1^2 + w_1^2 + u_2^2 + v_2^2 + w_2^2 + u_3^2 + v_3^2 + w_3^2 + \dots + u_N^2 + v_N^2 + w_N^2}{N}$

$= \bar{u}^2 + \bar{v}^2 + \bar{w}^2$

Molecules and kinetic energy

The mean **kinetic energy of a molecule of the gas** = total kinetic energy of all the molecules/total number of molecules

$$= \frac{\frac{1}{2}mc_1^2 + \frac{1}{2}mc_2^2 + \frac{1}{2}mc_3^2 + \dots + \frac{1}{2}mc_N^2}{N}$$

$$= \frac{\frac{1}{2}m(c_1^2 + c_2^2 + c_3^2 + \dots + c_N^2)}{N} = \frac{1}{2}mc_{rms}^2$$

The higher the temperature of a gas, the greater the mean kinetic energy of a molecule of the gas.

For an ideal gas, by assuming the mean kinetic energy of a molecule

$$\frac{1}{2}mc_{rms}^2 = \frac{3}{2}kT$$

where $k = \dfrac{R}{N_A}$, then $3kT = mc_{rms}^2$

Link

The idea that the mean kinetic energy of a particle is proportional to absolute temperature can be applied in many other situations, for example to explain why conduction electrons can't escape from a metal at room temperature. See *AS Physics* Topic 3.2.

Summary questions

$N_A = 6.02 \times 10^{23}\,\text{mol}^{-1}$,
$R = 8.31\,\text{J}\,\text{mol}^{-1}\,\text{K}^{-1}$,
$k = 1.38 \times 10^{-23}\,\text{J}\,\text{K}^{-1}$

1 a Explain in molecular terms why the pressure of a gas in a sealed container increases when its temperature is raised.

   b The molar mass of oxygen is $0.032\,\text{kg}\,\text{mol}^{-1}$. A cylinder of volume $0.025\,\text{m}^3$ contains oxygen gas at a pressure of $120\,\text{kPa}$ and a temperature of $373\,\text{K}$. Calculate:

   i   the number of moles of oxygen in the cylinder,

   ii   the total kinetic energy of all the gas molecules in the container.

2 Calculate:

   a the mean kinetic energy of a hydrogen molecule at $0\,°\text{C}$,

   b the root mean square speed of a hydrogen molecule at $0\,°\text{C}$,

   molar mass of hydrogen gas = $0.002\,\text{kg}\,\text{mol}^{-1}$.

3 Air consists mostly of nitrogen and oxygen in proportions 1:4 by mass.

   a Explain why the mean kinetic energy of a nitrogen molecule in air is the same as that of an oxygen molecule in the same sample of air.

   b Show that the root mean square speed of a nitrogen molecule in air is $1.07 \times$ that of an oxygen molecule in the same sample of air.

   molar masses:
   nitrogen = $0.028\,\text{kg}\,\text{mol}^{-1}$
   oxygen = $0.032\,\text{kg}\,\text{mol}^{-1}$

4 An ideal gas of molar mass $0.028\,\text{kg}\,\text{mol}^{-1}$ is in a container of volume $0.037\,\text{m}^3$ at a pressure of $100\,\text{kPa}$ and a temperature of $300\,\text{K}$. Calculate:

   a the number of moles,

   b the mass of gas present,

   c the root mean square speed of the molecules of a gas.

Substituting $3kT$ for mc_{rms}^2 in the kinetic theory equation $pV = \frac{1}{3}Nmc_{\text{rms}}^2$ therefore gives:

$$pV = \tfrac{1}{3}N \times 3kT = NkT$$

As $Nk = \dfrac{NR}{N_A} = nR$, we then obtain the ideal gas equation $pV = nRT$

We have derived the ideal gas equation (which is an experimental law) from the kinetic theory equation by assuming that the mean kinetic energy of an ideal gas molecule $= \frac{3}{2}kT$

Therefore we can say for an ideal gas at absolute temperature T,

the mean kinetic energy of a molecule of an ideal gas $= \frac{3}{2}kT$,

where $k = \dfrac{R}{N_A}$. The constant k is referred to as the Boltzmann constant.

Its value $\left(= \dfrac{R}{N_A}\right)$ is $1.38 \times 10^{-23}\,\text{J}\,\text{K}^{-1}$

Notes:
Using the above equation,

- the total kinetic energy of 1 mole of an ideal gas $= N_A \times \frac{3}{2}kT = \frac{3}{2}RT$ (as $k = N_A/R$),

- the total kinetic energy of n moles of an ideal gas $= n \times \frac{3}{2}RT = \frac{3}{2}nRT$

The total kinetic energy of n moles of an ideal gas $= \frac{3}{2}nRT$

Worked example:

$k = 1.38 \times 10^{-23}\,\text{J}\,\text{mol}^{-1}\,\text{K}^{-1}$, $N_A = 6.02 \times 10^{23}\,\text{mol}^{-1}$

Calculate the root mean square speed of oxygen molecules at $0\,°\text{C}$. The molar mass of oxygen = $0.032\,\text{kg}\,\text{mol}^{-1}$

Solution

$T = 273\,\text{K}$

The mass of an oxygen molecule, $m = \dfrac{0.032}{6.02 \times 10^{23}} = 5.3 \times 10^{-26}\,\text{kg}$

Rearranging $\frac{1}{2}mc_{\text{rms}}^2 = \frac{3}{2}kT$ gives

$$c_{\text{rms}}^2 = \frac{3kT}{m} = \frac{3 \times 1.38 \times 10^{-23} \times 273}{5.3 \times 10^{-26}} = 2.13 \times 10^5\,\text{m}^2\,\text{s}^{-2}$$

$\therefore$ root mean square speed, $c_{\text{rms}} = (2.13 \times 10^5)^{\frac{1}{2}} = 461\,\text{m}\,\text{s}^{-1}$

How science works

Making assumptions

In deriving the kinetic theory equation, certain assumptions are made about the molecules of a gas in order to apply the laws of mechanics and knowledge of statistics to the molecular model of a gas. The ideal gas equation is then obtained by applying the further assumption that the mean kinetic energy of a gas molecule is directly proportional to the absolute temperature of the gas. Therefore, since the ideal gas law is an experimental law, the assumptions made in deriving it from the molecular model of a gas must be valid in any gas which obeys the ideal gas law. Under conditions where a gas does not obey the ideal gas equation (e.g. very high pressure), one or more of the assumptions is no longer valid. For example, a gas at very high pressure does not obey the ideal gas law. This is because its molecules are so close to each other, the volume of the molecules is significant and they do not behave as 'point molecules'.

1   The escape velocity v_{esc} of an object from a planet or moon is the minimum velocity the object must have to escape from the planet. For a planet or moon of radius R, it can be shown that $v_{esc} = (2gR)^{1/2}$, where g is the gravitational field strength at the surface of the planet or moon.

   (a) The radius of the Earth's moon is 1740 km and its surface gravitational field strength is 1.62 N kg^{-1}. Calculate the escape velocity from the Earth's moon.   *(2 marks)*

   (b) The average temperature of the lunar surface during the lunar day is about 400 K.

      (i)   Calculate the mean kinetic energy of a molecule of an ideal gas at 400 K.

      (ii) Show that the root mean square speed of a molecule of oxygen gas at this temperature is 560 m s^{-1}.

      (iii) Explain why gas molecules released on the lunar surface escape into space.   *(8 marks)*

   (c) Astronomers have discovered the existence of water vapour in a giant gas planet orbiting a star 64 light years from Earth. The astronomers observed the spectrum of infrared light from the star and discovered absorption lines due to water vapour which are present only when the planet passes across the face of the star.

      (i)   Why did astronomers conclude that the absorption lines were due to the planet rather than the star?

      (ii) Give **one** reason why it might not have been possible to detect such absorption lines if the planet's surface had been at the same temperature but the planet had been much smaller in diameter and in mass.   *(6 marks)*

2   (a) (i)   Sketch a graph of pressure against volume for a fixed mass of ideal gas at constant temperature. Label this graph O.

          On the *same axes* sketch **two** additional curves A and B, if the following changes are made:

      (ii) The same mass of gas at a lower constant temperature (label this A).

      (iii) A greater mass of gas at the original constant temperature (label this B).   *(3 marks)*

   (b) A cylinder of volume 0.20 m^3 contains an ideal gas at a pressure of 130 kPa and a temperature of 290 K. Calculate:

      (i)   the amount of gas, in moles, in the cylinder,

      (ii) the total kinetic energy of a molecule of gas in the cylinder,

      (iii) the total kinetic energy of the molecules in the cylinder.   *(5 marks)*

AQA, 2005

3   (a) State the equation of state for an ideal gas.   *(1 mark)*

   (b) A fixed mass of an ideal gas is heated while its volume is kept constant. Sketch a graph to show how the pressure, p, of the gas varies with the absolute temperature, T, of the gas.   *(2 marks)*

   (c) Explain in terms of molecular motion, why the pressure of the gas in part (b) varies with the absolute temperature.   *(4 marks)*

   (d) Calculate the average kinetic energy of the gas molecules at a temperature of 300 K.   *(2 marks)*

AQA, 2004

4 (a) The molecular theory model of an ideal gas leads to the derivation of the equation

$$pV = \tfrac{1}{3}Nmc_{rms}^{2}$$

Explain what each symbol in the equation represents. *(4 marks)*

   (b) One assumption used in the derivation of the equation stated in part (a) is that molecules are in a state of random motion.

   (i) Explain what is meant by random motion.

   (ii) State **two** more assumptions used in this derivation. *(4 marks)*

   (c) Describe how the motion of gas molecules can be used to explain the pressure exerted by a gas on the walls of its container. *(4 marks)*

AQA, 2002

5 The number of molecules in one cubic metre of air decreases as altitude increases. The table shows how the pressure and temperature of air compare at sea-level and at an altitude of 10 000 m.

altitude	pressure/Pa	temperature/K
sea-level	1.0×10^{5}	300
10 000 m	2.2×10^{4}	270

   (a) Calculate the number of moles of air in a cubic metre of air at:

   (i) sea-level,

   (ii) 10 000 m. *(3 marks)*

   (b) In air, 23% of the molecules are oxygen molecules. Calculate the number of extra oxygen molecules there are per cubic metre at sea-level compared with a cubic metre of air at an altitude of 10 000 m. *(2 marks)*

AQA, 2006

6 (a) **Figure 1** shows a helium atom of mass 6.8×10^{-27} kg about to strike the wall of a container. It rebounds with the same speed.

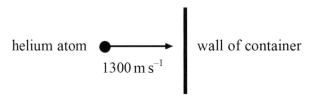

Figure 1

   (i) Calculate the momentum change of the helium atom.

   (ii) Calculate the number of collisions per second on each cm^2 of the container wall that will produce a pressure of 1.5×10^{5} Pa. *(5 marks)*

   (b) The molar mass of gaseous nitrogen is 0.028 kg mol^{-1}. The average kinetic energy for nitrogen molecules in a sample is 8.6×10^{-21} J.

   (i) Calculate the temperature of the sample.

   (ii) Calculate the mean square speed of the nitrogen molecules. *(5 marks)*

AQA, 2006 and 2007

7 The graph in **Figure 2** shows the best fit line for the results of an experiment in which the volume of a fixed mass of gas was measured over a temperature range from 20 °C to 100 °C. The pressure of the gas remained constant throughout the experiment.

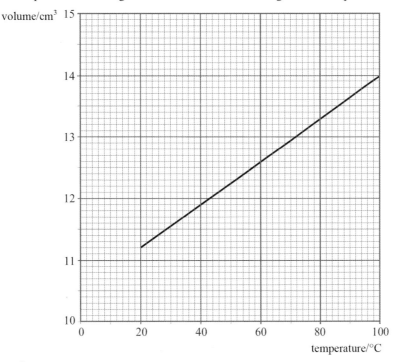

Figure 2

(a) Use the graph in **Figure 2** to calculate a value for the absolute zero of temperature in °C. Show clearly your method of working. *(4 marks)*

(b) Use data from the graph to calculate the mass of gas used in the experiment.
You may assume that the gas behaved like an ideal gas throughout the experiment.
gas pressure throughout the experiment $= 1.0 \times 10^5$ Pa
molar mass of the gas used $= 0.044$ kg mol^{-1} *(5 marks)*

(c) Use the kinetic theory of gases to explain why the pressure of an ideal gas decreases
   (i) when it is expanded at constant temperature,
   (ii) when its temperature is lowered at constant volume. *(5 marks)*

AQA, 2005 and 2006

8 (a) A cylinder of fixed volume contains 15 mol of an ideal gas at a pressure of 500 kPa and a temperature of 290 K.
   (i) Show that the volume of the cylinder is 7.2×10^{-2} m^3.
   (ii) Calculate the average kinetic energy of a gas molecule in the cylinder. *(4 marks)*

(b) A quantity of gas is removed from the cylinder and the pressure of the remaining gas falls to 420 kPa. If the temperature of the gas is unchanged, calculate the amount, in mol, of gas remaining in the cylinder. *(2 marks)*

(c) Explain in terms of the kinetic theory why the pressure of the gas in the cylinder falls when gas is removed from the cylinder. *(4 marks)*

AQA, 2003

Unit 5: Nuclear physics, thermal physics plus an optional topic

1   The equation

$$p \longrightarrow n + \beta^+ + \nu_e$$

represents the emission of a positron from a proton.

(a) Energy and momentum are conserved in this emission.
     What other quantities are conserved in this emission?   *(3 marks)*

(b) Draw the Feynman diagram that corresponds to the positron emission
     represented in the equation.   *(4 marks)*

(c) Copy and complete the following table using ticks ✓ and crosses ✗.

particle	meson	baryon	lepton
p			
n			
β^+			
ν_ε			

(4 marks)

AQA, 2005

2   (a) (i)   Alpha and beta emissions are known as *ionising radiations*. State and explain
                    why such radiations can be described as *ionising*.

              (ii) Explain why beta particles have a greater range in air than alpha particles.   *(4 marks)*

         (b) **Figure 1** shows the variation with time of the number of radon (^{220}Ra) atoms in a
              radioactive sample.

number of
atoms/10^{21}

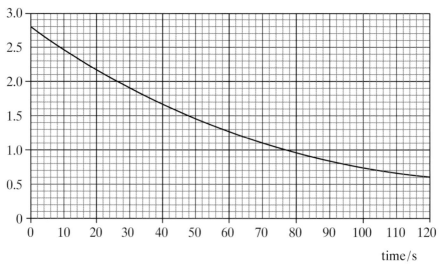

time/s

Figure 1

         (i)   Use the graph to show that the half-life of the decay is approximately 53 s.
               Show your reasoning clearly.

         (ii) The decay constant of ^{220}Ra is $1.3 \times 10^{-2}\,\text{s}^{-1}$. Use data from the graph to find
               the activity of the sample at a time $t = 72\,\text{s}$.   *(6 marks)*

(c) (i) State **two** origins of background radiation.

　　(ii) Suggest why it should be unnecessary to allow for background radiation when measuring the activity of the sample described in part (b)(ii). *(3 marks)*

AQA, 2005

3 A nucleus of plutonium ($^{240}_{94}$Po) decays to form uranium (U) and an alpha particle (α).

(a) Copy and complete the equation that describes this decay:

$$^{240}_{94}\text{Po} \longrightarrow$$ *(2 marks)*

(b) (i) Show that about 1 pJ of energy is released when one nucleus decays.

　　　mass of plutonium nucleus $= 3.986\,26 \times 10^{-25}\,\text{kg}$

　　　mass of uranium nucleus $= 3.919\,70 \times 10^{-25}\,\text{kg}$

　　　mass of alpha particle $= 6.642\,51 \times 10^{-25}\,\text{kg}$ *(3 marks)*

　　(ii) The plutonium isotope has a half-life of 2.1×10^{-11} s. Show that the decay constant of the plutonium is about $3 \times 10^{-12}\,\text{s}^{-1}$.

　　(iii) A radioactive source in a school laboratory contains 3.2×10^{21} atoms of plutonium.

　　　Calculate the energy that will be released in one second by the decay of the plutonium described in part (b)(i).

　　(iv) Comment on whether the energy release due to the plutonium decay is likely to change by more than 5% during 100 years. Support your answer with a calculation. *(12 marks)*

AQA, 2004

4 The table shows data for some nuclei.

element	Z	A	nuclear radius $r/10^{-15}$ m	binding energy per nucleon/MeV	emission (half-life)
beryllium	4	9	2.5	6.46	stable
sodium	11	23	3.4	8.11	stable
manganese	25	56	4.6	8.74	β^- (2.6 h)

(a) (i) Show that these data support the rule that

$$r = r_0 A^{1/3}$$

　　where r_0 is a constant.

　　(ii) The mass of a nucleon is about 1.7×10^{-27} kg. Calculate the density of nuclear matter. *(6 marks)*

(b) (i) Explain what is meant by the binding energy of a nucleus.

　　(ii) Show that the total binding energy of a sodium-23 nucleus is about 3×10^{-11} J.

　　(iii) Calculate the mass-equivalent of this binding energy. *(5 marks)*

(c) Nuclear structure can be explored by bombarding the nuclei with alpha particles. The de Broglie wavelength of the alpha particle must be similar to the nuclear diameter.

Calculate the energy of an alpha particle that could be used to explore the structure of manganese-56.

mass of an alpha particle $= 6.8 \times 10^{-27}$ kg *(4 marks)*

(d) (i) State the proton number and nucleon number of the nucleus formed by the decay of manganese-56.

　　(ii) The activity of a sample of manganese-56 varies with time according to the equation

$$A = A_0 e^{-\lambda t}$$

　　What value should be used for λ in calculations involving manganese-56 when t is in seconds? *(4 marks)*

AQA, 2007

5   (a)   When an α particle is emitted from a nucleus of the isotope $^{212}_{83}Bi$, a nucleus of thallium, Tl, is formed. Copy and complete the equation below.

$$^{212}_{83}Bi \longrightarrow \alpha + Tl$$

(2 marks)

(b)   The α particle in part (a) is emitted with 6.1 MeV of kinetic energy.

   (i)   The mass of the α particle is 4.0 u. Show that the speed of the α particle immediately after it has been emitted is $1.7 \times 10^7 \, m \, s^{-1}$. Ignore relativistic effects.

   (ii)   Calculate the speed of recoil of the daughter nucleus immediately after the α particle has been emitted. Assume the parent nucleus is initially at rest. *(6 marks)*

AQA, 2002

6   (a)   A solar panel of area $3.8 \, m^2$ is fitted to a satellite in orbit above the Earth. The panel produces a current of 2.8 A at a pd of 25 V when solar radiation is incident normally on it.

   (i)   Calculate the electrical power output of the panel.

   (ii)   Solar radiation on the panel has an intensity of $1.4 \, kW \, m^{-2}$. Calculate the efficiency of the panel. *(4 marks)*

(b)   The back-up power system of the satellite is provided by a radioactive isotope enclosed in a sealed container which absorbs the radiation from the isotope. Energy from the radiation is converted to electrical energy by means of a thermoelectric module.

   (i)   The isotope produces α particles of energy 4.1 MeV and the container absorbs energy from the α particles at a rate of $85 \, J \, s^{-1}$. Show that the isotope has an activity of $1.3 \times 10^{14} \, Bq$.

   (ii)   The half-life of the isotope is 200 years. Calculate the decay constant, λ, of this isotope. 1 year = $3.15 \times 10^7 \, s$.

   (iii)   The nucleon number of the isotope is 209. Calculate the mass of isotope needed for an activity of $1.3 \times 10^{14} \, Bq$. *(7 marks)*

AQA, 2006

7   The radioactive isotope $^{40}_{19}K$ decays by β^- emission to form a stable isotope of calcium (Ca) or by electron capture to form a stable isotope of argon (Ar).

(a)   (i)   Copy and complete the following equation which represents the B⁻ decay of $^{40}_{19}K$.

$$^{40}_{19}K \longrightarrow \beta^- + Ca + \bar{v}_e$$

   (ii)   Sketch the Feynman diagram for this process. *(4 marks)*

(b)   (i)   Copy and complete the following equation which represents electron capture by $^{40}_{19}K$.

$$^{40}_{19}K + e^- \longrightarrow Ar + v_e$$

   (ii)   Sketch the Feynman diagram for this process. *(3 marks)*

(c)   The isotope of argon formed as a result of electron capture by $^{40}_{19}K$ is found as a trapped gas in ancient rocks. The age of an ancient rock can be determined by measuring the proportion of this isotope of argon to $^{40}_{19}K$.

An ancient rock is found to contain 1 argon atom for every 4 atoms of $^{40}_{19}K$.

   (i)   The decay of $^{40}_{19}K$ by β^- emission is 8 times more likely than electron capture. Show that for every argon atom in this rock, there must have originally been 13 atoms of $^{40}_{19}K$.

   (ii) $^{40}_{19}K$ has a half-life of 1250 million years. Calculate the age of this rock. *(6 marks)*

AQA, 2004

8 (a) (i) Explain why, despite the electrostatic repulsion between protons, the nuclei of most atoms of low nucleon number are stable.

(ii) Suggest why stable nuclei of higher nucleon number have greater numbers of neutrons than protons.

(iii) All nuclei have approximately the same density. State and explain what this suggests about the nature of the strong nuclear force. *(6 marks)*

(b) (i) Compare the electrostatic repulsion and the gravitational attraction between a pair of protons the centres of which are separated by 1.2×10^{-15} m.

(ii) Comment on the relative roles of gravitational attraction and electrostatic repulsion in nuclear structure. *(5 marks)*

AQA, 2006

9 A beaker contains 1.3×10^{-4} m³ of water at a temperature of 18 °C. The beaker is placed in a freezer. The water cools to 0 °C and freezes in a total time of 1700 s.

(a) (i) Calculate the mass of water in the beaker.

density of water = 1000 kg m⁻³

(ii) Calculate the average energy per second transferred from the water. Assume the beaker has negligible heat capacity.

specific heat capacity of water = 4200 J kg⁻¹ K⁻¹

specific latent heat of fusion of ice = 3.3×10^5 J kg⁻¹ *(4 marks)*

(b) The freezer uses electrical energy from the mains at a rate of 25 J s⁻¹. Calculate the total energy transferred to the surroundings from the time the beaker of water is placed in the freezer to when it freezes completely. *(2 marks)*

AQA, 2005

10 A long vertical tube contains several small particles of lead, which rest on its base. When the tube is inverted the particles of lead fall freely through a vertical height equal to the length of the tube, which is 1.2 m.

(a) Describe the energy changes that take place in the lead particles during one inversion of the tube. *(3 marks)*

(b) The tube is made from an insulating material and is used in an experiment to determine the specific heat capacity of lead. The following results are obtained.

mass of lead: 0.025 kg   number of inversions: 50

length of tube: 1.2 m   change in temperature of the lead: 4.5 K

Calculate:

(i) the change in potential energy of the lead as it falls after one inversion down the tube,

(ii) the total change in potential energy after 50 inversions,

(iii) the specific heat capacity of the lead. *(4 marks)*

AQA, 2005

11 An electric shower heats the water flowing through it from 10 °C to 42 °C when the volume flow rate is 5.2×10^{-5} m³ s⁻¹.

(a) (i) Calculate the mass of water flowing through the shower each second.

density of water = 1000 kg m⁻³

(ii) Calculate the power supplied to the shower, assuming all the electrical energy supplied to it is gained by the water as thermal energy.

specific heat capacity of water = 4200 J kg⁻¹ K⁻¹. *(4 marks)*

(b) A jet of water emerges horizontally at a speed of 2.5 m s⁻¹ from a hole in the shower head. The hole is 2.0 m above the floor of the shower. Calculate the horizontal distance travelled by this jet. Assume air resistance is negligible. *(3 marks)*

AQA, 2004

12 (a) **Figure 4** shows an arrangement used to investigate the energy stored by a capacitor.

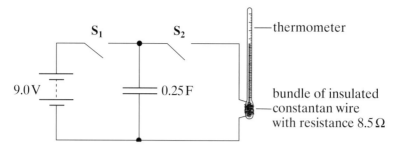

Figure 4

The bundle of constantan wire has a resistance of $8.5\,\Omega$. The capacitor is initially charged to a potential difference of $9.0\,\text{V}$ by closing S_1.

(i) Calculate the charge stored by the $0.25\,\text{F}$ capacitor.

(ii) Calculate the energy stored by the capacitor.

(iii) Switch S_1 is now opened and S_2 is closed so that the capacitor discharges through the constantan wire.

Calculate the time taken for the potential difference across the capacitor to fall to $0.10\,\text{V}$.

(7 marks)

AQA, 2006

(b) The volume of constantan wire in the bundle in **Figure 4** is $2.2 \times 10^{-7}\,\text{m}^3$.

density of constantan $= 8900\,\text{kg m}^{-3}$

specific heat capacity of constantan $= 420\,\text{J kg}^{-1}\text{K}^{-1}$

(i) Assume that all the energy stored by the capacitor is used to raise the temperature of the wire. Use your answer to part (a)(ii) to calculate the expected temperature rise when the capacitor is discharged through the constantan wire.

(ii) Give **two** reasons why, in practice, the final temperature will be lower than that calculated in part (b)(i).

(5 marks)

AQA, 2006

13 (a) A $3.0\,\text{kW}$ electric kettle heats $2.4\,\text{kg}$ of water from $16\,^\circ\text{C}$ to $100\,^\circ\text{C}$ in $320\,\text{s}$.

(i) Calculate the electrical energy supplied to the kettle.

(ii) Calculate the heat energy supplied to the water.

specific heat capacity of water $= 4200\,\text{J kg}^{-1}\text{K}^{-1}$

(iii) Give **one** reason why not all the electrical energy supplied to the kettle is transferred to the water.

(4 marks)

(b) The potential difference supplied to the kettle in part (a) is $230\,\text{V}$.

(i) Calculate the resistance of the heating element of the kettle.

(ii) The heating element consists of an insulated conductor of length $0.25\,\text{m}$ and diameter $0.65\,\text{mm}$. Calculate the resistivity of the conductor.

(5 marks)

AQA, 2004

14 (a) The air in a room of volume $27.0\,\text{m}^3$ is at a temperature of $22\,^\circ\text{C}$ and a pressure of $105\,\text{kPa}$.

Calculate:

(i) the temperature, in K, of the air,

(ii) the number of moles of air in the room,

(iii) the number of gas molecules in the room.

(5 marks)

(b) The temperature of an ideal gas in a sealed container falls. State, with a reason, what happens to the

(i) mean square speed of the gas molecules,

(ii) pressure of the gas.

(4 marks)

AQA, 2004

15 The table gives the average kinetic energy E_k of gas molecules at certain temperatures T.

$E_k/\text{J} \times 10^{-21}$	6.21	6.62	7.04	7.45	7.87	8.28
T/K	300	320	340	360	380	400

(a) (i) Plot a graph of E_k against T.

(ii) Determine the gradient of your graph and hence calculate a value for the Boltzmann constant. Show all your working. *(8 marks)*

(b) One of the assumptions of the kinetic theory is that collisions of gas molecules are elastic.

(i) State what is meant by an elastic collision.

(ii) State another assumption of the kinetic theory.

(iii) Explain how the data in the table leads to the concept of absolute zero. *(4 marks)*

AQA, 2002

16 (a) (i) State **three** assumptions concerning the motion of the molecules in an ideal gas.

(ii) For an ideal gas at a temperature of 300 K, show that the mean kinetic energy of a molecule is 6.2×10^{-21} J. *(5 marks)*

(b) (i) When no current passes along a metal wire, conduction electrons move about in the wire like molecules in an ideal gas.

Calculate the speed of an electron which has 6.2×10^{-21} J of kinetic energy.

(ii) Describe the motion of conduction electrons in a wire when a pd is applied across the ends of the wire. *(6 marks)*

AQA, 2007

17 A sample of air has a density of $1.24\,\text{kg m}^{-3}$ at a pressure of 1.01×10^5 Pa and a temperature of 300 K.

(a) Calculate the mean kinetic energy of an air molecule under these conditions. *(2 marks)*

(b) Calculate the mean square speed for the air molecules. *(3 marks)*

(c) Explain why, when the temperature of the air is increased to 320 K, some of the molecules will have speeds much less than that suggested by the value you calculated in part (b). *(2 marks)*

AQA, 2007

18 (a) (i) At the surface of a spherical planet of radius R, show that the gravitational potential, V_s, is related to the gravitational field of strength, g_s, by

$$V_s = -g_s R.$$

(ii) The gravitational field strength of the Moon at its surface is $1.6\,\text{N kg}^{-1}$. Show that the gravitational potential energy of an oxygen molecule at the surface is -1.4×10^{-19} J.

radius of the Moon = 1700 km   molar mass of oxygen = $0.032\,\text{kg mol}^{-1}$ *(5 marks)*

(b) Oxygen gas at 400 K is released on the surface of the Moon.

(i) Calculate the mean kinetic energy of an oxygen gas molecule at this temperature.

(ii) The maximum temperature of the surface of the Moon is about 400 K. Use the data from part (a)(ii) and the results of your calculations to explain why some of the oxygen gas released at the Moon's surface would escape into space. *(4 marks)*

AQA, 2005

Investigative and practical skills

Chapters in this unit

13 Practical work in A2 physics

14 Internal assessment in A2 physics

15 Mathematical skills for A2 physics

Moving on from AS level

Practical work is an integral feature of your A2 physics course just as at AS level because it helps you develop your understanding of important concepts and applications as well as learning how scientists work in practice and finding out how important discoveries were made and continue to be made in the subject. A2 practical skills embrace the practical skills you have developed in your AS course and you will develop them further in the context of the more demanding knowledge and understanding of the A2 course. For example, in your studies on radioactivity, you will learn how to use a Geiger counter when you study how to measure the effect of absorbers on different forms of ionising radiation. At AS level you learnt new analytical skills such as using measured data to plot a straight-line graph in order to confirm a theoretical relationship (e.g. load against extension graph for a spring). At A2, such skills are developed further by using them in the context of more complex theoretical relationships (e.g. measuring capacitor discharge and plotting ln V against time to confirm the decay is exponential).

Assessment overview

The assessment of A2 investigative and practical skills is undertaken in Unit 6 and carries the same percentage of the total A2 mark as Unit 3 (the corresponding AS Unit) does at AS level. The structure of Unit 6 is similar to that of Unit 3 in that the same two assessment schemes are available, namely scheme T (the PSA/ISA route) and scheme X (the board marked route). An outline of each scheme is given below. As at AS, your teacher will decide which scheme you and your fellow students will follow and this may or may not be the same scheme as you followed at AS level. For example, your assessment in Unit 3 might have been through scheme X and your A2 assessment might be through scheme T. Whichever scheme of assessment you follow, they both count for a total of 20% of the A2 mark and the structure and format is the same as at AS level, but the level of complexity is higher at A2 because the A2 topics are more complex and demanding. The differences in demand and complexity between internal assessment at AS and at A2 are explained in more detail in Chapter 14.

Scheme T The ISA/PSA scheme

This assessment scheme is in two parts:

1 **The investigative skills assignments (ISA)** consists of a practical task on a topic in the specification followed by a written test on your ability to analyse data and evaluate results. More details are given about A2 ISAs in Topic 14.1. The written test will ask you about the results of your own task and about given results from a related practical investigation. The practical task and the written test are both set by AQA and are taken under supervision after you have studied the relevant topic. The ISA counts for 41 out of the 50 marks for the Unit.

2 **The practical skills assessment (PSA)** will assess how well you can follow instructions and on how well you can make measurements. The assessment is made by your teacher **towards the end of your course** and is based on your practical work during the course, specifically your ability to follow instructions, your skill in using equipment and how well you can organise yourself and work safely in the laboratory. The PSA assessment counts for 9 out of the 50 marks for the Unit. More details are given about the PSA at A2 in Topic 14.1.

Scheme X The AQA-marked scheme

This AQA-marked scheme is in three parts.

Part 1 Practical skills verification
You are required to carry out 5 short practical exercises in normal class time on measuring tasks set by AQA. Your teacher will check that you have carried out each of these tasks satisfactorily. Some of the measuring skills in these tasks will be assessed in the AQA-set practical experiments in part 2.

Parts 2 and 3 Externally-marked practical assessment
These parts consist of practical experiments (part 2) and a written test (part 3) set and marked by AQA. You will need to obtain reliable and accurate results in the experiments as you have to analyse and evaluate them in the written test.

More details about scheme X at A2 are given in Topic 14.2.

13 Practical work in A2 physics

13.1 Comparison of physics practical work at A2 and at AS level

The notes that follow apply equally well to either scheme as the skills you need to develop before assessment are the same for both schemes. References below to PSA or ISA features in scheme T apply equally well to the corresponding features in scheme X unless specifically stated.

In any practical assessment at AS or at A2 level, you are assessed on your ability to:

- plan an investigation,
- carry out practical work,
- analyse data from practical experiments and investigations, and
- evaluate the results of practical experiments and investigations.

Planning

In assessment terms, this might be part of the practical task or activities that you have to carry out or it might be part of the written test in which you have to write about how you would improve an investigation or how you would carry out a different investigation in the same topic area. At A2, the topics are more complex than at AS level so you can expect assessment questions on planning to be more demanding than at AS level. For example,

- at AS level, after carrying out a practical task on how you would investigate the rebound height of a ball released from a certain height, you might be asked to say how you would investigate successive rebound heights to find out if there is a pattern.
- at A2, your practical task might involve timing the oscillations of a mass–spring system for different masses. You might then be asked in the written paper to describe how you would investigate the effect of damping on the oscillations of a mass–spring system. Thus the context of the A2 'planning' question is more complex than at AS as you have to describe how you would apply damping to a mass–spring system, how you would vary the degree of damping and how you measure the effect of the damping.

Carrying out practical work

At AS and at A2 you are required to set up apparatus and possibly rearrange it as part of the procedures you have to follow. You also have to make reliable and accurate measurements, selecting and using the appropriate measuring instruments in the process. The difference between what you have done at AS level and what you have to do at A2 lies once again in the more advanced topics in the A2 course and in the level of complexity of some of the instruments and procedures you have to use. For example,

▨ At AS level, you might be asked to investigate the electrical characteristics of a circuit in a sealed box by setting up a circuit, given the circuit diagram, and making a set of measurements of current and pd in the forward and reverse directions through the box. In addition, you would be asked to record your measurements in a table and, in this case, to plot a graph of your results.

▨ At A2, you might be asked to set up a circuit to charge a capacitor and discharge it through a resistor then make measurements of the capacitor pd at measured times as it charges or discharges. You would have to decide on the number of measurements to be made, the time interval between successive measurements and the exact procedure of how to make the measurements. The timing element in this investigation adds a further level of complexity beyond AS level.

▨ Analysing data

At AS level and at A2 you generally need to process the data (e.g. calculation of mean values) and plot a graph. In many investigations, the graph has to be related to an equation to check a theoretical relationship or to measure a physical property.

▨ At AS level, the theoretical equations you meet in the AS course are generally linear equations (e.g. $s = vt$ for a distance–time graph of an object falling in a viscous fluid at terminal speed) or sometimes simple non-linear equations (e.g. $s = \frac{1}{2}gt^2$ for a distance–time^2 graph of an object falling in air).

▨ At A2, there may be more variables than at AS level and the processing of the data might be more complicated, for example the calculation of log values. The graph plotting exercise requires the same skills as at AS level but the analysis might be more complicated. For example, you would probably be expected to plot a log graph in a capacitor discharge experiment and use it to determine the time constant RC of the discharge circuit or you might be expected to plot a log–log graph as explained in 15.3 (see Figure 2 in 15.3 and the related text) to establish if two variables x and y relate to each other according to an equation of the form $y = kx^n$.

▨ Evaluating your results

At AS and A2 this involves discussing the strength of your conclusions. From your work at AS level, you should now know how to:

▨ distinguish between systematic errors (including zero errors) and random errors,

▨ understand in respect of measurements what is meant by accuracy, uncertainty, sensitivity, linearity, reliability, precision and validity,

▨ estimate experimental uncertainties for each measured quantity and use them as outlined on the next page to estimate the overall percentage uncertainty of a result determined from the measured quantities.

If you are unsure about the meaning of any of the above terms, look them up in the glossary of practical terms at the end of this book.

How science works

Using experimental uncertainties

As explained in Topic 14.4 of the AS book,

- if two measurements are added or subtracted, the uncertainty of the result is the sum of the uncertainties of the two measurements,
- if a quantity in a calculation is raised to a power n, the percentage uncertainty is increased n times.
- In addition, if two or more quantities are multiplied or divided by each other in a calculation, the overall percentage uncertainty in the result is the sum of the uncertainties of each quantity. For example, if the % uncertainty in a resistance R is 5% and in a capacitance C is 4%, the % uncertainty in RC is 9%.

Clearly, the more demanding nature of the A2 topics compared with AS makes the evaluation of a practical investigation more demanding, but the same general features as outlined above still apply. For example,

- at AS level, you might be asked to investigate the motion of an object sliding down a slope by measuring the time taken by the object to slide different measured distances down the slope and plotting a distance–time^2 graph. In your evaluation, you might be asked to use a certain measurement (e.g. the smallest) to estimate the percentage uncertainty in the measurement of the dependent and independent variables so you could compare them and discuss how to improve the investigation.

- at A2, you might be asked to investigate the oscillations of a mass–spring system and to use the measurements to plot a graph of time period^2 against mass and show the uncertainty in each measurement on the graph, as outlined in *AS Physics* Topic 14.4. This would enable you to draw best-fit straight lines with a maximum and minimum gradient to enable you to determine the uncertainty in the gradient as well as its mean value. In this case, there is clearly more to discuss in terms of the closeness of the best-fit lines to the data than at AS level where only one best-fit line is drawn.

The above examples serve to illustrate the point that at A2, your practical skills build on your AS skills so you need to continue to practise all the practical skills you met at AS level. You need to be aware as you study each A2 topic that the topics are generally harder than at AS level and that consequently the practical work is more demanding, as outlined above.

13.2 More about measurements

At AS level, you should have learnt how to:

- measure lengths using a ruler, a vernier scale, a micrometer and callipers,
- weigh an object and determine its mass using a spring balance or a lever balance or a top pan balance,
- use a protractor to measure an angle and use a set square,
- measure time intervals using clocks, stopwatches and the time base of an oscilloscope,
- measure temperature using a thermometer,
- use ammeters and voltmeters with appropriate scales,
- read analogue and digital displays.

During your A2 course, as outlined in Topic 13.1, in addition to being able to use instruments and techniques that you used at AS level, you are also expected to be able to use instruments that are more complex. Such instruments might include the oscilloscope, the travelling microscope, the data logger, sensors and light gates, the Geiger–Müller tube with a scaler counter or ratemeter, and the spectrometer. In addition, you should know how to time multiple oscillations and how to avoid parallax errors when reading a scale.

Link

If you are unsure about how to use any of the above instruments, see Topic 14.3 in the AS book and consult your teacher.

An oscilloscope

This is used to display waveforms and to measure pds and time intervals. You will have probably used an oscilloscope in Unit 2 of your AS course when you studied alternating current. However, AS practical assessments in Unit 3 do not involve the use of an oscilloscope but your A2 assessment activities may do. In A2 topics such as capacitor discharge, you will use an oscilloscope to measure the pd across a discharging capacitor. When you use an oscilloscope, you should assume that the control dials for its time base and voltage gain are calibrated accurately. However,

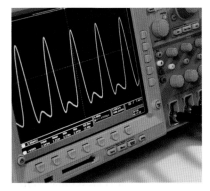

Figure 1 *The oscilloscope*

- always check if the oscilloscope has a variable control for either the time base or the voltage gain in addition to the fixed settings of each control dial. If so, you need to ensure that the variable control is at the correct setting (e.g. fully clockwise) for the calibration figure for each of the fixed settings to apply. See Topic 6.2 in the AS book if you need to revise the use of an oscilloscope.
- make sure if you are measuring direct pds that the oscilloscope input is set for direct pd measurements rather than for ac measurements. Likewise, if you are measuring an ac waveform, you should check the input is set for ac measurements rather than dc measurements.

In addition, when measuring

- an ac waveform, ensure the *y*-gain is adjusted so the vertical height of the waveform is as large as possible with the full waveform from top to bottom on the screen. When measuring a time period, ensure several cycles are displayed across the screen and that you measure across as many cycles as possible to reduce experimental uncertainty.
- dc potentials, for example in a capacitor discharge experiment, ensure the zero reading is correct for zero input pd and check it has not drifted during the investigation.

■ A travelling microscope

This is a microscope on an adjustable platform that can be moved vertically or horizontally by turning an adjustment screw. The microscope itself can usually be aligned vertically or horizontally, according to whether it is to be used to measure a vertical or a horizontal distance. The platform is fitted with a horizontal and a vertical vernier scale so its horizontal or vertical position can be measured to within ±0.1 mm. A travelling microscope would be used for example to measure the internal diameter of a glass tube (e.g. 1 mm bore) as a micrometer or a conventional vernier could not access the internal surface of the tube. Before use, a travelling microscope should be levelled using a spirit level in two perpendicular directions so its platform is horizontal. Otherwise, there could be a systematic error in the measurements.

■ A data logger

A data logger enables routine or remote measurements to be made as well as measurements over very long or short time scales. Electronic sensors connected to a data logger are necessary to record the variation of a physical property such as temperature. Ammeter and voltage sensors are necessary to measure currents and potential differences.

Data loggers vary considerably in complexity and ease of use. Assuming the data logger and sensors are set up, before using a data logger, you may need to choose:

■ the most appropriate time scale for the recording,

■ the time interval between successive recordings (or the number of recordings per second/minute/hour),

■ the most appropriate range of each sensor.

If a recording is too fast or too long or the sensors are out of range, the recording should be repeated if possible.

Most data loggers will be linked to computers which are loaded with appropriate software for recording, processing and/or plotting graphs of the results. You may need to print a graph out if you intend to use it to measure, for example, the gradient if it is a straight-line graph. However, the computer software may do such measurements for you.

Figure 2 *Using a data logger*

■ Light gates

These are used with a computer or a data logger or timer to remove some of the random errors associated with personal judgements when a moving object passes a certain position, for example, if you have to time an object to move from rest through a certain distance.

The effect of using light gates should be to reduce the range of the readings for a given measurement. However, light gates may not be suitable for every experiment in which a moving object has to be timed. For example, the time period of an oscillating object that repeatedly moves backwards and forwards through a light gate could only be timed for one half cycle of the object's motion, corresponding to the object moving through the light gate in one direction to start the timing and then in the opposite direction to stop the light gate. The light gate would need to be exactly at the centre of the oscillations otherwise the timing would not be exactly one half cycle. Repeated measurements of one half cycle could be made to give a more reliable mean value and this might give better results than using a stopwatch if the oscillations are too fast to time manually.

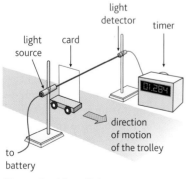

Figure 3 *Using a light gate*

The Geiger–Müller tube

This may be used with a **scaler counter** which counts the number of ionising particles that enter the tube or it may be used with a **ratemeter** which gives a read-out of the count rate (i.e. number of counts per unit time) of the particles entering the tube. The tube pd must be set at its operating pd which is normally in excess of 300 V. The number of counts in a certain time interval is measured by setting the counter to zero, then starting the counter and stopping it after a certain time.

Figure 4b shows how the count rate varies with the tube pd. The operating pd corresponds to the plateau of the graph sufficiently far from the minimum pd necessary for the tube to operate (i.e. the threshold pd) as to be unaffected by random fluctuations in the tube pd.

- When using the tube with a scaler counter, the number of counts in a given time (e.g. 100 s) should be measured several times to give a mean value of the count rate (i.e. counts per second). The bigger the total number of counts, the smaller the uncertainty in the measurement. If the time interval is too short, random errors that may occur in starting and stopping the counter could be more significant than if a longer time interval were used. If the time interval is too long, it would be difficult to tell if the activity of the source is decreasing or if an error in starting or stopping the timer has occurred.

- When using the tube with a ratemeter, ensure the ratemeter is set on the range which gives the largest reading. For example, if the range dial has three positions, 1, 10 and 100 counts per second, the range may need to be set at 1 count per second if the reading is very small on the '10' and '100' positions.

When using either a scaler counter or a ratemeter, remember to measure the background count rate and subtract it from the measurements made when the source is present.

a *a Geiger–Müller tube connected to a scaler counter*

Figure 4 *Using a Geiger–Müller tube*

b *a graph of count rate against tube pd*

A spectrometer

This is used to measure the wavelengths of a line emission spectrum or a line absorption spectrum. A spectrometer is fitted with a circular scale to measure the angle of diffraction of the lines of a spectrum. A spectrum analyser is used to obtain an intensity–wavelength (or frequency) display of the light detected by the spectrum analyser detector. Although neither instrument is specified in the AS or A2 unit specifications, you may be asked to use either instrument (given all the necessary instructions) to assess your ability to follow complex instructions.

14.1 The ISA/PSA scheme at A2 (scheme T)

The structure and format of the ISA/PSA scheme of internal assessment for Unit 6 summarised below is the same as for Unit 3. However, the assessment activities at A2 are based on A2 topics which are in general more demanding than at AS. Consequently, assessment at A2 is more demanding and so the assessment criteria are more demanding at A2 than at AS. The same is true in scheme X, the 'board marked scheme' of internal assessment.

Investigative skills assignments

Two A2 physics ISAs are set by AQA each year. You will be assessed using one of these ISAs if you are being assessed through the ISA/PSA scheme. As at AS level, an ISA counts for 41 marks out of the 50 mark total for Unit 3.

The ISA is carried out under supervision and is in two stages.

Stage 1 The practical task

The practical task requires you to carry out practical work using an AQA task sheet which outlines the investigation. The task sheet may be prescriptive, giving precise instructions or it may be more open-ended. Your teacher will tell you in advance when you will carry out the ISA. Also, your teacher will tell you a few weeks before the ISA test the general topic area which the ISA is in.

As at AS level, the task is carried out in the laboratory in a timetabled lesson (or lessons) under supervision and should take no more than about an hour. The task will require you to work on your own and to make measurements and present them in a table of your own design. You will be asked to process the measurement data and to use the data to draw a graph. Remember the demands at A2 are greater than at AS because the topics in the A2 course are more demanding than at AS.

You are not allowed to take work away from the ISA session and all completed work must be handed to your teacher who will assess the work using AQA marking guidelines. Your teacher is not allowed to write any marks or comments on your work as it will be returned to you for use in the written test. The practical task counts for 10 of the 41 marks on the ISA. Candidates are not allowed to redraft or repeat an ISA.

You will be provided with a complete set of practical equipment necessary for the practical task. This equipment should include familiar items that you have used at AS level (e.g. clamps, stands, ammeter, voltmeter, metre ruler, stopwatch, etc.) but it might include an item or materials specific to the task (e.g. conducting paper to investigate a specific electric field configuration). The task sheet will tell you what to do and what measurements to make. Read it carefully to make sure you set up and use the equipment correctly. If you think an item of equipment is not working, ask your teacher to check it.

Stage 2 The written test

You will take the written test in a timetabled lesson under supervision as soon as possible after completion of the practical task. The test is a 1 hour written paper set by AQA and counts for 31 of the 41 ISA marks. Lines to write your answer are provided after each part-question. Your teacher will mark your written test using AQA marking guidelines. In the 'exam room' just before the test begins, you will be provided with the test paper and your completed material from the practical task. The test is in two parts.

a **Section A** will consist of a number of general questions about the practical task. For example, you might be asked about the control variables in the task or about the precision of your measurements. You will not be required to plot a graph here as you will have already done this in the practical task. This section will not have as many marks allocated to it as at AS level although the total for the written paper will still be 31 marks.

b **Section B** will provide a further set of data on the practical task or a closely related task. The questions in this part will ask about methodology, analysis and evaluation of the data. You may be asked in your evaluation to suggest improvements or to discuss further work that could be done, for example to test a prediction. There will be more marks allocated for evaluation and analysis in this section compared with AS as A2 evaluation and analysis questions are more demanding than at AS level because the A2 topics are more demanding.

▨ The practical skills assessment

The skills in the PSA are assessed in practical activities that you will do throughout your course. The practical activities will give you opportunities to demonstrate your practical skills. You will be given some instructions when you carry out these activities and you will need to make decisions for yourself about how you organise yourself and how you use the equipment. You will be assessed on your ability to:

▨ **demonstrate safe and skilful practical techniques and processes,**

▨ **select appropriate methods and equipment,**

▨ **make measurements precisely and accurately,**

▨ **make and record reliable and valid observations and measurements,**

▨ **work with others in experimental activities.**

The paragraphs below shows how your PSA mark at A2 is determined. Note the criteria are more demanding than at AS level and so are worded differently. The three strands are each worth up to 3 marks, giving a total of 9 marks. Your teacher will assess the level you reach by the end of the course in each strand.

Following instructions and group work

▨ 3 marks are awarded if you are able to plan and work without guidance, select appropriate techniques, follow complex instructions and participate in group work. **If not, see below.**

▨ 2 marks are awarded if you are able plan and work without guidance, select appropriate techniques, follow instructions and participate in group work. **If not, see below.**

▨ 1 mark is awarded if you are able to plan and work with some guidance, select appropriate techniques and follow instruction. **If not, no marks are awarded.**

The standard laboratory apparatus you will use to make measurements might include:

▨ basic apparatus (metre rule, set square, protractors, stopclock or stopwatch),

▨ AS equipment such as electrical meters (analogue or digital), the micrometer, vernier callipers, a top pan electronic balance, measuring cylinders, thermometers and newtonmeters, and

▨ more complex instruments as listed in the notes overleaf.

Selection and use of equipment

- 3 marks are awarded if you can select and use suitable equipment with due regard for precision, including a wide range of at least 6 complex instruments **and** techniques appropriate to the A2 course. **If not, see below.**
- 2 marks are awarded if you can select and use suitable equipment, including more than 2 complex instruments **and** techniques appropriate to the A2 course. **If not, see below.**
- 1 mark is awarded if you can select and use suitable equipment, including at least 2 complex instruments **or** techniques appropriate to the A2 course. **If not**, no marks are awarded

Safety and organisation

- 3 marks are awarded if you consistently demonstrate safe working practices in the more complex procedures encountered on the A2 course. **If not, see below.**
- 2 marks are awarded if you demonstrate safe working practices in some of the more complex procedures encountered on the A2 course. **If not, see below.**
- 1 mark is awarded if you demonstrate safe working practices in using a range of equipment appropriate to the A2 course. **If not**, no marks are awarded.

Notes

1 **Complex instructions** or procedures or techniques refers to instructions or procedures or techniques which are not straightforward and which may involve

- following a set of instructions on the use of a complex instrument where different controls need to be adjusted or used (e.g. a Geiger–Müller tube connected to a scaler counter), or
- changing and measuring physical variables in a sequence while keeping other variables constant (e.g. altering a variable resistor in a capacitor discharge circuit to keep the discharge current constant to see the effect on the capacitor pd), or
- using a technique which involves several stages (e.g. measuring the count rate due to a radioactive source taking account of background radiation).

2 **Complex instruments** include an oscilloscope, a travelling microscope, a Geiger–Müller tube connected to a scaler counter or ratemeter, a data logger, electronic sensors (e.g. temperature, magnetic field, light intensity), light gates, a spectrometer or spectrum analyser.

3 **Safe working practices**: before you carry out a practical task, you should carry out a risk assessment to eliminate (if possible) or minimise any health and safety hazards. A risk assessment requires you to think about the possible hazards in an activity and plan to eliminate or minimise them. Your teacher ought to have made a risk assessment of every practical activity in advance to ensure the practical activities you undertake are safe.

Ionising radiation

if you are about to use a Geiger-Müller tube and a radioactive source, you must comply with the safety instructions your teacher will give you, including wearing disposable gloves and using long-handled tongs when you have to transfer the source from its container to a holder. Schools and colleges can only use sealed sources to prevent contamination of the laboratory or people inside the laboratory and you must keep as far from it as reasonably possible. Never look directly into a radioactive source as the eye is not protected by dead skin. You should be provided with eye protection which you should wear. However, you should also carry out your own risk assessment to ensure you use the apparatus you are given safely.

14.2 The AQA-marked scheme at A2 (scheme X)

The AQA-marked scheme is the same in structure and format as at AS. However, as with scheme T, the demands at A2 are higher because the A2 topics themselves are more demanding and experiments associated with A2 topics are more demanding than at AS level.

Part 1 (Practical skills verification)

This part is carried out under supervision in the laboratory during normal class time. You will be required to work individually and carry out 5 short practical exercises. The exercises for each year are set by AQA at the start of the year and each one may be carried out at any stage during the year during or after coverage of the relevant topic. Your teacher will tell you in advance when you are to do them. You will not be expected to spend more than 3 hours of laboratory time in total completing these exercises. The exercises will be typical of the normal practical work that would be expected to be covered as part of any A2 course.

In carrying out these exercises, you will be asked to use more complex instruments than at AS level, in addition to standard equipment you used at AS level. Such complex equipment could include an oscilloscope, a travelling microscope, a Geiger–Müller tube connected to a scalar counter or ratemeter, a data logger, electronic sensors (e.g. temperature, magnetic field, light intensity), light gates, a spectrometer or spectrum analyser.

Also, you might be asked to work together at times and you will be expected to follow complex instructions and procedures and to work safely. In addition, you are likely to be asked to make and record accurate measurements and assess the reliability and accuracy of your results.

At the end of each exercise, your results and observations are to be given to the teacher for verification purposes and may be returned to you for use during the remainder of the course. A sample set of part 1 exercises are listed below.

Sample set of part 1 exercises for A2 level		
	Exercise	Measuring equipment used
1	Measurement of g using a simple pendulum	stopwatch or stopclock, metre ruler
2	Capacitor discharge through a fixed resistor	oscilloscope or digital voltmeter, potential divider, stopwatch or stopclock
3	Measurement of magnetic flux density	top pan balance, U-shaped magnet, thick copper wire, ammeter, variable low voltage power supply
4	Absorption of β radiation by different thicknesses of aluminium foil	Geiger-Müller tube, scaler counter, micrometer, aluminium foil, stopclock or stopwatch
5	Measurement of specific heat capacity or specific latent heat	variable low voltage power supply, low voltage heater, metal block, thermometer, top pan balance, voltmeter, ammeter, stopclock or stopwatch

In Part 2 you will be required to use some of the practical skills from part 1 to undertake assessed practical activities. The measurements and results from these part 2 practical activities will be analysed and evaluated in Part 3, an AQA-set and marked written paper.

▨ Parts 2 and 3 Externally marked practical assessment

Part 2

In this part, you carry out a short practical activity and a longer practical activity, both based on physics from Unit 4 and/or from Unit 5A of the specification. The practical activities will be AQA set and marked. Once completed, you will not be able to attempt part 2 again. You can not carry forward written work from part 1 to these part 2 activities. The two activities will take around $1\frac{1}{2}$ hours.

Examples of some A2 longer practical activities for part 2 are listed below.

1   Investigation of the oscillations of a metre ruler as a loaded cantilever (use of stopwatch, metre rule, fiducial mark)

2   Investigation of the effect of varying the resistance in a capacitor charge and discharge circuit (digital voltmeter, capacitor, potential divider, low voltage supply, stopwatch or stopclock)

3   Measurement of the specific latent heat of ice by using ice to cool warm water.

Your teacher will tell you in advance when you are to carry out the part 2 experiment. This will be near the end of the course between March and the end of May. Because the experiment is a skills test like the 'on the road' part of the driving test, the experiment may be used to test other students at other times.

You have to work individually and be supervised throughout. You will be provided with a task sheet with sufficient information and instructions to enable you to obtain reliable measurements which you have to record, process and discuss. In carrying out the activities, you will be expected to:

▨ manipulate apparatus skilfully and safely,

▨ make reliable and accurate measurements,

▨ estimate experimental uncertainties,

▨ identify anomalous measurements,

▨ minimise or take account of the effects of random and any systematic error,

▨ tabulate the results in a well organised and systematic way, taking account of the expected conventions,

▨ process data,

▨ graph, or chart, these data as appropriate.

In addition, you will need to show your competence in following more complex procedures than at AS level and in recording and processing more complex data than at AS level.

At the end of the experiment, you have to hand in all your written work (i.e. table of results, calculations, graph, and discussion of errors). This will be returned to you for use in Part 3.

Part 3

This is an AQA-set and marked written paper of duration of 1 hour 15 minutes. Your teacher will arrange when you are to take this test, preferably as soon as possible after part 2. Before you commence the test, your written work from part 2 will be returned to you. At the end of the test, all your written work from parts 2 and 3 will be collected by your teacher who will send it to AQA for marking together with verification forms for part 1.

Some of the questions in the paper will require you to:

▦ use your part 2 results and graph to carry out further analysis in order to arrive at a conclusion,

▦ assess the overall accuracy of the outcome of the experiment.

In addition, you may be asked to:

▦ carry out error calculations on the data from part 2,

▦ describe procedures used to overcome errors in part 2,

▦ estimate the percentage uncertainty of a result,

▦ comment on the reliability of the evidence or procedures used during part 2,

▦ discuss all/some of the measurement techniques developed in part 1,

▦ make predictions about alternative outcomes,

▦ discuss ways of extending the range or reliability of the evidence produced during part 2 of the practical experiment,

▦ discuss how you would improve the experiment or how you would carry out a related investigation.

The work you produced in parts 2 and 3 will sent by your teacher to AQA for marking together with your part 1 verification forms.

15.1 Trigonometry

In this chapter, we consider only the A2 mathematical requirements of the specification that are beyond the requirements for AS level. If you need to check any of the mathematical skills specified for the AS course, you can use Chapter 16 'More on mathematical skills' in the AS book and/or use the on-line exercises that support the AS and A2 books.

Angles and arcs

The radian

The **radian** (rad) is a unit used to express or measure angles. It is defined such that 2π radians $= 360°$

When using a calculator to work out sines, cosines, tangents or the corresponding inverse functions, always check that the calculator is in the correct 'angle' mode. This is usually indicated on the display by 'deg' for degrees or 'rad' for radians. Your calculations will be incorrect if you work in one mode when you should be working in the other mode. For example, check for yourself that $\sin 30° = 0.5$ whereas $\sin(30\,\text{rad}) = -0.988$. You also need to know how to change from one mode to the other; read your calculator manual or ask you teacher if you can't do this.

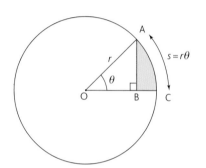

Figure 1 *Arcs and segments*

Note

Note that for $s = r$, $\theta = 1\,\text{rad}$

$$\left(= \frac{360}{2\pi} = 57.3°\right)$$

Arcs and segments

Consider an arc of length s on the circumference of a circle of radius r, as shown in Figure 1. The angle θ, in degrees, subtended by the arc to the centre of the circle is given by the equation

$$\theta/\text{degrees} = \frac{s}{2\pi r} \times 360$$

Because 2π radians $= 360°$, applying this conversion factor to the above equation for θ gives

$$\theta/\text{radians} = \frac{s}{r}$$

Rearranging this equation gives

$$\text{arc length } s = r\theta,$$

where θ is the angle subtended in radians.

The small angle approximation

For angle θ less than about 10°,

$$\sin\theta \approx \tan\theta \approx \theta \text{ in radians, and}$$

$$\cos\theta \approx 1$$

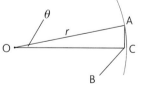

Figure 2 *The small angle approximation*

To explain these approximations, consider Figure 1 again. If angle θ is sufficiently small, then the segment OAC will be almost the same as triangle OAB, as shown in Figure 2.

- AB ≈ arc length s so $\sin\theta = \dfrac{AB}{OA} \approx \dfrac{s}{r} = \theta$ in radians, ∴ $\sin\theta \approx \theta$ in radians.

- OB ≈ radius r, so $\tan\theta = \dfrac{AB}{OB} \approx \dfrac{s}{r} = \theta$ in radians, ∴ $\tan\theta \approx \theta$ in radians.

- Also, $\cos\theta = \dfrac{OB}{OA} \approx \dfrac{r}{r} = 1$, ∴ $\cos\theta \approx 1$

Use a calculator to prove for yourself that for sin 10° = 0.1736, tan 10° = 0.1763 and 10° = 0.1745 rad. Also, cos 10° = 0.9848. So the small angle approximation is almost 99% accurate up to 10°.

The small angle approximation is used to show that the time period of a simple pendulum of length L is given by the formula $T = 2\pi\sqrt{\dfrac{L}{g}}$, provided the maximum angular displacement of the pendulum from equilibrium is less than about 10°. See Topic 3.4 for more about this equation.

Sine and cosine curves

Figure 3 shows how $\sin\theta$ and $\cos\theta$ change as θ increases. Notice that $\sin\theta \approx \theta$ and $\cos\theta \approx 1$ up to about 10°. The general shape of a cosine wave is the same as of a sine wave so we refer to them both as 'sinusoidal' waveforms. In addition, notice that:

- the sine wave starts at zero and rises to a maximum from $\theta = 0$ to $\theta = \frac{1}{2}\pi\,$rad $(= 90°)$ whereas the cosine wave starts at +1 and falls to zero from $\theta = 0$ to $\theta = \frac{1}{2}\pi\,$rad $(= 90°)$.

- the gradient of the sine wave is zero where the cosine wave is zero (i.e. where it crosses the horizontal axis) and the gradient of the cosine wave is zero where the sine wave is zero.

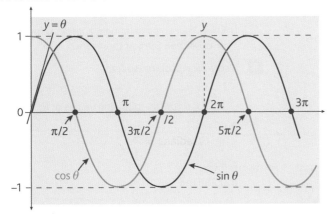

Figure 3 *Sine and cosine curves*

Equations that describe sine waves and cosine waves are often used to calculate, for example, the displacement of an oscillating particle at a certain time or of a wave at a particular position along the wave.

For example, consider the displacement x of a particle on a spring oscillating vertically in simple harmonic motion, as shown in Figure 4a. Let f represent its frequency and A its amplitude. Its displacement varies sinusoidally between a maximum value $+A$ and a minimum value $-A$. Also, suppose $x = +A$ at time $t = 0$. In other words, the object is held above the equilibrium position at displacement $x = +A$ and released at time $t = 0$.

■ Its displacement–time curve will therefore be a cosine wave, as shown in Figure 4b where its time period $T = 1/f$

■ At time t later, the particle will have gone through ft cycles of oscillation, corresponding to $\theta = 2\pi ft$ radians. Hence its displacement at time t is given by $x = A \cos 2\pi ft$

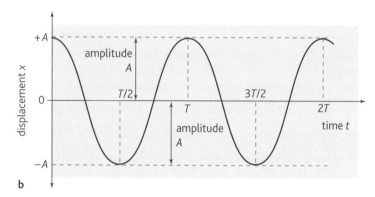

a

b

Figure 4 **a** *An object oscillating on a spring* **b** *Displacement–time curve for x = A cos 2πft*

Summary questions

1 **a** Convert the following angles from degrees into radians and express your answer to one further significant figure than in each question:

i 30°,

ii 50°,

iii 120°,

iv 230°,

v 300°.

b Convert the following angles from radians into degrees and express your answer to one further significant figure than in each question:

i 0.10 rad,

ii 0.50 rad,

iii 1.20 rad,

iv 2.50 rad,

v 6.00 rad.

2 **a** Measure the diameter of a 1p coin to the nearest millimetre. Calculate the angle subtended at your eye, in degrees, by a 1p coin held at a distance of 50 cm from your eye.

b i Estimate the angular width of the Moon, in degrees, at your eye by holding a millimetre scale at 50 cm from your eye and measuring the distance on the scale covered by the lunar disc.

ii The diameter of the Moon is 3500 km. The average distance to the Moon from the Earth is 380 000 km. Calculate the angular width of the Moon as seen from the Earth and compare the calculated value with your estimate in **b i**.

3 **a** Use the small angle approximation to calculate $\sin \theta$ for $\theta =$

i 2.0°,

ii 8.0°.

b Show that the small angle approximation for $\sin \theta$ is more than 99% accurate for $\theta = 10°$.

4 Use your calculator to find

i $\sin \theta$,

ii $\cos \theta$ for the following values of θ:

a 0.1 rad,

b 10°,

c 45°,

d 0.25π rad.

15.2 Algebra

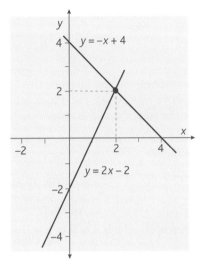

Figure 1 *A graphical solution*

Linear simultaneous equations

Two linear equations with two variable quantities, x and y, in each can be solved to find the values of x and y. Such a pair of equations are referred to as **simultaneous equations** because they have the same solution. They are described as **linear** because they contain terms in x and y and do not contain any higher order terms such as x^2 or y^2.

The general equation for a straight-line graph is $y = mx + c$, as explained in Topic 14.4 of the AS book. Two straight lines on a graph can be represented by two such equations. Provided the two lines are not parallel to one another, they cross each other at a single point. The coordinates of this point are the values of x and y that fit both equations. In other words, these coordinates are the solution of a pair of simultaneous equations representing the two straight lines. See Topic 14.4 in the AS book.

The graph approach to finding the solution of a pair of simultaneous equations is shown in Figure 1 and is described in Topic 12.4 in the AS book. However, plotting graphs takes time and is not as accurate as a systematic algebraic method. This method can best be explained by considering an example, as follows

$$2x - y = 2 \qquad \text{(equation 1)}$$

$$x + y = 4 \qquad \text{(equation 2)}$$

Make the coefficient of x the same in both equations by multiplying one or both equations by a suitable number. In the above equation, this is most easily achieved by multiplying equation 2 throughout by 2 to give $2x + 2y = 8$.

The two equations to be solved are now

$$2x - y = 2 \qquad \text{(equation 1)}$$

$$2x + 2y = 8 \qquad \text{(modified equation 2)}$$

Subtracting modified equation 2 from equation 1 gives

$$(2x - y) - (2x + 2y) = 2 - 8$$
$$\therefore -y - 2y = -6$$
$$-3y = -6$$
$$y = \frac{-6}{-3} = 2$$

Substituting this value into equation 1 or equation 2 enables the value of x to be determined. Using equation 2 for this purpose gives $x + 2 = 4$, hence $x = 4 - 2 = 2$.

The solution of the two equations is therefore $x = 2, y = 2$.

Linear simultaneous equations with two unknown quantities can arise in several parts of the A level physics course, for example

Hint

You can check this using the equations (e.g. $x = 2, y = 2$ is also a solution for $x + y = 4$).

■ $v = u + at$ in kinematics (see AS Topic 8.3),

■ $V = \varepsilon - Ir$ in electricity (see AS Topic 5.3),

■ $E_{Kmax} = hf - \phi$ (see AS Topic 3.2).

■ The quadratic equation

Any quadratic equation can be written in the form $ax^2 + bx + c = 0$, where a, b and c are constants. The general solution of the quadratic equation $ax^2 + bx + c = 0$ is

$$x = \frac{-b \pm \sqrt{(b^2 - 4ac)}}{2a}$$

Note that every quadratic equation has two solutions, one given by the + sign before the square root sign in the above expression, and the other given by the – sign. For example, consider the solution of the equation $2x^2 + 5x - 3 = 0$.

As $a = 2$, $b = 5$ and $c = -3$, then the solution is

$$x = \frac{-5 \pm \sqrt{(5^2 - (4 \times 2 \times -3))}}{2 \times 2} = \frac{-5 \pm \sqrt{49}}{4} = -5 \pm \frac{7}{4} = +0.5 \text{ or } -3$$

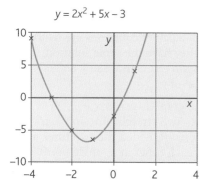

$y = 2x^2 + 5x - 3$

Figure 2 $y = 2x^2 + 5x - 3$

A graph of $y = 2x^2 + 5x - 3$ is shown in Figure 2. Note that the two solutions above are the values of the x-intercepts, which is where $y = 0$.

Quadratic equations occur in A level physics where a formula contains the square of a variable. The equation $s = ut + \frac{1}{2}at^2$ for displacement at constant acceleration is a direct example. Other examples can arise indirectly. For example, suppose the pd across a certain type of component varies with current I according to the equation $V = kI^2$. In a circuit with a battery of negligible internal resistance and a resistor of resistance R, the battery pd, $V_0 = IR + kI^2$. Given values of R, k and V_0, the current could be calculated using the solution for the quadratic equation with $a = k$, $b = R$ and $c = -V_0$.

Summary questions

1 Solve each of the following pairs of simultaneous equations.

a $3x + y = 6$; $2y = 5x + 1$

b $3a - 2b = 8$; $a + b = 2$

c $5p + 2q = 18$; $q = 2p$

2 Use the data and the given equation to write down a pair of simultaneous equations and so determine the unknown quantities in each case:

a For $v = u + at$, when $t = 3.0\,\text{s}$, $v = 8.0\,\text{m s}^{-1}$ and when $t = 6.0\,\text{s}$, $v = 2.0\,\text{m s}^{-1}$. Determine the values of u and a.

b For $\varepsilon = IR + Ir$, when $R = 5.0\,\Omega$, $I = 1.5\,\text{A}$ and when $R = 9.0\,\Omega$, $I = 0.9\,\text{A}$. Determine the values of ε and r.

3 Solve each of the following quadratic equations.

a $2x^2 + 5x - 3 = 0$

b $x^2 - 7x + 8 = 0$

c $3x^2 + 2x - 5 = 0$

4 Use the data and the given equation to write down a quadratic equation and so determine the unknown quantity in each case:

a $s = ut + \frac{1}{2}at^2$, where $s = 20\,\text{m}$, $u = 4\,\text{m s}^{-1}$ and $a = 6\,\text{m s}^{-2}$; find t.

b $P = V^2 \dfrac{R}{(R + r)^2}$, where $P = 16\,\text{W}$, $V = 12\,\text{V}$, $r = 2.0\,\Omega$; find R.

15.3 Logarithms

Logarithms and powers

Any number can be expressed as any other number raised to a particular power. You can use the y^x key on a calculator to show, for example that $8 = 2^3$ and $9 = 2^{3.17}$. In these examples, 2 is referred to as the base number and is raised to a different power in each case to generate 8 or 9. The power is defined as the **logarithm** of the number generated.

In general, for a number $\mathbf{n} = \mathbf{b}^p$ where b is the base number, then $\mathbf{p} = \log_b \mathbf{n}$ where $\log_b$ means a logarithm using b as the base number.

Note: $\log_b(b^p) = p$ as $b^p = n$ and $\log_b n = p$.

Applying the general definition above gives the following rules to remember when working with logs:

1 **For any two numbers m and n,**

$\log_b(nm) = \log_b n + \log_b m$

Let $p = \log_b n$ and let $q = \log_b m$ so $n = b^p$ and $m = b^q$

$\therefore nm = b^p b^q = b^{p+q}$ so $\log_b(nm) = p + q = \log_b m + \log_b n$

2 **For any two numbers m and n,**

$\log_b \dfrac{n}{m} = \log_b n - \log_b m$

Let $p = \log_b n$ and let $q = \log_b m$ so $n = b^p$ and $m = b^q$.

Therefore $\dfrac{1}{m} = \dfrac{1}{b^q} = b^{-q}$

$\therefore \dfrac{n}{m} = b^p b^{-q} = b^{p-q}$ so $\log_b\left(\dfrac{n}{m}\right) = p - q = \log_b n - \log_b m$

3 **For any number m raised to a power p,**

$\log_b(m^p) = p \log_b m$

This is because $m^p = m$ multiplied by itself p times.

$$\xleftarrow{\hspace{2cm}} p \text{ terms} \xrightarrow{\hspace{2cm}}$$

Therefore $\log_b m^p = \{\log_b m + \log_b m + \dots + \log_b m\} = p \log_b m$

Base 10 logarithms and natural logarithms are used extensively in physics and are explained below.

Base 10 logarithms

Base 10 logs are written as $\log_{10}$ or lg (or sometimes incorrectly as log).

For example,

- $100 = 10^2$ so $\log_{10} 100 = 2$
- $50 = 10^{1.699}$ so $\log_{10} 50 = 1.699$
- $10 = 10^1$ so $\log_{10} 10 = 1$
- $5 = 10^{0.699}$ so $\log_{10} 5 = 0.699$

The above examples illustrate the product rule for logs

(i.e. $\log_b nm = \log_b n + \log_b m$)

since $\log_{10} 50 = \log_{10} 5 + \log_{10} 10 = 0.699 + 1 = 1.699$.

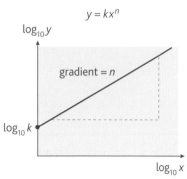

$y = kx^n$

$\log_{10} y$

gradient = n

$\log_{10} k$

$\log_{10} x$

Figure 1 *Using logs to test $y = kx^n$*

> ▰ **Hint**
>
> Note that natural logs could be used in Figure 1 instead of base 10 logs; the gradient would still be n but the y-intercept would be $\ln k$.

Uses of base 10 logs

In graphs where a **logarithmic scale** is necessary to show the full range of a variable that covers a very wide range, as shown in Figure 2. Notice in Figure 2 that the frequency increases by ×10 in equal intervals along the horizontal axis.

In data analysis where a relationship between two variables is of the form $y = kx^n$ and k and n are unknown constants. As explained on the previous page, for an equation of the form $y = kx^n$, then

$$\log_{10} y = \log_{10} k + \log_{10} x^n = \log_{10} k + n \log_{10} x$$

The graph of $\log_{10} y$ (on the vertical axis) against $\log_{10} x$ is therefore a straight line of gradient n with an intercept equal to $\log k$. Hence n and k can be determined.

In certain formulae where a ×10 scale is used. For example, the gain of an amplifier in decibels (dB) is a ×10 scale defined by the formula

$$\text{voltage gain/dB} = 10 \log_{10}\left|\frac{V_{out}}{V_{in}}\right|$$

where V_{out} and V_{in} are the output and input voltages, respectively. If $V_{out} = 50 V_{in}$, the gain of the amplifier is $17\,\text{dB}$ ($= 10 \log_{10} 50$).

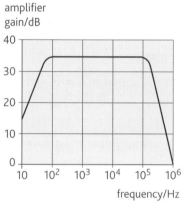

amplifier gain/dB

Figure 2 *Logarithmic scales*

▥ Natural logarithms

Natural logs are written as $\log_e$ or $\ln$, where e is the exponential number used as the base of natural logarithms and is equal to 2.718. For example,

- ▥ $2.718 = e^1$ so $\ln 2.718 = 1$
- ▥ $7.389 = e^2$ so $\ln 7.389 = 2$
- ▥ $20.009 = e^3$ so $\ln 20.009 = 3$
- ▥ In general, for any number n, if p is such that $n = e^p$, then $\ln n = p$

Uses of natural logarithms

Natural logs are used in the equations for radioactive decay (Topic 9.5) and capacitor discharge (Topic 6.3) or any other process where the rate of change of a quantity is proportional to the quantity itself. For example, the rate of decrease of pd across a capacitor discharging through a resistor is proportional to the pd across the capacitor. This type of change is described as an exponential decrease because the quantity decreases by the same factor in equal intervals of time.

> ▰ **Hint**
>
> The Richter scale for earthquakes is another example. A 'Richter scale 8' earthquake is ten times as powerful as a 'Richter scale 7' earthquake.

Applying the general rule (that if p is such that $n = e^p$, then $p = \ln n$) to the equation $x = x_0 e^{-\lambda t}$ gives $\ln x = \ln x_0 - \lambda t$.

Therefore, a graph of $\ln x$ (on the vertical axis) against t (on the horizontal axis) is a straight line with a gradient equal to $-\lambda$ and a y-intercept equal to $\ln x_0$.

Comparing the equation for capacitor discharge $Q = Q_0 e^{-t/RC}$ with the radioactive decay equation $N = N_0 e^{-\lambda t}$,

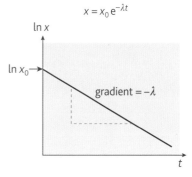

- for capacitor discharge, $\ln Q = \ln Q_0 - t/RC$ so a graph of $\ln Q$ (on the vertical axis) against t is a straight line which has a gradient $-1/RC$ and $\ln Q_0$ as its y-intercept,

- for radioactive decay, $\ln N = \ln N_0 - \lambda t$ so a graph of $\ln N$ (on the vertical axis) against t is a straight line which has a gradient $-\lambda$ and $\ln N_0$ as its y-intercept.

Figure 3 *Using logs to test $x = x_0 e^{-\lambda t}$*

Summary questions

1 **a** Use your calculator to work out

    i $\log_{10} 3$

    ii $\log_{10} 15$

  b Use your answers in **a** to work out

    i $\log_{10} 45$

    ii $\log_{10} 5$

2 The gain of an amplifier, in decibels, is given by the formula $10 \log_{10} \left(\dfrac{V_{out}}{V_{in}} \right)$.

  a Calculate the gain, in decibels (dB), for

    i $V_{out} = 12 V_{in}$

    ii $V_{out} = 5 V_{in}$

  b Show that the gain, in decibels, of an amplifier for which $V_{out} = 60 V_{in}$ is equal to the sum of the gain in **a i** and the gain in **a ii** above.

3 Write down the gradient and the y-intercept of a line on a graph representing the equation $\log_{10} y = n \log_{10} x + \log_{10} k$ for

  a $y = 3x^5$

  b $y = \frac{1}{2}x^3$

  c $y = x^2$

4 **a** Use your calculator to work out

    i $\ln 3$

    ii $\ln 15$

  b Use your answers in **a** to work out

    i $\ln 45$

    ii $\ln 5$

Rates of change

Consider a variable quantity y that changes with respect to a second quantity x as shown in Figure 1. The gradient of the curve at any point is the rate of change of y with respect to x at that point. This can be worked out from the graph by drawing a tangent to the curve at that point and measuring the gradient of the tangent. The rate of change of y with respect to x at point P is equal to the gradient of the tangent to the curve at P which is $\frac{\Delta y}{\Delta x}$.

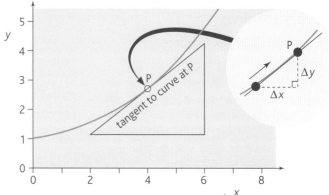

Figure 1 *Tangents and curves*

The rate of change of y with respect to x can be worked out algebraically if the equation relating y and x is known. This process is known as **differentiation.** For example,

▮ for $y = x^2$, then increasing x to $x + \Delta x$ increases y to $y + \Delta y$ where $y + \Delta y = (x + \Delta x)^2$

Multiplying out $(x + \Delta x)^2$ gives $y + \Delta y = x^2 + 2x\Delta x + \Delta x^2$

Subtracting $y = x^2$ from this equation gives $\Delta y = 2x\Delta x + \Delta x^2$

Dividing by Δx therefore gives $\frac{\Delta y}{\Delta x} = \frac{2x\Delta x + \Delta x^2}{\Delta x} = 2x + \Delta x$

Therefore, as $\Delta x \longrightarrow 0$, $\frac{\Delta y}{\Delta x} \longrightarrow 2x$ which is therefore the formula for the gradient at x.

This is written $\frac{dy}{dx} = 2x$, where $\frac{dy}{dx}$ is the mathematical expression for the rate of change of y with respect to x.

▮ for the general expression $y = x^n$, it can be shown that $\frac{dy}{dx} = nx^{n-1}$

For example, if $y = 3x^5$, then $\frac{dy}{dx} = 15x^4$

Exponential change

Exponential change happens when the change of a quantity is proportional to the quantity itself. Such a change can be an increase (i.e. exponential growth) or a decrease (i.e. exponential decay).

In both cases, the quantity changes by a fixed proportion in equal intervals of time. The A2 specification requires knowledge and understanding of the equations and graphs for exponential decrease and of graphs only for exponential growth. The notes below will therefore concentrate on exponential decrease.

In your studies of capacitor discharge (Topic 6.3) and of radioactive decay (Topic 9.5), you will have met and used the equation $\frac{dx}{dt} = -\lambda x$ and the solution of this equation $x = x_0 e^{-\lambda t}$.

Let's consider why the equation $\frac{dx}{dt} = -\lambda x$ represents an exponential decrease which is a change where the variable quantity x decreases with time at a rate in proportion to the quantity.

If x decreases by Δx in time Δt, the rate of change is $\frac{\Delta x}{\Delta t}$. This is written as $\frac{dx}{dt}$ in the limit $\Delta t \longrightarrow 0$.

For an exponential decrease, the rate of change is negative and is proportional to x, therefore $\frac{dx}{dt} = -\lambda x$, where λ is referred to as the decay constant.

Now consider why the solution of this equation is $x = x_0 e^{-\lambda t}$, where x_0 is a constant.

Look at the function:

$$x = x_0 \left(1 + t + \frac{t^2}{2 \times 1} + \frac{t^3}{3 \times 2 \times 1} + \frac{t^4}{4 \times 3 \times 2 \times 1} \right. $$
$$\left. + \text{ similar higher order terms} \right) \dots$$

Applying the rules of **differentiation** to it gives:

$$\frac{dx}{dt} = x_0 \left(0 + 1 + t + \frac{t^2}{2 \times 1} + \frac{t^3}{3 \times 2 \times 1} \right.$$
$$\left. + \text{ similar higher order terms} \right) \dots \text{ which is the same as } x.$$

So $\frac{dx}{dt} = x$ if x is the above function.

It can be shown that the function in brackets above may be written as n^t, where n is a specific number which is referred to as the exponential number e.

Therefore, $e^t = 1 + t + \frac{t^2}{2 \times 1} + \frac{t^3}{3 \times 2 \times 1} + \frac{t^4}{4 \times 3 \times 2 \times 1}$

$$+ \text{ similar higher order terms}$$

The value of e, the exponential number, can be worked out by substituting $t = 1$ in the above expression for e^t, giving $e = 1 + 1 + \frac{1}{2} + \frac{1}{6}$ + etc. $= 2.718$ to 4 significant figures.

To show that the solution of the equation $\frac{dx}{dt} = -\lambda x$ is $x = x_0 e^{-\lambda t}$, divide

both sides of the equation by $-\lambda$ to give $\frac{dx}{-\lambda dt} = x$

Substituting z for $-\lambda t$ therefore gives $\frac{dx}{dz} = x$ which has the solution

$x = x_0 e^z = x_0 e^{-\lambda t}$

The half-life $T_{1/2}$ of an exponential decrease is the time taken for x to decrease from x_0 to $\frac{1}{2} x_0$.

Substituting $x = \frac{1}{2} x_0$ and $t = T_{1/2}$ into $x = x_0 e^{-\lambda t}$ gives $x_0/2 = x_0 e^{-\lambda T_{1/2}}$

Applying logs to both sides gives $\ln x_0 - \ln 2 = \ln x_0 - \lambda T_{1/2}$

> **Note**
>
> Note that knowledge of the equation for the exponential function $e^t = 1 + t + \frac{t^2}{2 \times 1}$ + etc., is not required in the AS or the A2 specification. The information is provided to help you develop your understanding of the exponential number e and the exponential function e^{-x}.

which simplifies to $\lambda T_{1/2} = \ln 2$

$$\therefore T_{1/2} = \ln\frac{2}{\lambda} = \frac{0.693}{\lambda}$$

The time constant τ of an exponential decrease is the time taken for x to decrease from x_0 to $\frac{x_0}{e}$ $(= 0.368\, x_0$ as $\frac{1}{e} = 0.368)$.

Substituting $x = \frac{x_0}{e}$ and $t = \tau$ into $x = x_0 e^{-\lambda t}$ gives $\frac{x_0}{e} = x_0 e^{-\lambda \tau}$

Applying natural logs to both sides gives $\ln x_0 - \ln e = \ln x_0 - \lambda\tau$

which simplifies to $\tau = \frac{1}{\lambda}$ as $\ln e = 1$

For capacitor discharge, $\lambda = \frac{1}{CR}$ therefore $\tau = \frac{1}{\lambda} = CR$ (see Topic 6.3).

Testing exponential decrease

As explained on page 248, $\ln(e^{-\lambda t}) = -\lambda t$

Therefore, $\ln x = \ln(x_0 e^{-\lambda t}) = \ln x_0 + \ln(e^{-\lambda t}) = \ln x_0 - \lambda t$

Suppose two physical variables x and t are thought to relate to each other through an equation of the form $x = x_0 e^{-\lambda t}$. If so, a graph of $\ln x$ on the y-axis against t on the x-axis would be a straight line in accordance with the equation $\ln x = \ln x_0 - \lambda t$ where the gradient is $-\lambda$ and the y-intercept is $\ln x_0$.

Summary questions

1 a For each exponential decrease equation, write down the initial value at $t = 0$ and the decay constant:

   i $x = 2e^{-3t}$

   ii $x = 12e^{-t/5}$

   iii $x = 4e^{-0.02t}$

  b For each exponential decrease equation above, work out the half–life.

2 A radioactive isotope has a half-life of 720 s and it decays to form a stable product. A sample of the isotope is prepared with an initial activity of 12.0 kBq. Calculate the activity of the sample after:

  a 1 min,

  b 5 min,

  c 1 h.

3 A capacitor of capacitance 22 µF discharged from a pd of 12.0 V through a 100 kΩ resistor.

  a Calculate:

   i the time constant of the discharge circuit,

   ii the half-life of the exponential decrease.

  b Calculate the capacitor pd

   i 2.0 s, and

   ii 5.0 s after the discharge started.

4 A certain exponential decrease process is represented by the equation $x = 1000e^{-5t}$

  a i Calculate the half-life of the process.

   ii Calculate x when $t = 0.5$ s.

  b Show that the above equation can be rearranged as an equation of the form $\ln x = a + bt$ and determine the values of a and b.

15.5 Areas and integration

From the AS course, you should recall that the area under a line on a graph can give useful information if the product of the y-variable and the x-variable represents another physical variable. For example, the tension against extension graph for a spring is a straight line through the origin and the area under the line represents the work done to stretch the spring. See *AS Physics* Topic 10.1.

Table 1 gives some further examples where the area under a graph has physical significance

Table 1 *Areas in graphs*

examples (y-variable first)	area between the line and the x-axis	equation	units
power against time	energy transferred	energy transferred = power × time	$1W = 1Js^{-1}$
potential difference against charge (or stored)	electrical energy transferred	electrical energy transferred = pd × charge	$1V = 1JC^{-1}$
force against time	change of momentum (or impulse)	change of momentum = force × time	$1kgms^{-1} = 1Ns$
force against distance	work done	work done = force × distance	$1J = 1Nm$

To find the area under the line, we can either:

- count the squares of the grid under the line and multiply the number of squares by the amount of the physical variable that 1 square of area represents, or
- use the mathematical process known as **integration** as outlined below. The notes below are intended to give a deeper understanding of how areas under curves can be calculated. They are not part of the A2 Physics specification.

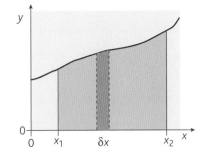

Figure 1 *Integration*

Consider Figure 1 which shows a y-variable that changes as the x-variable changes. A small increase of the x-variable, δx (δ for small) gives little or no change of the y-variable. The area under that section of the curve, $\delta A = y\,\delta x$ as it is a strip of width δx and height y. Note that rearranging $\delta A = y\,\delta x$ gives $y = \dfrac{\delta A}{\delta x}$.

Hence the total area under the line from x_1 to x_2 in Figure 1 is equal to the area of all the strips, each of width δx, from x_1 to x_2. The process of adding the individual strip areas together to give the total area is called **integration.**

In mathematical terms,

Total area $A = \displaystyle\int_{x_1}^{x_2} \delta A = \int_{x_1}^{x_2} y\,\delta x$, where $\int$ is the mathematical symbol for integration.

As $y = \frac{\delta A}{\delta x}$, then differentiating A in terms of x gives y. If we know the formula for y in terms of x, we can find the formula for A in terms of x by using the differentiation formula in Topic 15.4 in reverse.

For example, if $y = 2x$, then using the process of reverse differentiation gives $A = x^2$

Force-field curves, such as the inverse square law of force between two point charges, give areas that represent potential energy. We can use the ideas outlined above to obtain an exact formula for the potential energy of two point charges at a certain distance apart.

Consider the two point charges q_1 and q_2 at distance apart r. The force F between the charges is given by Coulomb's law

$$F = \frac{q_1 q_2}{4\pi\varepsilon_0} \times \frac{1}{r^2}$$

If the charges move so their distance apart changes by δr, the work they do in this movement $= F\delta r$. This is represented on Figure 2 by the narrow strip of width δr.

Since the work they do reduces their potential energy, their change of potential energy $\delta E_p = -F\delta r$

When the distance apart decreases to r_1 from infinite separation, the potential energy changes from zero at infinite separation to E_p at distance apart r_1. Since E_p is represented by the total area under the line from $r = $ infinity to $r = r_1$

$$E_p = \int_{\text{infinity}}^{r_1} \delta E_p = \int_{\text{infinity}}^{r_1} -F\delta r$$

Because the force is given by the inverse square law above,

$$E_p = \int_{\text{infinity}}^{r_1} \frac{-k}{r^2} \delta r$$

where $k = \frac{q_1 q_2}{4\pi\varepsilon_0}$

Therefore, $E_p = \frac{k}{r}$ because differentiating $\frac{1}{r}$ gives $\frac{-1}{r^2}$.

See Topic 15.4 if necessary.

Hence their potential energy at distance r_1 apart, $E_p = \frac{q_1 q_2}{4\pi\varepsilon_0 r_1}$

as the potential energy at infinity is zero.

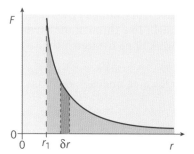

F

0 r_1 δr r

Figure 2 *The inverse square law of force*

Note

The inverse square law also applies to the gravitational force $F = \frac{GMm}{r^2}$ between two point masses M and m. The constant k is written as $-GMm$.

(The minus sign represents the attractive nature of the force.)

Therefore, for a small mass m at distance r from the centre of a spherical planet of mass M at or beyond its surface, the gravitational potential energy $E_p = -\frac{GMm}{r}$.

Summary questions

1 For a velocity–time graph, what physical variable is represented by:

a the gradient,

b the area under the line?

2 What physical variable is represented by:

a the area under a graph of acceleration against time,

b the area under a graph of current against time,

c What physical variable is represented by the area under a graph of pressure against volume for a gas?

d State the unit of

i pressure,

ii volume,

iii pressure × volume.

3 For the electric field near a point charge, what physical variable is represented by

a the area under the graph of electric field strength E against distance r in Figure 3a?

b the gradient of the graph of electric potential V against distance r in Figure 3b?

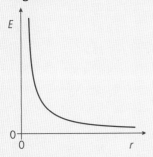

Figure 3a

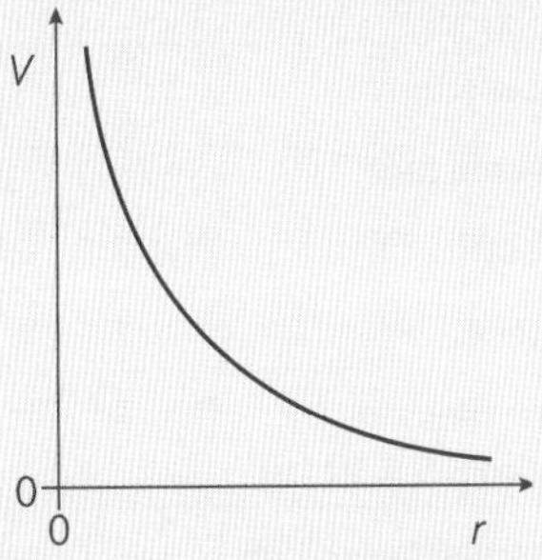

Figure 3b

4 a For the gravitational field strength near a spherical object, what physical variable is represented by

i the area under the graph of gravitational field strength g against distance r in Figure 4a,

ii the gradient of the graph of gravitational potential V_{grav} against distance r in Figure 4b?

b Which of the graphs shown in Figures 3 and 4 are inverse square curves?

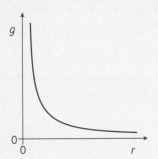

Figure 4a

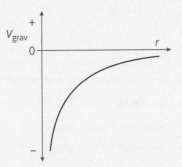

Figure 4b

Useful data for Physics (Specification A)

▨ Data

Fundamental constants and values

quantity	symbol	value	units
speed of light in vacuo	c	3.00×10^8	$m\,s^{-1}$
permeability of free space	μ_0	$4\pi \times 10^{-7}$	$H\,m^{-1}$
permittivity of free space	ε_0	8.85×10^{-12}	$F\,m^{-1}$
charge of electron	e	-1.60×10^{-19}	C
Planck constant	h	6.63×10^{-34}	$J\,s$
gravitational constant	G	6.67×10^{-11}	$N\,m^2\,kg^{-2}$
Avogadro constant	N_A	6.02×10^{23}	mol^{-1}
molar gas constant	R	8.31	$J\,K^{-1}\,mol^{-1}$
Boltzmann constant	k	1.38×10^{-23}	$J\,K^{-1}$
Stefan constant	σ	5.67×10^{-8}	$W\,m^{-2}\,K^{-4}$
Wien constant	α	2.90×10^{-3}	$m\,K$
electron rest mass (equivalent to $5.5 \times 10^{-4}\,u$)	m_e	9.11×10^{-31}	kg
electron charge/mass ratio	e/m_e	1.76×10^{11}	$C\,kg^{-1}$
proton rest mass (equivalent to $1.007\,28\,u$)	m_p	$1.67(3) \times 10^{-27}$	kg
proton charge/mass ratio	e/m_p	9.58×10^7	$C\,kg^{-1}$
neutron rest mass (equivalent to $1.008\,67\,u$)	m_n	$1.67(5) \times 10^{-27}$	kg
gravitational field strength	g	9.81	$N\,kg^{-1}$
acceleration due to gravity	g	9.81	$m\,s^{-2}$
atomic mass unit ($1\,u$ is equivalent to $931.3\,MeV$)	u	1.661×10^{-27}	kg

Astronomical data

body	mass/kg	mean radius/m
Sun	1.99×10^{30}	6.96×10^8
Earth	5.98×10^{24}	6.37×10^6

Geometrical equations

arc length $= r\theta$

circumference of circle $= 2\pi r$

area of circle $= \pi r^2$

surface area of cylinder $= 2\pi rh$

volume of cylinder $= \pi r^2 h$

area of sphere $= 4\pi r^2$

volume of sphere $= \frac{4}{3}\pi r^3$

A2 formulae (for Unit 4 and Unit 5A only)

Momentum

force	$F = \dfrac{\Delta(mv)}{\Delta t}$
impulse	$F\Delta t = \Delta(mv)$

Circular motion

angular velocity	$\omega = \dfrac{v}{r}$
	$\omega = 2\pi f$
centripetal acceleration	$a = \dfrac{v^2}{r} = \omega^2 r$
centripetal force	$F = \dfrac{mv^2}{r} = m\omega^2 r$

Oscillations

acceleration	$a = -(2\pi f)^2 x$
displacement	$x = A\cos(2\pi ft)$
speed	$v = \pm 2\pi f\sqrt{A^2 - x^2}$
maximum speed	$v_{max} = 2\pi fA$
maximum acceleration	$a_{max} = (2\pi f)^2 A$
for a mass-spring system	$T = 2\pi\sqrt{\dfrac{m}{k}}$
for a simple pendulum	$T = 2\pi\sqrt{\dfrac{l}{g}}$

Gravitational fields

force between two masses	$F = \dfrac{Gm_1 m_2}{r^2}$
magnitude of gravitational field strength	$g = \dfrac{F}{m}$
	$g = \dfrac{GM}{r^2}$
gravitational potential	$\Delta W = m\Delta V$
	$V = -\dfrac{GM}{r}$
	$g = -\dfrac{\Delta V}{\Delta r}$

Electric fields and capacitors

force between two point charges	$F = \dfrac{Q_1 Q_2}{4\pi\varepsilon_0 r^2}$
force on a charge	$F = EQ$
field strength for a uniform field	$E = \dfrac{V}{d}$
force strength for a radial field	$E = \dfrac{Q}{4\pi\varepsilon_0 r^2}$
electric potential	$W = QV$
	$V = \dfrac{Qq}{4\pi\varepsilon_0 r}$
capacitance	$C = \dfrac{Q}{V}$
decay of charge	$Q = Q_0 e^{-t/RC}$
time constant	RC
capacitor energy stored	$E = \frac{1}{2}QV = \frac{1}{2}CV^2$
	$= \dfrac{1}{2}\dfrac{Q^2}{C}$

Magnetic fields

force on a current	$F = BIl$
force on a moving charge	$F = BQv$
magnetic flux	$\Phi = BA$
magnetic flux linkage	$N\Phi = BAN$
induced emf	$\varepsilon = N\dfrac{\Delta\Phi}{\Delta t}$
emf induced in a rotating coil	$N\Phi = BAN\cos\theta$
	$\varepsilon = BAN\omega\sin\omega t$
transformer equations	$\dfrac{N_s}{N_p} = \dfrac{V_s}{V_p}$
efficiency	$= \dfrac{I_s V_s}{I_p V_p}$

Radioactivity and nuclear physics

the inverse square law for γ variation $\quad I = \dfrac{k}{x^2}$

radioactive decay $\quad \dfrac{\Delta N}{\Delta t} = -\lambda N \quad N = N_0 e^{-\lambda t}$

activity $\quad A = \lambda N$

half-life $\quad T = \dfrac{\ln 2}{\lambda}$

nuclear radius $\quad R = r_0 A^{1/3}$

energy–mass equation $\quad E = mc^2$

Gases and thermal physics

gas law $\quad pV = nRT$

$\quad pV = NkT$

kinetic theory model $\quad pV = \frac{1}{3} N m c^2_{rms}$

kinetic energy of a gas molecule $\quad \frac{1}{2} m c^2_{rms} = \frac{3}{2} kT$

$\quad = \dfrac{3RT}{2N_A}$

energy to change temperature $\quad Q = mc\Delta T$

energy to change state $\quad Q = ml$

AS formulae

Particle physics

Rest energy values

class	name	symbol	rest energy / MeV
photon	photon	γ	0
lepton	neutrino	ν_e	0
		ν_μ	0
	electron	$e^\pm$	0.510 99
	muon	$\mu^\pm$	105.659
mesons	π meson	$\pi^\pm$	139.576
		π^0	134.972
	K meson	$K^\pm$	493.821
		K^0	497.762
baryons	proton	p	938.257
	neutron	n	939.551

Properties of quarks
Antiparticles have opposite signs

type	charge	baryon number	strangeness
u	$+\frac{2}{3}e$	$+\frac{1}{3}$	0
d	$-\frac{1}{3}e$	$+\frac{1}{3}$	0
s	$-\frac{1}{3}e$	$+\frac{1}{3}$	-1

Properties of leptons

lepton	lepton number
particles: $e^-, \nu_e; \mu^-, \nu_\mu$	+1
antiparticles: $e^+, \overline{\nu}_e; \mu^+, \overline{\nu}_\mu$	-1

Photons and energy levels

photon energy $\quad E = hf = \dfrac{hc}{\lambda}$

photoelectricity $\quad hf = \phi + E_{K(max)}$

energy levels $\quad hf = E_1 - E_2$

de Broglie wavelength $\quad \lambda = \dfrac{h}{p} = \dfrac{h}{mv}$

Electricity

current and pd $\quad I = \dfrac{\Delta Q}{\Delta t}$

$\quad V = \dfrac{W}{Q}$

$\quad R = \dfrac{V}{I}$

emf $\quad \varepsilon = \dfrac{E}{Q}$

$\quad \varepsilon = I(R + r)$

resistors in series $\quad R = R_1 + R_2 + R_3 + ...$

resistors in parallel $\quad \dfrac{1}{R} = \dfrac{1}{R_1} + \dfrac{1}{R_2} + \dfrac{1}{R_3} + ...$

resistivity $\quad \rho = \dfrac{RA}{L}$

power $\quad P = VI = I^2 R = \dfrac{V^2}{R}$

alternating current $\quad I_{rms} = \dfrac{I_0}{\sqrt{2}}$

$\quad V_{rms} = \dfrac{V_0}{\sqrt{2}}$

Mechanics

Moments	$\text{moment} = Fd$
velocity and acceleration	$v = \dfrac{\Delta s}{\Delta t}$
	$a = \dfrac{\Delta v}{\Delta t}$
equations of motion	$v = u + at$
	$s = \dfrac{(u + v)t}{2}$
	$v^2 = u^2 + 2as$
	$s = ut + \tfrac{1}{2}at^2$
force	$F = ma$
work, energy and power	$W = Fs\cos\theta$
	$E_K = \tfrac{1}{2}mv^2$
	$\Delta E_p = mg\,\Delta h$
	$P = \dfrac{\Delta W}{\Delta t} \quad P = Fv$

$$\text{efficiency} = \frac{\text{useful output power}}{\text{input power}}$$

Materials

density	$\rho = \dfrac{m}{V}$
Hooke's law	$F = k\Delta L$
Young modulus	$= \dfrac{\text{tensile stress}}{\text{tensile strain}} = \dfrac{FL}{A\Delta L}$
energy stored	$E = \tfrac{1}{2}k\Delta L^2 = \tfrac{1}{2}F\Delta L$

Waves

wave speed	$c = f\lambda$
period	$T = \dfrac{1}{f}$
fringe spacing	$w = \dfrac{\lambda D}{s}$
diffraction grating	$d\sin\theta = n\lambda$
refractive index of a substance s,	$n_s = \dfrac{c}{c_s}$

For two different substances of refractive indices n_1 and n_2,

law of refraction	$n_1\sin\theta_1 = n_2\sin\theta_2$
critical angle	$\sin\theta_c = \dfrac{n_2}{n_1} \quad \text{for } n_1 > n_2$

Glossary

A glossary of practical terms follows this glossary.

A

absolute scale: temperature scale in kelvins (K) defined in terms of *absolute zero*, 0 K, and the triple point of water, 273.16 K, which is the temperature at which ice, water and water vapour are in thermal equilbrium.

absolute zero: the lowest possible temperature, the temperature at which an object has minimum internal energy.

absolute temperature T: in kelvin = temperature in °C + 273(.15).

activity A: of a radioactive isotope, the number of nuclei of the isotope that disintegrate per second. The unit of activity is the becquerel (Bq), equal to 1 disintegration per second.

alpha (α) decay: change in an unstable nucleus when it emits an α particle which is a particle consisting of two protons and two neutrons.

alpha radiation: particles that are each composed of two protons and two neutrons. An alpha (α) particle is emitted by a heavy unstable nucleus which is then less unstable as a result. Alpha radiation is easily absorbed by paper, has a range in air of no more than a few centimetres and is more ionising than beta (β) or gamma (γ) radiation.

amplitude: the maximum displacement from equilibrium of an oscillating object.

angular displacement: the angle an object in circular motion turns through. If its time period is T and its frequency is f, its angular displacement in time t, in radians = $2\pi ft = 2\pi t/T$

angular speed ω: the rate of change of angular displacement of an object in circular (or orbital or spinning) motion.

angular frequency ω: for an object oscillating at frequency f in simple harmonic motion, its angular frequency = $2\pi f$.

atomic mass unit u: correctly referred to as the unified atomic mass constant; $\frac{1}{12}$th of the mass of an atom of the carbon isotope $^{12}_{6}$C, equal to 1.661×10^{-27} kg.

atomic number Z: of an atom of an element is the number of protons in the nucleus of the atom. It is also the order number of the element in the Periodic Table.

Avogadro constant N_A: the number of atoms in 12 g of the carbon isotope $^{12}_{6}$C. N_A is used to define the mole. Its value is 6.02×10^{23} mol^{-1}.

B

back emf: emf induced in the spinning coil of an electric motor or in any coil in which the current is changing (e.g. the primary coil of a transformer). A back emf acts against the applied pd.

background radiation: radiation due to naturally occurring radioactive substances in the environment (e.g. in the ground or in building materials or elsewhere in the environment). Background radiation is also caused by cosmic radiation.

beta (β) decay: change in a nucleus when a neutron changes into a proton and a β^- particle and an antineutrino are emitted if the nucleus is neutron-rich or a proton changes to a neutron and a β^+ particle and a neutrino are emitted if the nucleus is proton-rich.

beta-minus (β^-) radiation: electrons (β^-) emitted by unstable neutron-rich nuclei (i.e. nuclei with a neutron/proton ratio greater than for stable nuclei). β^- radiation is easily absorbed by paper, has a range in air of no more than a few centimetres and is less ionising than alpha (α) radiation and more ionising than gamma (γ) radiation.

beta-plus (β^+) radiation: positrons (β^+) emitted by unstable proton-rich nuclei (i.e. nuclei with a neutron/proton ratio smaller than for stable nuclei). Positrons emitted in solids or liquids travel no further than about 2 mm before they are annihilated.

binding energy of a nucleus: the work that must be done to separate a nucleus into its constituent neutrons and protons. Binding energy = mass defect $\times$ c^2. Binding energy in MeV = mass defect in u $\times$ 931.3.

binding energy per nucleon: the average work done per nucleon to separate a nucleus into its constituent parts. The binding energy per nucleon of a nucleus = the binding energy of a nucleus/mass number A. The binding energy per nucleon is greatest for iron nuclei of mass number about 56. The binding energy curve is a graph of binding energy per nucleon against mass number A.

boiling point: the temperature at which a pure liquid at atmospheric pressure boils.

Boyle's law: for a fixed mass of gas at constant temperature, its pressure $\times$ its volume is constant. A gas that obeys Boyle's law is said to be an *ideal gas*.

Boltzmann constant k: the molar gas constant divided by the Avogadro number (i.e. R/N_A). See *kinetic energy of the molecules of an ideal gas*.

Brownian motion: the random and unpredictable motion of a particle such as a smoke particle caused by molecules of the surrounding substance colliding at random with the particle.

C

capacitance: the charge stored per unit pd of a capacitor. The unit of capacitance is the farad (F), equal to 1 coulomb per volt. For a capacitor of capacitance C at pd V, the charge stored, $Q = CV$.

capacitor energy: energy stored by the capacitor, $E = \frac{1}{2}QV = \frac{1}{2}CV^2 = \frac{1}{2}Q^2/C$

capacitor discharge: through a fixed resistor of resistance R; time constant $= RC$; exponential decrease equation for current or charge or pd; $x = x_0e^{-t/RC}$

Celsius scale: temperature, in degrees Celsius or °C, is defined as absolute temperature in kelvins −273.15. This definition means that the temperature of pure melting ice (ice point) is 0 °C, and the temperature of steam at standard atmospheric pressure (steam point) is 100 °C.

centripetal acceleration: 1. For an object moving at speed v (or angular speed ω) in uniform circular motion, its centripetal acceleration $a = v^2/r = \omega^2 r$ towards the centre of the circle. 2. For a satellite in a circular orbit, its centripetal acceleration $v^2/r = g$

centripetal force: the resultant force on an object that moves along a circular path. For an object of mass m moving at speed v along a circular path of radius r, the centripetal force $= mv^2/r$ towards the centre of the circle.

chain reaction: a series of reactions in which each reaction causes a further reaction. In a nuclear reactor, each fission event is due to a neutron colliding with a $^{235}_{92}$U nucleus which splits and releases two or three further neutrons that can go on to produce further fission. A steady chain reaction occurs when one fission neutron on average from each fission event produces a further fission event.

Charles' law: for an ideal gas at constant pressure, its volume is directly proportional to its *absolute temperature*.

collisions: see *elastic collision*.

conservation of momentum: for a system of interacting objects is the total momentum of the objects remains constant provided no external resultant force acts on the system.

control rods: rods made of a neutron-absorbing substance such as cadmium or boron that are moved in or out of the core of a nuclear reactor to control the rate of fission events in the reactor.

coolant: a fluid that is used to prevent a machine or device from becoming dangerously hot. The coolant of a nuclear reactor is pumped through the core of the reactor to transfer thermal energy from the core to a heat exchanger.

Coulomb's law of force: for two point charges Q_1 and Q_2 at distance apart r, the force F between the two charges is given by the equation $F = Q_1Q_2/4\pi\varepsilon_0 r^2$, where ε_0 is the permittivity of free space.

count rate: the number of counts per unit time detected by a Geiger Müller tube. Count rates should always be corrected by measuring and subtracting the background count rate (i.e. the count rate with no radioactive source present).

critical mass: the minimum mass of the fissile *isotope* (e.g. the uranium *isotope* $^{235}_{92}$U) in a nuclear reactor necessary to produce a *chain reaction*. If the mass of the fissile isotope in the reactor is less than the critical mass, a chain reaction does not occur because too many fission neutrons escape from the reactor or are absorbed without fission.

D

damped oscillations: oscillations that reduce in *amplitude* due to the presence of resistive forces such as friction and drag. 1. For a lightly damped system, the amplitude of oscillations decreases gradually. 2. For a heavily damped system displaced from equilibrium then released, the system slowly returns to equilibrium without oscillating. 3. For a critically damped system, the system returns to equilibrium in the least possible time without oscillating.

de Broglie wavelength: a particle of matter has a wave-like nature which means that it can behave as a wave. For example, electrons directed at a thin crystal are diffracted by the crystal. The de Broglie wavelength, λ, of a matter particle depends on its momentum, p, in accordance with de Broglie's equation $\lambda = h/p = h/mv$.

decay constant λ: the probability of an individual nucleus decaying per second.

decay curve: an exponential decrease curve showing how the mass or activity of a radioactive isotope decreases with time.

differentiation: mathematical process of finding the gradient of a line from its equation.

diffraction: the spreading of waves when they pass through a gap or round an obstacle. X-ray diffraction is used to determine the structure of crystals, metals and long molecules. Electron diffraction is used to probe the structure of materials. High-energy electron scattering is used to determine the diameter of the nucleus.

displacement: distance in a given direction.

dissipative forces: forces that transfer energy which is wasted.

dose equivalent: a comparative measure of the effect of each type of *ionising radiation*, defined as the energy that would need to be absorbed per unit mass of matter from 250 k of X-radiation to have the same effect as a certain 'dose' of the *ionising radiation*. The unit of dose equivalent is the sievert (Sv).

dynamo rule: See Fleming's *right-hand rule*.

E

eddy currents: unwanted induced currents in the metal parts of ac machines.

elastic collision: an elastic collision is one in which the total kinetic energy after the collision is equal to the total kinetic energy before the collision.

electrical conductor: an object that can conduct electricity.

electric field strength E: at a point in an electric field, is the force per unit charge on a small positively charged object at that point in the field.

electric potential V: at a point in an electric field is the work done per unit charge on a small positively charged object to move it from infinity to that point in the field.

electromagnetic induction: the generation of an emf when the *magnetic flux linkage* through a coil changes or a conductor cuts across magnetic field lines.

electron: a *lepton* of rest mass 9.11 $\times$ 10^{-31} kg and electric charge -1.60 $\times$ 10^{-19} C (to 3 significant figures).

electron capture: a proton-rich *nucleus* captures an inner-shell electron to cause a *proton* in the nucleus to change into a *neutron*. An electron *neutrino* is emitted by the nucleus. An X-ray *photon* is subsequently emitted by the atom when the inner shell vacancy is filled.

equilibrium: state of an object when at rest or in uniform motion.

equipotential: a line or surface in a field along which the electric or gravitational potential is constant.

excited state: an atom which is not in its ground state (i.e. its lowest energy state).

explosion: when two objects fly apart, the two objects carry away equal and opposite momentum.

exponential change: exponential change happens when the change of a quantity is proportional to the quantity itself. For an exponential decrease of a quantity x, $dx/dt = -\lambda x$, where λ is referred to as the decay constant. The solution of this equation is $x = x_0 e^{-\lambda t}$ where x_0 is an initial value of x.

F

Faraday's law of electromagnetic induction: the induced emf in a circuit is equal to the rate of change of *magnetic flux linkage* through the circuit. For a changing magnetic field in a fixed coil of area A and N turns, the induced emf $= -NA\dfrac{\Delta B}{\Delta t}$

field line: see *line of force*.

fission: the splitting of a $^{235}_{92}$U *nucleus* or a $^{235}_{94}$Pu nucleus into two approximately equal fragments. Induced fission is fission caused by an incoming *neutron* colliding with a $^{235}_{92}$U nucleus or a $^{235}_{94}$Pu nucleus.

fission neutrons: neutrons released when a nucleus undergoes fission and which may collide with nuclei to cause further fission.

Fleming's left-hand rule: rule that relates the directions of the force, magnetic field and current on a current-carrying conductor in a magnetic field.

Fleming's right-hand rule: rule that relates the directions of the induced current, magnetic field and velocity of the conductor when the conductor cuts across magnetic field lines and an emf is induced in it.

force: = rate of change of *momentum*

$$= \frac{\text{change of momentum}}{\text{time taken}}$$

(= mass $\times$ acceleration for fixed mass).

free electrons: electrons in a conductor that move about freely inside the metal because they are not attached to a particular atom.

free oscillations: oscillations where there is no damping and no periodic force acting on the system so the amplitude of the oscillations is constant.

forced oscillations: oscillations of a system that is subjected to an external periodic force.

frequency: of an oscillating object is the number of cycles of oscillation per second.

fusion (nuclear): the fusing together of light nuclei to form a heavier nucleus.

fusion (thermal): the fusing together of metals by melting them together.

G

gamma (γ) radiation: electromagnetic radiation emitted by an unstable nucleus when it becomes more stable.

geostationary satellite: a satellite that stays above the same point on the Earth's equator as it orbits the Earth because its orbit is in the same plane as the equator, its period is exactly 24 h and it orbits in the same direction as the Earth's direction of rotation.

gold leaf electroscope: a device used to detect electric charge.

gravitational constant G: the constant of proportionality in *Newton's law of gravitation*.

gravitational field: the region surrounding an object in which it exerts a gravitational force on any other object.

gravitational field strength g: the force per unit mass on a small mass placed in the field.

1. $g = F/m$, where F is the gravitational force on a small mass m.

2. At distance r from a point mass M, $g = GM/r^2$

3. At or beyond the surface of a sphere of mass M, $g = GM/r^2$ where r is the distance to the centre.

4. At the surface of a sphere of mass M and radius R, $g_s = GM/R^2$

gravitational force: an attractive force that acts equally on any two objects due to their mass.

gravitational potential V: at a point in a gravitational field is the work done per unit mass to move a small object from infinity to that point. At distance r from the centre of a spherical object of mass M,

$$V = -\frac{GM}{r}$$

gravitational potential energy: at a point in a gravitational field is the work done to move a small object from infinity to that point. The change of gravitational potential energy of a mass m moved through height h near the Earth's surface, $\Delta E_p = mg\Delta h$

grid system: the network of transformers and cables that is used to distribute electrical power from power stations to users.

ground state: the lowest energy state of an atom.

H

half-life $T_{1/2}$: the time taken for the mass of a radioactive isotope to decrease to half the initial mass or for its activity to halve. This is the same as the time taken for the number of nuclei of the isotope to decrease to half the initial number.

Hall probe: a device used to measure *magnetic flux density*.

heat Q: energy transfer due to a difference of temperature.

heat capacity: the energy needed to change the temperature of an object by 1 K

heat exchanger: a steel vessel containing pipes through which hot coolant in a sealed circuit is pumped, causing water passing through the steel vessel in separate pipes to turn to steam which is used to drive turbines.

I

ideal gas: a gas under conditions such that it obeys *Boyle's law*.

ideal gas equation: $pV = nRT$, where p is the gas pressure, V is the gas volume, n is the number of moles of gas, T is the absolute temperature and R is the *molar gas constant*.

impulse: of a force acting on an object, force × time for which the force acts.

induced emf: see *electromagnetic induction*.

induced fission: see *fission*.

insulating materials: an electrical insulator is a material that cannot conduct electricity; a thermal insulator is a material that is a poor conductor of heat.

integration: mathematical process of finding the area under a curve from its mathematical equation.

intensity of radiation: at a surface is the radiation energy per second per unit area at normal incidence to the surface. The unit of intensity is $J\,s^{-1}\,m^{-2}$ or $W\,m^{-2}$.

internal energy: of an object is the sum of the random distribution of the kinetic and potential energies of its molecules.

ionising radiation: radiation that produces ions in the substances it passes through. It destroys cell membranes and damages vital molecules such as DNA directly or indirectly by creating 'free radical' ions which react with vital molecules.

isotopes: of an element are atoms which have the same number of protons in each nucleus but different numbers of neutrons.

inverse square laws: 1. Force: *Newton's law of gravitation* and *Coulomb's law* of force between electric charges are inverse square laws because the force between two point objects (masses in the case of gravitation and charge in the case of charges) is inversely proportional to the square of the distance between the two objects. Because these two laws are inverse

square laws, the field strength due to a point mass or a point charge varies with distance according to the inverse of the square of the distance to the point object.

2. Intensity: the intensity of γ radiation from a point source varies with the inverse of the square of the distance from the source. The same rule applies to radiation from any point source that spreads out equally in all directions and is not absorbed.

K

Kepler's third law: for any planet, the cube of its mean radius of orbit r is directly proportional to the square of its time period T. Using *Newton's law of gravitation*, it can be shown that $r^3/T^2 = GM/4\pi^2$

kinetic energy: the energy of a moving object due to its motion. For an object of mass m moving at speed v, its kinetic energy $E_K = \frac{1}{2}mv^2$, provided $v << c$ (the speed of light in free space).

kinetic energy of the molecules of an ideal gas: 1. Mean kinetic energy of a molecule of an *ideal gas* $= \frac{3}{2}kT$, where the Boltzmann constant $k = R/N_A$

2. Total kinetic energy of n moles of an ideal gas $= \frac{3}{2}nRT$

kinetic theory of a gas:

1. Assumptions; a gas consists of identical point molecules which do not attract one another. The molecules are in continual random motion colliding elastically with each other and with the container.

2. The pressure p of N molecules of such a gas in a container of volume V is given by the equation $pV = \frac{1}{3}Nmc^2_{rms}$, where m is the mass of each molecule and c^2_{rms} is the mean square speed of the gas molecules.

3. Assuming that the mean kinetic energy of a gas molecule $\frac{1}{2}mc^2_{rms} = \frac{3}{2}kT$, where $k = R/N_A$, it can be shown from $pV = \frac{1}{3}Nmc^2_{rms}$ that $pV = nRT$, which is the *ideal gas law*.

kinetic theory of gases equation: $pV = \frac{1}{3}Nmc^2_{rms}$

L

latent heat of fusion: the energy needed to change the state of a solid to a liquid without change of temperature. See *specific latent heat of fusion*.

latent heat of vaporisation: the energy needed to change the state of a liquid to a vapour without change of temperature. See *specific latent heat of vaporisation*.

Lenz's law: when a current is induced by electromagnetic induction, the direction of the induced current is always such as to oppose the change that causes the current.

line of force or a field line: a line followed by a small mass in a gravitational field (or a small positively charged object in an electric field or a free north pole in a magnetic field) acted on by no other forces than the force due to the field.

logarithms: for a number $n = b^p$ where b is the base number, then $p = \log_b n$
$\log(nm) = \log n + \log m$,
$\log(n/m) = \log n - \log m$,
$\log(m^p) = p \log m$
natural logs: for $n = e^p$, then $\ln n = p$
base 10 logs: for $n = 10^p$, then $\log_{10} n = p$

logarithmic scale: a scale such that equal intervals correspond to a change by a constant factor or multiple (e.g. ×10).

log graphs: 1. For $y = kx^n$, $\log_{10} y = \log_{10} k + n \log_{10} x$; the graph of $\log_{10} y$ (on the vertical axis) against $\log_{10} x$ is therefore a straight line of gradient n with an intercept equal to $\log_{10} k$;
2. For $x = x_0 e^{-\lambda t}$, $\ln x = \ln x_0 - \lambda t$; the graph of $\ln x$ (on the vertical axis) against t is a straight line with a gradient equal to $-\lambda$ and a y-intercept equal to $\ln x_0$

M

magnetic flux Φ: $\Phi = BA$ for a uniform magnetic field of flux density B that is perpendicular to an area A.

magnetic flux density B: the magnetic force per unit length per unit current on a current carrying conductor at right angles to the field lines. The unit of magnetic flux density is the tesla (T). B is sometimes referred to as the magnetic field strength.

magnetic flux linkage $N\Phi$: through a coil of N turns, $= N\Phi = NBA$ where B is the magnetic flux density perpendicular to area A. The unit of magnetic flux and of flux linkage is the weber (Wb), equal to $1\,T\,m^2$ or $1\,V\,s$.

magnetic force: 1. $F = BIl\sin\theta$ gives the force F on a current-carrying wire of length l in a uniform magnetic field B at angle θ to the field lines, where I is the current. The direction of the force is given by *Fleming's left-hand rule* where the field direction is the direction of the field component perpendicular to the wire.
2. $F = BQv\sin\theta$ gives the force F on a particle of charge Q moving through a uniform magnetic field B at speed v in a direction at angle θ to the field. If the velocity of the charged particle is perpendicular to the field, $F = BQv$. The direction of the force is given by Fleming's left-hand rule, provided the current is in the direction that positive charge would move in.
3. $BQv = mv^2/r$ gives the radius of the orbit of a charge moving in a direction at right angles to the lines of a magnetic field.

mass defect: of a nucleus is the difference between the mass of the separated nucleons (i.e. protons and neutrons from which the nucleus is composed) and the nucleus.

mean kinetic energy: for a molecule in a gas at absolute temperature T, its mean kinetic energy = $\frac{3}{2}kT$, where k is the Boltzmann constant ($= R/N_A$)

melting point: the temperature at which a pure substance melts.

metastable state: an excited state of the nuclei of an isotope that lasts long enough after α or β emission for the isotope to be separated from the parent isotope (e.g. technetium $^{99}_{43}Tc$).

moderator: substance in a thermal nuclear reactor that slows the fission neutrons down so they can go on to produce further fission.

mole: one mole of a substance consisting of identical particles is the quantity of substance that contains N_A particles of the substance.

molar gas constant: R See *the ideal gas equation*.

molarity: the number of moles in a certain quantity of a substance. The unit of molarity is the mol.

molar mass: the mass of one mole of a substance.

momentum: mass × velocity. The unit of momentum is $kg\,m\,s^{-1}$

motor effect: the force on a current-carrying conductor due to a magnetic field.

N

natural frequency: the frequency of free oscillations of an oscillating system.

neutron: an uncharged particle that has a rest mass of 1.674×10^{-27} kg. Neutrons are in every atomic nucleus except that of hydrogen ^1_1H.

Newton's law of gravitation: the gravitational force F between two point masses m_1 and m_2 at distance r apart is given by $F = Gm_1m_2/r^2$.

Newton's laws of motion: first law: an object continues at rest or in uniform motion unless it is acted on by a resultant force. Second law: the rate of change of momentum of an object is proportional to the resultant force on it. Third law: when two objects interact, they exert equal and opposite forces on one another. Newton's second law may be written as $F = \Delta p/\Delta t$, where p is the momentum ($= mv$) of the object and F is the force in newtons. For constant mass, $\Delta p = m\,\Delta v$ so $F = m\,\Delta v/\Delta t = ma$.

nuclear fission: see *fission*.

nuclear fusion: see *fusion (nuclear)*.

nucleon: a neutron or a proton in the nucleus.

nucleus: the relatively small part of an atom where all the atom's positive charge and most of its mass is concentrated.

nuclide of an isotope $^A_Z X$: a *nucleus* composed of Z protons and $(A - Z)$ neutrons, where Z is the proton number (and also the atomic number of element X) and A is the mass number (i.e. the number of protons and neutrons in a nucleus).

P

pair production: when a gamma *photon* changes into a particle and an antiparticle.

periodic force: a *force* that varies regularly in magnitude with a definite time period.

permittivity of free space ε_0: the charge per unit area in coulombs per square metre on oppositely charged parallel plates in a vacuum when the *electric field strength* between the plates is 1 volt per metre. See *Coulomb's law of force*.

phase difference: in radians, for two objects oscillating with the same time period, T_p, the phase difference $= 2\pi\Delta t/T_p$, where Δt is the time between successive instants when the two objects are at maximum displacement in the same direction.

photon: electromagnetic radiation consists of photons. Each photon is a wave packet of electromagnetic radiation. The energy of a photon, $E = hf$, where f is the frequency of the radiation and h is the Planck constant.

positron: a particle of antimatter that is the antiparticle of the electron.

potential gradient: at a point in a field is the change of potential per unit change of distance along the field line at that point. The potential gradient $= -$ the field strength at any point.

power: rate of transfer of energy $= \dfrac{\text{energy transferred}}{\text{time taken}}$

pressure: the force per unit area that a gas or a liquid or a solid at rest exerts normally on (i.e. at right angles to) a surface. Pressure is measured in pascals (Pa), where $1\,Pa = 1\,N\,m^{-2}$

pressure law: for a fixed mass of an ideal gas at constant volume, its pressure is directly proportional to its absolute temperature.

principle of conservation of momentum: when two or more bodies interact, the total *momentum* is unchanged, provided no external forces act on the bodies.

principle of conservation of energy: in any change, the total amount of energy after the change is always equal to the total amount of energy before the change.

proton: a particle that has equal and opposite charge to the electron and has a rest mass of 1.673 × 10^{-27} kg which is about 1836 times that of the electron. Protons are in every atomic nucleus. The nucleus of hydrogen ${}^{1}_{1}$H is a single proton. The proton is the only stable baryon.

R

radial field: a field in which the *field lines* are straight and converge or diverge as if from a single point.

radian: 1 radian = 360/2π degrees

reactor core: the fuel rods, control rods, and the absorber rods of a nuclear reactor which together with the moderator substance are in a steel vessel through which the coolant (which is also the moderator in 'pressurised water reactor') is pumped.

renewable energy: energy from a source that is continually renewed. Examples include hydroelectricity, tidal power, geothermal power, solar power, wave power and wind power.

resonance: the amplitude of vibration of an oscillating system subjected to a periodic force is largest when the periodic force has the same frequency as the resonant frequency of the system. For a lightly damped system, the frequency of the periodic force = natural frequency of the oscillating system. At resonance, the system vibrates such that its velocity is in phase with the periodic force.

resonant frequency: the frequency of an oscillating system in resonance.

root mean square speed, c_{rms}: square root of the mean value of the square of the molecular speeds of the molecules of a gas.

$$c_{rms} = \left(\frac{c_1^2 + c_2^2 + \dots + c_N^2}{N}\right)^{1/2}$$

where $c_1, c_2, c_3 \dots c_N$ represent the speeds of the individual molecules and N is the number of molecules in the gas.

Rutherford's α-particle scattering experiment: demonstrated that every atom contains a positively charged nucleus which is much smaller than the atom and where all the positive charge and most of the mass of the atom is located.

S

satellite: a small object in orbit round a larger object.

satellite motion: for a satellite moving at speed v in a circular orbit of radius r round a planet, its centripetal acceleration, $v^2/r = g$. Substituting $v = 2\pi r/T$, where T is its time period, and $g = GM/r^2$, where M is the mass of the planet, $T^2 = (4\pi^2/GM)r^3$. See *geostationary satellite*.

simple electric motor: an electric motor with an armature consisting of a single coil of insulated wire.

simple harmonic motion: motion of an object if its acceleration is proportional to the displacement of the object from equilibrium and is always directed towards the equilibrium position.
1. The acceleration, a, of an object oscillating in simple harmonic motion is given by $a = -(2\pi f)^2 x = -\omega^2 x$, where x = displacement from equilibrium, and f = frequency of oscillations and ω = the angular frequency = $2\pi f$.
2. The solution of this equation depends on the initial conditions. If $x = 0$ and the object is moving in the + direction at time $t = 0$, then $x = A\sin(2\pi ft)$. If the object is at maximum displacement, $+A$, at time $t = 0$, then $x = A\cos(2\pi ft)$

simple harmonic motion applications: 1. For a simple pendulum of length L, its time period $T = 2\pi(L/g)^{1/2}$
2. For an oscillating mass m on the end of a vertical spring, its time period $T = 2\pi(m/k)^{1/2}$, where k is the spring constant.

sinusoidal curve Any curve with the same shape as a sine wave (e.g. a cosine curve).

specific heat capacity c: of a substance is the energy needed to raise the temperature of 1 kg of the substance by 1 K without change

of state. To raise the temperature of mass m of a substance from T_1 to T_2, the energy needed, $Q = mc(T_2 - T_1)$, where c is the specific heat capacity of the substance.

specific latent heat of fusion: of a substance is the energy needed to change the state of unit mass of a solid to a liquid without change of temperature.

specific latent heat of vaporisation: for a substance is the energy needed to change the state of unit mass of a liquid to a vapour without change of temperature. To change the state of mass m of a substance without change of temperature, the energy needed $Q = ml$, where l is the specific latent heat of fusion or vaporisation of the substance.

strong nuclear force: force that holds the nucleons together. It has a range of about 2–3 fm and is attractive down to distances of about 0.5 fm. Below this distance, it is a repulsive force.

sublimation: the change of state when a solid changes to a vapour directly.

T

temperature: the degree of hotness of an object.

thermal energy: the internal energy of an object due to temperature.

thermal equilibrium: when no overall heat transfer occurs between two objects at the same temperature.

thermal nuclear reactor: nuclear reactor which has a moderator in the core.

time constant: the time taken for a quantity that decreases exponentially to decrease to 0.37 (= 1/e) of its initial value. For the discharge of a capacitor through a fixed resistor, the time constant = resistance × capacitance.

time period or period: time taken for one complete cycle of oscillations.

transformer: converts the amplitude of an alternating pd to a different value. It consists of two insulated coils, the primary coil and the secondary coil, wound round a soft iron laminated core; **step-down transformer:** a transformer in which the rms pd across the secondary coil is less than the rms pd applied to the primary coil; **step-up transformer:** a transformer in which the rms pd across the secondary coil is greater than the rms pd applied to the primary coil.

transformer rule: the ratio of the secondary voltage to the primary voltage is equal to the ratio of the number of secondary turns to the number of primary turns.

transformer efficiency: for an ideal transformer (i.e. one that is 100% efficient), the output power (= secondary voltage × secondary current) = the input power (= primary voltage × primary current). Transformer inefficiency is due to: resistance heating of the current in each coil; the heating effect of eddy currents (i.e. unwanted induced currents) in the core; and repeated magnetisation and demagnetisation of the core.

uniform circular motion: motion of an object moving at constant speed along a circular path.

uniform field: a region where the field strength is the same in magnitude and direction at every point in the field.
1. The **electric field** between two oppositely charged parallel plates is uniform. The electric field strength $E = V/d$, where V is the pd between the plates and d is the perpendicular distance between the plates.
2. The **gravitational field** of the Earth is uniform over a region which is small compared to the scale of the Earth.
3. The **magnetic field** inside a solenoid carrying a constant current is uniform along and near the axis.

universal constant of gravitation: see *gravitational constant*.

velocity: change of displacement per unit time.

work done: work is energy transferred by means of a force. The work done W by a force F when its point of application moves through displacement s at angle θ to the direction of the force is given by $W = Fs\cos\theta$

wave particle duality: 1. Matter particles have a wave-like nature, for example, electrons directed at a thin crystal are diffracted by the crystal, and particle-like behaviour, such as electrons in a beam deflected by a magnetic field. See *de Broglie wavelength*.
2. Photons have a particle-like nature, as shown in the photoelectric effect, as well as a wave-like nature as shown in *diffraction* experiments.

X-rays: electromagnetic radiation of wavelength less than about 1 nm. X-rays are emitted from an X-ray tube as a result of fast-moving electrons from a heated filament as the cathode being stopped on impact with the metal anode. X-rays are ionising and they penetrate matter. Thick lead plates are needed to absorb a beam of X-rays.

Glossary of practical terms

accepted value: value of the most accurate measurement available, sometimes referred to as the 'true value'.

accuracy: measure of confidence in a measurement, often expressed as the uncertainty or probable error of the measurement.

dependent variable: a physical quantity whose value depends on the value of another physical variable.

errors: 1. Random errors vary randomly with no recognisable pattern or trend or bias.
2. Systematic errors differ systematically and show a pattern or trend or bias.

independent variable: physical quantities whose values are selected or controlled by the experimenter.

linearity: an instrument that gives readings that are directly proportional to the magnitude of the quantity being measured.

mean value of a set of readings: sum of the readings divided by the number of readings.

percentage uncertainty:
$$= \frac{\text{uncertainty}}{\text{mean value}} \times 100\%$$

precision of a measurement: the degree of exactness of a measurement, usually expressed as the uncertainty of the readings used to obtain the measurement.

precision of an instrument: the smallest non-zero reading that can be measured using the instrument.

range of a set of readings: the difference between the largest and the smallest reading.

reliability: an experiment or measurement is reliable if a consistent value is obtained each time it is repeated under identical conditions. The reliability of an experiment is increased if random and systematic errors have been considered and eliminated and, where approriate, a more precise best fit line has been obtained.

sensitivity of an instrument: output response per unit input quantity.

uncertainty of a measurement: half the range of the readings used to obtain the measurement.

valid measurement: measurements that give the required information by an acceptable method.

zero error of an instrument: a systematic error due to a non-zero reading when the quantity to be measured is zero.

Answers to summary questions

1.1

1 a i $1.2 \times 10^{-18}\,\text{kg m s}^{-1}$ ii $0.050\,\text{kg m s}^{-1}$
    iii $14\,\text{kg m s}^{-1}$
   b i $6.0\,\text{kg}$ ii $20\,\text{m s}^{-1}$

2 a $3.6 \times 10^{5}\,\text{kg m s}^{-1}$ b $60\,\text{s}$

3 a $5.4 \times 10^{6}\,\text{kg m s}^{-1}$ b $45\,\text{s}$

4 a $9.0 \times 10^{3}\,\text{kg m s}^{-1}$
   b i $-8.4 \times 10^{3}\,\text{kg m s}^{-1}$ ii $1.0\,\text{m s}^{-1}$

1.2

1 a $1600\,\text{kg m s}^{-1}$ b $3200\,\text{N}$

2 a $3000\,\text{kg m s}^{-1}$ b $7.5\,\text{kN}$

3 a $-4.2 \times 10^{-23}\,\text{kg m s}^{-1}$ b $-1.9 \times 10^{-13}\,\text{N}$

4 a $-2.1 \times 10^{-23}\,\text{kg m s}^{-1}$ b $-9.5 \times 10^{-14}\,\text{N}$

1.3

1 $0.72\,\text{m s}^{-1}$,

2 $0.7\,\text{m s}^{-1}$ in the same direction

3 $0.05\,\text{m s}^{-1}$ in the direction the $1.0\,\text{kg}$ trolley was moving in

4 $-0.63\,\text{m s}^{-1}$ in the opposite direction to its initial direction.

1.4

2 a $9.0\,\text{m s}^{-1}$ in the same direction   b $24\,\text{kJ}$

3 a $1.1\,\text{m s}^{-1}$ in the reverse direction   b $20\,\text{J}$

4 a i $1.0\,\text{m s}^{-1}$ b The driver of the $250\,\text{kg}$ car experiences a force from his/her car which slows him/her down; the other driver experiences a force from his/her car that accelerates him/her.

1.5

1 $0.35\,\text{m s}^{-1}$

2 a $0.25\,\text{m s}^{-1}$; the mass of A and X was greater than the mass of B, so B moved away faster.

3 a i $0.10\,\text{m s}^{-1}$ ii $15\,\text{mJ}$ b $0.19\,\text{m s}^{-1}$

4 a $9.0\,\text{m s}^{-1}$ b i $1.1\,\text{J}$ ii $81\,\text{J}$

2.1

1 a $1.75 \times 10^{-3}\,\text{rad}$ b $0.105\,\text{rad}$ c $6.28\,\text{rad}$

2 a $20\,\text{ms}$ b i $0.31\,\text{rad}$ ii $310\,\text{rad}$

3 a $465\,\text{m s}^{-1}$ b i $0.0042°$ ii $7.3 \times 10^{-5}\,\text{rad}$

4 a $7.0\,\text{km s}^{-1}$ b i $0.050°$ ii $8.7 \times 10^{-4}\,\text{rad}$

2.2

1 a $0.23\,\text{m s}^{-1}$ b i $7.9 \times 10^{-4}\,\text{m s}^{-2}$ ii $5.1 \times 10^{-2}\,\text{N}$

2 a $0.53\,\text{m s}^{-1}$, $0.66\,\text{m s}^{-2}$ b $9.9 \times 10^{-2}\,\text{N}$

3 a i $3.0 \times 10^{4}\,\text{m s}^{-1}$ ii $6.0 \times 10^{-3}\,\text{m s}^{-2}$
   b i $7.9 \times 10^{3}\,\text{m s}^{-1}$ ii $5.1 \times 10^{3}\,\text{s}$

4 a $8.4\,\text{m s}^{-1}$ b $88\,\text{m s}^{-2}$ c $175\,\text{N}$

2.3

1 a $6.7\,\text{m s}^{-2}$ b $3.8\,\text{kN}$

2 a $4.1\,\text{m s}^{-2}$ b $3.0\,\text{kN}$

4 a $40\,\text{m s}^{-1}$

2.4

1 a $30\,\text{m s}^{-1}$ b i $11.3\,\text{m s}^{-2}$ ii $690\,\text{N}$

2 a $25\,\text{m s}^{-1}$ b $20\,\text{m s}^{-2}$ c $2000\,\text{N}$

3 a $13\,\text{m s}^{-1}$ b $13\,\text{m s}^{-2}$ c $240\,\text{N}$

4 $-0.04\,\text{N}$

3.1

3 a $0.48\,\text{s}$ b $2.1\,\text{Hz}$

4 a $\frac{\pi}{2}$ radian   b π radian

3.2

1 a $+25\,\text{mm}$, changing direction from up to down

   b 0, moving down

   c $-25\,\text{mm}$, changing direction from down to up

   d 0, moving up

2 a $0.5\,\text{Hz}$ b i $-0.25\,\text{m s}^{-2}$ ii 0 iii $0.25\,\text{m s}^{-2}$

3 a $0.5\,\text{Hz}$ b $-0.32\,\text{m s}^{-2}$

4 a $-32\,\text{mm}$ $0.32\,\text{m s}^{-2}$ b $0, 0$

3.3

1 a $0.33\,\text{Hz}$ b $0.25\,\text{m s}^{-2}$

2 a i $12\,\text{mm}$ ii $0.63\,\text{s}$ b $6.5\,\text{mm}$

3 a $2.1\,\text{Hz}$ b $0.057\,\text{m}$

4 a $3.7\,\text{Hz}$

   b i $-8.2\,\text{mm}$ towards maximum negative displacement
     ii $-0.7\,\text{mm}$ towards maximum positive displacement.

3.4

1 a i $0.33\,\text{s}$ ii $3.1\,\text{Hz}$
   b i 0 ii $-3.7\,\text{m s}^{-2}$ iii $-7.5\,\text{m s}^{-2}$

2 a i $3.0\,\text{Hz}$ ii $0.33\,\text{s}$ b $f_2 < f_1 \therefore m_2 > m_1$

3 a i $70\,\text{mm}$ ii $21\,\text{N m}^{-1}$ b ii $0.53\,\text{s}$

4 a i $1.25\,\text{N}$ ii $2.5\,\text{m s}^{-2}$ b ii $1.1\,\text{Hz}$, $+47\,\text{mm}$

5 a i $2.0\,\text{s}$ ii $1.0\,\text{s}$ b $5.0\,\text{s}$

3.5

1 a i $1.50\,\text{s}$ ii $0.56\,\text{m}$ iii $0.029\,\text{J}$
   b See Figure 2

2 a i $60\,\text{N m}^{-1}$ ii $0.54\,\text{s}$
   b i $75\,\text{mJ}$ ii $75\,\text{mJ}$ iii $0.50\,\text{m s}^{-1}$

3 a i light   ii heavy

4 b $82\,\text{mm}$ d $44\,\text{mm}$

3.6

2 a $27\,N\,m^{-1}$ b $1.7\,Hz$
4 b $2.8\,m\,s^{-1}$

4.1

2 a i $33\,N$ ii $160\,N$
  b i $16\,N\,kg^{-1}$ ii $4.0\,N\,kg^{-1}$

4.2

1 a $235\,J$
2 a $2.0\,MJ\,kg^{-1}$ b i $-61\,MJ\,kg^{-1}$ ii $2.2 \times 10^9\,J$
3 a i $-250\,J$ ii $-200\,J$ iii $-200\,J$
  b i $50\,J$ ii 0
4 b $5\,N\,kg^{-1}$ c $25\,MJ$

4.3

1 a $1.3 \times 10^{-6}\,N$ b $5.4\,mm$
2 a $780\,N$ b $6.0 \times 10^{24}\,kg$
3 a $54\,N$ b $0.24\,N$
4 a i $16.6\,N$ ii $0.2\,N$
  b $16.4\,N$ towards the centre of the Earth

4.4

1 a $7.35 \times 10^{22}\,kg$
2 a i $272\,N\,kg^{-1}$ ii $5.9 \times 10^{-3}\,N\,kg^{-1}$
3 a $0.028\,N\,kg^{-1}$ c $7.1 \times 10^6\,J$
4 $2.8\,MJ\,kg^{-1}$, $1410\,MJ$

4.5

2 a $3.4 \times 10^6\,m$ b $3.0\,m\,s^{-2}$ c $5.2 \times 10^{23}\,kg$
3 b i $9.5\,N\,kg^{-1}$ ii $7.9\,km\,s^{-1}$ iii $5200\,s$
4 b ii $7100\,s$

5.1

2 b i $75\,nA$ ii 1.9×10^{11}

5.2

1 a $1.4 \times 10^{-3}\,N$ b $4.0 \times 10^4\,V\,m^{-1}$
2 a i negative ii $1.3 \times 10^{-7}\,C$
  b i $7.3 \times 10^{-3}\,N$ ii towards the metal surface
3 a i $9.0 \times 10^4\,V\,m^{-1}$ ii $7.2 \times 10^{-14}\,N$ b $80\,mm$
4 a $2.9\,kV$ b i $5.6 \times 10^{-15}\,N$

5.3

1 a i $-8.0 \times 10^{-18}\,J$ ii $+7.2 \times 10^{-17}\,J$ b $+8.0 \times 10^{-17}\,J$
2 a $-1.8 \times 10^{-3}\,J$ b $+1.2 \times 10^{-3}\,J$
3 a i $250\,V\,m^{-1}$
  ii $8.0 \times 10^{-17}\,N$ (towards the negative plate)
  b $-8.0 \times 10^{-19}\,J$
4 b i $3000\,V\,m^{-1}$

5.4

1 a $3.7 \times 10^{-11}\,N$ b $2.6 \times 10^{-10}\,N$
2 a i $69\,mm$ ii $3.6 \times 10^{-6}\,N$
  b $2.5 \times 10^{-5}\,N$ repulsion
3 a $6.1\,nC$, negative   b $2.2 \times 10^{-2}\,N$
4 a $2.7\,nC$, attract   b $6.2 \times 10^{-2}\,m$, repel

5.5

1 a $5.3 \times 10^6\,V\,m^{-1}$ b $10\,mm$
2 a i $3.7 \times 10^8\,V\,m^{-1}$ ii $5.6 \times 10^{-3}\,N$ towards Q_1
3 a i $4.5 \times 10^8\,V\,m^{-1}$ towards Q_2
  ii $2.6 \times 10^8\,V\,m^{-1}$ away from Q_1
  b ii $11\,mm$ from Q_1, $9\,mm$ from Q_2
4 a $-9.0 \times 10^6\,V$
  b ii $2.0 \times 10^9\,V\,m^{-1}$ directly towards Q_2

6.1

1 a $5.0\,\mu F$ b $2.2\,V$ c $9.9\,mC$
  d $1.4\,\mu F$
2 a $264\,\mu C$ b $106\,s$
3 a $27.5\,\mu C$ b $5.5\,\mu F$
4 a $0.91\,\mu C$ b $0.22\,\mu F$
  c $700\,\mu C$ d $7.4\,V$

6.2

1 a $30\,\mu C$, $45\,\mu J$ b $60\,\mu C$, $180\,\mu J$
2 a $0.45\,C$, $2.0\,J$ b $10\,W$
3 a i $6.6\,\mu C$, $9.9\,\mu J$ ii $6.6\,\mu C$, $19.8\,\mu J$
4 a $56\,\mu C$, $338\,\mu J$
  b i $2.2\,\mu F$; $18\,\mu C$, $4.7\,\mu F$; $38\,\mu C$ ii $8.2\,V$
  c $2.2\,\mu F$; $73\,\mu J$, $4.7\,\mu F$; $157\,\mu J$

6.3

1 a i $300\,\mu C$ ii $5.0\,s$
  b i $5\,s$ approx   ii $20\,k\Omega$
2 a i $0.61\,mC$ ii $0.45\,mA$ b $0.23\,V$, $11\,\mu A$
3 a $13\,\mu C$, $40\,\mu J$ b $0.62\,V$, $0.42\,\mu J$
4 a i $60\,mA$ ii $0.34\,mJ$
  b $1.4\,s$ c $0.32\,mJ$

7.1

1 a $2.4 \times 10^{-2}\,N$; west   b $4.5\,A$; east to west
  c $0.20\,T$; vertically down   d $8.0 \times 10^{-3}\,N$; due south
2 a $22\,mN$ due east   b $4.0\,A$ west to east
3 Short sides; zero, long sides; $2.72\,N$ vertically up on one side
  and vertically down on the other side
4 a $58\,\mu T$ b $6.5 \times 10^{-5}\,N$ due east

7.2

1 b i $1.9 \times 10^{-13}\,N$ ii 0
2 $3.8 \times 10^{-23}\,N$ horizontal due East
4 b i $4.4\,m\,s^{-1}$ ii $8.5 \times 10^{-20}\,N$

7.3

1 a ii 21 mm   b 2.8 mT

2 a 4.7 mT   b 17.5 mm

3 b 1.2 MeV

4 a 8.0×10^6 C kg^{-1} b 1.4×10^7 C kg^{-1}

8.2

1 a i 1.1 mWb   ii 2.0 s   iii 0.54 mV

2 a 1.4 mWb   b 23 mV

3 a i 4.5×10^{-4} m^2 ii 1.5(4) mWb

   b i 3.1 mWb   ii 33 mV

4 a 8.0 µWb   b 40 µV

8.3

2 flux linkage 0, 0, $-BAN$; induced emf 0, $-\varepsilon_0$, 0

3 a 26 mWb

8.4

3 a 11.5 V   b i 0.26 A   ii 5.2 A

4 b i 17 A (16.7 A to 3 sig. fig.)   ii 56 kW

9.1

4 b 3×10^{-14} m   c 4.5×10^{-14} m

9.2

3 a 42 %   b 58 %

9.3

1 a $^{235}_{92}\text{U} \longrightarrow \ ^{234}_{90}\text{Th} + \ ^4_2\alpha$

   b $^{228}_{90}\text{Th} \longrightarrow \ ^{224}_{88}\text{Ra} + \ ^4_2\alpha$

2 a $^{64}_{29}\text{Cu} \longrightarrow \ ^{64}_{30}\text{Zn} + \ ^0_{-1}\beta \ (+ \bar{\nu})$

   b $^{32}_{15}\text{P} \longrightarrow \ ^{32}_{16}\text{S} + \ ^0_{-1}\beta \ (+ \bar{\nu})$

3 a $^{213}_{84}\text{Po}, \ ^{209}_{82}\text{Pb}, \ ^{209}_{83}\text{Bi}$

   b i 83 p + 130 n   ii 83 p + 126 n

4 a 3.2 counts per second   b 160 mm

9.5

1 a 40 s   b 6 mg

2 a i 9.0×10^{14} ii $2.2(5) \times 10^{14}$

   b i 9.0×10^{14} ii 15.8×10^{14}

   c 1.3×10^3 J

3 a 19 kBq   b 2.4 kBq

4 a 4.4×10^{21} b 1.1×10^{21} atoms

9.6

1 a 1.0×10^{-6} s^{-1} b 3.9×10^{16}

2 a 6.3×10^{-10} s^{-1} b 20.5 kBq

3 a 2.7×10^{24} b i 0.65 kg   ii 1.7×10^{24}

4 a 1.3×10^{-6} s^{-1} b 149 hours

9.7

1 b 1340 years

2 a i 730 kBq   ii 870 kBq   iii 1.9×10^{-13} kg

4 b i 5.2×10^{13} Bq   ii 3.3 J s^{-1}

9.8

2 a 82 p, 126 n

4 a

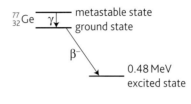

$^{77}_{32}\text{Ge}$ γ   metastable state   ground state

β$^-$

0.48 MeV excited state

$^{77}_{33}\text{As}$ ground state

   b 0.21 MeV, 0.27 MeV

9.9

2 a 3.2 fm   b 5.2 fm

3 b 6.5 fm, 1.2×10^{-42} m^3

4 b 2.5 fm, 3.4×10^{17} kg m^{-3}

10.1

1 a 2.18×10^{-15} kg

   b i 8.89×10^{-33} kg   ii 8.89×10^{-30} kg

2 6.2 MeV

3 0.56 MeV

4 1.68 MeV

10.2

2 a 7.4 MeV   b 8.8 MeV

3 a i 7.1 MeV   ii 2.6 MeV

4 a $p + p \longrightarrow \ ^2_1\text{H} + \ ^0_{+1}\beta + \nu$

   b 1.12 MeV

10.3

2 b i $a = 56, b = 98$ ii 206 MeV

3 b ii 0.43 MeV, 5.5 MeV

4 b 12.9 MeV

11.1

4 a i 273 K   ii 293 K   iii 77 K

   b i 328 K   ii 137 kPa

11.2

1 a 23 kJ   b 535 kJ

2 a 280 s   b 10.3 MJ

3 a 320 J   b 130 J kg^{-1} K^{-1}

4 3.2 kW (3.15 kW to 3 sig. figs)

11.3

2 0.16 kg

3 a $4.2\,\text{J s}^{-1}$ b 6500 s

4 a $22\,\text{J s}^{-1}$ b 6.5 kJ

12.1

1 126 kPa

2 79 kPa

3 $0.097\,\text{m}^3$

4 b $2.3 \times 10^{-5}\,\text{m}^3$, $1600\,\text{kg m}^{-3}$

12.2

1 a 1.1 moles   b 109 kPa

2 a 9.3×10^{-4} moles   b $2.1 \times 10^{-5}\,\text{m}^3$

3 b $1.3\,\text{kg m}^{-3}$

4 a $1.2\,\text{kg m}^{-3}$ b 2.5×10^{22}

12.3

1 b i 0.97 mol   ii 4.5 kJ

2 c $5.7 \times 10^{-21}\,\text{J}$ d $1.8 \times 10^3\,\text{m s}^{-1}$

4 a 1.48 mol   b $4.2 \times 10^{-2}\,\text{kg}$ c $5.2 \times 10^2\,\text{m s}^{-1}$

15.1

1 a i 0.524 rad   ii 0.873 rad
         iii 2.094 rad   iv 4.014 rad   v 5.236 rad
      b i 5.73°   ii 28.7°   iii 68.8°
         iv 143.2°   v 343.8°

2 a 20 mm, 2.3°   b ii 0.5°

3 a i 0.035   ii 0.140

4 a i 0.0998   ii 0.995
      b i 0.1736   ii 0.9848
      c i 0.7071   ii 0.7071
      d i 0.7071   ii 0.7071

15.2

1 a $x = 1, y = 3$ b $a = 2.4, b = -0.4$ c $p = 2, q = 4$

2 a $u = 14\,\text{m s}^{-1}, a = -2.0\,\text{m s}^{-2}$ b $r = 1.0\,\Omega, \varepsilon = 9.0\,\text{V}$

3 a 0.5 or –3   b 1.4 or 5.6
      c $-\frac{10}{6} = -1.67$ (to 3 sig. figs) or 1

4 a $t = -\frac{20}{6} = -3.33$ (to 3 sig. figs) or 2 s   b $R = 1$ or $4\,\Omega$

15.3

1 a i 0.477 ii 1.176   b i 1.653 ii 0.699

2 a i 10.8 dB ii 7.0 dB   b 17.8 dB

3 a $n = 5, k = 3$ b $n = 3, k = \frac{1}{2}$ c $n = 2, k = 1$

4 a i 1.10   ii 2.71   b i 3.81   ii 1.61

15.4

1 a i 2, 3   ii 12, 0.2   iii 4, 0.02
      b i 0.23 s   ii 3.5 s   iii 35 s

2 a 11.3 kBq   b 9.0 kBq   c 0.38 kBq

3 a i 2.2 s   ii 1.52 s   b i 4.83 V   ii 1.24 V

4 a i 0.14 s   ii 82   b $a = 6.9, b = -5$

15.5

2 d i Pa or N m^{-2} ii m^3 iii J

Index

A

absolute temperature scale **200**
absolute zero **200**
absorption tests, radiation **153, 157**
ac generators **127–9**
acceleration **24–5, 36–7, 113**
Advanced Gas-cooled Reactor (AGR) **192**
ALARA (as low as is reasonably achievable) **161**
alarm circuits **100**
algebra **245–6**
alpha particle tunnelling **185–6**
alpha radiation **151–60**
    dangers **159–60**
    emission **157, 165, 172, 183**
    nature of **156**
    nucleus, discovery **148**
    properties **151–5**
    radioactive decay **165, 172, 183**
    tracers **169**
alternating current (ac) generators **127–9**
alternators
    power stations **128**
    regenerative braking **123–4**
    three-phase **128**
aluminium **174**
ammeters **73, 94**
amplitude, oscillation **34, 36, 44–5, 47–8**
angles **242–3**
angular displacement **22–3**
angular frequency **34**
angular speed **22–3**
annihilation of particles **182**
antiparticles **156, 182**
applied frequency, oscillation **47**
AQA-marked assessment scheme **228–9, 239–41**
arcs of circles **242–3**
areas **253–5**
argon dating **169**
as low as is reasonably achievable (ALARA) **161**
assessment
    external **240–1**
    internal **236–41**
    overview **228–9**
    scheme T: ISA/PSA **228–9, 236–8**
    scheme X: AQA-marked **228–9, 239–41**

B

back emf **129, 131**
background radiation **160–2**
banked race tracks **27**
bar magnets **106, 123**
Barton's pendulums **48**
base ten logarithms **247–8**
batteries **123–4**
Becquerel, Henri **151**
beta radiation **151–9**
    danger **159**
    emission **158, 165, 172–3, 183**
    nature of **156**
    nucleus, discovery **148**
    properties **151–5**
    radioactive decay **165, 172–3, 183**
Big Dipper **28**
Big Wheel **22, 24–5, 28–9**
binding energy **185–9**
blood flow monitoring **175**
boiling point **205**
Boltzmann constant **214, 218**
bombs, atomic **160**
Boyle's law **210, 215**
braking **123–4**
bridge oscillations **48–9**
de Broglie wavelength **176**
Brown, Robert **212**
Brownian motion **212**

C

calibration of thermometers **201**
capacitors **94–105**
    capacitance **94–5**
    charge **94–101**
    constant current **95**
    discharge **98–101, 248–9, 251**
    energy storage **96–7**
    examination-style questions **102–5**
    fixed resistors **98–101**
    usage **95**
car suspension systems **46**
carbon dating **168**
Cavendish, Henry **61**

atomic bombs **160**
    see also explosions
atomic mass units **157–8, 183, 213**
atomic numbers **149**
atoms **148, 186, 198, 212–13**
Avogadro constant **163, 212**

cells, living **159–60**
Celsius temperature scale **200**
centripetal acceleration **24–5, 113**
centripetal force **24–9**
chain reactions **188**
change of state **205–7**
charge
    capacitors **94–101**
    like/unlike charges **72**
    microchips **74**
    point charges **86–8**
charged particles **110–15, 156**
Charles' law **211**
Chernobyl disaster **193**
circular motion **22–33**
centripetal force **24–9**
    examination-style questions **30–3**
    fairgrounds **28–9**
    road journeys **26–7**
    simple harmonic motion **38**
    uniform motion **22–3**
circular orbits **113–15**
cloud chambers **152–3**
coefficient of friction **27**
coils
    ac generators **127–8**
    Faraday's law **125–6**
    magnetic fields **108–9, 123, 125–6**
    transformers **130–1**
coldest places on earth **200–1**
collisions
    charged particles **110–11**
    elastic/inelastic **14–15**
    head-on **13**
    see also impact forces
complex instructions, PSA **238**
conductors
    current-carrying **106–9**
    electric fields **72, 77, 88**
    Faraday's law **124–5**
    magnetic fields **106–9, 124–5**
    superconductors **131, 201**
conservation of momentum **11–13**
constant of gravitation **60**
constant of proportionality
    Coulomb's law **84–5**
    electric fields **78, 84–5**
    Newton's law of gravitation **60**
    simple harmonic motion **37**
cooling **202**
cosine curves **38, 243–4**
Coulomb, Charles **83**

Coulomb's law **83–7**
  inverse square laws **61**, **84**
  point charges **86–7**
  radioactivity **149**
  strong nuclear force **183**
count rate **153**, **166**, **235**
crash barriers **13**
critical damping **45**
critical mass **192**
crosswinds **48**
crystals, salt **84**
Curie, Marie **151**
current
  ac/dc generator **127–9**
  conductors **106–9**
  eddy currents **130–1**
  electromagnetic induction **123**
  energy changes **120–1**
current-carrying conductors **106–9**
  couple on coil **108**
  force on wire **106–7**
  motor effect **106–7**
cycle dynamos **120**
cyclotrons **113–14**

D
D-shaped electrodes **113–14**
damping, oscillation **45–6**
dangers of radioactivity **159–61**
data analysis **248**
data loggers **234**
data for reference **256–9**
dating, radioactive **168–9**
dc generators **128**
de Broglie wavelength **176**
dead time, Geiger-Müller tube **153**
decay *see* radioactive decay
deep sea diving **211**
dees, cyclotrons **113–14**
deflection tubes, electron **110**
density
  gases **205**, **214**
  nuclear **177**
deuterium **189–90**
diameter of nucleus **150**, **176–7**
differentiation **250–1**
direct current (dc) generators **128**
discharge, capacitors **98–101**,
    248–9, **251**
displacement
  angular **22–3**
  energy-displacement graphs **45**
  simple harmonic motion **34**,
    36–42, **44–5**
dissipative forces **45**
diving, deep sea **211**
dynamo rule **122**
dynamos, cycles **120**

E
Earth
  gravitational fields **54–5**, **57**,
    63–7
  magnetic fields **106**
  satellite motion **66–7**
  see also planet
earthing, electricity **72**, **74**
eddy currents **130–1**
efficiency, transformers **130–1**
Einstein, Albert **4**, **182**
elastic collisions **14–15**
electric cars **124**
electric fields **56**, **72–93**
  between parallel plates **77–8**
  Coulomb's law **83–7**
  examination-style questions **90–3**
  field patterns **72–5**, **77–8**
  gravitational fields **81**, **87**, **89**
  mass spectrometers **115**
  point charges **86–8**
  potential **64**, **80–2**
  strength **76–9**, **82**, **84–7**, **97**
electric motors **108–9**, **120**, **129**
electric shocks **88**
electric showers **204**
electricity **120–2**
  energy changes **120–1**
  generation **120–2**
  power **132**
  specific heat capacity **203**
electromotive force (emf)
  ac generators **127–9**
  back emf **129**, **131**
  Faraday's law **124–6**
  generating electricity **120–1**
  transformers **130–1**
electromagnetic induction **120–36**
  ac generator **127–9**
  examination-style questions
    133–6
  generating electricity **120–2**
  laws **123–6**
  transformers **130–2**
electromagnets **109**, **128**
electron beams **110–11**, **121**
electron capture **158**, **183**
electron deflection tubes **110**
electron diffraction, nuclear radius
    176–7
electron guns **113**
electrons
  beta radiation **158**
  nuclear radius **176–7**
  nucleus, discovery **148**
  static electricity **72–3**
electroscope, gold leaf **73**
emf *see* electromotive force

energy
  capacitors **96–7**
  electrical **120–1**, **124**
  energy–displacement graphs **45**
  free oscillations **44**
  internal thermal **198–201**
  kinetic energy **14–15**, **44–5**
  radioactivity **157**, **164**, **182–3**
  renewable **194**
  simple harmonic motion **44–6**
  storage **44**, **96–7**
  see also nuclear energy
engine wear **170**
equilibrium **34**, **36**, **40**, **43**, **45**
equipment use, PSA **238**
equipotentials **57–8**, **81–2**, **87**
examination-style questions
  capacitors **102–5**
  circular motion **30–3**
  electromagnetic induction **133–6**
  gases **219–21**
  gravitational fields **68–71**
  magnetic fields **116–19**
  momentum **18–21**
  nuclear energy **195–7**
  radioactivity **178–81**
  simple harmonic motion **50–3**,
    90–3
  thermal physics **208–9**
  unit questions **137–45**, **222–7**
excitation of molecules **15**, **174**
experimental gas laws **210–11**
experimental uncertainties **231–2**
explosions **16–17**, **160**
exponential change **250–2**
exponential decrease **166**, **250–2**
exponential functions **99**, **166**, **251**
external assessment **229**, **240–1**

F
fairgrounds **28–9**
Faraday, Michael **121**
Faraday's law **124–6**
farads **78**, **95**
fields **2–145**
electric **56**, **64**, **72–93**, **115**
  gravitational **54–71**, **81**, **87**, **89**
  magnetic **106–36**, **151–2**, **157**
  planetary **62–5**
film badges **159–60**
fission **187–93**
fixed resistors **98–101**
Fleming's left-hand rule **107**,
    110–11, **113**
Fleming's right-hand rule **122**
flow of liquids and gases **205**
foil, metal **170–1**
footbridges **49**

force
  centripetal **24–9**
  friction **26–7, 44**
  impact **8–10**
  motor effect **106–7**
  periodic **47–8**
  restoring **40–2, 44**
  resultant **86–7**
  strong nuclear **172, 183–4**
  support **26–8**
  see also Coulomb's law; inverse
    square laws
force fields **54, 254**
force–time graphs **6, 9**
forced oscillations **47–9**
free electrons **72**
free fall **54–5**
free oscillations **34, 44**
frequency
  applied **47**
  natural **47–8**
  oscillation **34, 41–2, 47–8**
  resonant **48**
friction **26–7, 44**
further mechanics **2–145**
fusion **187–90, 205**

G

g-forces **29**
gamma radiation **151–61**
  dangers **159–61**
  emission of photon **158, 165,
    174**
  gamma camera **175**
  inverse square laws **156–7**
  nature of **156**
  nucleus, discovery **148**
  properties **151–5**
  technetium generator **174**
  tracers **169**
gases **210–21**
  assumptions about molecules
    218
  change of state **205–7**
  examination-style questions
    219–21
  excitation of molecules **15**
  experimental laws **210–11**
  ideal gas law **212–14**
  kinetic theory **215–18**
  molecules **15, 199, 212–13,
    215–18**
  pressure **201, 210–11, 215**
Geiger–Müller tube **153–4, 163,
  235, 238**
generators **80–1, 127–9**
geostationary satellites **66–7**
glossary **260–6**
gold leaf electroscope **73**
gradients, potential **57–8, 65, 81–2**

graphs
  areas under lines **253**
  base ten logs **248**
  energy–displacement **45**
  force–time **6, 9**
  log–log **177**
  simultaneous equations **245**
  temperature-time **206–7**
gravitational fields **54–71**
  electric fields **81, 87, 89**
  equipotentials **81**
  examination-style questions
    68–71
  field lines/patterns **54–5**
  field strength **54–5, 62–3, 65, 87**
  gravitational potential **56–8,
    63–5, 202**
  Newton's law of gravitation
    59–61, 87, 254
  planetary fields **62–5**
  satellite motion **66–7**
Grid system, National **131–2**
ground state, nuclear energy **174**
group work, PSA **237**

H

Hahn, Otto **149, 188**
half-life **162–3, 165–9, 171, 173,
  251–2**
Hall probes **111–12**
head-on collisions **13**
Health and Safety Executive (HSE) **29**
heat **202–6**
heavy damping **45**
helium **156, 189–90**
high energy electron diffraction
  176–7
hill tops **26–7**
Hooke's law **41**
HSE (Health and Safety Executive)
  29
hybrid vehicles **123–4**

I

ideal gases **210–15, 218**
impact forces **8–10**
  see also collisions
impulse, momentum **4–7**
induced fission **188–9**
induction, electromagnetic **120–36**
industrial use, radioactivity **170–1**
inelastic collisions **14–15**
insulators **72**
integration, areas **253–5**
intensity of radiation **156–7, 161**
internal assessment **236–41**
internal thermal energy **198–201**
International Thermonuclear
  Experimental Reactor (ITER)
  fusion reactor **190**

inverse square laws
  Coulomb's law **61, 84**
  electric field strength **87**
  gamma radiation **156–7**
  Newton's law of gravitation **60–1,
    84, 87, 254**
inversion tube experiment **202**
investigative skills **228–55**
  assignments (ISA) **228–9, 236–7**
ionisation, radiation **152, 154, 157,
  159–61, 238**
ISA (investigative skills
  assignments) **228–9, 236–7**
isothermal change **210**
isotopes
  Avogadro constant **212**
  induced fission **188**
  momentum **16**
  see also radioactive isotopes;
    uranium
ITER (International Thermonuclear
  Experimental Reactor) fusion
  reactor **190**

J

Joint European Torus (JET) fusion
  reactor **190**
joule **97, 203**

K

kelvin scale **200–1**
Kepler, Johannes **59**
Kepler's third law **59, 66**
kinetic energy **14–15, 44–5, 217–18**
kinetic theory of gases **215–18**

L

laboratory apparatus **237–8**
latent heat **205–6**
Lenz's law **123–4, 129**
light damping **45**
light gates **234**
lightening conductors **77, 88**
like charges **72**
linear simultaneous equations
  245–6
lines of force **54, 74, 81, 87, 106**
liquids **198, 203–7**
lithium **190**
living cells **159–60**
lodestones **106**
log–log graphs **177**
logarithms **247–9**
London Eye, The **22, 24–5**
  see also Big Wheel

M

magnesium **174**
magnetic fields **106–36**
  circular orbits **113–15**

current-carrying conductors
106–9
electromagnetic induction
120–36
examination-style questions
116–19
field lines/patterns 106–7
moving charges 110–12
radioactivity 151–2, 157
strength of field 107, 111–12
magnetic flux
ac generators 127–9
density definition 107
Faraday's law 124–6
transformers 130–1
magnets 106, 109, 123, 128
Mars 66
mass
atoms 186
critical 192
defect of nucleus 185
gases 212–14
mass-spring systems 40–2
molar 163, 213
nuclear energy 182–4
numbers 177
radioactive isotopes 165
spectrometers 114–15, 186
mathematical skills 242–55
algebra 245–6
areas 253–5
differentiation 250–1
exponential decrease 250–2
integration 253–5
logarithms 247–9
trigonometry 242–4
measurements 233–5
mechanics 2–145
melting point 205–7
metal foil 170–1
metals, specific heat capacity 203
metastable state 174
microammeters 73, 94
microchips 74
microscopes 234
Millennium Bridge, London 49
moderators 192
molar gas constant 213
molar mass 163, 213
molecules
assumptions 218
Avogadro constant 212
gases 15, 199, 212–13, 215–18
internal energy 199
kinetic energy 217–18
speed in gases 215, 217
momentum 4–21
conservation of 11–13
definition 4
elastic/inelastic collisions 14–15

examination-style questions
18–21
explosions 16–17
impact forces 8–10
impulse 4–7
monitoring
blood flow 175
metal thickness 170–1
radiation 159–60
Moon 66
motion
circular 22–33, 38
satellites 66–7
simple harmonic 34–53
see also Newton's laws
motor effect 106–7
moving charges 110–12
multistage rockets 64

N

National Grid system 131–2
natural frequency 47–8
natural logarithms 166, 248–9
neutrons
binding energy 185
fission 188
N–Z graph 172–3
radiation 156–7, 159
strong nuclear force 184
thermal reactors 191–2
Newton, Isaac 4, 59–60, 62, 66
newton 5
Newton's law of gravitation 4,
59–61, 84, 87, 254
Newton's laws of motion 4–6
first law 5
radioactivity 149
second law 5, 25, 216
third law 11
newtons per coulomb 76–7
newtons per kilogram 54
north-seeking poles, magnets 106
nuclear energy 182–97
binding energy 185–7
examination-style questions
195–7
excited state 174
fission 187–93, 188
fusion 187–90
ground state 174
mass and energy 182–4
nuclear reactions 182–3
solar energy 189
thermal reactors 191–4
nuclear physics 146–97
nucleons 172, 177, 184–7
nucleus
density 177
diameter 150, 176–7
discovery 148–50

mass numbers 177
N–Z graph 172–3
radioactive decay 163, 165,
172–3
radius 176–7
size 149–50
stability 172–3, 186–7
volume 177
see also nuclear energy
nuclides 157–8, 176–7, 187
N–Z graph 172–3

O

oil dampers, suspension 46
optional topics 147
oscillation 34–5
bridge spans 48–9
damped oscillation 45–6
forced 47–9
free oscillations 34, 44
mass-spring system 40–2
measurement 34
phase differences 35, 39
sine/cosine curves 243–4
springs 40–2, 47
oscilloscopes 100, 233

P

pair production 182
pendulums 42–5, 48
periodic force 47–8
periods see time periods
phase differences 35, 39, 47
photons 158, 165, 174
planetary fields 62–5
gravitational field strength 62–3,
65
gravitational potential 63–5
inside planets 63
potential gradients 65
planets 62–6
inside 63
motion 66
see also individual planets
plutonium 188
point charges 86–8
poles, magnets 106
positrons 110, 156, 158
potential
capacitors 96–7
electric 80–2
equipotentials 81–2
gradients 57–8, 65, 81–2
gravitational 56–8, 63–5, 202
simple harmonic motion 44–5
potential gradients
electric fields 81–2
gravitational fields 57–8
planetary fields 65

power
  electrical power 132
  radioactive decay 164, 171
  remote devices 171
power stations 128, 193–4
powers of numbers 247
practical assessment, scheme X 229,
  240–1
practical skills 228–55
  assessment (PSA) 228–9, 237–8
  verification 229, 239–40
practical task, ISA 236
practical work 230–5
  A2 vs AS level 230–2
  analysing data 231
  carrying work out 230–1
  evaluating results 231–2
  experimental uncertainties 231–2
  measurements 233–5
  planning 230
pressure, gases 201, 210–11, 215
pressurised water reactor (PWR)
  191–2
Principle of Conservation of
  Momentum 11–12
proportionality see constant of
  proportionality
protons
  binding energy 185
  fusion 189
  radiation 156–9
  radioactive decay 172–3
  strong nuclear force 183–4
PSA (practical skills assessment)
  228–9, 237–8
PWR (pressurised water reactor)
  191–2

Q

quadratic equations 246

R

race tracks 27
radial fields 55, 87–8
radian (rad) 22–3, 35, 39, 242
radiation
  alpha/beta/gamma 148, 151–61
  background 160–2
  dose limits 160
  ionisation 152, 154, 157,
    159–61, 238
  monitoring 159–60
  range in air 154–5, 157
radiation therapy 113
radioactive decay 162–75
  activity 163–6
  constant 165–7
  curves 162, 164
  dating 168–9

energy/mass in reactions 182–3
  exponential change 251–2
  half-life 162–3, 165–9, 171, 173,
    251–2
  natural logarithms 248–9
  nuclear energy levels 174
  N–Z graph 172–3
  power 164, 171
  random nature 163, 165–6
  series 173
  theory 165–7
  waste 167, 194
radioactive isotopes 168–71
  alpha emission 152
  argon dating 169
  carbon dating 168
  decay 162–3, 165–7
  N–Z graph 172–3
  tracers 169–70
  usage 168–71
radioactivity 148–81
  alpha/beta/gamma radiation 148,
    151–61
  dangers 159–61
  decay 162–75
  discovery 151
  equations for change 157–8
  examination-style questions
    178–81
  industrial usage 170–1
  isotopes 168–71
  nuclear radius 176–7
  nucleus, discovery 148–50
  Rutherford 148–9, 151–2, 156
  storage/usage of materials 161
  warning sign 159
radius of nucleus 176–7
radon gas 160
rad (radian) 22–3, 35, 39, 242
random processes 163, 165–6, 212
ratemeters 235
rates of change 250
reactions, nuclear 182–3
reactors 190–4
rebound impacts 9–10
recoil, explosions 16
reference data 256–9
regenerative braking 123–4
relativity, theory of 4, 182
remote devices 171
renewable energy 194
resistance 96, 98–101
resistors, fixed 98–101
resonance 47–9
restoring forces 40–2, 44
resultant forces 86–7
Richter earthquake scale 248
rides, fairground 28–9
road journeys 26–7
  banked tracks 27

over hill tops 26
  roundabouts 26–7
rockets 56–7, 64
root mean square speed 215, 217
roundabouts 26–7
Rutherford, Ernest 148–9, 151–2,
  156

S

safety
  fairground rides 29
  Health and Safety Executive 29
  nuclear reactors 193
  PSA working practices 238
  vehicles 8–9
salt crystals 84
satellite navigation (SATNAV) 67
satellites 25, 66–7
SATNAV (satellite navigation) 67
scalar counters 235
scattering experiments, Rutherford
  148–9
scheme T assessment 228–9, 236–8
scheme X assessment 228–9,
  239–41
segments of circles 242–3
Sellafield reprocessing plant 194
series, radioactive 173
shocks, electric 88
shuttling ball experiment 72–3
sideways friction 27
simple electric motors 108–9
simple harmonic motion 34–53
  applications 40–3
  energy 44–6
  examination-style questions 50–3
  principles 36–7
  resonance 47–9
  sine waves 38–9
  speed equation 44
  see also oscillation
simple pendulum 42–5
simultaneous equations 245–6
sine waves 38–9, 243–4
sinusoidal curves 39
small angle approximation 242
smoothing, capacitor discharge 100
soft iron 131
solar energy 189, 204
Solar System 59
  see also planets
solenoids 123
  see also coils
solids 198, 205–7
south-seeking poles, magnets 106
space stations 66
sparks 80, 88
specific heat capacity 202–4
specific latent heat 206–7
spectrometers 114–15, 186, 235

speed
  angular 22–3
  gas molecules 215, 217
  root mean square 215, 217
  simple harmonic motion 44
spherical planets 62–5
split ring commutator 128
springs
  car suspension systems 46
  energy storage 44
  forced oscillation 47
  frequency of oscillation 41–2
  mass–spring system 40–2
stability of nucleus 172–3, 186–7
standard laboratory apparatus 237–8
state, change of 205–7
static electricity 72–4
stationary charges 111
stationary waves 48
stators 128
step-up/down transformers 130–2
Strassmann, Fritz 188
strong nuclear force 172, 183–4
sublimation 206
Sun 66, 189
superconductors 132, 201
support forces 26–8
suspension systems 46
swings, fairgrounds 28

T
T scheme assessment 228–9, 236–8
Tacoma Narrows Bridge 48
technetium 169, 174–5
television 110
temperature 198–204
  gases 210–13, 215, 217
  internal energy 198–201
  scales 200
  specific heat capacity 202–4
  time graphs 206–7
tension
  simple pendulum 43
  springs 41

testing
  conservation of momentum 12
  model explosions 17
theory of gravitation 59–60
theory of radioactive decay 165–7
theory of relativity 4, 182
theory of simple pendulum 42–3
thermal energy 164, 198
thermal nuclear reactors 191–4
thermal physics 146, 198–209
  change of state 205–7
  examination-style questions
    208–9
  internal energy 198–201
  specific heat capacity 202–4
  temperature 198–204, 206–7
thermionic devices 113
thermometers 201
Thomson, J.J. 148
three-phase alternators 128
thunderclouds 97
time
  capacitor discharge 100
  constants 99–100, 252
  periods 34, 36–7, 39, 43, 45
  temperature graphs 206–7
torsion balance, Coulomb 83–4
tracers, radioactive 169–70
transformers 130–2
  efficiency 130–1
  step-up/down 130–2
  symbol 130
  transformer rule 130
travelling microscopes 234
trigonometry 242–4
tritium 190
Tsiolovski, Konstantin 64

U
uniform circular motion 22–3
uniform fields
  electric 75, 77–8
  gravitational 55, 57
universal constant of gravitation 60
universal laws 4

unlike charges 72
uranium 151, 173, 188, 191–2

V
Van de Graaff generator 80–1
vapour 205–7
vectors
  acceleration 24
  electric field strength 76, 86–7
  gravitational field strength 54
  velocity 24
vehicles
  regenerative braking 123–4
  safety 8–9
  SATNAV 67
velocity 24–5, 36
voltage
  capacitors 96
  Faraday 121
  Hall 111–12
  National Grid 132
volts per metre 77
volume
  gases 210–11, 212–13
  nuclear 177

W
waste, radioactive 167, 194
wavelengths, de Broglie 176
waves
  cosine 38, 243–4
  sine 38–9, 243–4
  stationary 48
weber 125
wind 48
written test, ISA 236

X
X scheme assessment 228–9,
  239–41
X-rays 159

Z
zero, absolute 200

Acknowledgements

Photograph Acknowledgements

The authors and publisher are grateful to the following for permission to reproduce photographs and other copyright material in this book.

Alamy/Ball Miwako: p 29; **Alamy/David Ball:** p 22; **Alamy/David Lyons:** p 64; **Alamy/Francisco Martinez:** p 49; **Alamy/imac:** p 124; **Alamy/ImageState:** p 54; **Alamy/Jon Arnold Images Ltd:** p 3; **Alamy/JupiterImages/Ablestock:** p 73; **Alamy/Philippe Hays:** p 67; **Alamy/Stephen Harrison:** p 198; **Alamy/Stocktrek Images:** p 66; **Alamy/Trip:** p 56; **Associated Press:** p 48; **Kevin 'Brindle' Briden, courtesy of Mike Subritzky:** p 16; **Associated Press:** p 48; **Martyn Chillmaid:** p 109, p 112; **Mary Evans Picture Library:** p 151; **Science Photo Library:** p 152 (left); **Science Photo Library/Andrew Lambert Photography:** p 234, 235; **Science Photo Library/Brookhaven National Laboratory:** p 110; **Science Photo Library/Canada-France-Hawaii Telescope/Jean-Charles Cuillandre:** p 147; **Science Photo Library/David Parker:** p 169; **Science Photo Library/David Parker & Julian Baum:** p 152 (right); **Science Photo Library/EFDA-Jet:** p 190; **Science Photo Library/Geoff Tompkinson:** p 201; **Science Photo Library/Giphotostock:** p 233; **Science Photo Library/Keith Kent:** p 77; **Science Photo Library/Lionel Bret/Eurelios:** p 68; **Science Photo Library/Maxmillian Stock Ltd:** p 170; **Science Photo Library/Mere Words:** p 194; **Science Photo Library/Ria Novosti:** p 193; **Science Photo Library/Science & Society Picture Library:** p 61; **Science Photo Library/Sheila Terry:** p 121; **UKAEA, courtesy of Emilio Segre Visual Archives:** p 149, p 159.

Every effort has been made to trace and contact all copyright holders and we apologise if any have been overlooked. The publisher will be pleased to make the necessary arrangements at the first opportunity.

I would like to thank my family for their support in the preparation of this book, particularly my wife, Marie, for secretarial support and cheerful encouragement. I am also grateful to the publishing team at Nelson Thornes, in particular Eleanor O'Byrne and Carol Usher who initiated the project. I am grateful to Ian Holt and Patrick Organ for their contributions and advice and I wish also to thank AQA for their support.

Jim Breithaupt